THE MONEY CO

TOP FUNDS

1999

A Winning Approach to Building Your Mutual Fund Portfolio

Riley Moynes

Michael Nairne

with...

Nick Fallon, CFA
David Hillock, Ph.D.
Garnet Anderson, CA

Addison Wesley Longman

ASHLAR HOUSE INC.

In order to avoid the appearance of a conflict of interest, both Optima Strategy and Artisan Funds have been excluded from this edition, as both Riley Moynes and Michael Nairne are officers of Equion Securities Canada Limited ,which distributes and manages these funds.

Editorial Coordination: Rosina Daillie

Design and Electronic Composition: Christine Gilham

Cover Design: Christine Gilham

Illustration and Computer Graphics: Christine Gilham, Kyle Gell, Kevin Ghiglione, Valentino Sanna, Dave Murphy, Adele Webster

Printing and Binding: Bryant Press

Although every effort has been made to ensure the accuracy and completeness of the information contained in this book, the authors and the publisher assume no responsibility for errors, inaccuracies, omissions or any inconsistency herein. Readers should use their own judgement and/or consult a financial expert for specific applications to their individual situations. Any slights of people or organizations are unintentional.

Canadian Cataloguing in Publication Data

Money Coach Guide to Top Funds

Annual.

1998-

Issues for 1999-   have title: The Money Coach's Guide to Top Funds.

ISSN 1483-1333

ISBN 0-201-47795-5 (1999 issue)

1. Mutual funds—Canada. I. Title: Money Coach's Guide to Top Funds.

HG5154.5.M68   332.63'27   C97-901118-3

ISBN 0-201-47795-5

Printed and bound in Canada

1 2 3 4 5 – BP – 03 02 01 00 99

CONTENTS

ACKNOWLEDGEMENTS

It is a pleasure to be a part of the Equion Group, which has taken the lead in funding research on "managed money" in Canada. Equion was the first company of its type to establish a Managed Money Research Department. Michael Nairne, Equion's President, provided personal support and vision for the creation of new models, new studies, and new frontiers for mutual fund research in Canada at a time when many others were not interested.

This commitment led to the creation of the Multi-Period Composite and the Style Grids which are used in this book, and to which Equion owns the rights. The Equion All-Fund Index, a new benchmark for reporting mutual fund returns which appear weekly in *The Globe and Mail*, and the Equion Balanced Portfolio are other industry-leading innovations, both of which are incorporated in this edition as well as in *The Money Coach*.

We are pleased to be able to share this leading-edge research with interested individuals across the country.

Many other individuals and organizations have contributed their time, support, and expenditure in the development of this project. Sincere thanks are extended to the Investment Funds Institute of Canada, Rosina Daillie, Cas Shields, Christine Gilham, Loring Ward Investment Counsel, Heather Latimer, Chris Moynes, Mike Connon, Michael Susser, Georgina Blight, and Nindy Singh.

In addition, we would like to thank Ralph Desai and Sue McDonell for their concentrated effort in both processing and validating the data. These are critical parts of the process, and their attention to detail was uncompromising.

Both Riley Moynes and Michael Nairne are officers of Equion Securities Canada Limited, a member of IDA and the TSE, which distributes units of Optima Strategy Funds as well as Artisan Funds. In order to avoid any appearance of a conflict of interest, neither family of funds is included in this edition, although several individual funds met the Top Funds criteria.

INTRODUCTION

Mutual funds are without doubt the fastest growing and most popular type of investment available today. And over the past few years, this rising popularity has spawned a number of good books on the subject of mutual funds.

So why do you need *this* book?

There are several reasons. We're constantly asked for advice on mutual funds and how to pick the "top" funds. Every day, we meet people who want comparative information on funds and fund managers, based on data that is relevant, well-researched, and up-to-date.

The problem we've found, however, is that the most common method of selecting funds today—that is, on the basis of published 1-, 3-, 5- and 10-year performance statistics—is not only inadequate, but can actually be misleading. So we've developed what we believe to be a better performance measurement system to identify the **real** Top Funds.

These funds are further qualified with other important information, including changes in fund management, management style, and expense ratios. How often has a fund been outperformed by "risk-free" investments like GICs— or lost money? These are simple questions that every investor should ask, and we try to provide the answers here. Finally, we've identified which management styles complement one another to create the best "package" of funds, so you can apply our analysis to make well-informed decisions as you build your portfolio.

Top Funds is based on innovative state-of-the-art research techniques and facilities which, to our knowledge are among the most sophisticated available. Remember, it's not the funds you own that counts; it's how they're put together. And while we start with research-proven data to reach our conclusions and recommendations, we've also added a good dose of common sense: we interviewed hundreds of managers and factored in our personal experience in research and in dealing with individual investors.

The *Top Funds* mix of quantitative and qualitative research is what makes this book unique. With over 1800 funds available today— we provide a way to cut through the hype and concentrate on only the best funds. The results: you save hours of your precious time!

Naturally, there were good funds that almost made the *Top Funds* list, but didn't quite—at least, not this year. And some of last year's *Top Funds* were edged out by stronger competitors, which just goes to show that the Top Funds list isn't cast in stone. We'll be reviewing all the funds over the next year and adjusting the list according to our findings.

Finally, we felt it was important to present the material as interestingly and simply as possible. So we took the approach that proved so popular in Riley's earlier book, *The Money Coach*, now in its Fifth Edition. The result, we think, combines rigorous research with an attractive format to provide clear and, ultimately, truly useful recommendations.

We wish to thank and acknowledge the support shown by our wives, Yvonne and Joanne, as we burned the midnight oil to meet the publishing deadlines.

Riley Moynes

Michael Nairne

MONEY MANAGEMENT IN THE '90s

• • • • • • • • • • •

The Canadian mutual fund industry has been one of the fastest growing industries in Canada over the last 10 years. According to the Investment Funds Institute of Canada, since 1986:

- the number of unitholder accounts has jumped from 1.7 million to over 21 million;
- assets under management have grown from $22 billion to over $300 billion;
- the number of funds has risen from 155 to well over 1800; and
- the number of fund managers has increased from 58 to 83.

What can account for such extraordinary industry growth? There are several factors which have had a major impact:

1. LOW INTEREST RATES

Since 1988 the prime rate has fallen from nearly 14% to 6.5%, lowering the yield on traditional investments to painfully unattractive levels. GIC investors have been forced, often against their will, to seek alternatives. Since 1991, mutual funds have grown far more quickly than traditional bank deposits (by 552% versus 157%).

2. DEMOGRAPHICS

The portion of the Canadian population between age 45 or over has risen steadily over the last 10 years and will continue to do so. This population shift has coincided with the remarkable growth in mutual fund assets. Typically, once an individual reaches his or her peak earning years at age 45 or older, mortgages and loans are paid off and the focus shifts to saving money for retirement.

The aging of the Canadian population has been well documented and publicized in books such as *Boom, Bust & Echo* by Professor David Foot of the University of Toronto. This aging segment of the population has another 20 years of earning and savings power and as a result, the mutual fund industry will likely continue to grow strongly at least over this period of time.

3. RETIREMENT PLANNING

The Canada Pension Plan (CPP) is running an increasingly large deficit and has reached the point where its payments to retirees have surpassed contributions by workers. Without changes to either benefits or contributions, this trend will continue. Motivated by growing concerns that expected benefits may not be made available, Canadians have begun to save for their own retirement, primarily through the use of RRSPs because of the tax free growth of assets as long as these stay within the plan.

Since most people see saving for retirement as a long-term proposition, Canadians are becoming increasingly long-term investors. With interest rates so low, stocks have grown in popularity, especially since they have proven to outperform interest-bearing investments over longer time frames.

Mutual funds offer investors a diversified portfolio of stocks—both domestic and international—along with professional money management; these are benefits most people probably could not afford otherwise.

4. PENSION SHIFTS

Over the past 10 years, savings have moved increasingly from defined benefit pension to defined contribution plans. This shift has provided people with the freedom to choose among various investment alternatives. At the same time, some companies, concerned with potential large pension liabilities, have encouraged this transfer of risk whereby the responsibility is on employees to generate sufficient returns to ensure their future well being. Again, mutual funds have benefited from this shift in savings.

5. EDUCATION

The pressures and changes outlined above have motivated Canadians to learn about investment alternatives. David Chilton's *The Wealthy Barber* published in 1989, and Riley Moynes' *The Money Coach*, first published in 1992, have sold hundreds of thousands of copies as people seek answers to these important issues. Mutual fund company advertising, newspaper attention to mutual funds—their returns, their management, and factors impacting returns—and books such as *Top Funds* have assisted in providing the information and knowledge which people seem so hungry to obtain.

As well several banks, faced with an erosion of their deposit bases, have become significant players in the field and have helped increase public awareness of mutual funds. In 1986, banks and trust companies had only about 16% mutual fund assets in Canada; by June of 1998 they controlled over 30% of industry assets.

These developments have helped the mutual fund industry to grow very rapidly over the last 10 years, and are expected to ensure continued strong growth over the next 20 years or so. A C.I.B.C. Wood Gundy research paper, "The Canadian Mutual Fund Industry: The Rising Tide", published in January 1997 projected mutual fund asset growth at about $650 billion within 10 years. On June 30, 1998 total assets under management by members of the Investment Funds Institute of Canada were at $322 billion.

FUND PHENOMENON

Actual and projected growth of the Canadian mutual fund industry

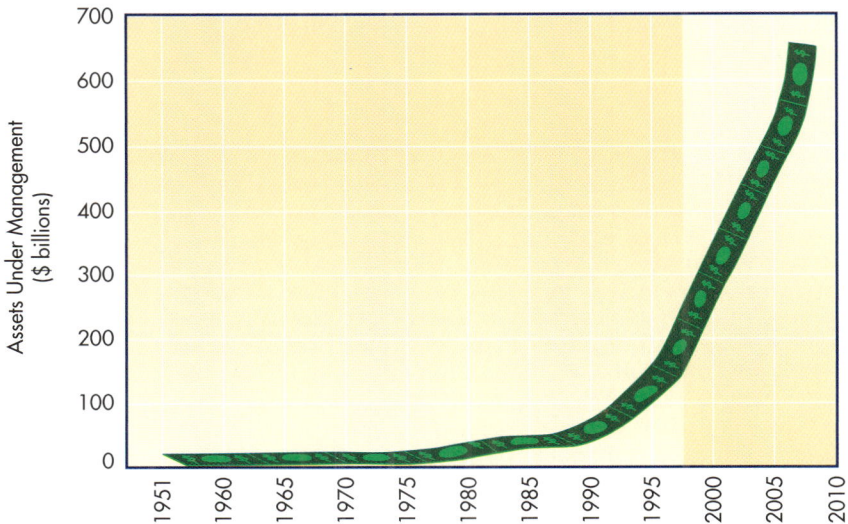

So, welcome to the era of "managed money"—an era that promises to offer you more investment choices than ever. And that's where we come in. Because it's our job to assist you in selecting the mutual fund or funds that best suit your needs.

If you are an experienced mutual fund investor, you may want to skip ahead to the next part of this book, where we provide the rationale for the recommended Top Funds. But if the whole business of mutual funds is relatively unfamiliar with you, let's take a moment to look at the basics.

WHAT IS A MUTUAL FUND?

A mutual fund is a "pool" of money to which thousands of people contribute. This pool of money is managed by professional money managers in accordance with the specific fund's investment objectives. Managers typically concentrate on one or more asset classes such as Treasury Bills (T-Bills), safe and secure government or corporate bonds, and in shares of generally proven Canadian and international corporations. They keep a watchful eye on the economy, on political, demographic and economic trends, and on international events in order to determine where and how the pool of money can be invested to produce the most solid, long-term growth.

THE BENEFITS OF MUTUAL FUNDS

● *Professional Money Management*

Most people haven't got the time to oversee their financial affairs effectively. And they're not trained to be expert money managers. But with an investment in mutual funds, they benefit from the experience and skills of some of the world's best money managers.

One of the most successful mutual funds ever, the **Templeton Growth Fund**, which is managed by Sir John Templeton and his team, provides a good example. If you had invested $10,000 in this fund when it began in 1954, you would have seen your investment grow to be worth $5.0 million by July 31, 1998. That's an average annual compounded growth rate of over 15.3%!

● *Diversification*

Most people aren't wealthy enough to be able to diversify properly on their own by buying stocks of various companies in a number of countries. Because of the size of the mutual fund "pool," often totalling millions or billions of dollars, investors can purchase a share of a vast array of securities, bonds, and other investments. This allows you to achieve the security that comes from "not putting all your eggs in one basket."

● *"Hands-Off" Investment*

As mentioned earlier, most people don't have the time, the inclination, or the expertise to do the research necessary to make wise investment decisions. This is all looked after for investors by professional money managers for whom this is a full-time job.

● *Lots of Choice*

Regardless of your circumstances, there are mutual funds that can meet your needs. Some people want income now; others, who will require income later, opt for growth now. Some investors are aggressive while others are much more conservative. Some select equity funds, others prefer real estate funds, and still others like mortgage funds — or a mixture of each. Some wish to invest in specialty funds like gold; others like to invest in specific foreign regions like Japan or Europe. With so many funds available to choose, there is truly a fund to meet just about every need.

● *Objectivity*

When it is your own money, there can be worry and anxiety associated with the endless decisions needed to manage a diversified portfolio. Is this stock over-priced and should I sell it? Should I build up cash reserves? The decisions are seemingly endless and for many, emotionally draining. By having professionals take over, you can have an objective expert making these decisions and take the emotional burden off your shoulders.

TYPES OF MUTUAL FUNDS

With over 1800 mutual and segregated funds now available in Canada, the job of finding the right ones can be very difficult. So we've outlined here the major types of funds and also given sub-groupings under the major headings. For example, we've categorized Canadian equity funds by the typical size of companies held or sectors of the market, and international funds by regional focus.

One perception that persists in the minds of many people is that a mutual fund is the same as a stock market investment. While this **may** be true (some funds do buy stocks) it is not **automatically** true. In fact, since there are mutual funds available to meet just about every investment preference (and for some people, that doesn't include stocks), many funds hold no stocks (or "equities") at all. These include funds that buy bonds, mortgages, Treasury Bills, gold, real estate, and other assets.

A WORLD OF CHOICE
The wide range of mutual funds available today provides something for virtually every type of investor.

In fact, with the proliferation in fund choices, there has also been an increase in the number of fund categories as more and more funds narrow their investment objectives. You can invest in funds which concentrate on a particular type of security such as short-term bonds or small-cap equities, a specific region of the globe such as European equities, a particular sector of the equity market such as global telecommunications; or in funds which invest in a diversified portfolio geared to a specific risk profile through an asset allocation approach.

Proper categorization of a fund is critical in building a portfolio and in evaluating that fund's performance and potential risk. To make "apple to apple" comparisons, you need to compare a fund to a similar peer group to really see if it is a top performer.

There's a saying that goes "If you want to win a tomato-growing contest, paint a cantaloupe red". This certainly applies to the fund industry where often the best way to have become a leading fund was to be miscategorized. For example, a number of years ago, Japanese funds were included with broadly diversified global funds under the loose definition of international funds. When Japan was soaring, no one really focused on the difference. Yet, as Japan deflated and North America and Europe took off, broadly diversified funds continued to grow while Japanese funds sunk into the red.

A more recent example is a fund such as AIC Advantage which has concentrated holdings in financial service stocks and mutual funds in particular. The soaring numbers of AIC had it well in front of diversified Canadian equity funds. Yet, it is really a sector fund where its narrower focus means that it can be much more volatile, winning big sometimes, but with the potential for much greater declines if the sector stumbles.

Chapter 4 reviews in more detail how fund categorization can help in building a portfolio. Here are the major groups:

MONEY MARKET FUNDS

These funds generally hold short-term debt securities of the highest quality, and therefore offer the lowest level of risk. They invest in government Treasury Bills or bank guaranteed deposits (GICs), and their purpose is to provide current income where necessary without taking any risks with the capital.

Not surprisingly, these funds are very popular when interest rates are high and less so when rates are lower. They are generally seen as temporary "parking spots" for money held by people seeking alternatives to savings accounts (which generally pay less than money market funds), and are not desirable as a long-term investment.

Money market funds come in several varieties:

● *Canadian money market funds* invest in a range of short-term vehicles. Among them are federal or provincial government guaranteed Treasury Bills (T-Bills) which are issued for terms up to one year. (T-Bills are sold at a discount and the return to the investor is the difference between the lower purchase price and the full face value paid when the bill matures.)

The advantage of investing in T-Bills through a mutual fund is that the fund can buy significantly larger quantities than you can (unless you have several million dollars in the bank), so the price is lower, and it's much more convenient. Some funds even offer chequing privileges, although at a cost.

Money market funds also invest in GICs, short-term promissory notes issued by major corporations (called "corporate paper"), and "bankers' acceptances." (The latter are promissory notes issued by corporations and guaranteed by a bank that the amount of the note will be paid in full on the date specified.)

As with T-Bills, all of these are short-term and highly liquid investments which are usually issued in amounts of several hundred thousand dollars, so most individual investors only have access to these vehicles through a mutual fund.

● *U.S. and International money market funds* are similar to their Canadian counterparts, although they can offer higher returns when U.S. interest rates are higher than those in Canada. These funds may be good for people who want to diversify into U.S. dollars as a hedge against the fall of the Canadian dollar, or who require U.S. or other foreign currencies on a frequent basis. Our own forecasts are calling for a rise in the Canadian dollar in the next several years, so be aware that currency losses can erode the superior interest rate returns.

RETURN EROSION

How U.S.$ Money Market Fund Returns Can Decline When the C$ Rises

Money market funds provide the highest degree of safety and liquidity but, over the long term, the lowest "real" rate of return (that is, after inflation). Also, outside of the tax-sheltered environment of a registered plan, money market returns are taxed at a higher rate than capital gains or dividends from Canadian corporations. The result is that after taxes and inflation have been taken into account, money market returns can actually be negative for many investors.

FIXED INCOME FUNDS

These funds generally hold assets that pay a fixed rate of return — such as bonds, mortgages, and money market vehicles. They are generally more secure than equity funds, and provide a reliable source of income, so they are popular with conservative investors and with retirees or other people who require a steady income. While there may be a capital gain to the investor if long-term interest rates decline (see *Top Funds Close Up, pg. 9*), the major objective of these funds is generally to achieve maximum income while preserving invested capital and minimizing risk.

Because they are sensitive to interest rates, fixed income funds will provide strong returns during times of declining rates and may actually lose value when rates rise. Because of this, these funds are

riskier than money market funds. On the other hand, they have the potential to provide higher returns than money market funds generally do. Here are the major types of fixed income funds.

● *Canadian Short-Term Bond Funds*

These are the most conservative type of bond funds focusing on fixed income securities with maturities of less than five years, which have been issued by the Government of Canada, provinces, municipalities, or corporations.

Although typically offering lower rates of return, these funds will stand up much better than their mid- to long-term cousins when inflation rears its head and interest rates rise. This is due to the fact that bonds with longer-term maturities decline much more substantially than short-term securities as rates rise.

Hence, these funds are suitable for very conservative investors or those who need to invest for a three- to five-year investment horizon with considerable safety. An example of the latter might be saving for a house in the next few years. In more broadly diversified portfolios, a very modest allocation to this category can improve returns in tough years when interest rates rise. 1994 is a great example where a sudden surge in rates produced the worst bond market in three decades. Short-term bond funds significantly outperformed other fixed income options.

● *Canadian Long-/Mid-Term Bonds*

These funds issued by Canadian corporations or governments invest primarily in fixed income securities with a maturity of five years or longer. Because Canadian bonds are offered for maturities as long as 30 years, there is a substantial range in the

Top Funds Close Up

What happens to the value of your investments if interest rates rise?

Dan Richards, president of Marketing Solutions, surveyed over 5,000 people in 1994 with this question. Surprisingly, 30% said that the value of their investments would go up with rising interest rates. Sorry folks — guess again. Higher interest rates have a negative impact on all fixed-income investments except cash (that is, money market funds). That's because no one would be as interested in buying your 9% bond when new bonds are available at 10%. So your old 9% issue (or those held by your bond fund) must fall in price to remain attractive to buyers on the bond market.

Stocks, too, often fall in value when interest rates rise. That's because companies who are big borrowers will face higher interest charges (and less profits) when rates rise. GICs can also fall in value, but their prices are generally not listed daily, so you may not notice the change.

In fact, there would be little point in tracking the value of a GIC, since you probably couldn't sell it anyway. Your money is completely locked in. Do GICs offer a higher return to compensate for this lack of liquidity and lack of pricing? No, not usually. Government bonds often yield higher rates of return, are liquid, and have higher credit quality, generally speaking, than bank GICs, which offer only limited deposit insurance.

Top Funds Scouting Report

Slamming the Doors on Labour Funds: What to Do Now

The deals were great — 40% cash back to invest in a high-growth asset class with important diversification benefits. But one fund abused the rules. Working Ventures invested too slowly and allowed money to still pour in, effectively creating a mostly T-Bill fund — subsidized at taxpayers' expense. Now, governments have cracked down on all labour-sponsored funds.

For Ontario-based investors, here are three high-quality venture capital funds with brief but strong track records, manageable size, and high-calibre management:
- C.I. Covington
- Capital Alliance Ventures
- Vengrowth

These funds remain attractive as holds or as new purchases, despite reduced tax credits (maximum combined credits now total 30%, depending upon the province, instead of 40%) and longer minimum holding periods (8 years, up from 5).

return potential as well as risk in these funds. As a general rule, the longer the maturity horizon and the higher the weighting of corporate to government securities, the more aggressive the fund.

It's important when evaluating mid- to long-term bond funds not to over-emphasize historic returns. Unlike equities, where over the long run a value management style can produce higher returns with less risk relative to other approaches, in bond funds higher returns are most often related to higher risk. So be aware that if you are reaching for higher returns in today's low interest rate environment, you are taking on greater risk.

From a portfolio perspective, bonds are much less risky than equities. The average Canadian bond fund is somewhere between 50% and 70% less volatile than a Canadian equity fund. Thus, bond funds serve as a real anchor in a broadly diversified portfolio. In bear markets, in particular, bond funds keep the total portfolio's decline from getting out of hand. So don't let the recent bull market in equities obscure this critical role.

● International Bond Funds

These funds have diminished in popularity recently, but deserve attention now for diversification reasons, and as the trend towards international investing picks up momentum again. These funds are similar to Canadian bond funds in their investment objectives, but hold bonds denominated in foreign currencies, including the pound sterling, deutschemarks, U.S. dollars, French francs, etc.

What type of international bond fund offers the best opportunities? Look for funds with exposure to foreign economies that are in recession — where interest rates are likely to decline, in which case bond prices should rise. Also, keep in mind that emerging market bond funds often offer eye-popping returns but are extremely risky.

Keep in mind, too, that Canada makes up only about 3% of the world's bond markets. And since a fixed income component is important to any well-balanced portfolio, one should probably include international bonds as part of a sound investment strategy.

● *Mortgage Funds*

Most mortgage funds concentrate on holding residential first mortgages. These generally include "conventional" mortgages, where the loan does not exceed 75% of the appraised value of the home. They may also include "insured" mortgages, in which the loan may exceed 75% of the appraised value but is insured against default by the Canada Mortgage and Housing Corporation (CMHC). Some mortgage funds also hold commercial mortgages while others also contain mortgage-backed securities, a liquid security backed by a basket of mortgages, often government-insured.

These funds are generally very conservative and offer comparatively modest risk. They are positioned between Canadian short-term and mid-/long-term bond funds. Returns are mostly in the form of interest income.

DIVIDEND FUNDS

These funds traditionally invest in high-quality preferred shares (which pay fixed dividends) of taxable Canadian corporations. They may also invest in the common shares of banks and utilities, which also pay regular dividends.

The dividends paid allow investors to take advantage of the dividend tax credit, allowing for tax-favoured treatment over interest income. In fact, dividends represent the lowest-taxed form of income in every province except Quebec.

Top Funds Scouting Report

Real estate for diversification

Open-end real estate funds, most notable for their price collapse a few years ago, suffered from a fatal design flaw. Basically, it's this: real estate is not a liquid investment, so if investors want to get their money out, the fund is forced to sell assets — which, in a depressed market, is almost certain to be at a loss. This is exactly what happened in 1992 to a number of real estate funds, including **First City RealFund, Counsel Real Estate Fund**, **MD Realty Fund**, and others. The fund managers were unable to unload the properties without wiping out much of the value of the funds. So investors were stuck, and redemptions frozen. The situation changed, however, when these funds finally switched to a closed-end format and began trading on a stock exchange.

Now, a number of real estate investment trusts are available in the Canadian markets, joining some 200 or so trading in the U.S. Real estate offers the potential for capital appreciation and tax-advantaged cash flow and through REITs, you get professional management and liquidity.

An important inflation hedge, these are a worthwhile vehicle for diversification.

11

Some dividend funds are now either including or focusing on higher yielding real estate investment trusts (REITs), royalty and income trust units. A portion of the cash distributed by trusts is often tax deferred due to real estate, resource or business deductions at the trust level. Tax advantages and higher yields are real pluses, but these are really equity investments and are higher risk than traditional preferred shares.

With the wide range of dividend fund types now available, you really must understand what you are investing in. Just because a fund focuses on producing income does not mean that it isn't volatile.

Because of the tax-favoured treatment, it's recommended that these funds be held in investment accounts and not as part of your RRSP or RRIF where the favoured tax treatment will be lost.

EQUITY FUNDS

If you own an equity (or growth) fund, you hope to see an increase in the value of your fund over a period of time. Most of that increase will be in the form of a capital gain.

As a result, equity funds are generally seen to be riskier in the short term. Over the longer term, however, they have historically produced better returns than other types of funds, and are generally more favourably taxed — two significant advantages.

We believe that as part of a well-balanced portfolio, ownership of some growth funds is absolutely essential.

Growth funds have one thing in common: they all hold stocks of Canadian and/or international companies. Beyond that, the differences can be bewildering. Here's how they can be organized to provide some order.

● *Canadian Equity Funds*

This group invests in the common shares of Canadian corporations. The vast majority are eligible for RRSP investing, although many still invest up to 20% of their holdings in U.S. or international equities to provide for greater diversity. In the Canadian equity category, however, there are a number of very distinct sub-categories. They are as follows:

Canadian Large Cap/Diversified Blend. These are funds that invest in a portfolio of common stocks and other equity securities of Canadian companies at a market capitalization above approximately $750 million. Further, this includes a range of diverse management styles such as growth at a reasonable price, sector rotation, momentum investing, and index funds.

Canadian Large Cap/Diversified Value. These funds concentrate on Canadian companies with a market capitalization in excess of $750 million. However, the focus of the managers is on buying value stocks. This means that the stocks they are buying are of companies that are out of favour or undervalued, based on financial measures such as price earnings and price-to-book ratios.

Canadian Large Cap/Diversified Growth. The concentration is on larger companies with a capitalization above approximately $750 million but in this category, managers seek stocks that they believe will grow at a faster rate than the market. In many instances, they are prepared to pay slightly higher prices but believe the expected faster rate of growth will more than compensate.

Canadian Small/Mid-Cap. These are funds that invest primarily in common stocks or other equity securities of Canadian companies with the market capitalization equal to less than 0.1% of the total capitalization of the TSE 300 (i.e., approximately $750 million). A range of styles including growth and value exist within this category. Investors are cautioned to include funds within this group as part of a broader portfolio. Although small cap funds can at times provide eye-popping returns, they can also incur steep losses given their inherent greater volatility.

Canadian Sector Funds. These are funds that invest in specific Canadian industry sectors such as financial services. They allow you to concentrate on a specific area of the market, but again, a caution flag should be raised. Such concentration brings with it the potential for higher returns, but only at significantly greater risk. Sector fund investing should only occur after you have built a broadly diversified portfolio.

Canadian Resources & Precious Metals. These are funds that concentrate on the Canadian resource sector including mining, oil and gas, and forestry as well as those funds that invest in gold and other precious metals through common stocks of Canadian mining companies, or which may actually invest directly in bullion certificates. Although funds in this area have been substantial under-performers of late because of chronicly-depressed commodity prices and an overall trend to disinflation, they still merit attention. Should, as many analysts suspect, inflation begin to perk up as this business cycle moves along, a small allocation to this area can provide an inflation hedge to your total portfolio.

● *U.S. Equity Funds*

These funds are varied in their approach, but invest almost exclusively in the U.S., the world's largest market. After 15 years of extraordinary growth, the medium-to-high teen returns of the past are likely not indicative of future performance. In fact, our prognosis and that of many other experts is that market returns in the U.S. are likely to average in the 9% to 11% range and going forward. This makes the selection of top funds with winning managers an even more vital part of your investment plan. We've subdivided the U.S. equity fund groups into the two following categories:

U.S. Large Cap/Diversified. This includes funds which invest a large portion of their assets in a portfolio of common stocks of U.S. companies with a market capitalization of U.S $2 billion or more. Some funds in this group concentrate on larger capitalization stocks, where the market cap is $9 billion or more

U.S.Small Cap Equity. These are funds which concentrate in common stocks of U.S. companies with a market capitalization of below U.S.$2 billion.

Research Tidbits

Other Countries Outperform

While Canadian stocks and equity mutual funds have produced strong returns recently, don't overlook the fact that over the last 20 years other markets had outperformed ours. The need for international diversification is clear, not only to improve returns but also to reduce risk by spreading your "eggs" among several geographic "baskets".

You will find that size distinction is very important in evaluating funds. Because larger capitalization companies have done so well over the past several years, it is really very important to separate managers, who concentrate on smaller company stocks from the others. Also, although U.S. small cap stocks are more volatile than their larger brethren, we believe there is greater relative value in this area of the market.

● *International Equity Funds*

These are funds that invest in the common stocks or other equity securities of companies outside of Canada. Again, however, there is a tremendous range in the type of international equity funds available. Here are some further categories:

Global Equity. These funds invest in common stocks

WORLD STOCK MARKETS
Compound Annual Return for the 20 Years Ended December 31, 1997 (C$)

Hong Kong	
United Kingdom	
France	
United States	
Italy	
Canada	
Japan	

0%   5%   10%   15%   20%   25%   30%

Source: Rothschild Asset Management Limited

of Canadian, U.S., or foreign companies with no particular concentration on a single country or region. Hence, you get a tremendous range in results in any given time span. Funds with a heavier weighting of Asia will have under-performed of late relative to those that have overweighted in either the U.S. or Europe. It is important, therefore, to look at the long-term track record as you want consistency above all else in your global manager.

International Equity. These are funds that invest in common stocks of companies located outside Canada and the U.S. Here, managers are also able to invest internationally, moving around Europe, Asia, and the emerging markets. Funds in this group, because they haven't been able to access the rich returns of the U.S. markets over the past several years, will tend to have somewhat weaker numbers. However, for individuals who want to pick specific U.S. funds, these are the perfect complement to provide total global coverage.

Global Sector. These are funds that focus on specific industry sectors such as telecommunications, technology, real estate, or financial services but do complete investing internationally including North America, Europe, and Asia.

One area that should demand interest is the growing number of funds that are investing in real estate. Real estate as a distinct asset class adds to the diversification of a portfolio. Many of the newer funds have got around the liquidity problems of the older real estate funds, which used to invest directly in properties by investing in Real Estate Investment Trusts (REITS). Since these are listed on public exchanges like the New York Stock Exchange, they overcome the liquidity problems inherent in real estate while providing access to top quality professional management and broader property diversification.

Regional Equity Funds. We have broken this into four categories including Latin America/Emerging Markets, European, North American, and Asia and the Pacific Rim. Regionally concentrated funds allow investors to overweight a particular area of the world based on anticipated higher returns. Over the past two years, the action has definitely been in Europe and North America. Asian funds have had a disastrous time since mid-1997, while the fallout of the Asian crisis has also hurt Latin America/Emerging Market Funds.

Remember, however, historic returns are no guarantee of future results. In fact, many experts believe that the value available in Asia and the emerging markets today merits attention in your portfolio. However, given the volatility of these funds and continued uncertainty, it is best to ease slowly into these markets by investing regularly on a monthly basis.

BALANCED FUNDS

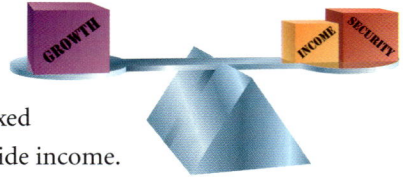

As the name suggests, these funds strive for a balance of assets: common stocks for growth and fixed income instruments like bonds and/or cash to provide income. A balanced fund should be less volatile than an equities-only fund, and will appeal to investors who want a variety of asset categories in their portfolio.

The managers of a balanced fund will generally hold different weightings of asset types, depending on current or anticipated economic developments. Most work within a framework of holding not more than 60% or less than 40% in equities or fixed income at any given time.

Read the fine print here. There is a world of difference between a fund confined to a 40% to 60% equity weighting with the balance in bonds to one which is allowed to go to much higher equity levels.

The more equity allowed in the fund objectives, the higher the potential reward but also the higher the risk. You want to make sure your balanced fund is tailored to your risk profile.

Philosophically, a balanced fund makes sense and Canadians have responded very positively to the 320 balanced funds available.

In fact, balanced funds are much more popular here than in the U.S. where they have never caught on. Perhaps, this is a reflection of our national character. Recently, there has also been a move to more and more international balanced funds as Canadians look for a conservative way to invest globally while still achieving growth in their portfolios.

We have broken balanced funds down into three distinct types.

Canadian Strategic Balanced. These are funds where the asset weighting is relatively stable over time and the manager invests in a blend of Canadian stocks and bonds. The stability of the stock and bond allocation in these funds allows an investor to build them into a long-term plan with greater confidence.

Canadian Tactical Balanced. Again, the managers invest in a blend of Canadian stocks and bonds but here they attempt to improve performance by switching between the asset classes as expected returns change. You should note that these are really tactical asset allocation or market timing funds and the caveats laid out in the following section on asset allocation funds apply.

Global Strategic Balanced. These are funds that invest in a blend of Canadian, U.S., and/or International stocks and bonds. Here again, asset class weightings remain relatively stable over time. Hence, these funds allow investors to access a globally diversified portfolio with much less volatility than a straight equity fund.

ASSET ALLOCATION FUNDS AND SERVICES

With the continuing growth in technology and increasing public awareness of portfolio management theory and practice, the diversification concept underlying balanced funds has evolved into a sophisticated range of asset allocation funds and services now available to Canadian investors.

There are **two** dramatically different types of asset allocation funds or services available. Although they share the same name, they are worlds apart philosophically, so you should know the difference between them and what it is you are buying.

The **first** type is called "tactical" asset allocation. This is essentially a market-timing approach where the manager attempts to move into the right asset group at the right time based on forecasts of superior short-term market performance. They differ from balanced funds in that their approach is frequently more quantitative and they tend to trade more frequently. Typically they have the right to go to 100% in cash, bonds, or equities. As such, their returns can be much more volatile than the average balanced fund, but when they are right, they can also achieve much higher returns.

Tactical asset allocation is implemented either directly in a fund through purchases of appropriate securities or by switching between members of a fund family. AGF, for example, has its Canadian and American tactical funds which buy and sell stocks, bonds, and cash within the fund, as well as its Canadian Asset Allocation Service, which implements its strategies using three of their Canadian funds.

The **second** type is called "strategic" asset allocation. Unlike "tactical" which tries to time the market—making one market call—for all investors, strategic asset allocation defines an optimal portfolio for investors based on their individual risk tolerance, age, return needs, and the like. In fact, clients must complete a detailed questionnaire to properly identify their needs.

Research Tidbits

Forget Market Timing

Mutual fund investors have shown a tendency to reallocate their assets/withdraw their funds entirely based on market movements; that is, they buy high and sell low. Over a 10-year period, investor returns were reduced by 1.1% a year through poor market timing.

"Source: "Buy High, Sell Low: Timing Errors in Mutual Fund Allocations", The Journal of Portfolio Management, vol.22, no.1 (Fall 1995). Stephen Nesbitt (Summer 1996 CFA Digest).

The optimal portfolio is based on quantitative models of long-term returns, volatility, and patterns of movement among the asset classes, which strive to achieve the highest possible return for a given level of risk. Hence, you get a range of portfolios from very conservative to very aggressive, and a client is directed to the portfolio which best suits his or her needs.

Mackenzie's STAR program which has developed 17 portfolios for different investor profiles has been a leader in this area. Among the no-load funds, the Bank of Montreal's Matchmaker program leads.

SEGREGATED FUNDS

Segregated funds have often been called the life insurance industry's "best kept secret". Well, that secret is now out in the open as numerous mutual fund companies working directly with insurance companies are launching segregated fund product lines.

Essentially, a segregated fund combines the features of an investment fund with the elements of an insurance contract. As a result, you end up with an open-ended investment fund that is combined with death benefits, maturity dates, and guarantees as in many other insurance contracts. The term "segregated" is a result of the requirement that assets in these funds must be kept *distinct* and *separate* from the other assets of the issuing insurance company.

Segregated funds have a number of advantages that have led to skyrocketing sales in the past year. *First*, these products usually provide a guaranteed return of anywhere from 75% to up to 100% of your initial investment, on the earlier of maturity (typically 10 years) or your death. The percentage death benefit guarantee often varies by age, so this should be examined in the specific contracts.

Lately, a number of companies have been allowing investors to reset their maturity guarantee several times a year. This means you are able to reset the time clock on the guaranteed return of your investment amount for a new term. This insures that the investor can update his return of principal guarantee on an ongoing basis. This feature has been particularly attractive to investors who are conservative or concerned with the high valuations of today's markets.

Second, segregated funds can provide an important element of creditor protection under certain circumstances. This is due to the fact that under provincial insurance laws, insurance monies may be protected from creditors, if certain conditions exist. For example, there has to be a named beneficiary who is the spouse, parent, child, or grandchild of the annuitant, or in the case of Quebec, the contract holder. Notably, there is always the potential for this creditor proofing to be nullified if the investor is insolvent at the time of the deposit into the plan. Additionally, there have been cases where family dependants have been able to access such monies. Hence, if credit protection is a factor in your decision to purchase a segregated fund, you should be consulting directly with your financial and legal advisors about your personal circumstances.

Third, if you name a beneficiary other than your estate, your investment will bypass the probate process, thereby saving fees. Again, probate fees vary radically by province and must be investigated at an individual level.

Are all these benefits there at no cost? Of course not. There is a charge for the maturity and death benefit elements on top of the normal management expense ratio (MER) charges for the investment element of the fund. For example, in the case of Trimark's recently announced family of segregated funds, the maturity and death benefits guarantee adds approximately 0.20% to the cost of fixed income funds, 0.45% to the cost of balanced funds, and 0.80% to the cost of equity funds. So you are paying a hefty extra charge for these benefits.

A major criticism of segregated funds is that a 10-year guarantee is of little real value, given the fact that with the exception of the Great Depression of the 30s, equities in Canada and in the U.S. have never lost money over a 10-year period, as measured by the major stock market benchmark indices. In fact, a recent study of over 500 mutual funds of all categories in Canada with at least 10 years of performance under their belt indicates that only nine actually ended up losing money.

For many individuals either younger or wealthier, buying term insurance combined with mutual funds may actually be a much cheaper approach. Finally, the benefits of credit proofing and avoidance of probate fees are individual specific. Depending on your occupation, age, and the province where you live, these factors may or may not be of benefit.

Nevertheless, segregated funds have brought a brand new package of benefits to the fund table. In recognition of this, the Monster Tables on pages 209-302 now identify these segregated funds by an (S) beside the fund name so that you can identify them for separate evaluation.

OPEN-END & CLOSED-END FUNDS

Although the emphasis in this book is on the more popular "open-end" fund, you may occasionally run across the "closed-end" type. These are not the same thing at all, and it's important to understand the differences.

In an "open-end" fund you can invest in, or take your money out of, the fund at any time. The money you invest is added to the money already contributed by others. The number of units you receive on purchase (or the amount you'll receive on sale) is determined by the value per unit (net asset value, or NAV, as it's called) when you buy or sell.

An open-end fund has an unlimited number of units and the NAV is determined by taking the current market value of all the assets of the fund, and dividing by the number of units or shares outstanding.

For example, if a fund had $100,000 in net assets and there were 10,000 units outstanding, the NAV would be $10. That's the price a seller would receive. Conversely, if someone had $1,000 to invest in the fund, they'd receive 100 units.

A fund's NAV is generally calculated and published each day. Because the fund issues additional units on demand, the value of already outstanding units is not reduced ("diluted") as a result of new purchases. Depending on the fund type, the return to an investor comes from dividends or interest earned from investments made by the fund (usually reinvested to buy more units) and/or from an increase in the market value of the fund's portfolio.

So in our example, assume that the original number of units had been increased over time to 115 as a result of reinvesting dividends to purchase more units (the usual strategy) and that the NAV on the day of sale had increased to $13 as a result of an increase in the underlying value of the assets. The amount received (ignoring possible redemption charges) would be $13 \times 115 = $1,495$.

The vast majority of funds sold today are open-end funds, but let's take a quick look at the other type — closed-end.

CLOSED-END FUNDS

Closed-end funds begin by raising capital from the public by offering shares in much the same way a public corporation does. The money raised is then invested by a fund manager as it is in an open-end fund.

However, once the money has been raised, the fund is "closed" and there are no

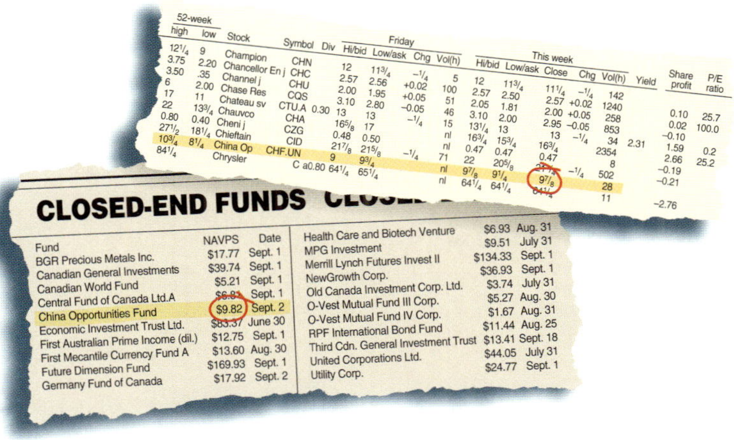

52-week							Friday					This week								
high	low	Stock	Symbol	Div	Hi/bid	Low/ask	Chg	Vol(h)		Hi/bid	Low/ask	Close	Chg	Vol(h)	Yield	Share profit	P/E ratio			
12¼	9	Champion	CHN		12	11¾		5	12	11¾		11¼	−¼	142						
3.75	2.20	Chancellor En j	CHC		2.57	2.56	−¼	100	2.57	2.50		2.57	+0.02	1240		0.10	25.7			
3.50	.35	Channel j	CHU		2.00	1.95	+0.02	51	2.05	1.81		2.00	+0.05	258		0.02	100.0			
6	2.00	Chase Res	CQS		3.10	2.80	+0.05	46	3.10	2.00		2.95	−0.05	853		−0.10				
17	11	Chateau sv	CTU.A	0.30	13	13	−0.05	15	13¼	13		13	−¼	34	2.31	1.59	0.2			
22	13¾	Chauvco	CHA		16⅝	17	−¼	nl	16¾	15¼		16¾		2354		2.66	25.2			
0.80	0.40	Cheni j	CZG		0.48	0.50		nl	0.47	0.47		0.47		8		−0.19				
27½	18¼	Chieftain	CID		21⅞	21⅝		71	22	20⅝				502		−0.21				
10¾	8¼	China Op	CHF.UN		9	9¾	−¼	nl	9⅞	9¼		9⅞		28						
84¼		Chrysler	C	a0.80	64¼	65¼		nl	64¼	64¼		64¼		11		−2.76				

CLOSED-END FUNDS CLO...

Fund	NAVPS	Date			
BGR Precious Metals Inc.	$17.77	Sept. 1	Health Care and Biotech Venture	$6.93	Aug. 31
Canadian General Investments	$39.74	Sept. 1	MPG Investment	$9.51	July 31
Canadian World Fund	$5.21	Sept. 1	Merrill Lynch Futures Invest II	$134.33	Sept. 1
Central Fund of Canada Ltd.A	$6.83	Sept. 1	NewGrowth Corp.	$36.93	Sept. 1
China Opportunities Fund	$9.82	Sept. 2	Old Canada Investment Corp. Ltd.	$3.74	July 31
Economic Investment Trust Ltd.	$83.37	June 30	O-Vest Mutual Fund III Corp.	$5.27	Aug. 30
First Australian Prime Income (dil.)	$12.75	Sept. 1	O-Vest Mutual Fund IV Corp.	$1.67	Aug. 31
First Mecantile Currency Fund A	$13.60	Aug. 30	RPF International Bond Fund	$11.44	Aug. 25
Future Dimension Fund	$169.93	Sept. 1	Third Cdn. General Investment Trust	$13.41	Sept. 18
Germany Fund of Canada	$17.92	Sept. 2	United Corporations Ltd.	$44.05	July 31
			Utility Corp.	$24.77	Sept. 1

Investor interest in China pushed up the market price of shares in the China Opportunities Fund to just over their net asset value per share (NAVPS). Such premiums are relatively rare among closed-end funds, which usually trade at a discount to NAVPS.

more units offered. If you want to sell, you can do so on a stock exchange or on the "over the counter" market; if you want to buy, you must buy from an owner of the fund's units who's willing to sell.

The NAV of these funds is generally calculated and published weekly in the Saturday edition of *The Globe and Mail*: Report on Business and the weekend *Financial Post*. Keep in mind, however, that the NAV does not represent the selling price of a closed-end fund's units. The price is set by supply and demand in the market and, often, the market bids the price down below the NAV — often 10% to 30% below — mostly because they are harder to sell, and are, therefore, considered to have a lower investment value.

Thus, while there may be opportunities for a sophisticated investor to profit by dealing in closed-end funds, for most investors they are less attractive options than an open-end fund because of their lack of flexibility, liquidity, and more limited choice.

COUNTING THE COST

There are two basic types of costs in the purchase of a mutual fund: *sales charges* and *management fees*. Both can have an impact upon your bottom-line returns. There may also be some miscellaneous charges that apply. In this section we'll provide an overview of these costs and offer some tips that may be helpful as you make these important decisions.

THE OBVIOUS COSTS: SALES CHARGES

● *Front-End Loads*

If you opt for a front-load fund, an agreed-upon percentage of your total investment will be deducted. So if you pay 4% on a $10,000 purchase, the actual amount invested will be ($10,000 − 4%) = $9,600.

While it used to be normal to pay loads of up to 9%, the situation is quite different today. It's now extremely unusual to pay more than 5% on even a small investment; on larger amounts, a lower rate can usually be negotiated between you and your broker or advisor. Of course, when you purchase a front-load fund, there is no percentage charge when you sell.

Large investors (for example, those with a quarter of a million dollars or more) can sometimes negotiate no front-end commissions at all. The advisor and his or her firm are compensated with modestly higher trailers or service fees from most fund companies when they select this option.

One exception to negotiable front-end loads is in the discount brokerage community — although here the loads are already quite low. For example, one discount broker advertises a rate of 2.5% on mutual fund investments under $5,000; 2% on orders from $5,000 to $25,000; and 1% on orders larger than $25,000. Other discount brokers are in the same range.

One important note regarding front-load funds is that every dollar taken off your investment will have a negative impact on growth over time: the higher the load, the greater that impact will be (assuming all other things including rate of return, operating and management costs are identical).

● *Back-End Loads*

Sometimes referred to as deferred sales charges (DSCs), these offer an advantage over front-load funds in that all of your money goes to work for you; nothing is deducted. This type of fund was introduced in 1987 and has become very popular over the intervening years.

Here's how it works. If you redeem these units before a certain period (usually about 7 years or so), you pay a fee based on the value of your investment. This percentage declines over time, as shown in the following example:

LOADS	4.5%	4.0%	3.5%	3.0%	2.5%	2.0%	1.0%	0
YEAR	1	2	3	4	5	6	7	...

Several companies charge the redemption fee on the original amount invested; a few, however, charge on the market value of funds when you cash them. In most cases (specifically, where you redeem the fund units for more than you paid), the former approach is preferable for the investor.

REDEMPTION CHARGES

Here's the way several of the larger fund companies currently handle their redemption charges:

Redemption Policy	Acquisition Cost	Redemption Value	Redemption Policy	Acquisition Cost	Redemption Value
AGF	✖		Investors		✖
Canadian International	✖		Mackenzie		✖
Dynamic		✖	Templeton	✖	
Fidelity		✖	Trimark	✖	
Global Strategy	✖		AIC	✖	✖ *
Guardian	✖		Spectrum/United	✖	

* Pre-July 1, 1998 based as acquisition cost; after July 1, 1998 based as redemption rules.

Due to the popularity of back-end load funds, many funds that used to charge only a front-end load can now be purchased either way. Trimark set up a new "Select" group of DSC funds to mirror their successful front-load funds such as the **Trimark Fund** (**Trimark Select Growth**) and the **Trimark Canadian Fund** (**Trimark Select Canadian Growth Fund**).

While it appears at first glance that the back-load approach is the way to go, there are **two** additional factors that should be considered before making a final decision.

Management fees. Some fund companies charge higher management expenses if funds are purchased on a back-load basis than if they are purchased on a front-load basis — often tacking on an extra 0.25% to 0.5%. **Trimark** is a striking example. Their back-load funds cost as much as 0.7% more annually to own. So investors should always choose the front-load option at Trimark.

These costs fall directly to the bottom line, meaning that the difference in net return can be significant. When compounded over several years, this can make a big difference in the value of the fund.

Despite this difference, people still tend to resist "up-front" costs. Indeed, our research shows they are opting overwhelmingly for back-load funds — over 90% of load-fund sales in recent years has been of the back-load variety.

No-Load Funds

Until very recently, no-load funds were available predominantly from banks and trust companies, as well as a few management companies (most notably **Altamira**) which sold directly to the public. In dealing with these companies, one is usually speaking with a salaried employee rather than an independent financial advisor. Not surprisingly, these employees are able to provide information only about the funds offered by their company.

INVESTMENT RETURNS

But there is growing evidence of ongoing change in the mutual fund industry. Only a few years ago, it was not unusual to pay a front load of up to 9% on a fund you purchased. Then came the back-end load funds and the practice of paying a front load on virtually any amount came abruptly to a halt.

There has been a similar trend toward no-load funds, though it comes in fits and starts. With nothing deducted on purchase and no redemption charges, this approach obviously has benefits for the investor. It is becoming increasingly popular in the U.S. and there are a number of fund companies in Canada that have introduced no-load options.

In this situation, the broker, mutual fund salesperson, or financial advisor receives little or no up-front commission from the fund company; instead, he or she receives a slightly higher than normal ongoing service or trailer fee. (See *Top Funds Close Up*). Typically available only to larger clients at this time, but likely to spread, this development will probably make life more difficult for newcomers to the business, since up-front commissions are likely to be significantly reduced. However, for those who have an established clientele, the increased trailer or service fees could generate substantially more ongoing income.

So it looks like we're soon going to see a situation that investors are really going to love: a much wider range of funds available on a no-load basis and ongoing financial advice at little or no direct cost.

WHAT YOU DON'T SEE: MANAGEMENT EXPENSES

The second, and less well understood, cost involved in the ownership of mutual funds is management fees. In fact, a Survey of Mutual Fund Fees conducted by Scudder Funds of Canada in late May of 1997 found that 45% of Canadians who purchased mutual funds during the past year believed their mutual fund did not charge management fees at all, while 8% were unsure.

Top Funds Close Up

The Dealer's Deal

On a front-load investment, the dealer (i.e., the investment company whose agent or representative sold the fund) receives the full amount of the load, which generally ranges from 2% to 5%. On a back-load investment, the range is about 4% to 5%.

Each dealer then pays its sales representatives a portion, generally from 40% to 80% of the dealer compensation. The remainder is retained to cover salaries and operating costs incurred by the dealer in carrying on business.

In many cases "trailer" or "service" fees are also paid to sales representatives. These are not paid by the investor, however (at least not directly), but are paid out of the management fees charged by the fund managers.

Critics of these charges say they could lead to increased management fees and/or higher expense ratios that affect an investor's return. While this is a possibility, it is not automatically true that an increase in management fees is charged to pay trailer fees.

To have the benefit of the skills and experience of several of the world's best money managers, combined with the ongoing advice and recommendations of a personal financial advisor is well worth 2% per year to growing numbers of investors.

<mark>Well, just like any business, mutual fund companies—including the no-load funds—charge these fees.</mark> They are the means by which the fund managers are reimbursed for their time, expertise, and (one hopes) the attractive returns they generate for their unitholders. They also reimburse the companies for costs incurred in establishing, maintaining, and promoting the fund, as well as for service fees paid to advisors and their firms.

Management fees generally range between 1% and 2.5% of the total assets under management. In some cases, this percentage will decline as the assets held by the fund increase. But most often the fees are determined by the type of assets held and, presumably, the work required to manage them — usually 2% for equity-based funds, and about 1% for cash management funds.

Management fees are typically charged directly to the fund, which means that investors do not receive a statement of the amount. But make no mistake — they do have an impact on the fund's return. For example, if a fund charges a 2% management fee and earns a 20% return in a given year, the investor's net return is 18%.

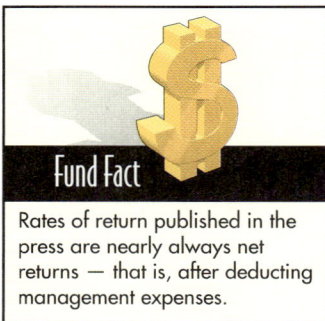

Fund Fact

Rates of return published in the press are nearly always net returns — that is, after deducting management expenses.

While some critics feel these fees are too high, there is a growing number of funds offering lower management fees. Scudder Funds of Canada ,which started in October 1995 and offers a family of no-load funds, is a prime example.

Further, many investors are looking for more than returns. First, they want guidance in selecting the right funds from the bewildering choice available in building a portfolio of funds suited to their needs. Also in today's complex world of ever changing economic and financial trends as well as tax and pension legislation, they want their funds integrated into a coherent financial plan and when implemented, want it accompanied by ongoing education, advice, and service.

Given these needs and the superlative returns of the past decade, the case against "higher" fees diminishes. Interestingly, it is the no-load funds—which typically do not involve advisors—which are much more expensive relative to their U.S. counterparts (see *Top Funds Close Up*/Comparing Management Expenses, page 24).

Fees, however, do matter. Investors have to pick the right funds and, if applicable, the right advisor to ensure they are getting value. Also, we believe that as the industry continues to grow and mature, we will see a trend towards lower fees emerging.

Investors should not pay as much attention to management fees as to the **management expense ratio**. This figure is expressed as a percentage of the fund's total assets and totals **all management fees** (those referred to above) **as well as** other expenses charged to the fund. Typically, these include legal, accounting, custodial, and safekeeping costs, as well as the costs of producing prospectuses and other reports. All else being equal, the higher the management expense ratio, the more money is being spent by the manager and the lower the return to the investor, so be sure to examine these factors when considering any fund purchase.

TRADING COSTS

One of the biggest hidden costs in any mutual fund is the commission cost or brokerage fee paid to trade the underlying stocks and bonds. Because these costs are buried in the price of the securities, they are not visible to the investor. Funds which move in and out of stocks and bonds on a frequent basis will have higher trading costs and hence, will have to perform that much better to deliver returns to investors.

THOSE LITTLE "EXTRAS"

There are a few other charges that may apply to the fund you are considering. These include:

● *Set-Up Fees*

This is a one-time fee often charged by "no load" companies. It's usually in the range of $40 or so.

● *Close-Out or Transfer Fees*

You may be charged a modest fee for closing out your account with a particular fund company. Many fund companies charge $20 on the termination or transfer out of a tax plan for an RRSP or a RRIF. Growing numbers of financial institutions are also charging this fee.

● *Trustee Fees for RRSPs, RRIFs, or RESPs (Registered Education Savings Plan)*

For these types of accounts, an annual trustee fee may be charged, usually about $25–$50. Some fund companies have eliminated their RRSP and RRIF fees altogether, so remember to enquire before you invest.

● *Systematic Withdrawal Fees/Charges*

A systematic withdrawal plan (SWP) allows investors to receive regular income from their fund. A few companies charge an annual fee, while others charge a fee for each withdrawal.

● *NSF Cheque Charge*

If you set up a regular investment program and invest monthly by preauthorized cheque, you may have to pay a service charge. If the identified bank account has insufficient funds to make the systematic investment, expect to pay a fee of about $15.

● *Switching Fees*

Nearly all companies allow switching from one fund to another within the same family. Often the prospectus will allow for a negotiable charge of between 0% and 2%. You should not usually expect to pay for occasional switches.

However, in order to control costs for the typical investor, many mutual fund companies are now charging a small fee for trades above a minimum level in a bid to ensure market timers and sector players pay for their own never-ending trading.

THE BIGNESS DEBATE: IS BIGGER BETTER?

Is a bigger fund a better investment than a smaller fund? Does size equal performance? We did some research to see if it was so. We looked at six major asset classes to see if the giants did outperform their smaller counterparts. We analyzed Canadian equity funds (large-cap and small-cap), bond funds, balanced funds, as well as U.S. equities, international bond and equity funds.

Our methodology was simple. We took the top 25% of funds in terms of assets and compared them against the top quartile performers over three and five years in their category. To make the comparisons more precise, the top quartile was adjusted based on the total number of funds which had three-and five-year histories. For example, there are 110 Canadian bond funds that have been around for three years. We, therefore, used the top quartile or 28 funds by asset size and compared their three-year performance against the top 28 funds ranked by percentage return. There are only 89 bond funds with five-year records, however, with a top quartile of only 23 funds. These 23 funds were compared against the top 23 five-year performers. If larger funds performed better than smaller funds, you would expect their names to pop up in the top performer group more often than their numbers would predict.

We then looked at the really big funds—the "Top Ten" in each category. Equally weighted portfolios of these "Top Ten" were created, and the average three- and five-year annual compound rates of return, as well as the management expense ratio were calculated. We then compared them to the numbers for the average fund in that asset class. Canadian small-cap funds are a relatively recent innovation and there are not many with five-year records. We, therefore, used the "Big Five."

After a rigorous and exhaustive study, our response to the "Is Bigger Better?" question is an unequivocal…probably.

Being top quartile by size does not seem to be particularly advantageous. Of our six asset classes, only the bigger U.S. and international equity funds outperformed their smaller cousins. The other four classes were either average or under performers. The "Top Ten" tells a different story, however. In all classes except international bonds, the "Top Ten" portfolios were also top performers over both three- and five-year periods.

It was a close race in Canadian fixed income, but the big bond funds won by a mere 0.4% over both time periods. At the other end of the scale, the Canadian small-cap "Top 5" returned 20.6% over three years versus 16.2% for the average small-cap fund, and 23.2% over five years versus 18.5% for the small fry. Over five years, this difference of 4.7% adds up to an extra $501 on a $1000 investment, so that's impressive.

Our research indicates that management fees are also lower in the big funds. This makes intuitive sense. Many of the fixed costs associated with running a mutual fund are pretty well the same whether the fund has $100 million or $500 million in assets. Economies of scale also come into play when a fund is trading securities in bulk. A big fund has more clout when negotiating commissions and fees. The "spread", or the difference between the buying and selling price, can tighten up for these preferred clients. The only exception to this "Bigger is cheaper" rule is our "Top Ten" balanced fund portfolio, which is actually 0.17% higher than the asset class average.

Why the performance gap between big and small funds? There are *three* key reasons, all having to do with success breeding success.

The **first** is simply great fund management. Not every big fund is superbly managed, or triumphs in every market climate. But consistency wins investor loyalty and builds a fund over time. While some funds balloon because of great marketing, lasting size is usually the result of investment success.

Second, lower expenses. Take bond funds, where expenses are so important. The average management expense ratio for the 13 largest bond funds is 1.5%—low, but still not low enough in our opinion—versus 1.7% for the rest of the pack. The economies created by size allow for a wider base across which to spread the fixed costs of managing a fund.

Research Tidbits

Mutual funds are a curious product: the highest quality is often found at the lowest price. Successful and established funds usually have lower expenses, while unproven upstarts often charge a bundle.

The **third** reason is trading and research economies. Bigger funds can afford more talent, whether in the form of more attention from brokerage analysts or more money for in-house analysts. And they pay even lower commissions on some trades than the already slim institutional rates.

The major argument against the bigger funds has been the "supertanker" analogy—that they lack the nimbleness necessary to make a change when conditions warrant it. Of course, supertankers don't need to make emergency course changes if the skipper and crew are professional seamen. They stay on course and don't take shortcuts on the way to their next port of call. Top funds are managed the same way.

We do believe that there is some validity to the argument that small-cap funds need to be nimble. Large funds require a proportionally large position in a stock in order to make the investment worthwhile. In a volatile market, there may be liquidity problems if the manager tries to sell or buy the stock without having an effect on the market price.

The bottom line? Don't use fund size as the main factor when choosing a fund. Many of our *Top Funds 1999* picks are big funds. Just as many are not big funds. Our methodology seeks out the outstanding performers, regardless of fund size.

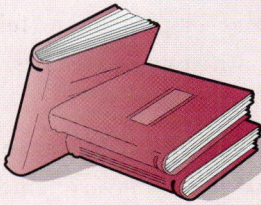

Research Tidbits

Big Is Beautiful

Many observers believe that large mutual funds should be avoided by investors because it's difficult for large funds to be nimble and outperform the market. Research by Value Line indicates just the opposite. Growth stock funds with over $1 billion in assets outperformed both those with less than $1 billion and those with less than $500 million over a ten-year period.

Time Frame	Greater than $1 billion Assets	Less than $1 billion and more than $500 million Assets	Less that $500 million Assets
3 years	16.7%	16.0%	15.9%
5 years	15.6%	13.7%	13.9%
10 years	13.8%	12.0%	12.1%
# of funds	61	139	181

Source: Value Line No-Load Fund Advisor, July 1996.
See also "The Bigness Debate," pages 24–26.

FUNDS DO BETTER

ALL-FUND INDEX TELLS BY HOW MUCH: 21 YEARS OF DATA

Tempted to abandon mutual funds for the seemingly more "secure" pastures of GICs? Think again. Over the past 20 years, or about four full market cycles, mutual funds have outperformed GICs.

By how much is revealed in the Equion All-Fund Index. It's a composite of all mutual funds in Canada, weighted by each fund size. Dating back to January 1, 1977, the index reveals that mutual funds have averaged an impressive growth of 12.5% compounded annually, while 5-year GICs have on average grown by 9.5% annually in the same period.

In dollar terms, a $1,000 investment in the All-Fund Index at its inception had grown to $13,124 by June 30, 1998 compared with only $6,936 for the average GIC. Updated weekly, the index level is reported in dollars to represent the value today of a $1,000 investment in all mutual funds in Canada at the start of 1977, and it is printed every week in *The Globe and Mail*.

From the index's 21-year history, investors can glean **three** important lessons.

The **first** is that mutual funds "collectively" deliver excellent value. They not only do better than GICs, they have outperformed the TSE stock index including dividends, and they have clobbered inflation. Not just over some lucky period when things were going well, but over a long time, through periods of inflation, deflation, war, recessions, referendums, 20% interest rates, and boom times.

The **second** lesson is that a balanced portfolio is the best blend of risk and return. The All-Fund Index is representative of such a portfolio because it is made up of all funds—equity, bond, resource, international, balance, mortgage, and sector funds. (The index excludes money market funds because they're just another way of holding cash.)

GICs or MUTUAL FUNDS?

Equion's All-Fund Index shows mutual funds beat GICs

January 1, 1977 to June 30, 1998

All-Fund ▮ $13,124 — 13.05% annual compound growth

5-year GIC ▮ $6,936 — 9.38% annual compound growth

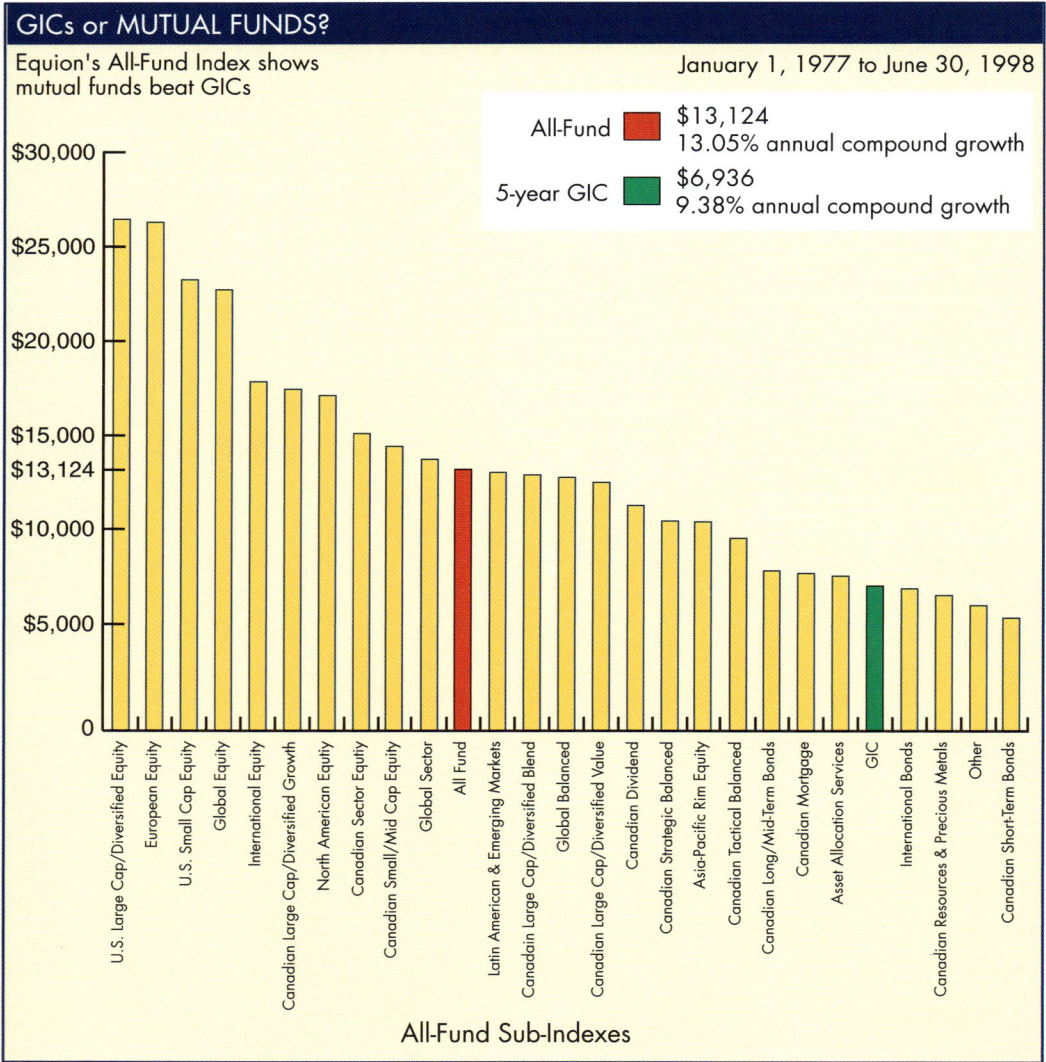

All-Fund Sub-Indexes

Source: THE EQUION GROUP

U.S. equity funds have been the best place to be, followed by European equity funds. A $1,000 investment in 1977 is now worth $26,533 in U.S. large cap equity funds. That's an average return of 17.4% annually. Next best were European equity funds where $1,000 has grown to $26,507. That's an annual return of 18.8%. But that came with more risk. Specifically, these funds showed about the same volatility as the Canadian stock market and about twice the volatility of Canadian bonds. The chart shows the average returns and dollar value for all the sub-indexes of the Equion All-Fund Index.

A balanced portfolio, however, manages to capture much of the extra return offered by equities without much of the risk. Magic? No, it's just plain math. Because some asset classes zig while others zag, balanced investors enjoy a smoother ride.

As the All-Fund Index shows, investors who diversify earn higher returns, with lower risk. The Index has a standard deviation of 8.8, about a third less risky than the TSE 300 total return index, but it shows a higher rate of return than the TSE. (Standard deviation is a widely used measure of risk.)

The **third** lesson from the 21-year history of the All-Fund Index: Don't even try to time the market. Even during the severe recession of 1980-82, contrary to what you might expect with the benefit of hindsight, the All-Fund Index did well. It rose 35% over that three-year period.

Instead of moving in and out of the market, hang in and put the market to work for you. The All-Fund Index has made money in 18 of the past 21 years, and beaten 5-year GICs in 15 of 20 years.

These types of results aren't an exaggeration of the merit of mutual funds. If anything, the All-Fund Index is a conservative growth yardstick. Because it includes all funds, it is a reasonable indicator of how much you should be able to make without taking big risks, picking strong-performing funds or adding value in any other way.

The truth is, bad funds did exist. But they've been folded, or merged with another fund. When that happens, the poor record vanishes and the merged fund adopts the record of the better fund. The All-Fund Index includes those poor funds, thus avoiding the upward bias of the monthly fund averages.

An index composed of every fund also avoids other selection biases. It doesn't just pick the good performers, or restrict itself to the big funds, which tend to do a little better than the overall fund universe.

In short, the All-Fund Index provides a snapshot of the big picture, something that investors often lose sight of. And the big picture is clear: Funds do better!

Judge Your Portfolio by Olympic Standards

You watch the Olympics when they are on TV, don't you? It's no surprise that most events are classified by gender, weight, distance, and the like. Sprinters and marathon runners are put into distinct events, for example, recognizing the very different objectives of these contests and the capabilities and skills of the participants.

Mutual funds are no different. Funds can be categorized by asset (e.g., equities versus bonds), market capitalization (e.g., small- versus large-capitalization stocks), management style, and geographic coverage.

Most importantly, each fund category varies materially in terms of the key investor objectives of long-run return potential and risk as measured by negative fluctuations.

For example, our research indicates Canadian bond funds have experienced an average annual return of 8.7% from January 1977 to June 30, 1998 compared to Canadian equity funds with a 13.2% return over the same period. Yet, the worst annual return for bond funds was a minus 4.4% return in 1994 compared to a minus 16.0% for Canadian equity funds in 1990.

In judging the performance of the funds in your portfolio, then, it is critical to evaluate them relative to the proper fund categories. Just as you can make the world's best marathon runners appear slow by putting them against a mediocre sprinter in the 100-metre dash, you can make a mediocre fund a hero by misclassifying it.

Here's a telling example. At a recent presentation, a particular fund was profiled as a big winner because its 20% plus returns so far this year dwarfed the TSE 300's 12% or so return. Great fund? Maybe so but not because of this comparison.

The fund in question was a Canadian small- to mid-cap equity fund. The more apt comparison would be Equion's Canadian small- to mid-cap equity fund sub-index which was up 22% over the same period. Sprinters should be judged by sprinting and not marathon standards. Everybody knows that in boxing it's the heavyweights that really count. It's the same in mutual funds.

Weight class is also critical to proper measurement. Everybody knows that in boxing it's the heavyweights that really count. It's the same in mutual funds.

Let's say, for the sake of an example, there are only two funds in a category; one is a heavyweight with a $1 billion in assets that does 1% in the year while the other is a newcomer with a $100 million that does 9%. What's the relevant average for performance comparison?

Well, if you picked 5%, you're wrong. That's the average fund experience, not the average investor experience. The more relevant number is a market weighted average that recognizes the fund that was ten times larger did one ninth as well. The market weighted average would be 1.7%—dramatically lower but really much more representative of the average investor experience in the group.

That's why Equion chose a market weighted approach in developing its All-Fund Index and its 25 sub-indexes. It allows a real read of investor experience, not a simple fund average. For example, as of June 30, 1998 the All-Fund Index was up 7.0% year to date. That's the average investor experience in Canadian mutual and segregated funds (excluding money market funds only) so far this year. How do your returns compare?

Also, to provide easier and more timely comparisons, Equion's Managed Money Research Department has reclassified the over 1800 funds that it monitors with a total current value of some $320 billion into the same categories as the new format of *The Globe and Mail*. That means each week you are able to easily track your fund price changes and performance relative to the appropriate sub-index.

So proper categorization, market weighting, comprehensiveness, and timeliness—it's all there so you can start picking the best sprinters, marathon runners, and other top performers to make your portfolio Olympic quality.

ANNOUNCEMENT

MACKENZIE/CUNDILL ALLIANCE

In early July 1998, Mackenzie and Cundill announced a 10-year contract whereby Cundill mutual funds would become the fourth fund family administered by Mackenzie; they currently handle Industrial, Ivy, and Universal funds.

According to the announcement, Peter Cundill is anxious that his team concentrate on investment management and research (what they do best), and leave the administration to Mackenzie, which has an outstanding reputation for marketing, innovation systems and client support.

The Cundill investment approach (a basically contrarian style) involves buying securities trading below their "true" value, following guidelines set by Benjamin Graham. The firm believes that this approach will make Cundill funds good choices for diversification to go along with the more traditional investment approaches used by Mackenzie.

Cundill administers about $900 million assets. Mackenzie manages over $31 billion on behalf of the over one million investors in Canada and the U.S.

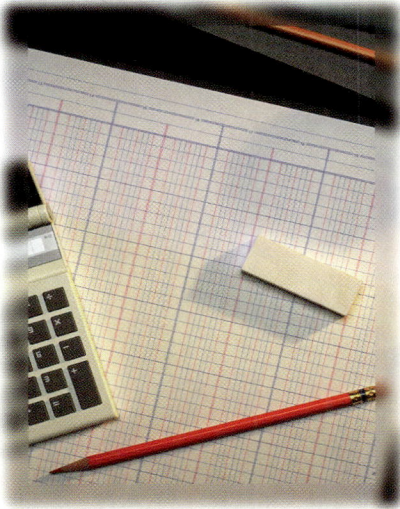

THE TOP FUNDS SELECTION METHOD

• • • • • • • • • • •

IN SEARCH OF "REAL" PERFORMANCE

Take a look at any mutual fund advertisement and chances are you'll find a lot of impressive numbers that attest to the fund's performance over the past six months, a year, three years, or five years — all of which makes the fund look like a pretty attractive investment. But take a look at the fine print down near the bottom of the ad, which usually reads something like this:

"The performance data represents past performance and is not necessarily indicative of future returns..."

So what gives? Well, the disclaimer comes to you courtesy of your provincial securities regulator, who recognizes that performance figures can be deceiving.

Consider, for example, a fund that advertises an average annual rate of return of 65% over one year, and 25% over three years. Sounds good, doesn't it? But these figures could reflect a disturbingly roller-coaster performance record — say, a 30% loss followed by a 50% gain, followed by a 65% gain. In this scenario, you would have done fine if you had held the fund for the entire three-year period. But what if you'd panicked and sold after the first-year loss? Or if you'd sold out after two years for an average gain of 2.5%?

The fact is that just about any fund can make itself look good if it chooses the right measurement period.

Research Tidbits

Superior Funds Persistently Superior... Or Are They?

Results of this study indicate that a portfolio constructed by buying funds with the highest four-year returns earned risk-adjusted returns 6.12% higher than the return on a benchmark weighted portfolio over a two-year investment horizon. Further analysis shows persistent "abnormal" returns during a one- to three-year investment horizon using three- and four-year evaluations. The results demonstrate the persistence of superior performing funds.

In another study on the same topic, the authors analyzed the quarterly investment returns of 54 no-load Canadian equity mutual funds from the fourth quarter of 1988 to the fourth quarter of 1993. Their research indicated no evidence of persistence in winners. They did not repeat their past performance and in no way mirror future returns. The authors conclude: "That can only mean, then, that an investor cannot actually devise a mutual fund strategy that will consistently generate excess returns".

Sources:
David A. Volkman and Mark Wohar. "Abnormal Profits and Relative Strength in Mutual Fund Returns", Review of Financial Economics, vol.5, no.2 (1996) (Spring 1997, CFA Digest). John Ramseyer and Lucy Ackert. "Win Some, Lose Some," Canadian Investment Review, vol. IX, no.3 (Fall 1996).

Fund Fact

Do people really rely on past performance that much? Absolutely, yes! Consider this. The top 10% of Canadian equity funds, based on performance over the three-year period ended December 31, 1992, enjoyed 90% greater sales during the boom of 1993 than all the other funds in that group. And this trend has persisted over the past couple of years as well.

So are the securities regulators right? Is past performance an unreliable indicator of future performance?

Well, most investors think that past performance is important. And so do we — but only if **the performance is measured properly**. The problem is that it's almost impossible to find that kind of performance data in conventional sources.

WHAT NEWSPAPER LISTINGS WILL (AND WON'T) TELL YOU

If you're one of the many people who spend hours comparing mutual funds in the monthly or quarterly surveys published by *The Globe and Mail:* Report on Business or *The Financial Post*, then we needn't tell you how seductive past performance figures can be. Past performance is, after all, the only tangible, comparative thing investors have to go on. It's also the easiest yardstick for comparison, making it seem very easy to find the *best* mutual fund in the paper. Trouble is, you've then got a handle on what *was* the best fund, over *that* particular period — whether that's six months or 10 years. You are by no means

UPS & DOWNS

Most mutual fund reviews measure a fund's volatility by the extent to which its monthly returns deviate from the average. Month-to-month consistency may be easy on the nerves, but only if the fund is making money!

CANADIAN EQUITY FUNDS

Fund Name	Fees	Exp. ratio	RRSP	Volatility	3 mo	6 mo	1 yr	2 yr	3 yr	5 yr	NAVPS
Admax Canadian Performance Fund	F9% or R7%	2.45	Y	3	-0.7		-0.38	11.09	7.93	N/A	6.00
All-Canadian Capital Fund	F9%	2%	Y	3		-0.1	11.70	15.99	12.0	7.27	2.36
All-Canadian Compound Fund	N	0%	N	3		-0.1	1.61	15.87	11.7	7.32	15.78
All-Canadian Consumer Fund	F9%	1.97%	N	4		-3.72	5.57	N/A	N/A	N/A	3.62
Altafund Investment Corp	N	2.8%	Y	4	-1.06	9.03	4.21	7.35	2.31	N/A	17.75
Altamira Capital Growth Fund	Y	2.03%	Y	4	3.47	2.93	12.8	1.40	1.09	1.22	13.72
Altamira Equity Fund	N	2.37%	Y		0.82	1.87	3.6	26.6	30.90	1.86	29.39
Altamira North American Recovery	N	1.81%	Y	4	0.17	-1.08	1.71	N/A	N/A	N/A	11.85
Altamira Special growth Fund	N	2.06%	Y	3	-10.44	-14.52	-13.03	14.86	20.52	15.	14.64
Associate Investors Ltd.	F5%	2.34%	Y	3	0.67	-3.80	3.32	8.04	7.01	3.	7.44
Atlas Large Cap Canadian Growth	N	2%	Y	5	1.30	-0.07	6.82	8.29	3.95	2.00	11.66
ABC Fundamental Value					-1.48	2.47	31.03	52.22	35.52	24.99	10.07

assured of having identified what fund is "best" for investors now.

The other problem that comes from looking at past performance figures is that we often compare them over the "wrong" time periods. Our research into the use of standard time periods shows that this factor has a remarkable effect in blurring the line between good and bad funds. In some cases, we've found that reliance on these periods can be worse than useless — it can be hazardous to your wealth!

THE FATAL FLAW: END-DATE BIAS

The one-, three-, five- and 10-year rates of return typically listed in the newspaper are all tied to a single ending day. To illustrate (albeit somewhat unrealistically) the weakness in this approach, let's imagine that a fund doubled in value on the day just prior to June 30, 1998 — the ending date for all the data in this edition of *Top Funds*. Now, that incredible one-day return will exaggerate (upward) historic returns. It would suddenly look as though the fund had done much better over three, five and 10 years — all because of the heavy weighting unconsciously given to the most recent performance.

In fact, this example is not as far-fetched as it sounds. In mid-1998 some funds were posting one-year returns of 50%–80%. Their historical performance appeared (as in the case above) to suggest that these funds had done well over the long term. The result was that they attracted a lot of investors, many of whom were unaware of the cyclical market forces that are inevitably poised to cool down those super-hot funds in a big hurry.

Fund Fact

Past performance is indicative of future returns.
But only if you measure it right.

THE SOLUTION:
MULTI-PERIOD COMPOSITES

To determine the Top Funds featured in this book, we've developed a simple mathematical model that eliminates end-date bias, and allows us to evaluate the past performance of funds in a fairer and much more informative way.

We call this approach the Multi-Period Composite (MPC), and it is not unlike the scoring system used to place athletes in multi-sports events such as the decathlon. Let's explore this analogy a little further.

In the decathlon, we don't add up the number of seconds that an athlete spends running the 100 metres and 400 metres, and compare that sum to that of the other athletes. We treat the events separately. Why? Simply because a one-second difference in time for the 100 metres is vastly more significant than a comparable difference in the 400.

Consequently, decathletes are awarded scores that reflect relative performance within each of their respective events. The overall winner is the individual whose average "place" is the highest.

Think of each year as a decathlon event and different mutual funds as decathletes and you have the essence of the MPC approach.

Not only does the MPC treat time periods as independent, incomparable events—which, after all, they are—it ranks only similar types of funds.

For example, each Canadian equity fund is ranked against other Canadian equity funds for as many years as the fund has been in existence—up to a maximum of fifteen years and a half (far back enough to include two market cycles). Then we just average the ranks to find the Top Funds.

In the decathlon, the best athletes are

those who are consistent. It's tough to win the decathlon with a first in jumps but a last-place finish in sprints. Likewise with mutual funds. It's better to do pretty well in most periods, and eventually earn a rank that is better than most, than it is to do spectacularly some times then horribly in others.

So past performance, properly measured, really does provide useful clues about the future.

But is that it? Is that all there is to finding tomorrow's best funds? Certainly not, although it's the first and most important step—if only because it eliminates over 80% of mutual funds from eligibility for *Top Funds 1999*. The result is that, even before refining our shortlist with more qualitative tests (which we'll get to later), we now have a nucleus of funds that have proven themselves to be consistent performers, and as such, they represent strong investment choices.

ASSESSING THE WINNERS

Every fund within our Top Fund group can be quite justifiably described as a "winner" within its asset category. However, the funds vary considerably in terms of size, longevity, current security holdings, availability of other funds in the same fund family, and volatility.

Therefore, although our Multi-Period Composite analysis substantially delineates the winners, it would be simplistic to rate funds on this measure alone. Instead, we've supplemented our MPC analysis with other quantitative as well as qualitative reviews. We have categorized these qualifiers under the headings of **consistency, risk, reward-to-risk relationship, efficiency,** and **style.**

Top Funds Close Up

Putting MPCs to the Test

The Multi-Period Composite (MPC) method sounds logical enough. But how long does it work in the real world? To find out, we tried a little back testing. Here are the results.

We studied 154 Canadian equity funds between 1980 and 1993. Our hypothesis was that the top funds selected by the MPC model would do better than others. Our control group was the market itself—the (unmanaged) TSE 300 Total Return Index.

The study needed to start at some point that would allow for both adequate *back* data and adequate *subsequent* data to evaluate the merit of these "dumb" or mechanical decisions. So we started the investing in 1988. That gave us enough information to make informed MPC choices and to monitor them for five years. The rule was simply that the funds required a three-year minimum track record up to 1988.

Sure enough, the MPC-selected top funds outperformed the returns of the MPC-selected median and bottom funds by a significant margin. Performance was improved further by taking a more active role, redoing the multi-period composite annually and trading into those funds newly suggested by the MPC study.

The performance of the top funds group also beat the performance of the TSE 300. Though not everything, this quantitative framework is a useful first step in fund selection.

TOP FUND QUALIFIER #1: CONSISTENCY

Consistency involves performance in both good and bad markets. It also has to do with consistency of people — that is, the people at the helm of the fund. Ideally we're looking for no turnover at all (or very little turnover) among managers, research assistants, and others.

Let's examine each of these consistency factors in turn.

PERFORMANCE

The MPC system evaluates a fund's performance history. Consequently, an older fund that had a few rough years in the beginning may not score as well as a younger fund — even if both funds performed equally well in more recent years. How do we overcome this "unfairness"? One way is to "deconstruct" the MPC formula, examining the performance rankings of each Top Fund relative to those in the same group for a given number of recent time periods.

For each category in the Top Funds listings, we provide comparative performance rankings for the years 1984 to June 30, 1998. This is shown graphically as a matrix consisting of 15 columns, each representing a year in the aforementioned time periods, and four rows, each representing the "performance quartile" for the time period. Consider the following example:

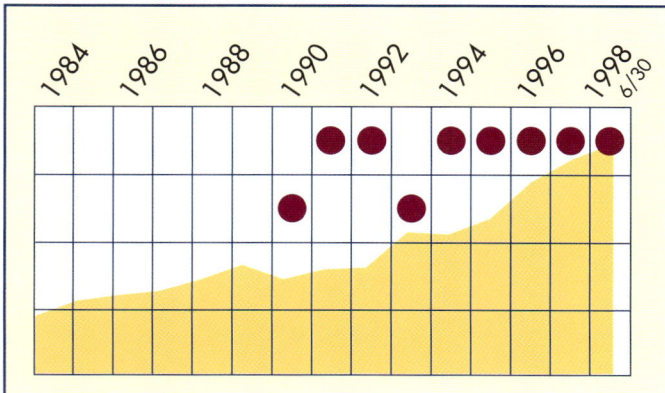

Here we see that in 1990, the fund started in the second performance quartile. In other words, it performed better than 50% of the funds (those in the third and fourth quartiles), but not as well as the 25% in the first quartile. In 1991, however, the fund moved up to the first quartile, outperforming 75% of funds in the same category. Note, too, the absence of data prior to 1990. This indicates either that the fund did not exist before this date, or that the number of funds in its category or "universe" was less than 20— a number below which quartile rankings are not meaningful.

Another benefit of comparing performance over discrete (that is, non-overlapping) time periods is that it allows us to see how similar funds fared in good and bad markets. Referring back to the figure on page 42, note the shaded graph in the background — indicating, in this example, the relative performance of the Canadian equity fund sub-index.

Appearing weekly in *The Globe and Mail* as well as other newspapers across the country, this sub-index is part of the Equion All-Fund Index, the most comprehensive measure of mutual fund performance of Canada. It measures the weighted average returns of all mutual and segregated funds in Canada which report their results.

In total, the index tracks nearly a quarter of a trillion dollars of money under management by funds. There are 27 sub-indexes that comprise the index which provides weighted average returns by asset category. These categories include:

① Canadian Large Cap/Diversified Blend
② Canadian Large Cap/Diversified Value
③ Canadian Large Cap/Diversified Growth
④ Canadian Small/Mid Cap Equity
⑤ Canadian Dividend
⑥ Canadian Sector Equity
⑦ Canadian Resources & Precious Metals
⑧ U.S. Large Cap/Diversified Equity
⑨ U.S. Small Cap Equity
⑩ International Equity
⑪ Global Equity
⑫ Global Sector
⑬ North American Equity
⑭ European Equity
⑮ Latin American & Emerging Markets
⑯ Asia-Pacific Rim Equity

⑰ Canadian Long/Mid-Term Bonds
⑱ Canadian Short-Term Bonds
⑲ Canadian Mortgage
⑳ International Bonds
㉑ U.S./International Money Market
㉒ Canadian Money Market
㉓ Canadian Tactical Balanced
㉔ Canadian Strategic Balanced
㉕ Global Balanced
㉖ Asset Allocation Services
㉗ Other

Top Funds Close Up

Why Quartiles Change

There is a logical reason why some funds' historic quartile rankings change. We've gotten letters on this, where a fund was given a third quartile for 1990 in one edition, then a second quartile for that same year in the next edition. Since the fund's performance didn't change, what did? — The comparison universe. As the fund world keeps exploding, more and more narrow peer-group universes can be created for comparison. Fund mergers affect historical comparisons also.

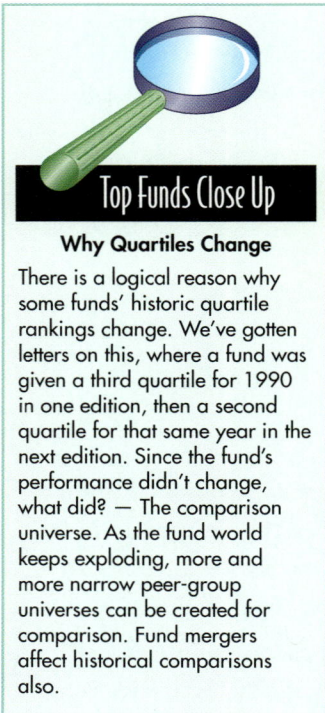

*Canadian and U.S./International Money Market Funds are tracked separately as they are not suitable long-term investments.

The use of these more precise and comprehensive benchmarks in this edition is another improvement over previous editions of *Top Funds*. It allows for "apple-to-apple" comparisons which ensure that a fund is being assessed correctly.

In our reviews of the 100 Top Funds, **the shaded graph in the background is always the appropriate sub-index**. This allows you to see how the particular fund category is performing. In the example shown, we see that the fund's performance has been relatively consistent through a variety of market conditions.

Simply stated, the markets were bad in 1990 and 1994. So our hypothetical fund's first-quartile performance in both 1991 and 1994 demonstrates an impressive degree of consistency throughout changing market conditions.

Examining relative performance over successive time periods also allows us to note any meaningful trends that may not be obvious from a fund's MPC score alone. For example, the data may show that the performance of a highly-ranked fund has declined marginally over the past few years, or that of a not-so-highly ranked fund has improved. Either may have an effect on your investment decision.

MEASURING MANAGEMENT STRENGTH

● *Talent or Luck?*

Will a .400 batter hit the ball every time at bat? Probably not. And yet such a hitter would be among the very best in the game.

Similarly, mutual fund managers provide no guarantees. But overall, a long-term investor will do well to stick with a manager or management team that has done well in the past (assuming a proper method of measurement, of course).

Poker, too, is a game of chance. On any given hand a professional player is as likely to get a great hand as is a novice. And yet over time, the professional will win more frequently.

We think talent exists. We believe that over the long term it manifests itself in superior fund performance. How do we know that talent exists? Well, let's take an example: Sir John Templeton turned $10,000 invested in the Templeton Growth Fund in 1954 into $5.0 million by July 31, 1998. George Soros, manager of the offshore-based Quantum Fund turned U.S. $10,000 in 1969 (at the top of the market — just before the biggest bear market in history) into more than U.S. $20 million by 1996.

Pure luck? We don't think so.

We believe that good managers (and good funds) can be identified by three fundamental characteristics:

① consistently beating the market,

② depth of talent in the management team,

③ solid research applied in a clear process.

Many institutional investors have given up looking for good money managers who are capable of beating the market; they simply try to do as well as the market. These institutions are hiring "passive" money managers who simply "buy the market" — that is, they buy every stock that makes up the TSE 300 Composite Index (in the case of Canadian equity funds) or Standard & Poor 500 Index (for U.S. equity funds) in proportion to the stock's weighting in that index.

Top Funds Close Up

Skill Benchmarks

Some types of funds are so specialized (single-country funds come to mind here) that they are virtually alone in their category, making peer-to-peer comparisons almost impossible. So how do you determine the relative skill of the fund manager?

One method is to identify a benchmark index that most closely tracks the asset type being managed by the fund. For example, in real estate you can use the real estate sector of the TSE 300 or in the U.S., the National Association of Real Estate Investment Trust's index. Then compare its value with that of the benchmark, thereby allowing you to see whether the manager was able to add value through his or her efforts. It's an instructive exercise. In some cases we've found that a fund's manager (and its unitholders) would have done better by buying the index and taking a year's vacation!

Nevertheless, we believe that good managers can be identified on the basis of past performance. We think that reasonable judgment can determine whether a good manager still seems to have everything in place for future success. On the other hand, it is also possible to spot, and avoid, bad managers.

How do you spot bad fund managers? They exhibit all the opposite characteristics of the Top Funds manager. They have:

① performance that has been consistently below average or swings wildly between hot and cold;

② high turnover of personnel because of poor environment, compensation, or structure;

③ funds with high fees;

④ no depth of personnel and few analysts, usually relying on second-hand research from others instead of conducting their own.

Top Funds Close Up

PH&N Priorities

Looking for fund managers who are motivated by investment — not just business — goals? A good example is **Phillips, Hager & North**, who closed off their **Vintage Fund** in 1993 because they felt that more assets would impede its ability to trade in illiquid small-cap markets.

The fund has subsequently continued to soar for the lucky few who own it. It has been selected as a Top Fund again this year.

● *Management Consistency*

Since the performance of a mutual fund depends so much on its people, consistent management is one of the most important things to look for in a potential investment. After all, when you buy a mutual fund you're buying the talent of the team running it. If the team leaves, then everything that you've bought has changed.

In the *Top Funds 1999* listings you'll find information about who manages each fund, and for how long. Investors should generally avoid **those funds with recent, significant changes in management,** just to see how the new "hot shot" settles in.

Of course, as the saying goes, sometimes a change is as good as a rest. If there ever was a fund that would qualify for a rest, it would be Spectrum United's Canadian Investment Fund. The oldest fund sold in Canada, it can trace its origins back to 1932 and its performance during the '70s and '80s could definitely be called sleepy. In 1996, however, Kim Shannon of AMI Partners took over the reins and used her fundamental value approach to kick start the fund, which is making its debut as a Top Fund in 1999.

For any Top Fund listed in this book, you can read our opinion of the management team and whether it's stable enough to make it a *reasonable* choice within its category. Other information that space does not allow us to include here — but which you may wish to look into yourself — involves things like whether the fund manager owns a piece of his or her investment firm. Such managers tend to seek the best long-term results for the fund (and its investors), rather than shooting for a terrific quarter to make a good bonus.

● *Evaluating the Management Firm*

Most often when we refer to a "fund manager" we tend to think of an individual who makes all the investment decisions. But even the most talented individuals rarely work alone; they are part of a team that works collaboratively within a management firm.

In addition to the qualities identified earlier, how do we identify a superior management firm?

● *Ten or more years in business.*

Generally, it's a good sign if the firm has been in existence for at least 10 years.

● *Large asset base.*

The firm should have enough assets under administration to buy and sell securities efficiently, and to attract the people that it needs. Look for total assets of $3 billion or more for bond managers, and $1 billion or more for equity managers.

● *Low turnover.*

A firm should not lose more than one senior investment professional every five years. The reasons for any turnover should be closely investigated.

● *Local expertise.*

This is particularly important for specialized funds that buy stocks or bonds in overseas markets, where conditions are often quite different from those at home. Look for a firm that has investment management offices and/or advisors located in the markets where it does business.

● *Efficient management structure.*

Although difficult for non-professionals to measure, this is something we examine very closely. In an ideal situation, an individual fund manager should have full and immediate discretion — within the limits of the fund's overall investment objectives — to react to rapid market changes. In more bureaucratically structured firms, a manager might have to wait for a committee meeting before taking action. Meanwhile, buying or selling opportunities could be missed.

TOP FUND QUALIFIER #2: RISK

While properly constructed performance statistics provide a good measure of how well a fund has done (and may do), they're less informative about the likelihood of the fund doing badly at any given time. This type of worst-case evaluation is now being pioneered in the U.S. by academics and investment practitioners. It's called "downside risk" and we believe that in a few years it will be as popular an investment buzzword as "asset allocation" is today.

In the *Top Funds 1999* listings we've laid out some easy-to-understand indicators of a fund's downside risk:

- how often a fund has beaten 5-year GICs,
- how often a fund has lost money,
- a fund's worst annual return.

Taken together, these indicators provide a more common sense picture of risk than accepted statistical measures such as standard deviation. And, they're easier to understand!

WHY STANDARD DEVIATION ISN'T
THE ONLY MEASURE OF RISK

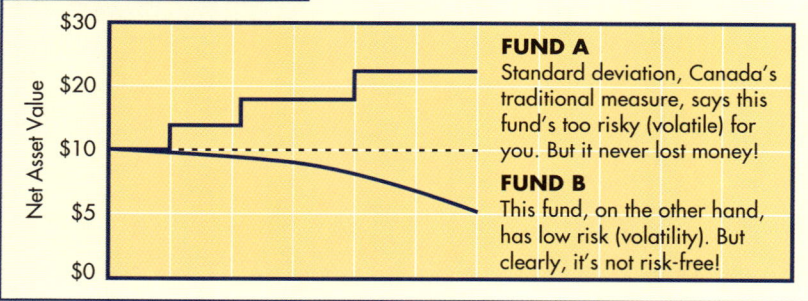

WHICH FUND IS RISKIER?

FUND A Standard deviation, Canada's traditional measure, says this fund's too risky (volatile) for you. But it never lost money!

FUND B This fund, on the other hand, has low risk (volatility). But clearly, it's not risk-free!

The mutual fund industry is letting investors down. It's continuing to support the use of a one-risk measure — one that unknowingly misleads you by not telling you how risky a fund really is. The measure is "standard deviation," which shows how widely a fund's monthly returns vary, or deviate, from a calculated norm — usually over a three-year trailing period. Standard deviation is the basis of the volatility scale used in most newspapers' monthly mutual fund tables. It's so widely accepted that few question its validity or usefulness.

But standard deviation alone doesn't do the job. It fails to distinguish between volatility associated with making money (gains) and volatility associated with losses — punishing a fund that makes money equally with a fund that loses money.

Standard deviation rewards consistent losers and punishes erratic gainers. Academics think using it as the only risk measure for investment performance can be problematic unless its limitations are understood.

Don't believe us? There are dozens of high-end journal articles with powerful arguments against standard deviation. And of course, as the regulators say, "nobody understands risk."

Understanding risk, in our view, is the most important determinant of your performance as an investor. When you lose money in a fund which you didn't figure would go down — or go down by much — you're more likely to sell at the bottom.

Why? Because all too often, investors buy at the peak and sell at the first setback. Dalbar Inc., a Boston-based consulting firm, has conducted one of the most comprehensive studies of investor behaviour. They found that investors underperform the market by as much as 40% due to mistiming their purchases and redemptions.

Should investors take all the blame for buying and selling at the wrong time, or could the industry be more helpful? Here's our suggestion. We recommend that the industry tell investors more about the risk of losing money, just like *Top Funds* has done for years: how much, how often, how long.

Cambridge Special Equity Fund, for example, is a Canadian small-cap equity offering for which these new measures of risk would be especially helpful. It has a standard deviation of 9.0, about double that of most similar funds, but is not the riskiest fund of its type.

Wouldn't it be nice to be warned that this fund lost money in four years of its nine-year history? In three of those years, it lost more than 20%, and in its worst year (1990) it lost 34.8%. In only four of the nine years did it outperform GICs.

Measuring downside risk is the new wave in investment research. Downside risk is a broad term that can describe elaborate measures of a fund's likelihood of underperforming some minimum rate of return. Or it can calculate the average loss.

Overall, downside risk is a framework that often uses calculus to explain the potential for investment pain. We've used a greatly simplified downside risk framework in this book, making the concept easy to understand and calculate.

Being told in advance of the frequent, temporary setbacks which even good funds suffer might help people weather those downturns better. Or it might scare the nervous nellies away. Either result is a good thing for both the investor and the industry.

Making new risk measures mandatory won't solve all the industry's problems. And these risk profiles will apply only to mature funds — with a history of four or more years. A disclaimer would have to be drafted for newer funds.

But we believe the fund industry owes it to investors to better disclose past risk, along with those seductive past returns it usually trumpets. And investors should start to demand more useful information about risk when they buy a fund.

TOP FUND QUALIFIER #3: REWARD-TO-RISK RELATIONSHIP

Despite its shortcomings, standard deviation does provide some insight into risk. Also, history has demonstrated that funds which soar upwards even for an extended period, are capable of crashing when a bear market eventually comes along. Japanese equity funds in the late 1980s are a telling example.

Thus, the degree to which a fund is volatile, even on the upside, provides clues as to its inherent risk—a risk that is easily disguised in a long-running bull market as we are experiencing currently.

Therefore, in *Top Funds 1999*, in addition to our measurement of downside risk, we've taken a hard look at volatility. But in our ongoing effort to provide increasingly research-driven data, we've gone one step further.

Measuring risk is important, but on its own, it fails to consider the reward-to-risk relationship. Here's an example to demonstrate this important point.

Let's say Fund A was 25% riskier than the typical fund in its category as measured by standard deviation. Would you consider buying it? Well, it depends on your risk profile. Maybe you would and maybe not.

Now, what if the same Fund A had earned a return 50% higher than the average fund over a prolonged period! Would that affect your decision? It very well might. In this example, Fund A is adding value in terms of return enhancement much greater than its risk increment. If you can handle the volatility, the managers are doing their job.

It works for poorer performing funds as well. Let's say a fund provides a return 10% less than the average in its category, yet it does so at a 30% reduction in risk. For a conservative investor, this is a better choice than the average fund despite its lower return; it has a better reward-to-risk relationship.

The point is **that risk as measured in relation to return can impact your decision on how a fund meets your needs.** Think of it like an airplane trip where there is both the smoothness of the flight (i.e., the volatility or risk) and the speed of getting to your destination (i.e., the returns).

Measuring them together helps you select the real winners— i.e., those who get you there faster (have higher returns) with less turbulence (below average volatility).

In order to measure the reward-to-risk ratio, we've relied on the Nobel prize-winning work of Bill Sharpe. He has developed an equation called the "Sharpe Ratio" which measures past return relative to risk that allows comparisons between mutual funds in a similar asset category.

We've used the Sharpe Ratio to rate all our Top Funds on a three- and five-year basis in terms of their reward-to-risk relationship, where data was available. In fact, we've also done this where the data was available for all funds in our Monster Tables starting on page 209.

Then in order to make it simpler for you, we ranked the funds within their respective categories in terms of their reward-to-risk capability. We used a quartile system, so the best 25% are in Quartile 1 declining to the bottom 25% in Quartile 4.

So, although it is critical to consider absolute performance potential and the downside risk when picking funds, it is also useful to measure the reward-to-risk relationship.

TOP FUND QUALIFIER #4: EFFICIENCY

EXPENSE ACCOUNTS: The Best and Worst MERs

Column A	Best	Column B	Worst
Canadian Large Cap/Diversified Blend Caldwell Canadian Equity Fund	0.50%	**Canadian Large Cap/Diversified Blend** Strategic Value RSP Fund	4.15%
Canadian Large Cap/Diversified Value Scudder Canadian Equity Fund	1.35%	**Canadian Large Cap/Diversified Value** Trans Canada Value Fund	3.52%
Canadian Large Cap/Diversified Growth Empire Equity Growth Fund	1.24%	**Canadian Large Cap/Diversified Growth** Great West Life Growth Equity Fund (A)	3.24%
Canadian Small/Mid Cap Equity Altamira Canada Aggressive Fund OTGIF Growth Section Fund	1.00% 1.00%	**Canadian Small/Mid Cap Equity** Cambridge Special Equity Fund	3.46%
Canadian Dividend Scotia Excelsior Dividend Fund	1.09%	**Canadian Dividend** Trans Canada Dividend Fund	3.51%
Canadian Sector Equity All-Canadian Consumer Fund	2.00%	**Canadian Sector Equity** Royal LePage Commercial Real Estate Fund	3.40%
Canadian Resources & Precious Metals Standard Life Natural Resources Fund All Canadian Resources Fund	2.00% 2.00%	**Canadian Resources & Precious Metals** First Heritage Fund	4.66%
U.S. Large Cap/Diversified Equity O.I.Q. Ferique American Fund	0.39%	**U.S. Large Cap/Diversified Equity** Elliott & Page U.S. Mid-Cap Fund	3.44%
U.S. Small Cap Equity Altamira Select American Fund	2.28%	**U.S. Small Cap Equity** Cambridge American Growth Fund	3.56%
International Equity Canada Trust International Equity Index Fund	0.53%	**International Equity** North West Life Ecoflex Investment Fund E	3.82%
Global Equity FMOQ International Equity Fund	0.81%	**Global Equity** 20/20 Aggressive Stock Fund	3.64%
Global Sector First Trust Pharmaceutical Trust 1996 Series	1.05%	**Global Sector** Allstar Adrian Day Gold Plus Fund	5.28%
North American Equity First Trust North America Technology Trust 1997 Series	1.15%	**North American Equity** Cambridge Americas Fund	3.50%
European Equity Green Line European Index Fund	0.90%	**European Equity** RCC Euro Fund	9.79%
Latin American & Emerging Markets Guardian Emerging Markets Fund	0.80%	**Latin American & Emerging Markets** Elliott & Page Emerging Markets Fund	4.69%
Asia-Pacific Rim Equity Green Line Japanese Index Fund	0.90%	**Asia-Pacific Rim Equity** Elliott & Page Asian Growth Fund	3.76%
Canadian Long/Mid-Term Bonds Scudder Canadian Bond Fund	0.25%	**Canadian Long/Mid-Term Bonds** CUMIS Life Memberfunds Canadian Bond Fund	3.00%
Canadian Short-Term Bonds Dynamic Government Income Fund	0.85%	**Canadian Short-Term Bonds** Acadia Bond Fund	2.16%
Canadian Mortgage Phillips, Hager & North Short Term Bond & Mortgage Fund	0.64%	**Canadian Mortgage** Great West Life Mortgage Investment Fund (G) NL	2.40%
International Bonds FMOQ Bond Fund	0.89%	**International Bonds** ABAX Bradys Bond Fund	6.50%
U.S./International Money Market C.I. U.S. Money Market Fund	0.51%	**U.S./International Money Market** AGF International Short Term Income Class Fund	2.69%
Canadian Money Market Altamira T-Bill Fund	0.24%	**Canadian Money Market** Maritime Life Money Market Fund (C)	2.00%
Canadian Tactical Balanced Mawer Canadian Diversified Investment Fund	1.08%	**Canadian Tactical Balanced** Trans Canada Pension Fund	3.48%
Canadian Strategic Balanced A.P.P. Q. (Fonds équilibre)	0.24%	**Canadian Strategic Balanced** Cambridge Balanced Fund	3.48%
Global Balanced FMOQ Investment Fund	0.64%	**Global Balanced** CUMIS Life Memberfunds Global Balanced Fund	3.00%
Asset Allocation Services n/a No standard reporting method		**Asset Allocation Services** n/a No standard reporting method	
Other Centrefire Growth Fund Inc.	1.60%	**Other** Innovacap Capital Corp. Fund	12.00%

The efficiency of a fund can be defined in many ways, but it's mostly about fees and other expenses that are charged against a fund, and thereby affect its performance.

These fees are distinct from sales commissions, which are somewhat more difficult to compare, since different advisors provide different levels of service — and, presumably, different levels of value for money. The bottom line is that we can't really compare the commissions paid on various funds. But we can speak about management fees.

Ultimately, it is much easier to predict a fund's fees than it is to predict a fund's investment returns. So if a fund's fees are reasonable, it is more likely — all else being equal — to do better in the future. This is especially true during periods when markets are relatively flat and every fraction of a percentage point gained or lost takes on a much greater significance.

In the *Top Funds 1999* listings we provide each fund's management expense ratio (MER), expressed as a dollar amount for every $100 in fund assets. (As you'll recall, the MER includes more than just management fees; it also includes all expenses charged to the fund, such as legal and accounting costs, custodial and safekeeping costs paid in carrying out the activities of the fund, and the costs of producing prospectuses and other reports.)

Since different types of funds require different levels of management activity, we should only compare MERs of similar funds. In the *Top Funds 1999* listings a colour-coded bar accompanies each fund's MER Rating — indicating whether it is above average (red), average (orange), or below average (green) in comparison to similar types of funds.

How much importance should you assign to the MER rating? Chances are you won't mind paying relatively high management expenses if the investment returns are correspondingly high. But as we said earlier, a high MER can have a significant effect in poor markets.

Still, there are some real MER bargains to be had among the Top Funds.

Phillips, Hager & North, for example, manage some outstanding funds with low management expense ratios.

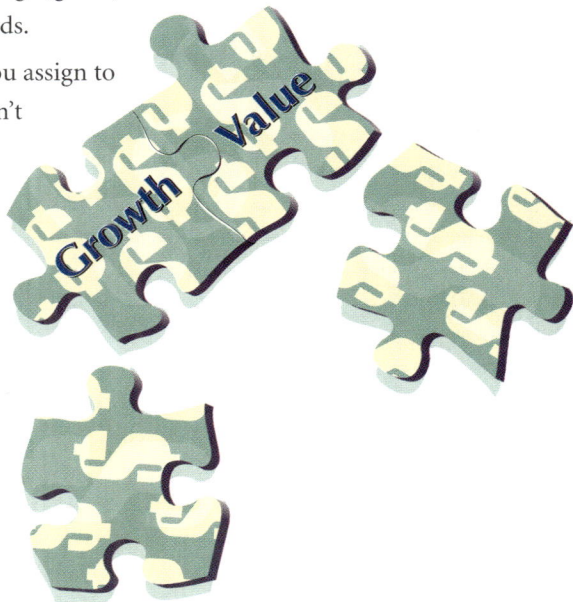

Also, you have to consider the level of advice and service you want. Management expenses for many funds include a trailer or service fee payable to an advisor and his or her firm for the ongoing work on your portfolio. The majority of Canadians prefer this kind of advisory relationship, so just getting the cheapest MER isn't the goal. It's getting a portfolio of funds tailored to your needs, integrated into your tax and estate plans, and adjusted as both our dynamic world and your goals evolve.

Top Funds Close Up

Interpreting Styles

In assigning a specific style to each of the Top Funds, we recognize that some managers may disagree with how we have categorized them. So let's take a moment to explore the kind of factors that went into making an assessment. We look at the portfolio ratios; price/earnings ratios, price/book-value ratios, and dividend yield. We compare these and other data to similar funds, including average capitalization of equities, asset mix and, for bonds, issuer quality and term to maturity.

Upon comparison, and within the framework of the style grids, we have made our own judgements about which style each fund employs. We also interviewed the portfolio managers to (among other things) solicit their opinions about their own style. This information was also factored in to the final judgement.

Discrepancies have been carefully studied to ensure a fair portrayal of each fund. There is an element of subjectivity to this, but we have tried to accommodate both opinions where discrepancies are significant.

TOP FUND QUALIFIER #5: STYLE

Style — or, more specifically, investment style — refers to the basic approach that a fund's manager takes in constructing his or her portfolio. Among equity funds, for example, one fund manager may feel that stocks of large, established (or "blue-chip") companies offer the best opportunities for returns. Another might prefer the growth potential of smaller, newer ("small-cap" or "junior") enterprises. Yet another may look for stocks that, for various reasons, have been undervalued by the market. And so on.

Did we rank the Top Funds based on style? Not really, since there is no particular style that is, in all circumstances, better than the rest. Still, investment style is important for you to consider when selecting one or more funds to add to your portfolio. There are several reasons for this:

● *A fund's investment style should be compatible with yours.*

If you're the sort of person who would normally choose conservative stocks, then you'll probably feel uncomfortable with an aggressively-managed fund that favours junior hi-tech or resource stocks — even if the fund has been remarkably successful with that approach.

● *A fund's investment style should complement those of other funds in your portfolio.*

Here we're talking about diversification — the process of spreading out your holdings to include a wide range of different investment types so that your overall risk is kept to a minimum. As we'll see in chapter 4, a good mutual fund portfolio will always contain some element of diversification, with assets allocated between cash (money market), fixed income, and equity investments. But within each of these investment types, you can (and should) diversify by investment style.

To illustrate why, let's say that you select three Top Funds with powerful performance, consistent management, low expenses — and a similar investment style. Now, the style of those funds may be "hot" when you buy the fund, but what happens when market and/or economic conditions change? Your entire portfolio will suffer.

On the other hand, if you diversify by investment style — by organizing your portfolio in two-fund pairs, where the style of one counterbalances the style of the other — you'll be less dependent on any given style, and your overall risk level will be reduced. That's what we call "complementary."

That's why, wherever possible, for every Top Fund, we've identified another Top Fund which will maximize your diversification within the asset category. That way you can still select top performers but ensure that you've got your risk **reduced**, not magnified, as you add more of them to your portfolio.

Top Funds Close Up

Why we like value over the long term

Is there a best style? In our opinion — and in the opinion of many others — it's value. Most long-term studies concur that value has done best. In a recently released 44-year study of performance in the U.S., value criteria were key in any winning strategy. Focusing on growth alone was a recipe for disappointment. In fact, the leading value strategy outperformed the S & P 500 by four times over the course of the study. Value stock indexes have done even better on a risk-adjusted basis. (That's when both returns and volatility are accounted for, essentially by discounting those returns earned by higher-risk securities.)

Why is value best? Or, you might ask, what's wrong with growth? Growth stocks trade at premium prices in relation to the value of assets and earnings represented by each share. Expectations are very high for these companies — so high, in fact, that much of the profit potential has been eliminated by the high price you're paying for tomorrow's good news. In such cases, you can only be surprised in one direction — down!

So, while value funds should be at the core of your investment portfolio, they should be complemented with other styles. A fund with a conservative growth manager, for example, would be a perfect complement to a value fund.

Top Funds Close Up

Big or Small?

In general, shares in small-companies suffer more during a market pullback than their big-cap rivals. But small-cap stocks have provided historically greater returns — over 12% annually since 1926, versus only 10% for big company shares. So while the return justifies the risk, we would still encourage people to mix large and small, and thus be insulated from the downdrafts of one of those sectors.

Home Alone

While we've tried to make the equity style grid as inclusive as possible, we've found that it is most useful when comparing funds that invest in North America. Equity styles are more difficult to assess in international markets, simply because these markets are not as efficient. And in an inefficient marketplace, sophisticated investors are able to come in and buy stocks that are relatively cheap, have relatively high growth, and represent a sector identified as "hot." The style of such managers could be accurately labelled as value, growth, and sector rotation.
Of course, some managers do have one style that remains consistent across all markets — domestic and foreign. In our efficient markets in North America, most investment managers have just one niche and stick to it exclusively.

UNDERSTANDING EQUITY STYLES

◉ *Value*

Managers with a value-based investment style usually use a "bottom-up" approach — that is, they pick securities using analysis of individual companies. Here managers look for companies with good products or services, as well as promising markets. They will (or should) perform detailed company

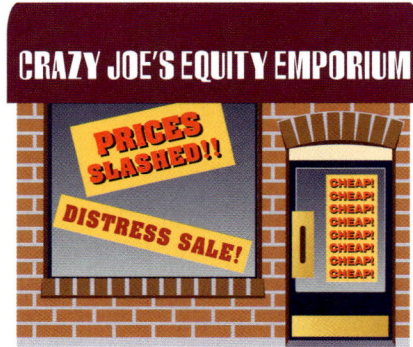

reviews — perhaps even inspecting the business on site — spending a great deal of time looking at a company's financial situation, interviewing customers, and getting to know the business intimately. Ultimately, value managers find such information to be more important than "top-down" factors such as GDP growth, inflation rates, or industrial sector performance.

Typically, they look for stocks that sell cheap because, for any number of reasons, they have fallen out of favour with investors. (Here, "cheap" means that share prices are lower than what one might expect given the company's earnings or assets per share.) Sir John Templeton is a classic value investor.

Within the value category, there are subcategories:

Conservative value. Portfolio managers employing this style will typically hold shares in companies with a very healthy financial position. Such companies will have substantial assets and little or no debt, as well as a solid earnings record — factors that are not reflected in share prices because of some other perceived weakness.

Aggressive value. This type of stock portfolio acquires shares in companies that are being shunned by investors, and are therefore extremely cheap. The basic aim is to capitalize on an expected turnaround in the company. However, such a strategy comes with certain risks: the turnaround, if it happens at all, may be a long time in coming. For this reason, aggressive value managers typically hold stocks for long periods — often four years or more. So while the performance of such funds can be very good over the long term, there can be long periods of under-performance that can try the patience (and nerves) of many investors. Peter Cundill is a typical aggressive value investor — because he's a real contrarian.

● *Growth*

Like their value-based counterparts, many growth managers also employ a "bottom-up" approach. But that's where the similarity ends. Growth managers buy shares in premium companies at premium prices. They look for companies that are doing things right; companies whose profits and sales are increasing rapidly — perhaps because of market expansion, new product development, or savvy packaging and service. For whatever reason, these companies are growing and their stocks trade at a premium because they are perceived as such.

Top Funds Scouting Report

What the Value-Growth Spread Tells Us

The value-growth spread is the difference between the cumulative average performance of value and growth funds. This spread can suggest potential market directions to the sophisticated or active investor.

When growth is ahead of value (beating it by, say, 3% in a year) it is more likely that growth will underperform sometime soon. Conversely, when value comes out ahead of growth, its cycle is more likely to slow down and underperform.

Right now our style tilt is towards value investing which has underperformed growth for most of 1997. In Canada we like bigger-cap stocks, and in the U.S. we like a blend of large- and small-cap funds.

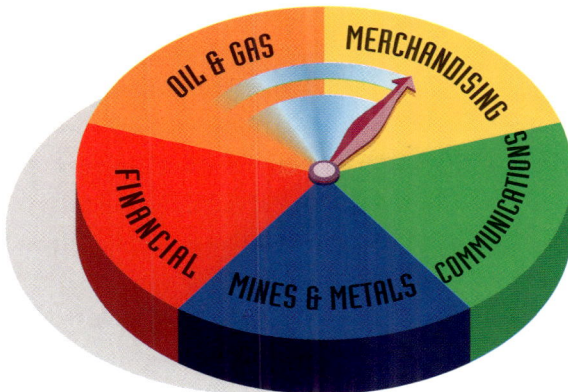

Typically, growth companies provide a lower dividend yield to shareholders, since so much of their excess earnings is put back into the business. These are glamour stocks in the truest sense of the word. They are financially healthy and successful. For many investors, the idea of paying a premium for such a stock is very easy to accept.

Aggressive growth. This portfolio management style tends to focus more on companies that are truly innovative within a specific area. They are therefore riskier, but this is offset to some degree by the companies' rapid sales and earnings momentum. Jim Broadfoot of Mackenzie's Universal group is typical of this style; he literally wrote the book on investing in emerging growth stocks.

● *Sector Rotation*

Top Funds Quote

"I skate to where the puck is going to be, not where it is."
—*Wayne Gretzky*

Managers with a sector rotation style frequently employ different types of inputs in their research and analysis, often using technical and macroeconomic research, with far less attention paid to company-specific data; they are "top-down" investors. Essentially, they look for broader trends in the economy — such as GDP growth, inflation, and major world developments in energy or population growth — and how these are likely to change various industrial sectors.

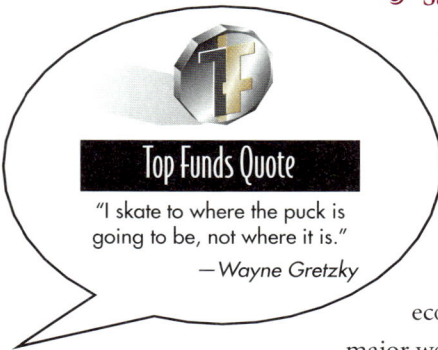

In general, a sector rotation manager will identify a number of sectors that appear to be most favourable, and will allocate the fund's portfolio accordingly. Within each sector, diversification is the key: rather than focusing on one or two "hot" companies within each sector, the manager will put money into a large number of stocks.

If the manager is successful in picking the right sectors, this approach can be very successful. In 1996, for example, just two sectors — oil and gas, and gold and silver — accounted for over 75% of the strong returns of the TSE 300. In fact, these two sectors nearly doubled in that one year. In 1996, small gold stocks were similarly ahead of the pack, pulling overweight managers up sharply, while in 1997, falling gold prices pummelled these same managers. Rising financial service stocks rewarded over weight funds during the same time frame.

As you might expect, the managers who correctly identified the right sectors came out of 1993 having done extremely well. And it would certainly have been tempting for investors to buy those winning funds. The problem is that economic forces change, and so does the relative strength of industry sectors. So it's never a great idea to load up on sector rotation funds exclusively. Sector rotation manager John Zechner of C.I., is an example of a hot manager from several years ago who has cooled recently. The key for him and for investors is consistency and patience.

58

THE EQUITY STYLE GRID

As you've probably realized by now, classifying equity fund styles is not an entirely straightforward task. For example, a fund manager may be value oriented, but also inclined to growth stocks. Another may take the value approach, but specialize in small companies. A growth manager may prefer big blue chips. And so on.

Style Grid

To simplify the classification process, we have used a style grid to indicate the different approaches taken by different mutual fund managers.

The style grid contains three columns, one for each general style category — value, growth, and sector rotation. Vertically, the grid is divided into three rows, each representing the size of companies the fund manager has tended to buy — large, medium, or small. So if a fund's portfolio contains mostly large (big-cap) value companies, the box at the intersection of "Value" (column) and "Big" (row) will be filled in.

And what if, in our estimation, the fund manager uses a blended style — that is, of value and growth? Simple. Both the Value and Growth squares will be filled in.

This visual approach offers a number of benefits besides simplicity. For instance, the relative aggressiveness of a fund manager can be identified just by looking at the position of the filled-in squares on the grid. More conservative companies tend to be in the upper left. As you move right and down, you find funds that take a more specialized approach which offers greater risks and rewards.

Also, as we'll see in chapter 4, style grids are exceptionally useful when it comes to selecting specific funds for your portfolio. Remember how we said earlier that funds should be purchased in complementary pairs? Well, again this year we actually name the Top Fund in the same category which has been scientifically identified as the best correlated (and, therefore, most complementary) to the Top Fund described. We also name the Top Fund most similar to the Top Fund being discussed. The universes we use to select from and to compare are Canadian equities, Canadian bonds, non-Canadian equities, non-Canadian bonds, and balanced funds; we're attempting to make reasonable "apples-to-apples" comparisons.

We think you'll find this a big help as you create you own portfolio.

UNDERSTANDING FIXED INCOME STYLES

There are **two** basic approaches to selecting bonds. One is *spread trading* and the other is *interest-rate anticipation*. Each approach has its own distinctive flavour.

● *Spread Trading*

Spread trading is the more conservative of fixed income styles, just as value is a more conservative equity strategy than sector rotation. Here, a manager tries to profit from small changes in the yields of various bonds or other debt instruments.

These funds aren't making big bets about the direction of interest rates. They profit most from changes in economic and cyclical factors affecting bonds. For example, as the economy has strengthened over the past year and eight of our 10 provinces have actually begun to run budget surpluses, two major things have happened to the spread traders: they've profited from buying corporate and provincial bonds, which have risen relatively in price as companies' and governments' finances have improved (what Bay-streeters call "spread-tightening").

In most cases, however, spread traders don't need a major economic change to make a profit: even small, day-to-day changes in yields — often just a fraction of a percentage point — translate into big dollars when you deal in million-dollar bond transactions. Add to these incremental capital gains the coupon income (interest paid) on the bonds themselves, and you have the makings of a strong bond fund.

● *Interest-rate Anticipation*

Interest-rate anticipation is more of a "big picture" strategy, where a manager uses macroeconomic analysis (amongst various other techniques) to predict changes in interest rates.

Top Funds Close Up

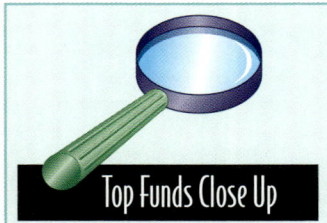

How risky is your bond fund?

When interest rates rise, bonds — and bond funds — go down. But by how much? A bond fund's average term to maturity can tell you approximately how sensitive that fund will be to changes in interest rates. Here's the rule of thumb: take 75% of your fund's average term to maturity to get the probable loss for every percentage point rise in interest rates. (On the plus side, it will also give you the approximate gain for a one-percentage point fall in interest rates!)

This rule of thumb won't always be right on, but it will give you an idea of what to expect in different market environments. For example:

	Medium-term bond fund	Long-term bond fund
Average term to maturity (years)	6	20
X		
75%	4	15
=		
Approx. loss/ gain if rates (%) rise/fall 1%	4	15

Generally, this comes down to a decision as to whether the manager should buy short- or long-term bonds. If he or she expects interest rates to rise, the manager will buy short-term bonds, since they can be turned over relatively quickly and are the least sensitive to changes in interest rates. (Remember that when interest rates go up, bond prices go down.) If the manager anticipates that interest rates will fall, he or she will rush in and buy long-term bonds; since their prices are the most sensitive to interest rates, they offer the best profit opportunity.

Fund Fact

Information about a bond fund's average term to maturity is easy to get from your fund company or *The Financial Post's* quarterly mutual fund survey.

Successful rate anticipation can deliver some very hefty profits — as it did in the early 1990s, when interest rates fell precipitously and bond-fund investors enjoyed three years of 20% annual returns in some of the better funds.

● *Blend*

Some managers use a blend of spread trading and rate anticipation — typically when the fund has an established policy of buying bonds with a particular term. If you think about it, you can see why. Let's say that a fund is mandated to buy long bonds. Clearly, the fund's style will be dictated by what's happening with interest rates — that is, if there's no money to be made from buying long bonds in anticipation of falling rates, the manager will have to resort to spread trading.

Research Tidbits

Good News In Rising Interest Rates?

The author contends that rising interest rates actually benefit most bond holders, despite the conventional view that as interest rates rise, bond holders suffer capital losses with no increase in income. He argues that rising interest income exceeds the injury from capital losses for holders of short- to medium-term bonds. Investors who are net savers are helped the most, while those who are spending capital at rapid rates lose the most.

Source: David A. Levine. "The Benefits of Rising Interest Rates", The Journal of Portfolio Management, vol.22, no.2, Winter 1996.

Top Funds Quote

Q: What's the difference between a bond and a bond fund manager?

A: Eventually a bond matures.

—*old Wall Street joke*

THE FIXED INCOME STYLE GRID

The format of the style grid for bond (and other fixed income) funds is much like that discussed earlier for equity funds. The difference is that the columns represent (from left to right) spread trading, blend, and rate anticipation styles. From top to bottom, the rows represent the term of bonds held in the fund.

Also, like its equity counterpart, the bond style grid starts in the top left corner with the most conservative style, representing what should be an investor's core assets. These funds typically hold securities with a short-term average maturity. "Short" is anything between one to just under four years.

Moving downward to the bottom right corner, we find the most aggressive, specialized types of funds. These typically hold longer-dated bonds ("long" defined as 10 years or more to maturity) with the aim of achieving capital gains on top of their interest income. While offering a higher potential return, these funds are appropriate only for someone with investment experience and sufficient assets to have diversified into other, less aggressive instruments.

TOP FUNDS 1999

• • • • • • • • • • •

Here's where it all comes together. The numbers have been crunched, the trends analyzed, and the final cuts made. What remains is an admittedly elite group—funds that have proven themselves as the best of the best.

In this section, you'll find the 100 Top Funds selected for 1999, grouped according to *fund category* (this is indicated by a coloured tab in the margin), and presented in *alphabetical order*.

THE TOP FUNDS LEGEND

Each full-page listing is provided in a concise, standardized format. Here's how to navigate your way through:

- **Fund Name** is the official name of the fund.
- **Fund Manager/Firm** (where applicable): The manager's name and the year when he or she assumed responsibility for the fund, plus the name of the fund management company. "Inception" means that the manager has looked after the fund since it began.
- **RRSP Eligibility.** An unstroked maple leaf indicates that the fund meets Revenue Canada's "Canadian content" rules, and can therefore make up to 100% of the total value of your RRSP or RRIF. A maple leaf with an oblique stroke indicates that the fund is considered "foreign content" which must not exceed 20% of the value of your RRSP or RRIF.

- **New in 1999.** Funds listed for the first time are labelled "NEW."
- **Top Fund in previous years:** This is indicated by the year in which the fund was on the *Top Funds* List.
- **Performance trend.** This graphic shows the fund's rankings by quartile for the calendar years where data was available from 1984 to the first half of 1998.

  A first quartile position indicates that the fund beat 75% of its direct competitors. A second quartile ranking means that it beat 50% of the others, but was beaten by 25%. The graph in the background indicates the relative performance of the appropriate sub-index of the **Equion All-Fund Index.**

  On occasion, you may notice that a fund, which you know has been in existence for a number of years, is shown on the Performance Trend for fewer years. The reason is that for a period of time the number of funds in the category was less than 20; this is the smallest number on which we believe quartile rankings to be meaningful.

- **Risk** indicators are self-explanatory except to note that the reference to the number of years is based on calendar years.

- **Reward-to-Risk Relationship/Sharpe Ratio Quartile Rankings**

  The Sharpe Ratio is a means of measuring risk-adjusted returns. It is the average annual return for 3 and 5 years less the 3- and 5-year average annual return of Government of Canada T-Bills (a "risk-free" investment) divided by the annual standard deviation of the particular fund.

  To simplify for you, this chart shows how this fund compares against its peers with respect to the Sharpe Ratio. As with the performance trend, **the higher the quartile ranking the better.** A 1st quartile ranking is the most desirable while a 4th quartile ranking is the least desirable.

  (Note that the chart shows comparative quartile performance rather than the more complicated Sharpe Ratio itself.)

- **Efficiency/Management expenses (MER),** shown as the amount charged by the fund managers for every $100 in assets managed. Since different categories of funds require different levels of managerial effort, the colour-coded stoplight model shows whether the MER for a given fund is high (i.e., above average) or low (below average) relative to other funds in the same category. If it's high, there is a red light; if it's average, there's an orange light; and if it's low, there's a green light.

- **Style Grid** categorizes the fund by investment style. In the example shown, the style leans towards large companies with a value approach. Note that this sample style is for funds that hold primarily **equity** or stock investments.

  A different grid is used for **fixed income** (bond, mortgage, money market) funds. Labels for this grid are shown at right.

- Specific suggestions of a **complementary** fund and a **similar** fund for each of the funds is also indicated.

Fund Name

Fund Manager/Firm

RRSP Eligibility

Top Fund in previous year(s)

New Top Fund

1998 RRSP 🍁

IVY CANADIAN FUND
Jerry Javasky (1997)/Mackenzie Financial Corporation

Performance Trend

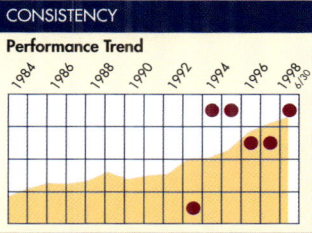

CONSISTENCY

Performance Trend

1984 1986 1988 1990 1992 1994 1996 1998 6/30

Risk Indicators

RISK

How often fund outperformed GICs	**4 years in 5**
How often fund lost money	**0 years in 5**
Worst year's rate of return	**5.0% (1994)**

Risk-Adjusted Returns

RISK-ADJUSTED RETURNS
SHARPE RATIO QUARTILE RANKINGS

3-Year	**1**
5-Year	**1**

Management Expenses (MER)

EFFICIENCY/MER

Management expense/$100

$2.32

○ above average
● average
○ below average

Style Grid

	Value	Growth	Sector Rotation (SR)
Company Size Big			
Medium			
Small			

STYLE

	Value	Growth	Sector Rotation (SR)
Company Size Big			
Medium			
Small			

Complementary Fund:
Colonia Special Growth Fund

Similar Fund:
Maxxum Dividend Fund of Canada

This high-profile Canadian value fund, managed solely by Jerry Javasky after the 1997 departure of Gerry Coleman, has accumulated $5.6 billion dollars in assets; this volume has helped grind the MER down to 2.32%. The fund was slow out the gates and was a complete stinker in 1993. Once it found its legs though, it has been leading the pack while posting some excellent numbers. Being a value fund, it has been true to form as the fund's volatility has been significantly lower than the average fund or the TSE 300.

The combined objectives of above-average returns with below-average risk has led Javasky to hike the cash position all the way up to 35% of the fund, as he opines that there is little room for error at the current valuation levels. The result was that while the market continued ahead with a full head of steam in the first quarter of 1998, the fund under performed. When choppiness returned in the second quarter, the fund recovered most of the lost ground. Such is the nature of value investing with an overlay of high cash reserves. While we prefer that managers hold no more than a transactional level of cash, Javasky's attempts to look after "investors' money" by controlling risk is at least noble.

Instead of trying to forecast the economic and sectoral tides, Javasky's approach is to invest in companies where the management is capable of anticipating economic and competitive changes and reacting to it. Like a good business manager, he believes in hiring the best, and delegating responsibility.

If you're a conservative investor or are anxious about the market's lofty heights, consider knocking on Jerry's door and buying some of what he's offering.

TOP FUNDS 1999

The following is a list of the 100 Top Funds of 1999, arranged by **category** and in **alphabetical order** within each category. An (✓) beside a fund indicates that it is a new Top Fund in 1999.

CANADIAN LARGE CAP/DIVERSIFIED BLEND

✓Atlas Canadian Large Cap Growth Fund	68
Bissett Canadian Equity Fund	69
Ethical Growth Fund	70
✓First Canadian Growth Fund	71
✓Green Line Canadian Equity Fund	72
✓Investors Summa Fund	73
McLean Budden Equity Growth Fund	74
✓Phillips, Hager & North Canadian Equity Fund	75
✓Standard Life Equity Mutual Fund	76

CANADIAN LARGE CAP/DIVERSIFIED VALUE

Ivy Canadian Fund	77
✓Spectrum United Canadian Investment Fund	78

CANADIAN LARGE CAP/DIVERSIFIED GROWTH

✓AIC Diversified Canada Fund	79
✓Clean Environment Equity Fund	80
Phillips, Hager & North Vintage Fund	81

CANADIAN SMALL/MID-CAP EQUITY

Bissett Small Cap Fund	82
✓Chou RRSP Fund	83
Colonia Special Growth Fund	84
✓Fidelity Canadian Growth Company Fund	85
✓Millennium Next Generation Fund	86

CANADIAN DIVIDEND

AGF Dividend Fund	87
Bissett Dividend Income Fund	88
Industrial Dividend Growth Fund	89
Maxxum Dividend Fund of Canada	90
Phillips, Hager & North Dividend Income Fund	91
Royal Dividend Fund	92

CANADIAN SECTOR EQUITY

AIC Advantage Fund	93

CANADIAN RESOURCES & PRECIOUS METALS

20/20 Canadian Resources Fund	94
Maxxum Natural Resource Fund	95
Royal Precious Metals Fund	96
✓Universal Canadian Resource Fund	97

U.S. LARGE CAP/DIVERSIFIED EQUITY

AGF American Growth Class Fund	98
AIC Value Fund	99
Fidelity Growth America Fund	100
✓Green Line U.S. Index Fund	101
✓Spectrum United American Growth Fund C$	102

U.S. SMALL CAP EQUITY

BPI American Small Companies Fund	103

INTERNATIONAL EQUITY

✓AIC World Equity Fund	104
✓Great West Life International Equity Inv (P) DSC	105
Templeton International Stock Fund	106

GLOBAL EQUITY

AGF International Value Fund	107
✓BPI Global Equity Value Fund	108
Canada Life U.S. & Int'l Equity Fund S-34	109
Fidelity International Portfolio Fund	110
✓Investors Growth Portfolio Fund	111
Templeton Global Smaller Companies Fund	112
Templeton Growth Fund Ltd.	113
Trimark Fund	114

GLOBAL SECTOR

AIM Global Health Sciences Fund	115
Dynamic Real Estate Equity Fund	116

NORTH AMERICAN EQUITY

✓Chou Associates Fund	117

EUROPEAN EQUITY

✓AGF International Group Germany Class Fund	118
Dynamic Europe Fund	119
Fidelity European Growth Fund	120
✓Universal European Opportunities Fund	121

LATIN AMERICAN & EMERGING MARKETS

20/20 Latin America Fund	122
✓AIM GT Latin America Growth Class Fund	123
✓C.I. Emerging Markets Fund	124
Spectrum United Emerging Markets Fund	125
Templeton Emerging Markets Fund	126

NEW

RRSP 🍁

ATLAS CANADIAN LARGE CAP GROWTH FUND
Fred Pynn (inception)/Bissett & Associates Investment Management Ltd.

CONSISTENCY

Performance Trend

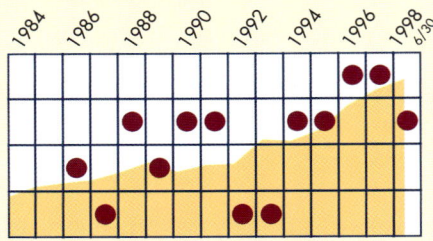

1984 1986 1988 1990 1992 1994 1996 1998 6/30

RISK

How often fund outperformed GICs	**7 years in 12**
How often fund lost money	**3 years in 12**
Worst year's rate of return	**-10.7% (1990)**

REWARD-TO-RISK RELATIONSHIP
SHARPE RATIO QUARTILE RANKINGS

3-Year	**1**
5-Year	**1**

EFFICIENCY/MER

Management expense/$100

$2.45

○ above average
● average
○ below average

STYLE

Company Size: Big / Medium / Small
Value Growth / Sector Rotation (SR)

Complementary Fund:
Chou RRSP Fund

Similar Fund:
Bissett Canadian Equity Fund

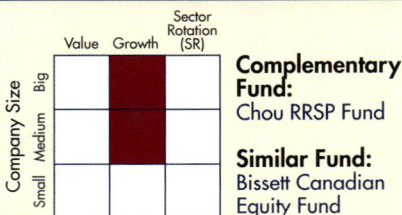

What a difference a manager makes! After plodding along for many years with less than sparkling returns, Atlas Canadian Large Cap Growth has been reborn. In 1994, Atlas hired Bissett & Associates to manage this fund and the turnaround was remarkable. Returns have been 1st or 2nd quartile ever since and in 1997, the fund ranked 18th in a 204 fund universe. Some of the fund's success can be attributed to the fact that manager Fred Pynn doesn't hesitate to add mid-cap issues to the portfolio. Ironically, this actually hurt performance in the first half of 1998 as Canadian mid-caps lagged their large-cap counterparts.

The fund's top holdings are Toronto 35 Index Participation Units or TIPS. Pynn didn't want to miss the boat in a bull market and decided to put the large cash inflows that new investors were providing into TIPs, until other opportunities arose. This is in sharp contrast to many managers who let the cash accumulate, sometimes to the 20%—30% level, with the commensurate drag on portfolio returns. Pynn's cash holdings are a measly 1.7%.

As is always the case with Bissett-managed funds, the management style is a fundamentals-orientated, bottom-up growth approach that is balanced with stringent value criteria. Volatility is low, and the holdings in over 90 securities are diversified broadly among Toronto Stock Exchange listed stocks.

BISSETT CANADIAN EQUITY FUND

Michael Quinn (1986) + Fred Pynn (1994)/Bissett and Associates

CANADIAN LARGE CAP/DIVERSIFIED BLEND

CONSISTENCY

Performance Trend

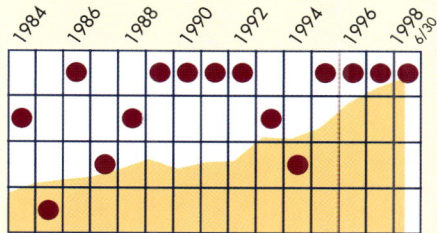

1984 1986 1988 1990 1992 1994 1996 1998 6/30

RISK

How often fund outperformed GICs	9 years in 14
How often fund lost money	3 years in 14
Worst year's rate of return	-8.5% (1990)

REWARD-TO-RISK RELATIONSHIP
SHARPE RATIO QUARTILE RANKINGS

3-Year	1
5-Year	1

EFFICIENCY/MER

Management expense/$100

$1.33

○ above average
○ average
● below average

STYLE

Complementary Fund:
Chou RRSP Fund

Similar Fund:
Atlas Canadian Large Cap Growth Fund

Michael Quinn and Fred Pynn have successfully managed this fund by employing a bottom-up approach to security selection. They have focused on growth stocks which is the stock type that has propelled both the U.S. and Canadian indices recently. The fund's stated objective is to earn above-average long-term returns through capital appreciation by investing in a diversified portfolio of Canadian and U.S. equities. If the fund's 15-year history is any indication of their ability to meet objectives, hop on board. While past returns are not an indicator of future returns, these two have been able to historically add significant value to the fund. Contributing to the fund's added value over the market has been the quite low MER.

Investors who hold this fund outside their RRSPs will like the style used by these two gentlemen. The fund's average holding period is three years which helps to defray trading charges as well as defer capital gains. In fact, the pre-tax and after-tax returns in 1997 were identical at 31.5%. While it is possible to buy at inopportune times and pay taxes on gains that you didn't get the benefit of, it has been shown that longer holding periods generally lead to greater after-tax returns.

One of the other benefits of investing in this fund is that it is part of a very strong 11 fund family, very few of which perform poorly. This allows you, should you wish, to move to another family member that will likely be a strong performer too. The alternative is that with the absence of any deferred sales charges, you can redeem your funds completely from Bissett without a penalty.

ETHICAL GROWTH FUND
Larry Lunn (1986) + Martin Gerber (1991)/Connor Clark and Lunn

CANADIAN LARGE CAP/DIVERSIFIED BLEND

CONSISTENCY

Performance Trend

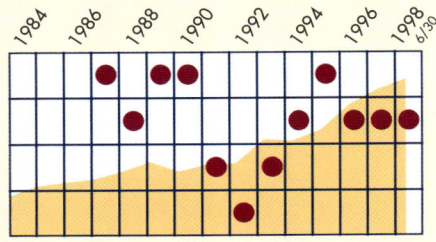

1984 1986 1988 1990 1992 1994 1996 1998 6/30

RISK

How often fund outperformed GICs	**7 years in 11**
How often fund lost money	**3 years in 11**
Worst year's rate of return	**-4.3% (1992)**

REWARD-TO-RISK RELATIONSHIP
SHARPE RATIO QUARTILE RANKINGS

3-Year	**1**
5-Year	**1**

EFFICIENCY/MER

Management expense/$100

$2.10

○ above average
● average
○ below average

STYLE

	Value	Growth	Sector Rotation (SR)
Big			
Medium			
Small			

Company Size

Complementary Fund:
Chou RRSP Fund

Similar Fund:
First Canadian Growth Fund

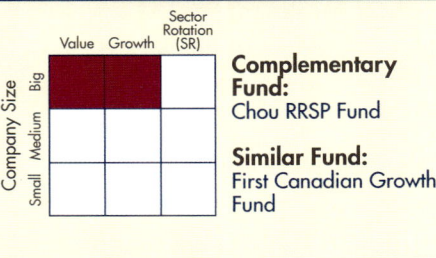

Not all of us will accumulate enough wealth to leave a huge legacy to foundations for saving the whales or the ozone layer. Spurred on by the desire to make a difference, more and more people are devoting portions of their portfolios to ethical funds. As evidence, the Ethical Growth Fund now has over $800 million in assets.

Martin Gerber and Larry Lunn manage the fund. The fund's benchmark is the TSE 300 (82.5%) and the Morgan Stanley World Index excluding Canada (17.5%). The fund is almost equally balanced between growth and value Canadian stocks, while avoiding companies involved in tobacco, liquor, nuclear power, national defense, or companies with poor histories on the environment or in labour relations.

Gerber and Lunn currently favour the financial services sector as they estimate that the group is trading at 60% of the market multiple based on projected earnings for 1998. While the fund managers contend that the economy is not recession-bound, economic growth is slowing and they are keeping an eye on the rising risk levels in the market.

The foreign component, of which France and Italy are the current favourites, is efficiently achieved by using country index futures in a disciplined manner.

One of the fund's hallmarks is its latitude (for an equity fund) in allocating amounts to cash, bonds and debentures. In fact, at times in the past it has held significant non-stock positions at very opportune times.

So if you want to feel good about yourself without sabotaging your portfolio, consider this fund, but factor in the fund's 27% cash position into your overall portfolio mix.

NEW

FIRST CANADIAN GROWTH FUND
Michael Stanley (inception)/Jones Heward Investment Counsel Inc.

CANADIAN LARGE CAP/DIVERSIFIED BLEND

CONSISTENCY

Performance Trend

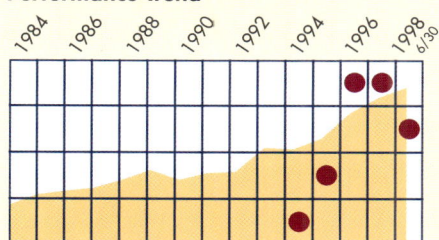

RISK

How often fund outperformed GICs	**3 years in 4**
How often fund lost money	**1 year in 4**
Worst year's rate of return	**-5.4% (1990)**

REWARD-TO-RISK RELATIONSHIP
SHARPE RATIO QUARTILE RANKINGS

3-Year	**1**
5-Year	**N/A**

EFFICIENCY/MER

Management expense/$100

$2.20

○ above average
● average
○ below average

STYLE

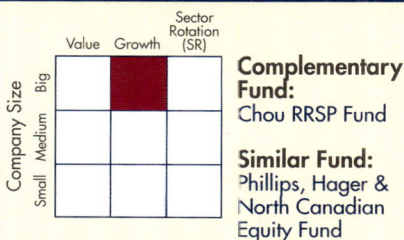

Complementary Fund:
Chou RRSP Fund

Similar Fund:
Phillips, Hager & North Canadian Equity Fund

Veteran manager Michael Stanley of Jones Heward Investment Counsel Inc. has a simple investment philosophy. Select companies according to the outlook for the industry, analyze the earnings record, weigh the strength of management, and determine the firm's growth potential. The result, in Stanley's case, is a portfolio of 20 to 40 blue-chip Canadian equities that have provided Top Fund investment returns. The holding period is one to two years, indicating that Stanley and his Jones Heward team have a rigid sell discipline and are not afraid to pull the trigger if an investment fails to meet his criteria. Stanley has been forced by the rich valuations in the market to seek out relative value, rather than buy stocks that are actually cheap.

BCE Inc. is the top holding, representing 7.2% of total assets. Four of the Big Five banks round out the top five, which of course has almost been a guarantee of investment success over the past few years. Ironically, Bank of Montreal, parent of First Canadian Funds, is the bank seen as not worthy of inclusion in the portfolio.

(left margin) CANADIAN LARGE CAP/DIVERSIFIED BLEND

NEW

GREEN LINE CANADIAN EQUITY FUND

John Weatherall (inception) + Phil Stafford/TD Asset Management Inc.

CONSISTENCY

Performance Trend

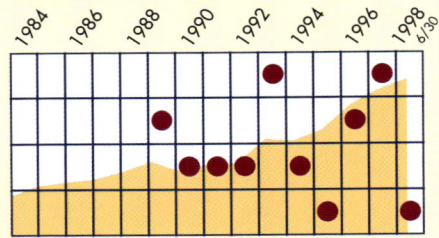

1984 1986 1988 1990 1992 1994 1996 1998 6/30

RISK

How often fund outperformed GICs	**6 years in 9**
How often fund lost money	**3 years in 9**
Worst year's rate of return	**-14.7% (1990)**

REWARD-TO-RISK RELATIONSHIP
SHARPE RATIO QUARTILE RANKINGS

3-Year	**2**
5-Year	**2**

EFFICIENCY/MER

Management expense/$100

$2.10

○ above average
● average
○ below average

STYLE

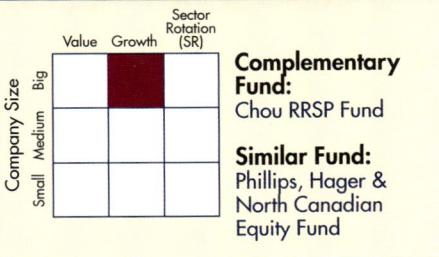

Company Size: Big / Medium / Small
Value / Growth / Sector Rotation (SR)

Complementary Fund:
Chou RRSP Fund

Similar Fund:
Phillips, Hager & North Canadian Equity Fund

Manager John Weatherall of TD Asset Management Inc. is helping to refute the myth that bank-owned mutual funds aren't up to snuff. Weatherall and his co-manager Phil Stafford have produced a top performer in Green Line Equity.

Their style is bottom-up stock selection, and they look for securities with high growth potential. The holdings total over 200 and are fully diversified by sector and capitalization. Currently, the fund is overweighted to the energy, communications, merchandising, and consumer products sectors.

Unfortunately, an underweighting to the red hot financial sector, as well as other interest rate sensitive sectors hurt performance in early 1998, although the single largest holding is actually Bank of Nova Scotia. The fund is fully invested, with minimal cash holdings. An attempt is made to maximize the 20% foreign content component of the fund, with an emphasis on U.S. equities.

NEW

INVESTORS SUMMA FUND
Allan Brown (1997)/Investors Group Inc.

CANADIAN LARGE CAP/DIVERSIFIED BLEND

CONSISTENCY

Performance Trend

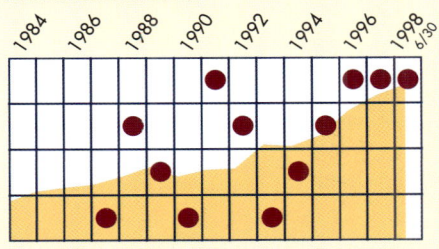

1984 1986 1988 1990 1992 1994 1996 1998 6/30

RISK

How often fund outperformed GICs	**7 years in 11**
How often fund lost money	**3 years in 11**
Worst year's rate of return	**-15.5% (1990)**

REWARD-TO-RISK RELATIONSHIP
SHARPE RATIO QUARTILE RANKINGS

3-Year	**1**
5-Year	**1**

EFFICIENCY/MER

Management expense/$100

$2.48

○ above average
● average
○ below average

STYLE

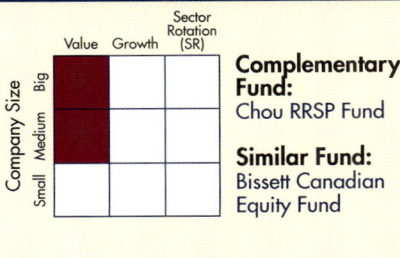

Sector Rotation (SR)
Value Growth
Company Size: Big / Medium / Small

Complementary Fund:
Chou RRSP Fund

Similar Fund:
Bissett Canadian Equity Fund

What a great time to be an ethical/environmental/green fund! One of the biggest surprises of this bull market has been the weakness in commodity prices and the resultant poor performance of industries dependent on raw materials prices, such as steel makers, mining companies, pulp and paper producers, and oil firms. By and large, these are also the types of businesses that most ethical type funds avoid like the plague. The result has been superior performance for this fund. Of course, a resurgence in commodity prices could seriously erode the top ranking of these funds.

Four of the top five holdings are banks and the fund is underweighted in the resource sector. Manager Allan Brown has also been active in the small- to-mid-cap area, looking for investments with superior growth opportunities. With about 50% of the TSE forbidden to Brown because of the ethical restrictions, he must dig deeper to turn up undervalued securities, and has been successful in doing so.

McLEAN BUDDEN EQUITY GROWTH FUND
McLean Budden Equity team (inception)

CONSISTENCY

Performance Trend

1984 1986 1988 1990 1992 1994 1996 1998 6/30

RISK

How often fund outperformed GICs	**6 years in 9**
How often fund lost money	**2 years in 9**
Worst year's rate of return	**-12.5% (1990)**

REWARD-TO-RISK RELATIONSHIP
SHARPE RATIO QUARTILE RANKINGS

3-Year	**1**
5-Year	**2**

EFFICIENCY/MER

Management expense/$100

$1.75

○ above average
○ average
● below average

STYLE

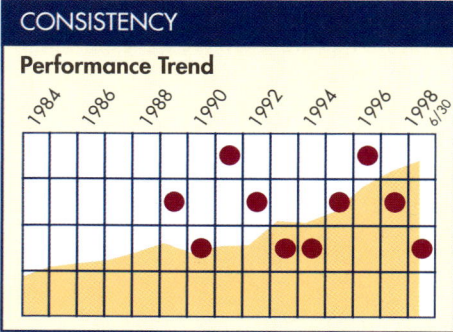

Complementary Fund:
Chou RRSP Fund

Similar Fund:
Phillips, Hager & North Canadian Equity Fund

This fund is on the bubble. The McLean Budden Canadian Equity team generally charges after growth stocks based on strong ground-up research. These are the types of stocks that have excelled over the past few years, yet this fund ranked only a third quartile for the year ending June 1998. Few funds exceed the average year in and year out, but if this aberration continues into next year, its Top Fund status will likely be revoked.

One of the team, Lewis Jackson, has been quoted as saying that growth investors will have nowhere to hide if earnings growth dissipates, given the current high multiples and valuations. He contends that if market gyrations give you an ulcer, step down to the more defensive value funds. If you can't stand the thought of any correction at all, stick to cash. The man has obviously received enough phone calls from nervous investors to know that investor risk tolerance in bear markets is a different beast than when the good times are rolling.

The managers attempt to lock in steady and consistent returns over the long haul instead of spotty bouts of spectacular growth. Although they tend to focus on a manageable number of stocks (currently 45), the portfolio is spread among the various sectors. The two heaviest exposures are industrial products (29%) and financial services (22%). Ranking third is the oil and gas sector (14%), which could rebound nicely when oil prices recover.

CANADIAN LARGE CAP/DIVERSIFIED BLEND

NEW

PHILLIPS HAGER & NORTH CANADIAN EQUITY FUND
Peter Guernsey (1971)/Phillips, Hager & North Investment Management Ltd.

CONSISTENCY

Performance Trend

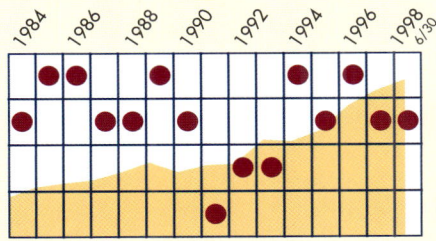

1984 1986 1988 1990 1992 1994 1996 1998 6/30

RISK

How often fund outperformed GICs	**13 years in 21**
How often fund lost money	**4 years in 21**
Worst year's rate of return	**-10.4% (1990)**

REWARD-TO-RISK RELATIONSHIP
SHARPE RATIO QUARTILE RANKINGS

3-Year	**2**
5-Year	**1**

EFFICIENCY/MER

Management expense/$100

○ above average
○ average
● below average

$1.09

STYLE

Value Growth Sector Rotation (SR)

Company Size: Big, Medium, Small

Complementary Fund: Chou RRSP Fund

Similar Fund: First Canadian Growth Fund

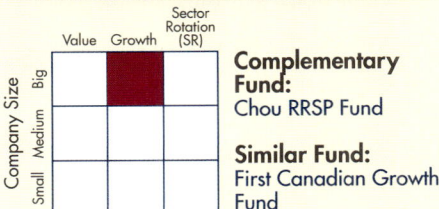

It was Teddy Roosevelt, the U.S. president in the early 1900s who said: "Speak softly and carry a big stick". That famous saying pretty well characterizes Phillips, Hager & North. Named Fund Company of the Year in 1997 by Investment Executive newspaper, the Vancouver-based PH&N has no superstar managers, advertises very little and, due to its no load status, receives scant promotion from investment industry salespeople. Yet it continues to offer a broad array of superior funds.

PH&N Canadian Equity is one of those superior funds. A rigorous analytical approach selects securities with above average growth potential as well as a high average return on shareholders' equity. Balance sheet profitability and management capabilities are also key. The portfolio customarily holds between 60 and 75 different securities, representing over 10 industry groups. Interestingly, PH&N also analyzes corporate life cycles, avoiding firms that are either at the beginning or the end of their cycles.

75

CANADIAN LARGE CAP/DIVERSIFIED BLEND

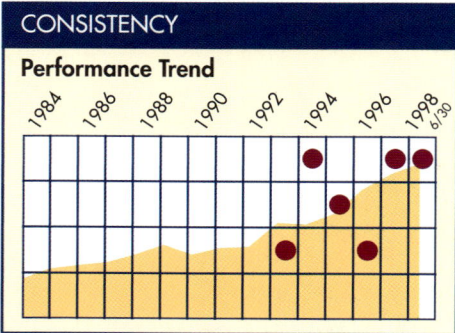

NEW

RRSP 🍁

STANDARD LIFE EQUITY MUTUAL FUND
Standard Life Portfolio Management (inception)

CONSISTENCY

Performance Trend

1984 1986 1988 1990 1992 1994 1996 1998 6/30

RISK

How often fund outperformed GICs	**4 years in 5**
How often fund lost money	**1 year in 5**
Worst year's rate of return	**0.6% (1994)**

REWARD-TO-RISK RELATIONSHIP
SHARPE RATIO QUARTILE RANKINGS

3-Year	**1**
5-Year	**1**

EFFICIENCY/MER

Management expense/$100

$2.00

○ above average
○ average
● below average

STYLE

Company Size: Big / Medium / Small
Value / Growth / Sector Rotation (SR)

Complementary Fund:
Chou RRSP Fund

Similar Fund:
Atlas Canadian Large Cap Growth Fund

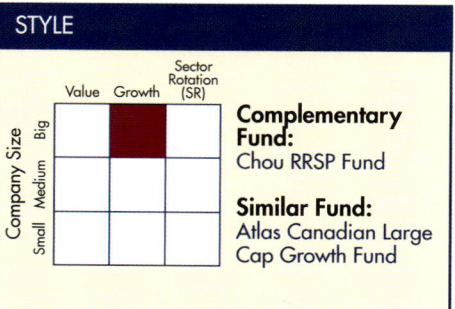

The management team at Standard Life Portfolio Management has two objectives: long-term capital growth and controlling short-term risk. The former is accomplished through a disciplined top-down approach, and the latter is achieved by owning a broadly diversified portfolio of blue-chip stocks.

The managers feel that the current economic setting in North America favours domestically-oriented groups and sectors that will continue to benefit from lower interest rates. They are avoiding the commodity industries, fearing the effect of the Asian slowdown on the exports of raw materials. BCE Inc. is the largest holding, but its weighting of only 2.7% in the portfolio confirms the presence of a large number of stocks, currently over 100 strong. Cash levels are a low 4.9%.

The fund tries to maximize the 20% foreign content limit, through exposure to U.S. markets. The currency exposure is not hedged and therefore the fund provides investors with a little bit of relief against further weakness in the Canadian dollar.

IVY CANADIAN FUND

Jerry Javasky (1997)/Mackenzie Financial Corporation

CANADIAN LARGE CAP/DIVERSIFIED VALUE

CONSISTENCY

Performance Trend

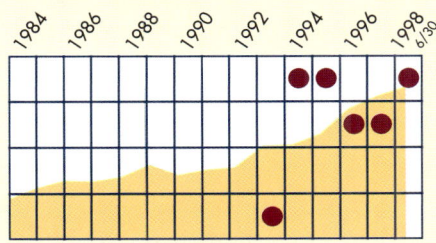

1984 1986 1988 1990 1992 1994 1996 1998 6/30

RISK

How often fund outperformed GICs	**4 years in 5**
How often fund lost money	**0 years in 5**
Worst year's rate of return	**5.0% (1994)**

RISK-ADJUSTED RETURNS
SHARPE RATIO QUARTILE RANKINGS

3-Year	**1**
5-Year	**1**

EFFICIENCY/MER

Management expense/$100	○ above average
	● average
$2.32	○ below average

STYLE

	Value	Growth	Sector Rotation (SR)
Big			
Medium			
Small			

Company Size

Complementary Fund:
Colonia Special Growth Fund

Similar Fund:
Maxxum Dividend Fund of Canada

This high-profile Canadian value fund, managed solely by Jerry Javasky after the 1997 departure of Gerry Coleman, has accumulated $5.6 billion dollars in assets; this volume has helped grind the MER down to 2.32%. The fund was slow out the gates and was a complete stinker in 1993. Once it found its legs though, it has been leading the pack while posting some excellent numbers. Being a value fund, it has been true to form as the fund's volatility has been significantly lower than the average fund or the TSE 300.

The combined objectives of above-average returns with below-average risk has led Javasky to hike the cash position all the way up to 35% of the fund, as he opines that there is little room for error at the current valuation levels. The result was that while the market continued ahead with a full head of steam in the first quarter of 1998, the fund under performed. When choppiness returned in the second quarter, the fund recovered most of the lost ground. Such is the nature of value investing with an overlay of high cash reserves. While we prefer that managers hold no more than a transactional level of cash, Javasky's attempts to look after "investors' money" by controlling risk is at least noble.

Instead of trying to forecast the economic and sectoral tides, Javasky's approach is to invest in companies where the management is capable of anticipating economic and competitive changes and reacting to it. Like a good business manager, he believes in hiring the best, and delegating responsibility.

If you're a conservative investor or are anxious about the market's lofty heights, consider knocking on Jerry's door and buying some of what he's offering.

RRSP 🍁

SPECTRUM UNITED CANADIAN INVESTMENT FUND
Kim Shannon (1996)/ AMI Partners Inc.

CANADIAN LARGE CAP/DIVERSIFIED VALUE

CONSISTENCY

Performance Trend

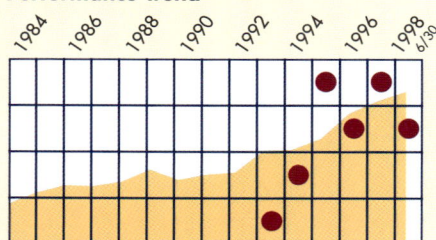

1984 1986 1988 1990 1992 1994 1996 1998 6/30

RISK

How often fund outperformed GICs	**11 years in 21**
How often fund lost money	**4 years in 21**
Worst year's rate of return	**-12.9% (1990)**

RISK-ADJUSTED RETURNS
SHARPE RATIO QUARTILE RANKINGS

3-Year	**1**
5-Year	**1**

EFFICIENCY/MER

Management expense/$100

$2.33

○ above average
● average
○ below average

STYLE

	Value	Growth	Sector Rotation (SR)
Big	■		
Medium			
Small			

Company Size

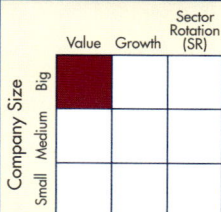

Complementary Fund:
Colonia Special Growth Fund

Similar Fund:
Maxxum Dividend Fund of Canada

It's been quite a turnaround for Canada's oldest mutual fund. Formed in 1932, it went through some lean years until Spectrum United decided to rejuvenate the fund in 1995. Manager Kim Shannon of AMI Partners Inc. changed the investment style from high yielding blue chips to a pure value, almost contrarian, approach with a focus on capital preservation. Her portfolio is large-cap weighted and has benefited from a hefty exposure to bank stocks—a common ingredient for success in 1997 and 1998. Her biggest position is in BCE Inc, but banks make up five of the next six largest holdings. Shannon believes that banks are still undervalued on a price-to-book (P/B) and price-to-earnings (P/E) basis. Her approach uses both quantitative and qualitative analyses. Shannon's quantitative model follows 425 stocks and applies the traditional value indicators, P/B, P/E and Return on Equity (ROE), while the qualitative side involves interviews with company officers in order to get a peek behind the scenes.

Total holdings exceed 200, which may seem a little excessive and is well above normal. The 20% foreign component is usually maximized and actually consists of two separate, fully diversified large-cap value portfolios: U.S. and international. Each holds 50-75 issues. The Canadian equity component is thus only 50-70 names.

Shannon feels that current market valuations are "extreme" and that increased volatility is the order of the day. She is in the process of "winterizing" her portfolio, i.e., looking for candidates with good upside and limited downside risk.

NEW

AIC DIVERSIFIED CANADA FUND

Jonathan Wellum+Michael Lee-Chin+Neil Murdoch (inception)/AIC Limited

CONSISTENCY

Performance Trend

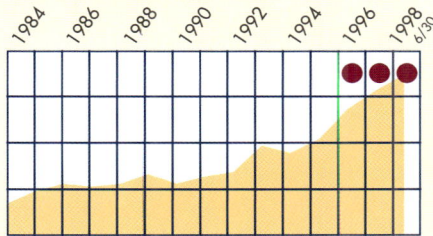

1984 1986 1988 1990 1992 1994 1996 1998 6/30

RISK

How often fund outperformed GICs	**2 years in 2**
How often fund lost money	**0 years in 2**
Worst year's rate of return	**32.1% (1977)**

RISK-ADJUSTED RETURNS
SHARPE RATIO QUARTILE RANKINGS

3-Year	**1**
5-Year	**N/A**

EFFICIENCY/MER

Management expense/$100

$2.39

○ above average
● average
○ below average

STYLE

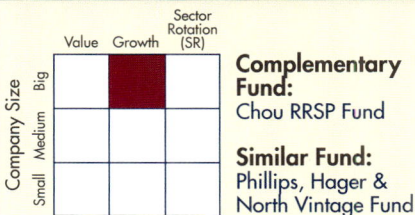

Value Growth Sector Rotation (SR)

Company Size: Big / Medium / Small

Complementary Fund:
Chou RRSP Fund

Similar Fund:
Phillips, Hager & North Vintage Fund

This the first year of eligibility for AIC Diversified Canada as a Top Fund and its inclusion was, from our perspective, a foregone conclusion. Unlike its better known sibling, AIC Advantage, this fund is not a sector fund masquerading as a core holding. Like AIC Advantage, though, performance has been superb since day one. Investors have also noticed this; asset growth has been exponential and the portfolio size has now reached almost $2 billion.

Manager Jonathan Wellum has a large cap focus with a long-term time frame. Portfolio turnover is low and the fund is therefore tax efficient. In fact, Wellum and his team expect the average security holding period to be a rather startling 12-15 years; time will tell. Total holdings are fewer than 40, which is below average for a Canadian equity fund.

Wellum's investments all have a significant international presence, allowing additional foreign diversification without exceeding the foreign content rules. Although a bottom-up manager, Wellum expects some sectors to outperform over the next few years. He sees health care, financial services, communications/media, and industrial products leading the way; we agree.

CANADIAN LARGE CAP/DIVERSIFIED GROWTH

NEW

CLEAN ENVIRONMENT EQUITY FUND

Ian Ihnatowycz (inception)/Acuity Investment Management Inc.

CANADIAN LARGE CAP/DIVERSIFIED GROWTH

CONSISTENCY

Performance Trend

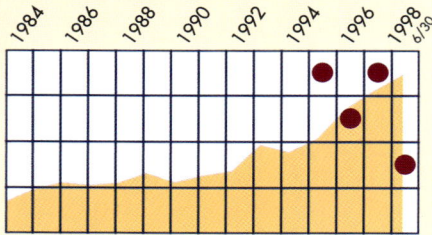

1984 1986 1988 1990 1992 1994 1996 1998 6/30

RISK

How often fund outperformed GICs	**4 years in 5**
How often fund lost money	**1 year in 5**
Worst year's rate of return	**-13.7% (1994)**

RISK-ADJUSTED RETURNS
SHARPE RATIO QUARTILE RANKINGS

3-Year	**1**
5-Year	**N/A**

EFFICIENCY/MER

Management expense/$100

$2.60

● above average
○ average
○ below average

STYLE

Company Size: Small, Medium, Big
Value, Growth, Sector Rotation (SR)

Complementary Fund:
Phillips, Hager & North Dividend Income Fund

Similar Fund:
Investors Summa Fund Ltd.

Don't let the name scare you off. Clean Environment Equity may conjure up images of a fringe fund appealing only to Birkenstock-wearing tree huggers, but the reality is that this is truly an excellent fund. Manager Ian Ihnatowycz and his team at Acuity Investment Management have put together a portfolio that meets the seemingly incongruous goals of holding securities that meet both stringent financial and environmental criteria. Candidates must use technologies that are not destroying the planet, have a strong strategic market position, and have significant growth potential. The result is a mixed cap, growth/value fund with an eclectic group of holdings, ranging from Fairfax Financial through Yogen Fruz to GEAC Computer Corp. The lack of any significant exposure to the Canadian banking industry, the driving force behind the market in 1997 and early 1998, makes Clean Environment's performance even more impressive.

Ihnatowycz feels that the relatively small size of the fund ($305 million) allows a nimbleness and flexibility that a larger fund can't match. He also believes that the reason his approach is so successful is that companies that use environmentally-friendly technologies and approaches are making sound business decisions.

PHILLIPS, HAGER & NORTH VINTAGE FUND
Ian Mottershead (inception)/PH & N Investment Management

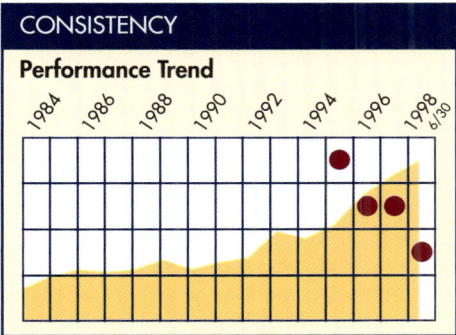

CONSISTENCY

Performance Trend

1984 1986 1988 1990 1992 1994 1996 1998 6/30

RISK

How often fund outperformed GICs	**8 years in 11**
How often fund lost money	**2 years in 11**
Worst year's rate of return	**-5.1% (1990)**

RISK-ADJUSTED RETURNS
SHARPE RATIO QUARTILE RANKINGS

3-Year	**2**
5-Year	**N/A**

EFFICIENCY/MER

Management expense/$100

$1.76

○ above average
○ average
● below average

STYLE

Sector Rotation (SR)
Value Growth
Company Size: Big / Medium / Small

Complementary Fund:
Chou RRSP Fund

Similar Fund:
Phillips, Hager & North Canadian Equity Fund

With a $10,000 initial investment minimum for an RRSP and $25,000 for a non-RRSP account, this is not the type of fund that most can afford to just dip their toe into. But if you decide to take the plunge and history is any indication, you could be well rewarded. The water may be a little turbulent as the fund has a history of above average volatility, but the returns have fairly consistently placed the fund within the top half of Canadian equity funds.

Like most Canadian equity funds, banks litter the top ten holdings. As a counterbalance, the fund also has allocations toward real estate, gold and precious metals as the fund seeks representation from the country's various business components. This is the result of P H & N's approach of choosing investments based on its views of economic events and its disciplined approach to security selection.

It's up to the individual investor if the additional return justifies the heightened volatility. If you intend to hold the fund long term and can see yourself through the various peaks and valleys, this fund should be considered.

CANADIAN LARGE CAP/DIVERSIFIED GROWTH

BISSETT SMALL CAP FUND
David Bissett (1992-inception)/Bissett and Associates

CANADIAN SMALL/MID-CAP EQUITY

CONSISTENCY

Performance Trend

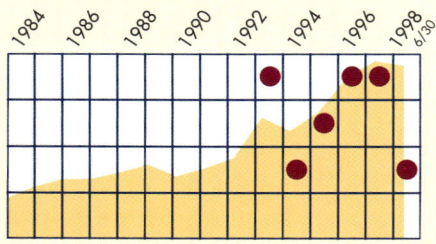

RISK

How often fund outperformed GICs	**4 years in 5**
How often fund lost money	**1 year in 5**
Worst year's rate of return	**-8.6% (1994)**

RISK-ADJUSTED RETURNS
SHARPE RATIO QUARTILE RANKINGS

3-Year	**1**
5-Year	**1**

EFFICIENCY/MER

Management expense/$100

$1.90

○ above average
○ average
● below average

STYLE

Complementary Fund:
Phillips, Hager & North Dividend Income Fund

Similar Fund:
Green Line Canadian Equity Fund

There are only a few fund managers who can consistently post good numbers in the small-cap class given the rapid pace of development, competition, and managerial changes in targeted industries and companies. David Bissett, who has managed Bissett Small Cap since its 1992 inception, has risen to the challenge. Although the first half of 1998 has been somewhat rough, in past years David has been able to squeeze out additional returns without stretching the fund's risk level and turning its performance into a roller coaster.

The Bissett Small Cap Fund has managed a couple of home runs as it returned 51% and 113% in 1996 and 1993 respectively. The price paid for the home runs has been a palatable loss of 3% for the first six months of 1998 and a mild 9% drubbing in 1994.

How does he do it? The fund focuses on growth companies with market capitalizations between $75 and $500 million. This diversification is exemplified by the fact that the fund's biggest position, Prudential Steel, accounts for only 3% of the fund's value. While free to invest anywhere, he favours his own Western Canada backyard where his in-depth knowledge of the players is an added bonus.

He discounts the potential of any significant interest rate hikes in the near term, and expects that the Canadian economy will continue to grow while maintaining its low inflation rate. These are all positives for growth hungry small-to-mid-cap stocks that need access to cheap capital in order to meet growing demand levels.

NEW

CHOU RRSP FUND
Francis Chou (inception)/Chou Associates Investment Inc.

CONSISTENCY

Performance Trend

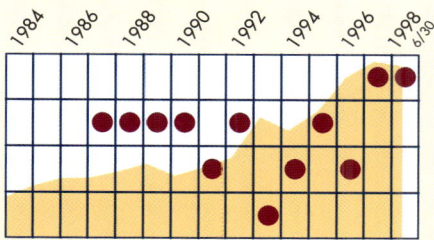

1984 1986 1988 1990 1992 1994 1996 1998 6/30

RISK

How often fund outperformed GICs	**7 years in 11**
How often fund lost money	**2 years in 11**
Worst year's rate of return	**-11.4% (1990)**

RISK-ADJUSTED RETURNS
SHARPE RATIO QUARTILE RANKINGS

3-Year	**1**
5-Year	**1**

EFFICIENCY/MER

Management expense/$100

$2.02

○ above average
○ average
● below average

STYLE

Company Size: Small, Medium, Big
Value, Growth, Sector Rotation (SR)

Complementary Fund:
AIC Diversified Canada Fund

Similar Fund:
Clean Environment Equity Fund

We're reminded of the line in the movie, *Butch Cassidy and the Sundance Kid*. As the Pinkerton agents relentlessly pursue our heroes day and night, over mountain and desert, through rain and under scorching sun, Butch turns to Sundance and asks: "Who are those guys?"

Who are these guys, indeed. Manager Francis Chou of Toronto-based Chou Associates Management Inc. has returned stellar results over the past few years. A small (less than $2.2 million) fund with an even smaller level of public awareness, this fund had the highest return of any non-leveraged fund in Canada in 1997 at 50.6%. The expense ratio is also reasonable, which is surprising in a small fund. The only problem is that when this fund is good, it is very good and when it's bad, it's horrid. In 1993 and 1994, its performance was abysmal.

We suspect that this fund will continue to make a name for itself. It had better, because Chou Associates haven't really done a great job in marketing their mutual funds. Information on the fund is difficult to obtain and, in fact, our requests for background data were ignored.

CANADIAN SMALL/MID-CAP EQUITY

COLONIA SPECIAL GROWTH FUND
Empire Financial Group (1998)

CANADIAN SMALL/MID-CAP EQUITY

CONSISTENCY

Performance Trend

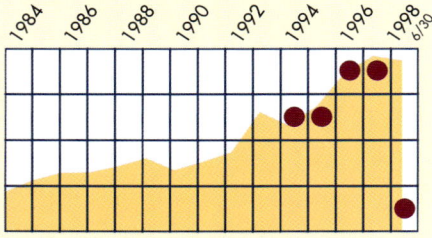

1984 1986 1988 1990 1992 1994 1996 1998 6/30

RISK

How often fund outperformed GICs	**3 years in 4**
How often fund lost money	**1 year in 4**
Worst year's rate of return	**-5.0% (1994)**

RISK-ADJUSTED RETURNS
SHARPE RATIO QUARTILE RANKINGS

3-Year	**1**
5-Year	**N/A**

EFFICIENCY/MER

Management expense/$100

$2.27

○ above average
○ average
● below average

STYLE

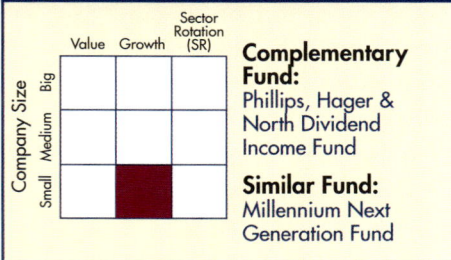

Sector Rotation
Value Growth (SR)

Company Size: Big / Medium / Small

Complementary Fund:
Phillips, Hager & North Dividend Income Fund

Similar Fund:
Millennium Next Generation Fund

We trumpeted this fund last year when Charles Roth managed it. Effective January 1, 1998, this fund has been managed by Empire Life and the results in the first six months of their tenure have not been stellar.

Empire will no doubt try to emulate Roth's performance by selecting leading-edge, smaller companies that will provide opportunities for long-term capital appreciation. The fund's current portfolio is somewhat distinct given its heavier (23%) allocation to merchandising, but it does hold a number of quality small-to-mid size stocks.

Just as we would not advise an investor to buy a fund with a six-month record, we would be hard pressed to suggest selling a position based on a six-month performance. Accordingly, although Empire Life is not new to investment management, we would not advise injecting new money into this fund until the dust settles. For those who already own the fund, you should be able to decide whether to hold or fold by comparing this fund to its small-to-mid cap peers at the end of 1998.

NEW

FIDELITY CANADIAN GROWTH COMPANY FUND
Allan Radlo (1995)/Fidelity Investments Ltd.

CONSISTENCY

Performance Trend

1984 1986 1988 1990 1992 1994 1996 1998 6/30

RISK

How often fund outperformed GICs	**3 years in 3**
How often fund lost money	**0 years in 3**
Worst year's rate of return	**20.5% (1996)**

RISK-ADJUSTED RETURNS
SHARPE RATIO QUARTILE RANKINGS

3-Year	**1**
5-Year	**N/A**

EFFICIENCY/MER

Management expense/$100

$2.47

○ above average
● average
○ below average

STYLE

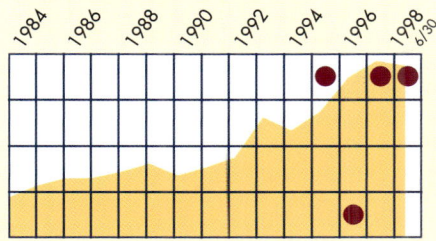

Company Size: Big / Medium / Small
Value / Growth / Sector Rotation (SR)

Complementary Fund:
Royal Dividend Fund

Similar Fund:
Green Line Canadian Equity Fund

Proponents of the "efficient markets hypothesis" feel that because so many brilliant analysts and resources are involved in the investment business, it is impossible to be privy to information about a company or industry that nobody else has. It should therefore also be impossible to consistently beat the market, because the market, especially these days, actually consists of all those other brilliant people who have the same information that you have. Now, this may be true in the case of the large blue-chip stocks which are followed by all the major money managers, but is not the case in the world of small-cap investing. There are simply too many investment choices available.

Manager Alan Radlo has the weight of Fidelity's renowned research capability behind him and the result is a top performing fund. Although nominally a small-cap fund, Radlo also searches for lesser known larger companies that are "poised for growth". For example, Power Corp of Canada, Teleglobe, and Air Canada are all top ten holdings. A bottom-up, growth manager, Radlo has been fortunate to avoid the resource and commodity issues that have been the bane of many other managers' existence in 1997 and 1998. His broadly diversified holdings total over 130.

Radlo feels that the small-cap market is relatively undervalued and believes that his holdings are inefficiently priced, given their P/E ratios and growth rates.

RRSP

MILLENNIUM NEXT GENERATION FUND
Les Williams (1993)/Morrison Williams Investment Management Ltd.

CANADIAN SMALL/MID-CAP EQUITY

CONSISTENCY

Performance Trend

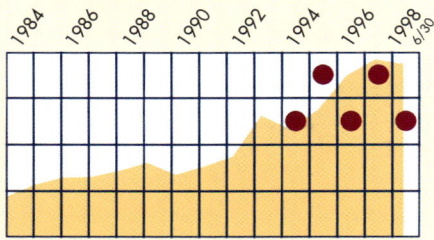

1984 1986 1988 1990 1992 1994 1996 1998 6/30

RISK

How often fund outperformed GICs	**3 years in 4**
How often fund lost money	**1 year in 4**
Worst year's rate of return	**-5.9% (1994)**

RISK-ADJUSTED RETURNS
SHARPE RATIO QUARTILE RANKINGS

3-Year	**1**
5-Year	**N/A**

EFFICIENCY/MER

Management expense/$100

$2.50

○ above average
● average
○ below average

STYLE

	Value	Growth	Sector Rotation (SR)
Big			
Medium			
Small		■	

Company Size

Complementary Fund:
Phillips, Hager & North Dividend Income Fund

Similar Fund:
Bissett Small Cap Fund

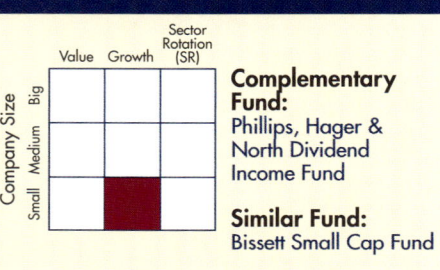

A rarity in the small cap world, Millennium Next Generation takes a top-down approach to investing. Manager Les Williams of Toronto-based Morrison Williams Investment Management Ltd. takes a macro economic view to determine his investment themes. Currently, he favours financial services and consumer stocks as he believes that secular disinflation will result in still lower interest rates. Williams then uses bottom-up fundamental research to identify the best individual prospects. He looks for above average growth, a clean balance sheet, and low P/E ratios.

The fund has only $37.3 million in assets and about 30 names in the portfolio, which allows significant positions in promising companies. This may change if continued investment success encourages new investors. His top holding is Softkey, with 3.9% of the portfolio. Noma Industries, Vincor International, Cogeco Cable, and CHC Helicopter make up the rest of the top five names.

Williams' cash positions usually speak volumes about his market views. In late 1996, he was 67% cash in anticipation of trouble in the market; this fell to 17% cash in mid 1997, and is presently only 7.8% cash.

His 20% foreign content is fully invested in the U.S stock market.

AGF DIVIDEND FUND
Gord MacDougall (inception) + Martin Gerber/CC & L

CONSISTENCY

Performance Trend

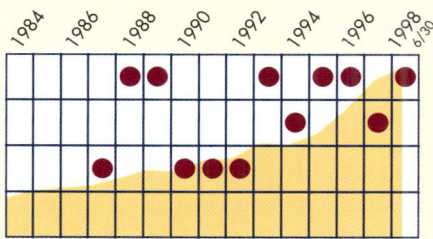

RISK

How often fund outperformed GICs	**7 years in 11**
How often fund lost money	**1 year in 11**
Worst year's rate of return	**-5.1% (1990)**

REWARD-TO-RISK RELATIONSHIP
SHARPE RATIO QUARTILE RANKINGS

3-Year	**4**
5-Year	**3**

EFFICIENCY/MER

Management expense/$100

$1.87

○ above average
● average
○ below average

STYLE

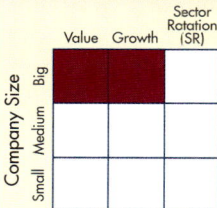

Complementary Fund:
Colonia Special Growth Fund

Similar Fund:
Spectrum United Canadian Investment Fund

This fund has performed particularly well over the past five and a half years. Longstanding managers Gord MacDougall and Martin Gerber describe their investment style as top down growth where high growth, potential sectors are singled out before the individual securities are selected. Their strategy includes sub-dividing the portfolio into three components: income stocks paying solid dividends; cyclical stocks paying larger dividends; and growth stocks for capital appreciation. The result is that for a dividend fund, the fund is highly sensitive to the general direction of the market as the duo have concentrated on common shares of high-profile Canadian and American companies. By purposely ramping up this sensitivity to the general market direction, the fund has done well for investors while the bull has run.

This is not to say that MacDougall and Gerber are letting the fund roar ahead without regard to risk. They have currently set aside about 20% of the fund's value in cash equivalents. Their concern, like many other fund managers, is that valuations are high and they want to maintain a cushion in case they can buy at lower prices in the future. While we applaud managers who attempt to control their risk levels, we prefer that the investor, in conjunction with their financial planner if applicable, dictate the level of cash reserves in attempting to meet the client's risk objectives.

CANADIAN DIVIDEND

BISSETT DIVIDEND INCOME FUND
Fred Pynn (1991)/Bissett and Associates

CONSISTENCY

Performance Trend

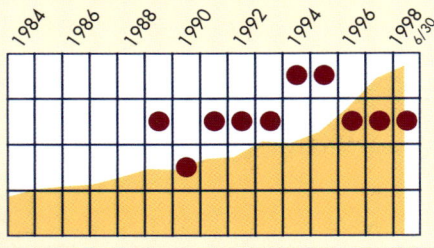

RISK

How often fund outperformed GICs	**6 years in 9**
How often fund lost money	**1 year in 9**
Worst year's rate of return	**-7.2% (1990)**

REWARD-TO-RISK RELATIONSHIP
SHARPE RATIO QUARTILE RANKINGS

3-Year	**1**
5-Year	**1**

EFFICIENCY/MER

Management expense/$100

$1.50

○ above average
○ average
● below average

STYLE

Complementary Fund:
Colonia Special Growth Fund

Similar Fund:
Spectrum United Canadian Investment Fund

Dividend funds have undergone a change in focus over recent years. They seem to have migrated toward dividend-yielding common stocks and away from higher yielding preferred shares that do not benefit from increased profits or price run-ups. The result has been that total returns posted by dividend funds have been healthy despite plummeting dividend yields. Unfortunately, without the backstop of the preferred dividend payments and their relatively stable prices, the inherent risk of these funds has increased while the downside protection has been reduced.

Bissett Dividend Income has not migrated as far toward commons as competing funds have; it still has approximately 27% of the fund in higher quality and higher yielding preferreds. Fred Pynn, who has run the fund since 1991, also considers higher yielding industrial products, consumer products, and financial services common shares. Pynn maintains that with the low inflation and interest rate environment continuing, the expected moderate economic growth should prevail. Such an environment should provide some room in the future for dividend payment levels of common shares to grow.

While the firm's stated benchmark is the Scotia Universe (35%), TSE 300 (50%), and the S&P 500 (15%), a simple comparison to the TSE 300 shows investors yielding comparable returns but at approximately half the risk.

INDUSTRIAL DIVIDEND GROWTH FUND LIMITED
Bill Proctor (1994)/Mackenzie Financial Corporation

CONSISTENCY

Performance Trend

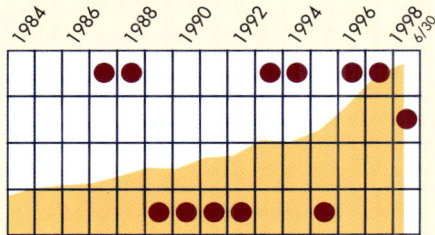

1984 1986 1988 1990 1992 1994 1996 1998 6/30

RISK

How often fund outperformed GICs	**12 years in 21**
How often fund lost money	**5 years in 21**
Worst year's rate of return	**-19.7% (1990)**

REWARD-TO-RISK RELATIONSHIP
SHARPE RATIO QUARTILE RANKINGS

3-Year	**3**
5-Year	**3**

EFFICIENCY/MER

Management expense/$100

$2.38

● above average
○ average
○ below average

STYLE

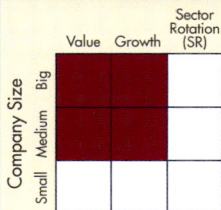

Company Size: Big / Medium / Small
Value Growth Sector Rotation (SR)

Complementary Fund:
Chou RRSP Fund

Similar Fund:
Atlas Canadian Large Cap Growth Fund

If you owned this fund during the 1989–1992 period, you are probably already turning the page. Stop! Things have changed. Ignoring the blip, or actually the blight, in 1995, this fund has flourished under the tutelage of Bill Proctor.

Uncharacteristically for a dividend fund, Mackenzie has stated that low-yielding but high-growth, potential stocks are fair game (currently at 5%). As well, convertible debentures can be held. At least they are direct in their disclosure about the fund's objectives, but the effect is to make the standard dividend fund comprised mostly of preferred shares a distant memory.

Being a value manager in a highly-valued market can makes things tough. Despite the market's dividend yields hitting record lows, Proctor still maintains that the investment environment is generally a positive one. But with a scarcity of high-yielding stocks, his views that earnings are sputtering and that inflation may have hit a low has induced him to increase the fund's cash balance to 13%.

Ignoring our classification qualms, this fund has outperformed the TSE 300 over the three-year period while chalking up lower volatility numbers.

Before you pull the trigger and integrate this holding with the balance of your Canadian equities, be sure to recognize that this is a large-cap equity fund, and not a conservative play on higher ranking and dividend yielding preferred shares that are more resilient in a correction.

CANADIAN DIVIDEND

MAXXUM DIVIDEND FUND
Jackie Pratt (1995)/London Fund Management

CANADIAN DIVIDEND

CONSISTENCY

Performance Trend

RISK

How often fund outperformed GICs	**6 years in 11**
How often fund lost money	**1 year in 11**
Worst year's rate of return	**-9.3% (1990)**

REWARD-TO-RISK RELATIONSHIP
SHARPE RATIO QUARTILE RANKINGS

3-Year	**3**
5-Year	**1**

EFFICIENCY/MER

Management expense/$100

$1.73

○ above average
● average
○ below average

STYLE

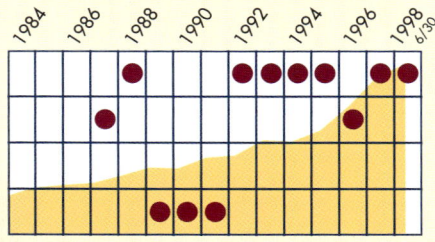

Complementary Fund:
Chou RRSP Fund

Similar Fund:
Spectrum United
Canadian Investment
Fund

As part of the purchase of Prudential Insurance's Canadian subsidiary, London Life acquired the Maxxum funds in 1996. Fortunately, they also inherited veteran Jacqueline Pratt who has been in charge of this fund since early 1995.

Like many dividend fund managers, Pratt has loaded up on dividend-paying commons in order to take advantage of the TSE's positive momentum. Pratt employs a bottom-up and value-based style of security selection. You'll find the usual roster of banks, pipelines, and utilities within her holdings. But Pratt also spreads the wealth across most other sectors in an attempt to diversify. Why invest here? Because with total expenses at a low 1.73%, you're buying a quality manager who analyzes and selects quality stocks at wholesale prices.

It's no secret that it is the large caps and the banks that have paced the TSE 300's ascent over the past few years, and Pratt does not anticipate that this will change much in the near future. She expects large stable stocks to continue their foray, as inflation remains subdued on a worldwide basis, and investors react to the Asian crisis.

PHILLIPS, HAGER & NORTH DIVIDEND INCOME FUND
PH & N Management team (inception)

CONSISTENCY

Performance Trend

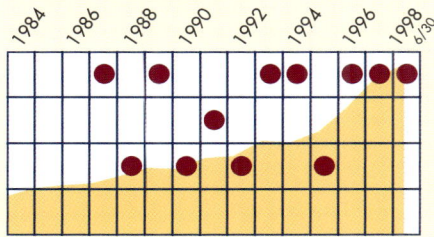

1984 1986 1988 1990 1992 1994 1996 1998 6/30

RISK

How often fund outperformed GICs	**12 years in 20**
How often fund lost money	**3 years in 20**
Worst year's rate of return	**-7.2% (1981)**

REWARD-TO-RISK RELATIONSHIP
SHARPE RATIO QUARTILE RANKINGS

3-Year	**1**
5-Year	**1**

EFFICIENCY/MER

Management expense/$100

$1.21

○ above average
○ average
● below average

STYLE

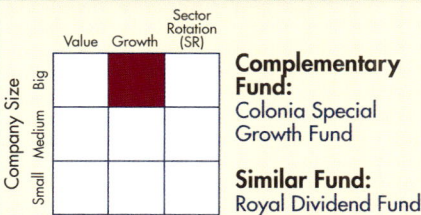

Sector Rotation (SR)
Value Growth
Company Size: Big / Medium / Small

Complementary Fund:
Colonia Special Growth Fund

Similar Fund:
Royal Dividend Fund

CANADIAN DIVIDEND

It's a tough hunt these days for dividend yields. As stock prices continue skyward, the hunt intensifies. Believing that upside remains, P H & N has staked this fund's reputation on continued capital appreciation instead of on yield. While the fund's managers have sought out the highest dividend paying common shares (which can continue to increase in price if earnings grow or the price-to-earnings ratios expand), they have turned a blind eye toward preferred shares which constitute only 0.7% of the portfolio. This approach has worked well in a rising market.

In trying to extract whatever yield they can out of Canadian common shares, the fund management team has focused on utilities and banks that have demonstrated a desire to gradually increase dividend levels instead of embarking on acquisition sprees or share buyback programs. The fund selection has been consistent with the objective of selecting stocks based on long-term earnings growth potential.

Make no mistake about it, P H & N has proven that it can manage Canadian equity portfolios along with the best of them; just be aware that this may not be the safest fund to hide in if you think bad times are ahead.

ROYAL DIVIDEND FUND
John Kellet (1993-inception)/Royal Bank Investment Management

CONSISTENCY

Performance Trend

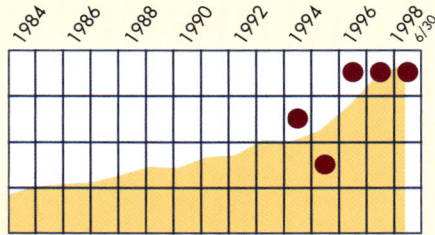

1984 1986 1988 1990 1992 1994 1996 1998 6/30

RISK

How often fund outperformed GICs	**3 years in 4**
How often fund lost money	**1 year in 4**
Worst year's rate of return	**-0.7% (1994)**

REWARD-TO-RISK RELATIONSHIP
SHARPE RATIO QUARTILE RANKINGS

3-Year	**2**
5-Year	**1**

EFFICIENCY/MER

Management expense/$100

$1.77

○ above average
● average
○ below average

STYLE

	Value	Growth	Sector Rotation (SR)
Big			
Medium			
Small			

Company Size

Complementary Fund:
Colonia Special Growth Fund

Similar Fund:
Phillips, Hager & North Dividend Income Fund

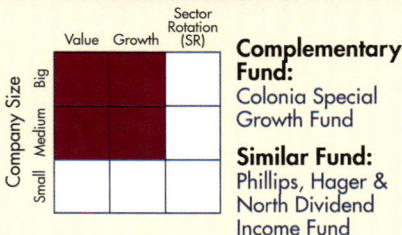

You would expect that any listing of top Canadian funds would have at least some representation from Canada's largest bank and no-load mutual fund company. This is one of only two that make the grade.

John Kellett manages an interesting dividend fund. His concern over the current excessive equity valuations has caused him to ramp up his bond allocation to almost 20%. Kellett's conviction is that the low inflation and interest rate environment will continue to prevail, which will benefit interest sensitive sectors like financial services, pipelines, and utilities. Kellett has no qualms about favouring his areas of comfort as the fund is slanted toward financials (34%), pipelines (9%), and utilities (14%).

This type of concentration has caused the fund to be slightly more volatile than the average Canadian dividend fund, but investors have been amply rewarded over the past two and a half years.

Kellett has geared this fund toward investors seeking a lower risk exposure to the stock market, but that is still desirous of modest long-term growth of capital.

AIC ADVANTAGE FUND
Jonathan Wellum (1990)/AIC Limited

CONSISTENCY

Performance Trend

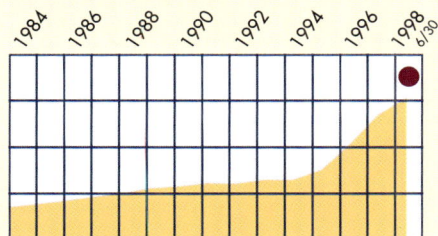

1984 1986 1988 1990 1992 1994 1996 1998 6/30

RISK

How often fund outperformed GICs	**8 years in 12**
How often fund lost money	**3 years in 12**
Worst year's rate of return	**-18.6% (1990)**

REWARD-TO-RISK RELATIONSHIP
SHARPE RATIO QUARTILE RANKINGS

3-Year	**N/A**
5-Year	**N/A**

EFFICIENCY/MER

Management expense/$100

$2.31

○ above average
○ average
● below average

STYLE

Company Size: Big / Medium / Small
Value / Growth / Sector Rotation (SR)

Complementary Fund:
Chou RRSP Fund

Similar Fund:
AIC Diversified Canada Fund

CANADIAN SECTOR EQUITY

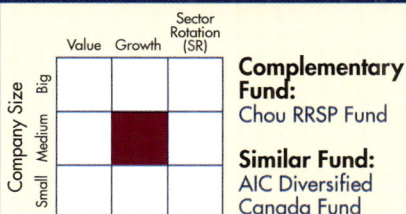

This fund was originally structured to be heavily weighted in the non-bank financial services industry; it bought stock in mutual fund companies like Mackenzie and Trimark, rather than taking large positions in bank stocks. This was done in anticipation of the greater level of savings and investments that will be made by the Baby Boomers as they prepare for retirement. This has begun to happen, and AIC Advantage has posted some eye-popping numbers. Of the three managers listed, it is Jonathan Wellum who is generally regarded as the prime mover.

The Warren Buffett-like investment style employed entails a thorough bottom-up analysis approach. Investments are made in leading companies in growth markets and are intended to be held for the very long term. Paying homage to the master, Berkshire Hathaway, which is managed by Buffett, is the fund's fourth largest holding.

Financial services stocks can get particularly battered in down markets as attested to by the fund's 1994 loss of 12.6%. Perhaps with some divine insight, theology-trained Wellum has reduced the fund's financial services exposure to 65% by redeploying capital into other quality companies. Despite the additional sector diversification, this fund should not be your core Canadian equity holding but could make a good fine-tuning addition, and offer some "pop" to your holdings.

20/20 CANADIAN RESOURCES FUND LIMITED
Bob Farquharson (1960-inception)/AGF Funds Inc.

CANADIAN RESOURCES & PRECIOUS METALS

CONSISTENCY

Performance Trend

RISK

How often fund outperformed GICs	**12 years in 21**
How often fund lost money	**9 years in 21**
Worst year's rate of return	**-29.4% (1981)**

REWARD-TO-RISK RELATIONSHIP
SHARPE RATIO QUARTILE RANKINGS

3-Year	**1**
5-Year	**1**

EFFICIENCY/MER

Management expense/$100

$2.88

● above average
○ average
○ below average

STYLE

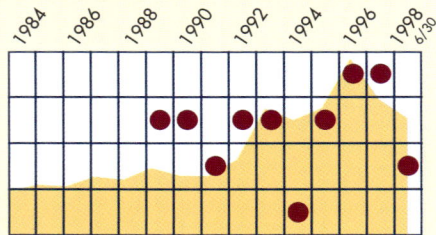

Complementary Fund:
Royal Precious Metals Fund

Similar Fund:
Universal Canadian Resource Fund

One of the old timers on the Canadian resources scene, this fund has been providing healthy returns since 1960. All the while, Bob Farquharson has been at the helm steering the fund through the cyclical highs and lows. A relatively high management expense ratio has been justified by the success Farquharson has had in implementing his bottom-up approach to hunting down high growth resource stocks.

He did a commendable job shielding investors from the large losses that many resource funds registered in 1997, as commodity prices unravelled. The carnage in commodities continued into 1998 as the resource-hungry Asian economies failed to be revived. Farquharson contends that one of the first beneficiaries of any recovery in the tiger economies will be the energy sector, and accordingly has almost half of the fund's holdings in the oil and gas sector. While he does not anticipate a spike in oil prices in the short term, he does anticipate that natural gas prices will remain solid in the interim. This exposure to the petroleum industry has hurt performance to date in 1998. The fund also has a significant exposure to gold and metals stocks that have been hammered lately on fundamentals, but that will again have their day in the sun.

Even in these down markets for resources, this fund has remained fully invested leaving the asset allocation decision with the fund investor. This demonstrates both management discipline and commitment to the eventual recovery.

This fund was formerly known as the AGF Canadian Resources Fund.

MAXXUM NATURAL RESOURCE FUND
Jackie Pratt (1995)/London Fund Management

CONSISTENCY

Performance Trend

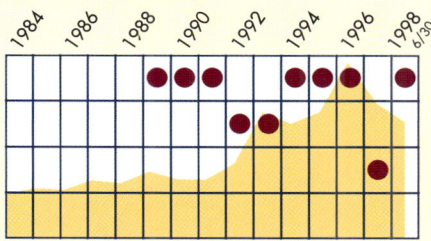

RISK

How often fund outperformed GICs	**5 years in 9**
How often fund lost money	**3 years in 9**
Worst year's rate of return	**-39.2% (1997)**

REWARD-TO-RISK RELATIONSHIP
SHARPE RATIO QUARTILE RANKINGS

3-Year	**2**
5-Year	**2**

EFFICIENCY/MER

Management expense/$100

$2.23

○ above average
○ average
● below average

STYLE

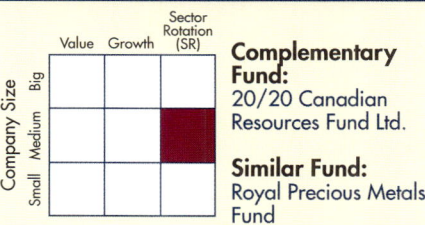

Complementary Fund:
20/20 Canadian Resources Fund Ltd.

Similar Fund:
Royal Precious Metals Fund

CANADIAN RESOURCES & PRECIOUS METALS

There is no dispute that the natural resources sector has been rocked over the past few years for various fundamental reasons. The sector has always been classified as a cyclical one given its roller-coaster ride between the peaks and valleys. So what's going to be your ticket for hitching a ride back to the top, if you decide at some point to hop on board?

Some resource funds lean a little more to the speculative side, banking on the next drill hole or management's past successes. Not this fund. Sure some of its holdings are currently down, but Pratt concentrates on market leaders that she has confidence will be capable of riding out the downturn. But this doesn't imply that she holds them for a long time, as she generally turns over her portfolio at least once a year.

Pratt's bottom-up growth orientation currently has the fund heavily invested in the oil and gas, and gold and precious metals areas. She contends that the Asian situation is already mostly priced into Canadian resource stocks, and that the contagion will not push Canada into a recession which would only compound the current pricing woes affecting commodities.

For the first time since the fund's inception in 1988, it under performed the median in 1997. Although the under performance was substantial, we contend that this is an aberration and not a reflection on Pratt's skill.

ROYAL PRECIOUS METALS FUND
John Embry (1994-inception)/Royal Bank Investment Management

CANADIAN RESOURCES & PRECIOUS METALS

CONSISTENCY

Performance Trend

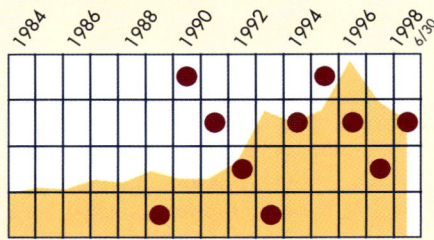

1984 1986 1988 1990 1992 1994 1996 1998 6/30

RISK

How often fund outperformed GICs	**3 years in 9**
How often fund lost money	**4 years in 9**
Worst year's rate of return	**-33.7% (1997)**

REWARD-TO-RISK RELATIONSHIP
SHARPE RATIO QUARTILE RANKINGS

3-Year	**1**
5-Year	**1**

EFFICIENCY/MER

Management expense/$100

$2.41

○ above average
● average
○ below average

STYLE

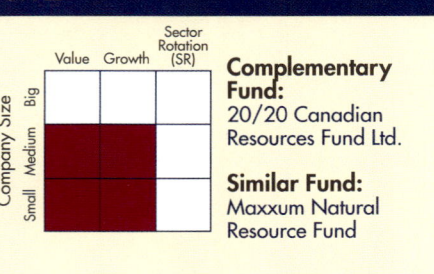

Company Size: Big, Medium, Small
Value, Growth, Sector Rotation (SR)

Complementary Fund:
20/20 Canadian Resources Fund Ltd.

Similar Fund:
Maxxum Natural Resource Fund

One of the Royal Bank Investment Management's leading lights, John Embry certainly runs an interesting fund, as its prospectus allows for holdings in coins and bullion while imposing a maximum exposure of 20% to silver and platinum.

Embry currently appears to be employing Mohammed Ali's "rope-a-dope" method of standing back and absorbing the punches while he awaits his opportunity to pounce. The fund's net asset value continues to get waylaid, yet Embry remains fully invested in areas such as gold and silver certificates (combined total of over 24% of fund's value), established producers and some not-so-established producers.

Foolish? No, it's his mandate and we respect him for fulfilling it. Embry contends that the heavy sales of gold by central banks will subside and bullion prices will rise again. He is also buoyed by the relatively high valuations of financial assets relative to hard assets such as precious metals.

The fund may have fallen to the third quartile in 1997, and the volatility may induce gray hair, but if you want to add some contrarian spice to your already diversified portfolio, this fund certainly fits the bill. We would not advise loading up excessively on this fund, but it will likely make the highlight reel again one day.

UNIVERSAL CANADIAN RESOURCE FUND
Fred Sturm (1986)/Mackenzie Financial Corporation

CONSISTENCY

Performance Trend

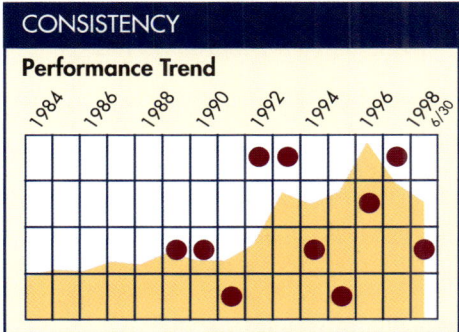

RISK

How often fund outperformed GICs	**9 years in 19**
How often fund lost money	**8 years in 19**
Worst year's rate of return	**-24.5% (1981)**

REWARD-TO-RISK RELATIONSHIP
SHARPE RATIO QUARTILE RANKINGS

3-Year	**2**
5-Year	**2**

EFFICIENCY/MER

Management expense/$100

$2.39

○ above average
● average
○ below average

STYLE

Complementary Fund:
Royal Precious Metals Fund

Similar Fund:
20/20 Canadian Resources Fund Ltd.

Manager Fred Sturm finds himself in the middle of a country fair hog contest instead of a beauty contest. The recent focus in the energy and resources category has been not how much you made but how much you managed to avoid losing. Universal Canadian Resources Fund has managed to lose only 25.8% for the year ending June 30, 1998.

Slower global economic growth and the disappearance of growing demand out of Asia has cast a pall over this classification's funds. If you are both a contrarian and patient, you will have bragging rights one day if you have the audacity to wade into the storm now, while commodity prices are at 12-year lows. Sturm believes that a number of commodities have already established their lows and are starting to stagger toward a recovery.

The fund exposure is slanted toward the oil and gas sector (36%), given their depressed prices and the chance for a hearty comeback. The fund is also focused on the out-of-favour gold and precious metals sector to the tune of 19%. Sturm has reduced some of his larger positions recently in order to generate cash (investors have been timid with new funds since the pummeling began) and take up positions in some new opportunities.

If you have the intestinal fortitude and can hang in for a while, give this fund a second thought. While Sturm concedes that the catalyst required for the resources sector to rebound remains elusive at present, he is highly optimistic. Remember that the smart ones buy low and sell high.

CANADIAN RESOURCES & PRECIOUS METALS

AGF AMERICAN GROWTH CLASS FUND
Steve Rogers (1993)/AGF Funds Inc.

CONSISTENCY

Performance Trend

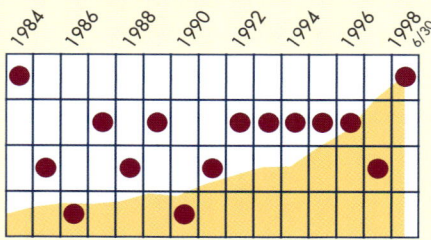

RISK

How often fund outperformed GICs	**13 years in 21**
How often fund lost money	**4 years in 21**
Worst year's rate of return	**-9.3% (1990)**

REWARD-TO-RISK RELATIONSHIP
SHARPE RATIO QUARTILE RANKINGS

3-Year	**3**
5-Year	**2**

EFFICIENCY/MER

Management expense/$100

$2.78

● above average
○ average
○ below average

STYLE

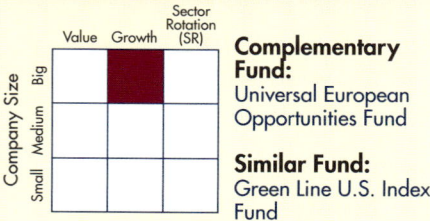

Complementary Fund:
Universal European Opportunities Fund

Similar Fund:
Green Line U.S. Index Fund

U.S. LARGE CAP/DIVERSIFIED EQUITY

If you want a fund with a long track record, this could be the one: it has been around since 1957. Steve Rogers has managed the fund since 1993 and earns his wages by being a stock picker of well-established American growth stocks. True to the fund's name, growth stocks permeate throughout the portfolio, as the top four holdings are large computer or technology stocks, while the fifth largest is a pharmaceutical company. One benefit of this fund is that given its gearing toward capital gains, it is tax effective for investors holding it outside their RRSPs.

Steve views the Asian crisis as almost a positive since it has lowered inflation expectations and preempted the U.S. Federal Reserve from hiking interest rates, an initiative that could cause widespread bloodshed among growth stocks. Despite a little trepidation regarding the short-term earnings outlook and the increased market volatility, Rogers is steadfast in his belief that his selections will fare well over the long term.

This fund will continue to boost portfolio returns as long as growth stocks dominate the American equity landscape as they have over the past five years.

AIC VALUE FUND
Jonathan Wellum + team (1990)/AIC Limited

CONSISTENCY

Performance Trend

1984 1986 1988 1990 1992 1994 1996 1998 6/30

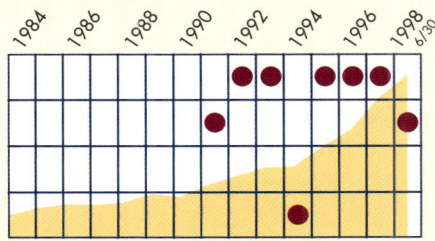

RISK

How often fund outperformed GICs	**6 years in 7**
How often fund lost money	**1 year in 7**
Worst year's rate of return	**-4.2% (1994)**

REWARD-TO-RISK RELATIONSHIP
SHARPE RATIO QUARTILE RANKINGS

3-Year	**1**
5-Year	**1**

EFFICIENCY/MER

Management expense/$100

$2.44

○ above average
● average
○ below average

STYLE

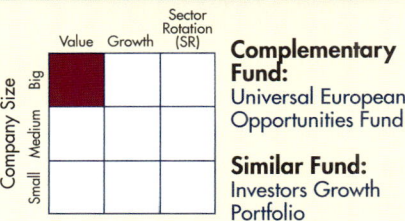

Company Size: Big, Medium, Small
Value, Growth, Sector Rotation (SR)

Complementary Fund:
Universal European Opportunities Fund

Similar Fund:
Investors Growth Portfolio

U.S. LARGE CAP/DIVERSIFIED EQUITY

The AIC managers have been successful in developing their long-term investing platform and applying it to different markets. These Warren Buffett "wannabes" (and who doesn't want to be like multi-billionaire Buffett these days) would make the grand master proud with the results they have posted since the fund's inception in 1990.

Taking advantage of the depth of the U.S. market to seek out market leaders has been a task successfully completed. Like a song that you can't get out of your mind, this fund has a strong financial services tilt to it like other AIC funds. Given the current rapid consolidation in the U.S. financial services sector, this overweighting could serve investors well in the future. But be cognizant that earnings of financial services companies often turn down in a stock market correction; accordingly this fund may suffer more than most when such a correction occurs. As we would suggest for most funds, adopt a long-term approach to investing in this fund. If you don't think that you can afford to carry a losing position until the eventual recovery, this fund, like many other equity funds, may not be for you.

FIDELITY GROWTH AMERICA FUND
Brad Lewis (1990-inception)/Steve Snider (1998)/Fidelity Management & Research Co.

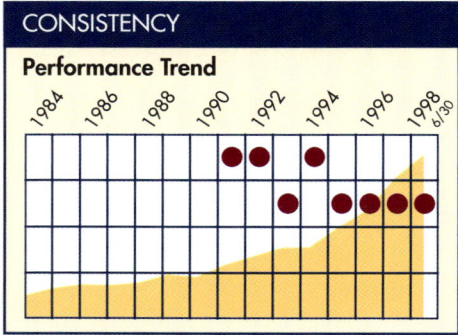

CONSISTENCY

Performance Trend

RISK

How often fund outperformed GICs	**6 years in 7**
How often fund lost money	**0 years in 7**
Worst year's rate of return	**6.2% (1994)**

REWARD-TO-RISK RELATIONSHIP
SHARPE RATIO QUARTILE RANKINGS

3-Year	**2**
5-Year	**2**

EFFICIENCY/MER

Management expense/$100

$2.34

○ above average
● average
○ below average

STYLE

Complementary Fund:
Universal European Opportunities Fund

Similar Fund:
Green Line U.S. Index

U.S. LARGE CAP/DIVERSIFIED EQUITY

This fund has under performed the average U.S. equity fund in the first half of 1998 but co-managers Brad Lewis and Steve Snider aren't feeling blue. With concerns over the price-to-earnings multiples and the sketchiness of the outlook for earnings, they have dropped back to the blue line to play some defense. Instead of loading up on cash to meet this goal, they have adjusted their weighting to the various sectors, and have managed to ratchet down the fund's weighted average P/E to 16 times versus 21 times for the S & P 500 on a 12-month, risk-adjusted basis. The portfolio is overweight in cheaper durables, financials, retail, and transport stocks while it has reduced its proportionate holdings in the non-durables, health, and technology sectors. The fund also has a small-to-mid-cap slant, currently cheaper than large-caps, as its average market capitalization is about half that of the S & P 500.

The 200 plus companies held by the fund are a subset of 3000 that are renewed daily using proprietary software. Lewis and Snider focus on finding undervalued companies which are supported by earnings growth and a healthy ownership disposition in the company by officers and directors. While they don't consider themselves sector rotators, Lewis and Snider try to maintain a healthy level of industry diversification.

These maneuvers infer that if a correction is in the offing, this fund should hold its value relative to others. The two-minute penalty for this conservatism has been the level of returns. On a risk-return basis though, this fund is worth a second glance.

NEW

GREEN LINE U.S. INDEX FUND
Enrique Cuyegkeng+Tim Thompson (1992)/TD Asset Management Inc.

CONSISTENCY

Performance Trend

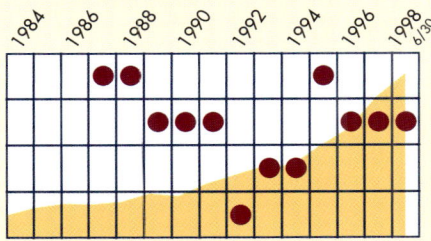

1984 1986 1988 1990 1992 1994 1996 1998 6/30

RISK

How often fund outperformed GICs	**7 years in 11**
How often fund lost money	**1 year in 11**
Worst year's rate of return	**-4.2% (1990)**

REWARD-TO-RISK RELATIONSHIP
SHARPE RATIO QUARTILE RANKINGS

3-Year	**2**
5-Year	**2**

EFFICIENCY/MER

Management expense/$100

$0.66

○ above average
○ average
● below average

STYLE

Company Size: Small / Medium / Big
Value / Growth / Sector Rotation (SR)

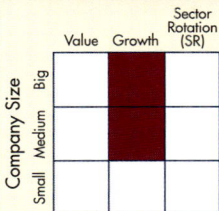

Complementary Fund:
Universal European Opportunities Fund

Similar Fund:
AGF American Growth Class

We have mixed feelings about index funds. It's true history shows that active fund managers have a difficult time outperforming the indexes in the efficient U.S.market. While the low expenses are compelling, and there is some satisfaction in knowing that you will never perform worse than the "market", there is also some downside to these types of funds. No cash reserves means volatility. As well the index being tracked doesn't necessarily represent the broad market.

Having said that, they can have a place within a diversified portfolio and Green Line U.S. Index Fund would be an excellent choice as a complement to an actively managed foreign fund. The MER is only .66%, making the task of tracking the S&P 500 Total Return Index, which excludes fees, an easier one to fulfil.

An additional benefit from a portfolio perspective is the natural hedge that the fund provides against a weakening Canadian dollar. Purchased in U.S. dollars, the fund will appreciate in value if the Canadian currency continues to falter.

U.S. LARGE CAP/DIVERSIFIED EQUITY

RRSP

SPECTRUM UNITED AMERICAN GROWTH FUND C$
John Ballen+Toni Shimura (1995)/MFS Institutional Advisors

CONSISTENCY

Performance Trend

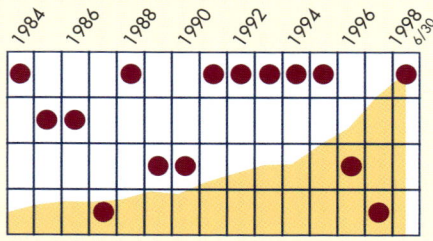

RISK

How often fund outperformed GICs	**15 years in 21**
How often fund lost money	**3 years in 21**
Worst year's rate of return	**-14.4% (1987)**

REWARD-TO-RISK RELATIONSHIP
SHARPE RATIO QUARTILE RANKINGS

3-Year	**3**
5-Year	**3**

EFFICIENCY/MER

Management expense/$100

$2.35

○ above average
● average
○ below average

STYLE

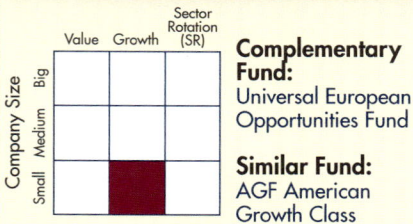

Complementary Fund:
Universal European Opportunities Fund

Similar Fund:
AGF American Growth Class

This fund is a clone of MFS Emerging Growth Fund, a U.S. mutual fund that has been highly rated south of the border. In fact, Smart Money magazine picked MFS Emerging Growth as one of the top six mutual funds for 1998. Spectrum United was smart enough to let John Ballen and Toni Shimura of MFS, the oldest mutual fund company in the U.S., continue to use their winning approach in Canada.

MFS believes that active management and bottom-up fundamental research are the keys to achieving consistent above-benchmark returns. For the American Growth fund, they also seek companies that are early in their life cycle and have the potential to be major corporations. Typically holding 100-150 securities, Ballen and Shimura are currently focusing on technology, business services, leisure, retailing, and health care. The largest holding is HFS, followed by Computer Associates International, and Oracle Corp. The average security holding period is four years—unusual for any fund and especially a small-cap growth fund.

The fund is restricted to holding no more than 20% of the portfolio assets in cash. MFS aren't market timers, however, and their goal is to be fully invested at all times. The fund doesn't hedge the currency exposure, and therefore is particularly suited for investors who are bearish on the Canadian dollar.

U.S. LARGE CAP/DIVERSIFIED EQUITY

BPI AMERICAN SMALL COMPANIES FUND
Thomas Sudyka (1997)/BPI Global Asset Management

CONSISTENCY

Performance Trend

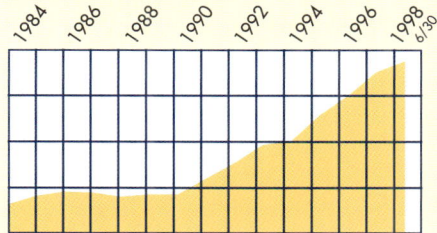

1984 1986 1988 1990 1992 1994 1996 1998 6/30

RISK

How often fund outperformed GICs	**7 years in 9**
How often fund lost money	**1 year in 9**
Worst year's rate of return	**-0.3% (1990)**

REWARD-TO-RISK RELATIONSHIP
SHARPE RATIO QUARTILE RANKINGS

3-Year	**N/A**
5-Year	**N/A**

EFFICIENCY/MER

Management expense/$100

$2.56

● above average
○ average
○ below average

STYLE

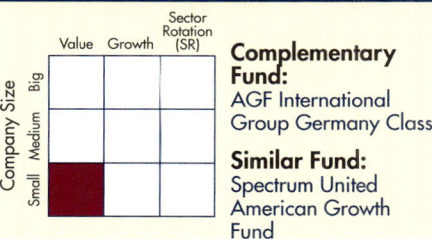

Company Size: Big / Medium / Small
Value / Growth / Sector Rotation (SR)

Complementary Fund:
AGF International Group Germany Class

Similar Fund:
Spectrum United American Growth Fund

A good example of BPI's small-cap expertise. Managed by Thomas Sudyka, the objective of the fund is to achieve above average growth of capital through investment in North American companies with market capitalization of less than U.S.$1 billion.

Sudyka employs a bottom-up, value approach and laments the difficulty currently of finding attractively priced securities. The fund holdings of 65 securities is low for the small-cap category, where many managers employ the scatter-gun approach, in order to provide both portfolio diversification and to increase the odds of an unexpected, but always welcome, hot performance from an individual stock.

Sudyka hasn't made many changes in the portfolio, which he inherited last May from Lazard Frères Asset Management's Michael Rome. His main asset weightings are in consumer products and commercial services.

U.S. SMALL CAP EQUITY

NEW

AIC WORLD EQUITY FUND

Jonathan Wellum+Michael Lee-Chin (inception) +Neil Murdoch (1994)/AIC Limited

CONSISTENCY

Performance Trend

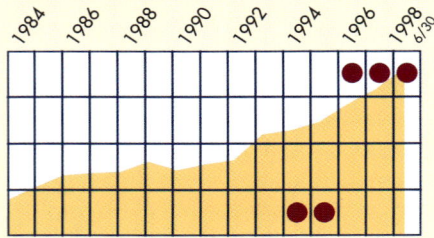

RISK

How often fund outperformed GICs	**2 years in 4**
How often fund lost money	**1 year in 4**
Worst year's rate of return	**-7.0% (1994)**

REWARD-TO-RISK RELATIONSHIP
SHARPE RATIO QUARTILE RANKINGS

3-Year	**1**
5-Year	**N/A**

EFFICIENCY/MER

Management expense/$100

$2.70

● above average
○ average
○ below average

STYLE

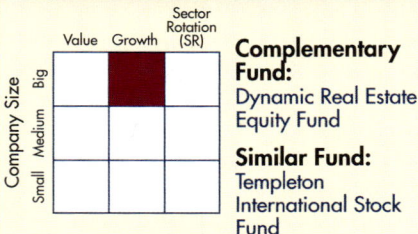

Complementary Fund:
Dynamic Real Estate Equity Fund

Similar Fund:
Templeton International Stock Fund

INTERNATIONAL EQUITY

AIC takes its approach to the world stage with this fund. Still with a focus on the wealth management and financial services, AIC World is predominantly non-North American with an emphasis on Europe. Manager Neil Murdoch feels that demographics, the demise of state-run pension systems and low penetration rates for the managed-money industry spells big opportunities in Europe. He currently favours the U.K, Switzerland, Italy, Sweden, Germany, and the Netherlands.

The fund has also taken positions in companies that Murdoch and his team feel are global, "blue chip" in nature and that have predominant positions in their respective industries. For example in 1997, Novartis, the healthcare giant and the fund's first foray in this sector, was added to the portfolio and now comprises 4.7% of the portfolio.

The largest holding in the 30 stock portfolio is Perpetual PLC. Cash levels are 28%, which is more a function of the popularity of this fund with investors than a statement about Murdoch's view on the market.

As is always the case with AIC, the holding periods are incredibly long: 12 to 15 years with minimal turnover. The result is nice tax efficiency, with minimal taxable capital gains for non-RRSP investors.

NEW

GREAT WEST LIFE INT'L EQUITY FUND INV. (P) DSC
John Storkerson (1998)/The Putnam Advisory Company Inc.

CONSISTENCY

Performance Trend

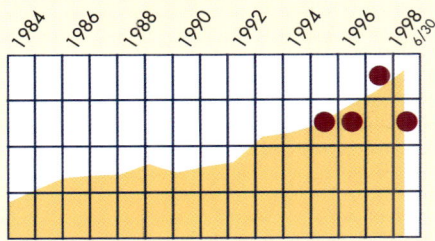

1984 1986 1988 1990 1992 1994 1996 1998 6/30

RISK

How often fund outperformed GICs	**3 years in 3**
How often fund lost money	**0 years in 3**
Worst year's rate of return	**8.1% (1995)**

REWARD-TO-RISK RELATIONSHIP
SHARPE RATIO QUARTILE RANKINGS

3-Year	**1**
5-Year	**N/A**

EFFICIENCY/MER

Management expense/$100

$2.69

● above average
○ average
○ below average

STYLE

Company Size: Small, Medium, Big
Value, Growth, Sector Rotation (SR)

Complementary Fund:
Chou Associates Fund

Similar Fund:
BPI Global Equity Value Fund

Like so many top quartile international funds over the past few years, the success of Great West Life International Equity can be traced to a bias towards European investments. Manager John Storkerson of Boston-based Putnam Advisory Company Inc. feels that there are fundamental changes occurring in Europe that continue to support equity investments there. In fact, his top ten holdings are all European companies. Why? Mergers are creating bigger, more efficient firms with improved strategic advantages, underperforming business lines are being sold off, and profits continue to grow. The impending Monetary Union is also expected to increase efficiencies for European companies.

Storkerson hasn't completely avoided the rest of the world however. He has small positions in South America and, much to his regret, still has a 9.6% representation in that Asian investment sinkhole, Japan. He is bearish on Japan, but does have some new investments in Hong Kong and Singapore companies. He generally avoids the rest of Southeast Asia.

Storkerson looks for mispriced securities. He has no growth versus value bias and uses a blend of both top-down and bottom-up approaches.

INTERNATIONAL EQUITY

TEMPLETON INTERNATIONAL STOCK FUND
Don Reed (1989-inception)/Templeton Asset Management Ltd.

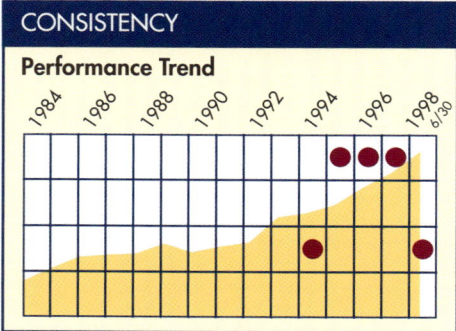

CONSISTENCY

Performance Trend

RISK

How often fund outperformed GICs	**6 years in 8**
How often fund lost money	**1 year in 8**
Worst year's rate of return	**-11.5% (1990)**

REWARD-TO-RISK RELATIONSHIP
SHARPE RATIO QUARTILE RANKINGS

3-Year	**1**
5-Year	**1**

EFFICIENCY/MER

Management expense/$100

$2.49

○ above average
◉ average
○ below average

STYLE

Complementary Fund:
Chou Associates Fund

Similar Fund:
AGF International Value Fund

Manager Don Reed has some impressive bench support available in searching the world outside of Canada and the United States for undervalued companies. Few could question the success that the $5.2 billion dollar fund has enjoyed.

Leveraging Templeton's global knowledge base, Reed assesses the relative value of a particular company in a particular market by comparing it to its global competitors. Enhanced by face-to-face meetings with company management, internal valuations are generated. If prices are favourable, the stock is bought and patiently held three to five years until other investors catch on and bid up the price.

The hunt for value can be time consuming as the fund currently has 15% in cash pending deployment.

Although a bottom-up approach is used, no significant sector tilts have developed, although there is a current fondness for European offerings. Derivatives are occasionally used to guard against undesirable currency fluctuations.

Those hunting for higher long-term total returns and global diversification will want to examine this fund carefully. We really like it.

INTERNATIONAL EQUITY

AGF INTERNATIONAL VALUE FUND Charles Brandes
+ Jeff Busby (1994-inception)/Brandes Investment Partners

CONSISTENCY

Performance Trend

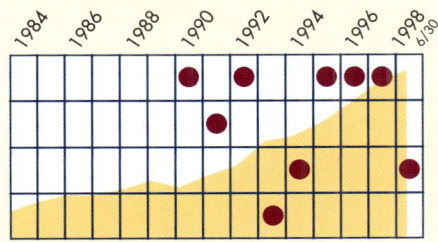

1984 1986 1988 1990 1992 1994 1996 1998 6/30

RISK

How often fund outperformed GICs	**6 years in 8**
How often fund lost money	**1 year in 8**
Worst year's rate of return	**-2.8% (1990)**

REWARD-TO-RISK RELATIONSHIP
SHARPE RATIO QUARTILE RANKINGS

3-Year	**1**
5-Year	**1**

EFFICIENCY/MER

Management expense/$100

$2.77

● above average
○ average
○ below average

STYLE

Company Size: Big, Medium, Small
Value, Growth, Sector Rotation (SR)

Complementary Fund:
Chou Associates Fund

Similar Fund:
Templeton International Stock Fund

This is one fund that you can comfortably buy for the long haul. The fund's shepherds, Charles Brandes and Jeff Busby, have been around the investment block a few times and have certainly learned the value of patience. Disciples of the famed value investor, Benjamin Graham, these two look for undervalued securities that may take time for their true value to show through. They are also disciplined in selling positions once they determine that the value was been wrung out of a stock by the arrival of investors jumping on the bandwagon. The key to successful investing is not only knowing what and when to buy, but when to sell. It is something like knowing when to hold them and when to fold them.

As an example, their second largest geographical weighting is in Japan because despite the current turmoil, Brandes and Busby feel that the leading Japanese firms will emerge from the debacle strong and competitive. With values in Japan being relatively cheap, they're willing to bet the upside outweighs the risk of further short-term corrections.

The fund's largest exposure is naturally in the U.S. with an over-weighting in Europe that has served the fund's unitholders well over the last year. The strong performance in these foreign markets has translated into even greater returns for unitholders since the fund does not hedge its returns; accordingly, all else remaining constant, it gains as the Canadian dollar falls.

GLOBAL EQUITY

NEW   RRSP

BPI GLOBAL EQUITY VALUE FUND
Daniel Jaworski (1997)/BPI Global Asset Management

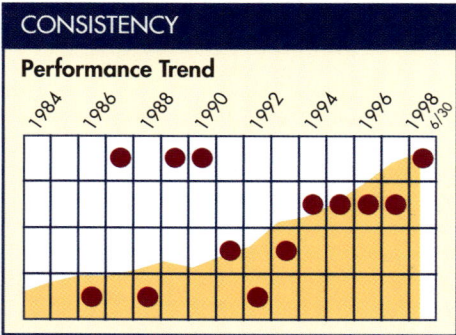

CONSISTENCY

Performance Trend

RISK

How often fund outperformed GICs	**6 years in 12**
How often fund lost money	**1 year in 12**
Worst year's rate of return	**-11.4% (1988)**

REWARD-TO-RISK RELATIONSHIP
SHARPE RATIO QUARTILE RANKINGS

3-Year	**1**
5-Year	**1**

EFFICIENCY/MER

Management expense/$100

$2.43

○ above average
● average
○ below average

STYLE

Complementary Fund:
Dynamic Real Estate Equity Fund

Similar Fund:
Great West Life International Equity Inv. (P) DSC

Manager Dan Jaworski of BPI Global Asset Management feels that individual stock selection will be the main driver of performance for international investors. While very aware of the possible continuation of volatile markets, Jaworski believes that good buying opportunities still exist, and he will continue to seek out companies with strong fundamentals and sustainable advantages that are trading at attractive levels.

A bottom up, value investor with a large-cap bias, Jaworski's view is that the best values are to be found in the financial services and consumer products sectors, mostly in North America and Europe. Having said that, the valuations in U.S. markets are a source of concern and he is currently slightly underweighted there compared to the Morgan Stanley World Index, which is his benchmark index. For the same reasons, he is overweighted in Europe and has very little Asian or emerging market exposure.

Jaworski generally holds 75-95 securities in his portfolio and no single position represents more than 3.0% of the total. Currently, his largest position is in Time Warner Inc., followed by ING Groep NV, the Dutch financial services conglomerate. Jaworski is fully invested, with only minimal cash and cash equivalents in the portfolio.

GLOBAL EQUITY

CANADA LIFE U.S. & INTERNATIONAL EQUITY (S-34) FUND
Thomas Tibbles + Diana Haflidson (1997)/Indago Capital Management

CONSISTENCY

Performance Trend

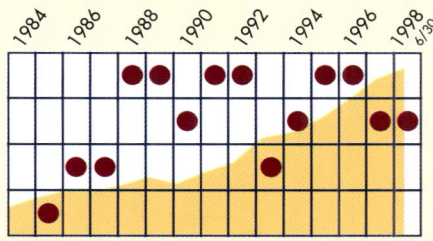

1984 1986 1988 1990 1992 1994 1996 1998 6/30

RISK

How often fund outperformed GICs	**10 years in 13**
How often fund lost money	**2 years in 13**
Worst year's rate of return	**-6.1% (1990)**

REWARD-TO-RISK RELATIONSHIP
SHARPE RATIO QUARTILE RANKINGS

3-Year	**1**
5-Year	**1**

EFFICIENCY/MER

Management expense/$100

$2.40

○ above average
● average
○ below average

STYLE

	Value	Growth	Sector Rotation (SR)
Big			
Medium	■	■	
Small			

Company Size

Complementary Fund:
Universal European Opportunities Fund

Similar Fund:
Fidelity International Portfolio Fund

With the fund's management company being spun off from Canada Life last year and renamed INDAGO, investors may have had some inhibitions, but we believe there's no need to worry. Thomas Tibbles, INDAGO's foreign equity team leader, and Diana Haflidson are the current fund managers. With a few exceptions, this fund has annually ranked as a first quartile fund within its category.

The key to their performance has been the successful managing of the mix between cash, U.S. equities, and non-North American equities that has not only produced strong returns, but has limited the number of losing years to two out of thirteen. The duo has managed to navigate the allocation between these widely varying classes without capsizing the fund's performance.

The first step is to determine their allocation to the various regions using a rigorous top down, country-by-country analysis that considers the current economic cycle, the underlying fundamentals and long-term market momentum. This is completed within the parameters that exposure to the U.S. can never fall below 30% (currently 47%), and that the fund must have exposure to at least five different currencies. Once the country allocation is out of the way, they focus on companies that sport attractive price-to-earnings ratios compared to growth rates. In an attempt to control risk, the minimum number of investments is 75.

One interesting note regarding this global fund is that although limited to 15%, it considers emerging markets as part of its mandate.

GLOBAL EQUITY

FIDELITY INTERNATIONAL PORTFOLIO FUND
Dick Habermann (1993-inception)/Fidelity Management & Research Co.

CONSISTENCY

Performance Trend

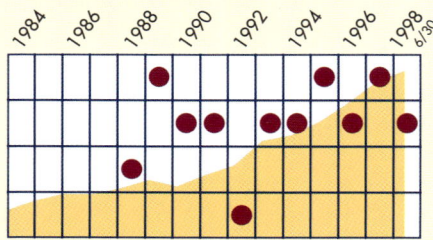

1984 1986 1988 1990 1992 1994 1996 1998 6/30

RISK

How often fund outperformed GICs	**6 years in 10**
How often fund lost money	**1 year in 10**
Worst year's rate of return	**-8.8% (1990)**

REWARD-TO-RISK RELATIONSHIP
SHARPE RATIO QUARTILE RANKINGS

3-Year	**1**
5-Year	**1**

EFFICIENCY/MER

Management expense/$100

$2.69

● above average
○ average
○ below average

STYLE

Value Growth Sector Rotation (SR)

Company Size: Big / Medium / Small

Complementary Fund:
Universal European Opportunities Fund

Similar Fund:
Canada Life U.S. & Int'l Equity Fund (S-34)

GLOBAL EQUITY

In Fidelity-speak, International means mostly American. No wonder our friendly neighbours to the South can never be accused of having a Canadian-like inferiority complex.

The fund's 50% allocation to the U.S. has obviously caused its returns over the past four years to sparkle. A substantial shift is unlikely given the outlook for positive economic and corporate earnings growth. Showing his agility at gauging the changing economic winds, manager Dick Habermann has allocated 25% of the fund toward Europe as he maintains that the potential for earnings growth there exceeds that of U.S. companies as they continue to restructure and adapt to the pending European Monetary Union. Within Europe, Habermann has chosen to focus on Spain, Ireland, Italy, and the Nordic countries.

While he thinks the Asian situation is a little overdone, he has yet to walk the talk as the fund has a neutral weighting of 12% in Japan.

Compared to the vast majority of global funds, Fidelity International has outperformed the benchmark index while realizing lower volatility levels over the past three years. Balancing the risk return relationship is what Habermann excels at. If Habermann can continue to successfully navigate the course, unitholders will be well served.

NEW

INVESTORS GROWTH PORTFOLIO FUND
Bob Darling (1989)/Investors Group Inc.

CONSISTENCY

Performance Trend

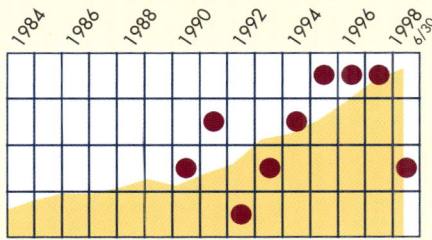

RISK

How often fund outperformed GICs	**5 years in 8**
How often fund lost money	**1 year in 8**
Worst year's rate of return	**-10.2% (1990)**

REWARD-TO-RISK RELATIONSHIP
SHARPE RATIO QUARTILE RANKINGS

3-Year	**1**
5-Year	**1**

EFFICIENCY/MER

Management expense/$100

$2.61

○ above average
● average
○ below average

STYLE

Complementary Fund:
Universal European Opportunities Fund

Similar Fund:
Fidelity International Portfolio Fund

Investors Group have had great success with their "fund of funds" concept. It gives retail investors the opportunity to reap all the benefits of diversification and still hold only one fund in their portfolio. Investors Growth Portfolio, for example, consists of five underlying Investors funds: 10% North American Growth Fund, 20% U.S. Growth Fund, 10% Special Fund, 20% Canadian Equity Growth Fund, and 40% Global Fund. The result is broadly diversified (>370 stocks) and low in volatility.

Manager Bob Darling is actually more of an administrator; he has no actual fund management responsibility as the component funds are stand alone entities managed by their own managers.

GLOBAL EQUITY

TEMPLETON GLOBAL SMALLER COMPANIES FUND
Norman Boersma + team (1997)/Templeton Asset Management Ltd.

CONSISTENCY

Performance Trend

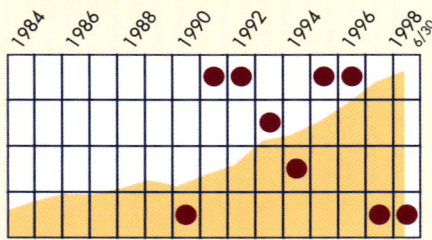

1984 1986 1988 1990 1992 1994 1996 1998 6/30

RISK

How often fund outperformed GICs	**6 years in 8**
How often fund lost money	**1 year in 8**
Worst year's rate of return	**-17.1% (1990)**

REWARD-TO-RISK RELATIONSHIP
SHARPE RATIO QUARTILE RANKINGS

3-Year	**3**
5-Year	**2**

EFFICIENCY/MER

Management expense/$100

$2.61

○ above average
● average
○ below average

STYLE

	Value	Growth	Sector Rotation (SR)
Big			
Medium			
Small			

Company Size

Complementary Fund:
Chou Associates Fund

Similar Fund:
BPI American Small Companies Fund

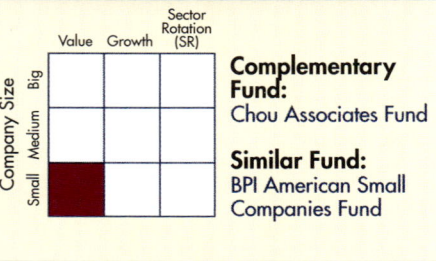

If you believe the studies which indicate that smaller capitalized stocks outperform their larger brethren in the global environment, consider this fund as an extension of your current global exposure.

Fund manager Norman Boersma has successfully implemented the long-standing Templeton approach to finding undervalued securities that possess long-term growth potential. Despite the historical contention that smaller caps tend to be more volatile, this fund has experienced relatively modest value swings.

Without the ability to load up on large cap stocks like banks and telephone utilities, the fund has smallish weightings in all the various sectors as Boersma has whittled down the universe of 15,000 stocks to 200. It also has a 15% geographic allocation to that bastion of entrepreneurship, the U.S.

The fund's ranking slipped somewhat in 1997 as it was the big boys who led the ticker tape parade while smaller-caps trailed. This situation will be remedied when either market confidence is renewed and small caps catch up, or if confidence is undermined and the higher-valued big stocks fall back.

GLOBAL EQUITY

TEMPLETON GROWTH FUND LTD.
Mark Holowesko (1987)/Templeton Global Advisors Ltd.

CONSISTENCY

Performance Trend

1984 1986 1988 1990 1992 1994 1996 1998 6/30

RISK

How often fund outperformed GICs	**16 years in 21**
How often fund lost money	**3 years in 21**
Worst year's rate of return	**-13.6% (1990)**

REWARD-TO-RISK RELATIONSHIP
SHARPE RATIO QUARTILE RANKINGS

3-Year	**4**
5-Year	**3**

EFFICIENCY/MER

Management expense/$100

$2.00

○ above average
○ average
● below average

STYLE

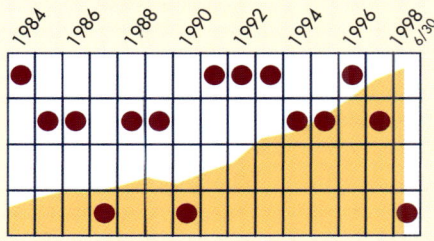

	Value	Growth	Sector Rotation (SR)
Big			
Medium			
Small			

Company Size

Complementary Fund:
AIM Global Health Sciences Fund

Similar Fund:
Trimark Fund

This fund is one of the mainstays on the Canadian investment scene. Few advisors land themselves in hot water for suggesting this fund and it has yet to disappoint. With the world as his canvas, Mark Holowesko has painted a pretty rosy picture for investors using a disciplined and established (since 1954) bottom-up, value-oriented approach to security selection.

With few investment limitations, Holowesko has been able to successfully wield the behemoth $11 billion dollar fund into and out of stocks, sectors, and countries. The fund is widely diversified with its 250 security positions well spread out among the sectors; industrial product companies are pervasive throughout the portfolio currently. Although just over 20% of the portfolio is in U.S. stocks, a number of other countries are represented. With a particular slant toward Europe currently, Holowesko awaits some further declines in the Asian market before locking in on some targets on his radar screen in that area.

If you were only going to select one global fund, we would contend that this is the one.

GLOBAL EQUITY

TRIMARK FUND Robert Krembil (1981) + Angela Eaton (1994) + Richard Jenkins (1994)/Trimark Investment Management

CONSISTENCY

Performance Trend

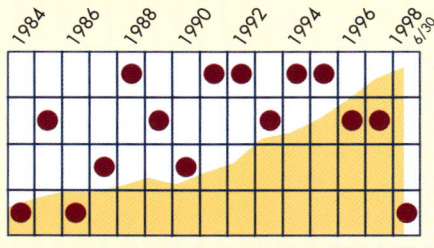

RISK

How often fund outperformed GICs	**13 years in 16**
How often fund lost money	**2 years in 16**
Worst year's rate of return	**-9.9% (1990)**

REWARD-TO-RISK RELATIONSHIP
SHARPE RATIO QUARTILE RANKINGS

3-Year	**3**
5-Year	**1**

EFFICIENCY/MER

Management expense/$100

$1.52

○ above average
○ average
● below average

STYLE

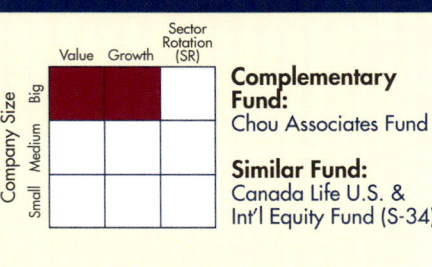

Complementary Fund:
Chou Associates Fund

Similar Fund:
Canada Life U.S. & Int'l Equity Fund (S-34)

GLOBAL EQUITY

In the hunt for strong reliable capital growth, Krembil, Eaton and Jenkins search the world for value but have found that North America has the most to offer. Although their value tests have resulted in about 53% of the portfolio being invested in the U.S. and just over 1% in Canada, an in-depth review determined that only 30% of the revenue earned by the companies in the portfolio originated from North America. Accordingly, they are buying global diversification without having to stray too far from home.

The management team has also found undervalued good companies that have significant opportunities for growth in Japan (17% of the portfolio) and Germany (10% of the portfolio). These allocations reflect their conviction as to where they can find leading international companies whose technology, inventiveness , or entrepreneurship gives them a leg up on their global competitors.

The cost of hiring this trio is a modest 1.52% which, in addition to good returns at enviable risk levels, is part of what has attracted $3 billion into the fund.

AIM GLOBAL HEALTH SCIENCES FUND
John Schroer (1996) + Carol Werther/Invesco Global Asset Management

CONSISTENCY

Performance Trend

1984 1986 1988 1990 1992 1994 1996 1998 6/30

RISK

How often fund outperformed GICs	**4 years in 5**
How often fund lost money	**1 year in 5**
Worst year's rate of return	**4.2% (1994)**

REWARD-TO-RISK RELATIONSHIP
SHARPE RATIO QUARTILE RANKINGS

3-Year	**N/A**
5-Year	**N/A**

EFFICIENCY/MER

Management expense/$100

$2.94

● above average
○ average
○ below average

STYLE

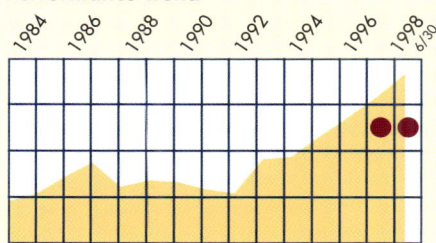

Company Size: Small / Medium / Big
Value / Growth / Sector Rotation (SR)

Complementary Fund:
Universal European Opportunities Fund

Similar Fund:
Spectrum United American Growth Fund C$

For those of you with creaky joints and who want to tweak your portfolio, this fund attempts to parlay the aging of North America's population into profits. The fund, managed by John Schroer since 1996, focuses on companies in the health services sector such as pharmaceuticals and medical products. In fact, non-health sciences companies are limited to 20% of the portfolio as are cash and money products.

Although the management fee expense ratio is higher than most, Schroer has been able to add value on a net basis. The fund focuses on well-capitalized companies within the sector that have proven to be defensive in light of constant demand during economic recessions and booms. Still, the sector is also resident to numerous smaller research-oriented companies that are naturally more volatile than the general market, given their strong growth component, and the propensity to disappoint on failed drug trials or Medicare scares.

Schroer, who uses a fundamental bottom-up approach, currently favours large-cap pharmaceuticals because of an improved regulatory process and the large number of potential new drugs currently in the product pipeline. Stocks of medical devices companies are also drawing Schroer's attention as earnings continue to grow strongly. John feels the long-term outlook for this sector is positive given growing demand and a supply process that is increasingly efficient.

Over the long-term, demographics alone should make Schroer an investment hero.

The fund was formerly known as the Admax Global Health Sciences Fund.

GLOBAL SECTOR

DYNAMIC REAL ESTATE EQUITY FUND
Goodman & Co. Investment Counsel

CONSISTENCY

Performance Trend

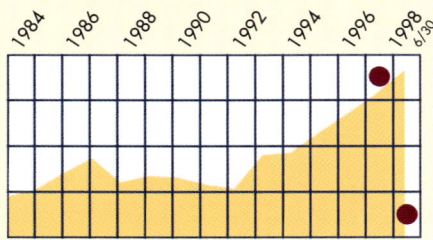

1984 1986 1988 1990 1992 1994 1996 1998 6/30

RISK

How often fund outperformed GICs	**2 years in 2**
How often fund lost money	**0 years in 2**
Worst year's rate of return	**38.5% (1997)**

REWARD-TO-RISK RELATIONSHIP
SHARPE RATIO QUARTILE RANKINGS

3-Year	**N/A**
5-Year	**N/A**

EFFICIENCY/MER

Management expense/$100

$2.72

○ above average
● average
○ below average

STYLE

Company Size: Big, Medium, Small
Value, Growth, Sector Rotation (SR)

Complementary Fund:
AGF American Growth Class

Similar Fund:
Templeton International Stock Fund

GLOBAL SECTOR

One of the earliest real estate mutual funds out of the starting blocks, this fund's stated objective is to profit from the long-term recovery of the real estate market after its meltdown in the early to mid-1990s. The managers are confident that despite some frothy returns in 1996 and 1997, upside potential still remains as the industry continues to recover from the devastating blows (higher interest rates, overbuilding, and slowing economy) that reduced real estate values well below replacement costs.

It is important to note that the fund does not invest directly in real estate projects that would serve to hamper liquidity and valuations. Instead, the fund concentrates on stocks and real estate investment trusts as well as some real estate bonds. This approach allows Goodman & Co. to employ their standard bottom-up approach to analyzing investment opportunities.

Although the mandate is global, the fund focuses mostly on North America with 74% invested in the "who's who" of the U.S. real estate scene, and 24% in Canada. The fund is RRSP-eligible as part of the foreign content component.

The benefit of this fund, and of its competitors, is that real estate is a separate asset class that adds to a portfolio's diversification; the result is that, by adding a fund like this, we can reduce portfolio risk. Despite the fact that real estate's business cycle tends to differ from the normal business cycle due to the long building development lead times, the class is more akin to equities than it is to fixed income vehicles.

NEW

CHOU ASSOCIATES FUND
Francis Chou (inception)/Chou Associates Management Inc.

CONSISTENCY

Performance Trend

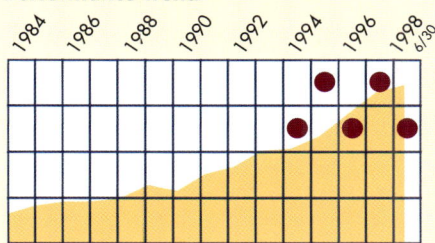

1984 1986 1988 1990 1992 1994 1996 1998 6/30

RISK

How often fund outperformed GICs	8 years in 11
How often fund lost money	2 years in 11
Worst year's rate of return	-10.7% (1990)

REWARD-TO-RISK RELATIONSHIP
SHARPE RATIO QUARTILE RANKINGS

3-Year	1
5-Year	1

EFFICIENCY/MER

Management expense/$100

$1.86

○ above average
○ average
● below average

STYLE

Complementary Fund:
AGF International Group Germany Class

Similar Fund:
AIC Value Fund

A top quartile performer over the past three years, this fund is not afraid to put most of its eggs in a few baskets. The top three holdings, Freddie Mac paper, Travelers Group, and Rothmans comprise a whopping 36% of total assets. Manager Francis Chou takes a value approach; looking for undervalued securities on the basis of P/E ratios and other value criteria. Chou will also buy short- term fixed income and cash securities if he feels that capital preservation is about to become an issue.

Fund assets are still small, just under $11 million, which allows a nimbleness that larger funds can't match. With a $25,000 minimum initial investment, many potential investors might avoid this fund. That would be a shame, because this fund is a gem.

NORTH AMERICAN EQUITY

117

NEW

RRSP

AGF INTERNATIONAL GROUP GERMANY CLASS FUND
Nils Wittenhagen (inception)/Deutsche Asset Management

CONSISTENCY

Performance Trend

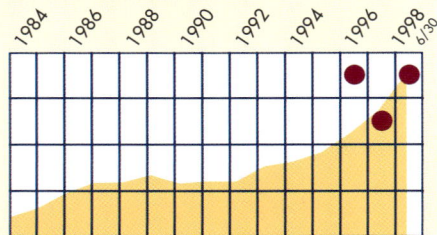

1984 1986 1988 1990 1992 1994 1996 1998 6/30

RISK

How often fund outperformed GICs	**2 years in 2**
How often fund lost money	**0 years in 2**
Worst year's rate of return	**24.2% (1997)**

REWARD-TO-RISK RELATIONSHIP
SHARPE RATIO QUARTILE RANKINGS

3-Year	**3**
5-Year	**N/A**

EFFICIENCY/MER

Management expense/$100

$2.99

● above average
○ average
○ below average

STYLE

Sector Rotation (SR)
Value Growth
Company Size: Big Medium Small

Complementary Fund:
Chou Associates Fund

Similar Fund:
Fidelity European Growth Fund

Thank geography for the success of this fund. With Germany ideally situated between Western Europe and the newly emerging Eastern European economies, markets there continue to hit all time highs and AGF Germany Class is reaping the benefits.

Managed by Nils Wittenhagen of Deutsche Asset Management (DBAM), this fund employs a bottom-up growth style driven by a focus on stock picking. Wittenhagen also feels that the restructuring of the German pension system to one that emphasizes personal savings will benefit equities, especially if bond yields continue to be low. The fund has an 18% exposure to other European markets, providing a diversification effect as well as the opportunity to enhance returns.

DYNAMIC EUROPE FUND
Joe Evershed (1994)/Goodman & Co. Investment Counsel

CONSISTENCY

Performance Trend

1984 1986 1988 1990 1992 1994 1996 1998 6/30

RISK

How often fund outperformed GICs	**3 years in 8**
How often fund lost money	**3 years in 8**
Worst year's rate of return	**-9.6% (1990)**

REWARD-TO-RISK RELATIONSHIP
SHARPE RATIO QUARTILE RANKINGS

3-Year	**3**
5-Year	**3**

EFFICIENCY/MER

Management expense/$100

$2.50

○ above average
● average
○ below average

STYLE

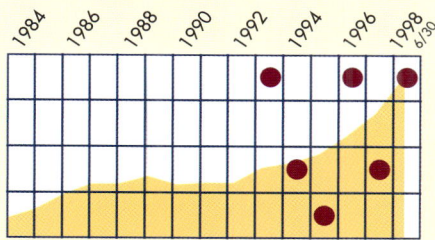

Company Size: Big / Medium / Small
Value / Growth / Sector Rotation (SR)

Complementary Fund:
Dynamic Real Estate Equity Fund

Similar Fund:
Universal European Opportunities Fund

Within a category where many funds have had trouble consistently beating the index, Dynamic Europe is a good choice. The investment strategy is the same as that applied by Dynamic across the board: long-term value investing based on individual stock picking. The fund mangers do not try to determine the next hot country or sector, but instead focus on companies with good growth prospects and that are trading at decent valuation levels.

Within the fund, Goodman tries to ferret out companies, both large and small, that will benefit the most from Europe's upcoming monetary union and the restructuring that is currently underway. They believe that telecommunications and technology information stocks will likely be key beneficiaries and have accordingly purchased some for the fund. With an increased focus on creating shareholder value, expectations of the continued low interest rate environment should continue to spell good news for European stocks.

While the fund invests primarily in established European markets, it does not confine itself to the largest markets as its two heaviest exposures are Sweden (17%) and Finland (14%). (We wonder if they do any scouting on the side for NHL teams). It also feels comfortable injecting some emerging Eastern European companies into the mix.

EUROPEAN EQUITY

FIDELITY EUROPEAN GROWTH FUND Sally Walden
(inception) + Thierry Serero (1998)/Fidelity Management & Research Co.

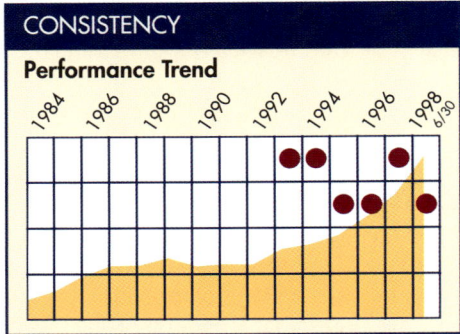

CONSISTENCY

Performance Trend

1984 1986 1988 1990 1992 1994 1996 1998 6/30

RISK

How often fund outperformed GICs	**5 years in 5**
How often fund lost money	**0 years in 5**
Worst year's rate of return	**10.1% (1994)**

REWARD-TO-RISK RELATIONSHIP
SHARPE RATIO QUARTILE RANKINGS

3-Year	**1**
5-Year	**1**

EFFICIENCY/MER

Management expense/$100

$2.72

● above average
○ average
○ below average

STYLE

Company Size: Small / Medium / Big
Value / Growth / Sector Rotation (SR)

Complementary Fund:
Chou Associates Fund

Similar Fund:
AGF Int'l Group
Germany Class

The Fidelity brand name came to Canada in 1987 and has not looked back as the success factors of the American parent have been replicated and/or adapted for the Canadian investing public. Its dedication to research and its global presence place it at the forefront of the mutual fund industry. The European Growth Fund is managed by Sally Walden (since inception) and Thierry Serero (new in 1998) who make good use of the proven Fidelity bottom-up formula. This approach entails focusing first on the company itself, including the strength of its balance sheet, then the sector and finally the country.

Consistent first and second quartile results have been the key to the fund accumulating $2.4 billion of unitholder funds. While the fund's MER remains at a hefty 2.72%, Walden has been successful in adding value. In fact, the combination of reaping strong returns within the context of controlling risk has yielded some of the highest Sharpe ratios amongst the Top Funds.

In sync with the roaring first half performance of Europe in 1998, this fund returned 29.9% led by its large exposure to the U.K. (28%) and France (12%). Within various targeted countries, Serero and Walden have found banking, software, and health care stocks that have met their criteria.

The pervasive sentiment is that as European companies continue to restructure and focus more on corporate governance and shareholder value, the outlook remains positive. Walden also maintains that the newfound interest in equities by Europeans will help drive prices upward.

NEW

UNIVERSAL EUROPEAN OPPORTUNITIES FUND

Stephen Peak+Tim Stevenson (inception)/Henderson Investment Management

CONSISTENCY

Performance Trend

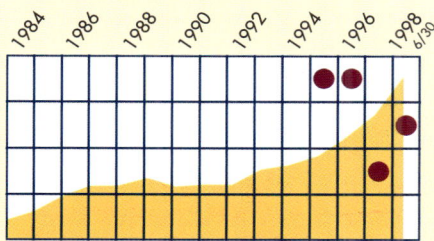

1984 1986 1988 1990 1992 1994 1996 1998 6/30

RISK

How often fund outperformed GICs	**3 years in 3**
How often fund lost money	**0 years in 3**
Worst year's rate of return	**20.0% (1997)**

REWARD-TO-RISK RELATIONSHIP
SHARPE RATIO QUARTILE RANKINGS

3-Year	**1**
5-Year	**N/A**

EFFICIENCY/MER

Management expense/$100

$2.48

○ above average
● average
○ below average

STYLE

Company Size: Big, Medium, Small
Value, Growth, Sector Rotation (SR)

Complementary Fund:
Green Line U.S. Index

Similar Fund:
Dynamic Europe Fund

Universal European Opportunity takes a rather fearless approach to investing. It searches for companies in areas that other money managers usually avoid. The fund's three investment themes are: 1. Small companies in mature economies; 2. Emerging markets; and 3. Special situations. The result is a portfolio with an eclectic mix of holdings, diversified by industry, size, and location. The fund is managed by Stephen Peak and Tim Stevenson of Henderson Investment Management, who temper their approach with a bottom-up, value style that offsets some of the riskiness inherent in small-cap and emerging market investing.

EUROPEAN EQUITY

LATIN AMERICAN AND EMERGING MARKETS

20/20 LATIN AMERICA FUND
Peter Gruber (1994-inception)/Globalvest Management Corp.

CONSISTENCY

Performance Trend

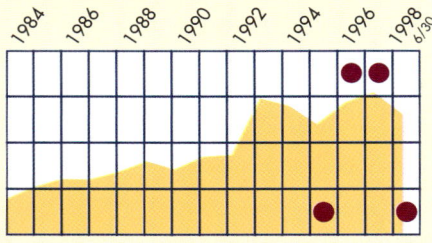

RISK

How often fund outperformed GICs	**2 years in 3**
How often fund lost money	**1 year in 3**
Worst year's rate of return	**-29.4% (1990)**

REWARD-TO-RISK RELATIONSHIP
SHARPE RATIO QUARTILE RANKINGS

3-Year	**2**
5-Year	**N/A**

EFFICIENCY/MER

Management expense/$100

$3.24

● above average
○ average
○ below average

STYLE

Complementary Fund:
C.I. Emerging Markets Fund

Similar Fund:
AIM GT Latin America Growth Class Fund

Investors in this fund are relying on the proven experience and skill of manager Peter Gruber, who has specialized in Latin America since 1972. This fund is not for the faint of heart, as Gruber has no qualms in significantly slanting his portfolio toward his favourite targets, which has led to higher volatility in this fund than many of its peers.

The Latin American markets have been whipsawed by the "Asian contagion" as global investors scaled back their allocations in riskier markets. In an attempt to roll with the punches, Gruber uses a top-down country approach to determine geographic allocations. Once he has settled on the countries of his choice, he then uses a bottom-up approach to select specific securities.

The current focus of Gruber's attention is Brazil, which continues to occupy about 75% of the portfolio. As a value investor, Gruber is excited about the attractive deals that are now available and has zeroed in on the banks, energy, and telecommunications sectors. If Brazil maintains its fiscal discipline, which includes an aggressive schedule of privatizations of state-owned businesses, Gruber's portfolio decisions could pay off handsomely as they did in the year ending June 30, 1997 when the fund returned a whopping 67.3%. Lest you think that the thrills come without some spills, the fund lost 35.9% the following year!

NEW

AIM GT LATIN AMERICA GROWTH CLASS FUND
Soraya Betterton + David Manuel (1997)/LGT Asset Management Inc.

LATIN AMERICAN AND EMERGING MARKETS

CONSISTENCY

Performance Trend

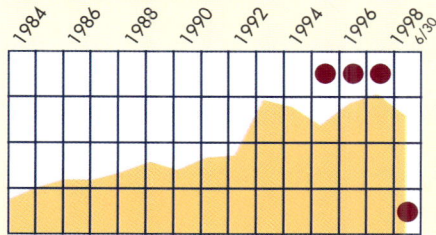

RISK

How often fund outperformed GICs	**2 years in 3**
How often fund lost money	**0 years in 3**
Worst year's rate of return	**4.0% (1995)**

REWARD-TO-RISK RELATIONSHIP
SHARPE RATIO QUARTILE RANKINGS

3-Year	**1**
5-Year	**N/A**

EFFICIENCY/MER

Management expense/$100

$2.86

○ above average
● average
○ below average

STYLE

Complementary Fund:
Templeton Emerging Markets Fund

Similar Fund:
Spectrum United Emerging Markets Fund

Talk about guilt by association. Despite being on the other side of the world, Latin America has been stung badly by the Asian crisis. Investors have deserted most emerging markets and Latin America has been no exception. This despite the fact that most of the Latin American economies, with the exception of Brazil, are doing just fine. Manager David Manuel of LGT Asset Management feels that the economic and structural reforms are proceeding well and that GDP growth in the region should be in the 3-4% range.

A contrarian who uses a blend of top-down and bottom-up styles, Manuel believes that Brazil has bottomed out and now is ripe for some great buys. In fact, over 41% of the portfolio is invested there, followed by Mexico with 28%, and Argentina 11%. His largest holding is Telecomunciacoes Brasileiros, the Brazilian state-owned telecommunications company.

RRSP

C.I. EMERGING MARKETS FUND
Nandu Narayanan (1997)/BEA Associates

CONSISTENCY

Performance Trend

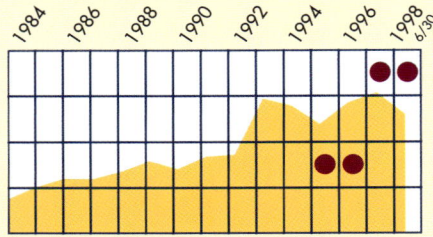

RISK

How often fund outperformed GICs	**4 years in 6**
How often fund lost money	**2 years in 6**
Worst year's rate of return	**-15.6% (1995)**

REWARD-TO-RISK RELATIONSHIP
SHARPE RATIO QUARTILE RANKINGS

3-Year	**2**
5-Year	**N/A**

EFFICIENCY/MER

Management expense/$100

$2.72

○ above average
● average
○ below average

STYLE

Complementary Fund:
20/20 Latin America Fund

Similar Fund:
Spectrum United Emerging Markets Fund

Someone once said that the light at the end of the tunnel could actually be that of an oncoming locomotive. That somewhat pessimistic viewpoint reflects the investment style of Krishnamurthy Narayanan of BEA Associates, manager of C.I. Emerging Markets. Unwilling to believe that the worst is over in Southeast Asian markets and fearful of the spillover effect to other emerging markets, Narayanan has parked over 37% of the fund assets in cash. Normally, we aren't thrilled with cautious management styles that involve the hoarding of cash, believing that investors are paying managers to invest. In this case however, given the current Asian instability, we approve. Narayanan does find some value (a relative term in emerging markets) in Latin America, as well as India and Russia. His biggest position is in Global Telesystems Inc., a Russian company.

SPECTRUM UNITED EMERGING MARKETS FUND
Ewen Cameron-Watt (1996)/Mercury Asset Management

CONSISTENCY

Performance Trend

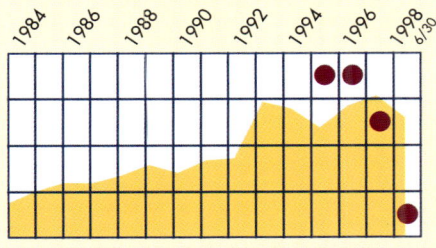

1984 1986 1988 1990 1992 1994 1996 1998 6/30

RISK

How often fund outperformed GICs	**2 years in 4**
How often fund lost money	**2 years in 4**
Worst year's rate of return	**-14.0% (1994)**

REWARD-TO-RISK RELATIONSHIP
SHARPE RATIO QUARTILE RANKINGS

3-Year	**2**
5-Year	**N/A**

EFFICIENCY/MER

Management expense/$100

$2.66

○ above average
○ average
● below average

STYLE

Company Size: Small / Medium / Big
Value / Growth / Sector Rotation (SR)

Complementary Fund:
C.I. Emerging Markets Fund

Similar Fund:
Templeton Emerging Markets Fund

If you want a high-powered investment team going to bat for your emerging markets exposure, this fund fits the bill. Manager Ewen Cameron-Watt leads a team of 11 professionals. A review of their investment criteria underscores why their depth is critical. The fund currently holds securities in 33 different countries with 25 being the minimum. In order to obtain the appropriate degree of diversification, they have 146 holdings with exposure in Latin America (39%), Europe (22%), Asia (20%), the Middle East/Africa (16%), and with the balance in cash.

How do they bring a semblance of order to such chaotic opportunity? They review a country's desirability based on fundamentals, liquidity, and investment opportunities. While aware of the benchmark weightings, these managers are no shrinking violets when it comes to over- and under-weighting regions.In early 1997, they started to reduce their Asian exposure; they also do not think that the pain is over for the region's currencies, and remain only lightly invested there.

Then they get down to the country level, where they perform a valuation and expectation ritual. They also retain a strong awareness of sectoral trends that may cross borders. Access to key corporate executives is critical to their decision to move forward on a particular company. Pricing and liquidity then affect the magnitude of their investment.

Like most emerging markets funds, and especially true lately, this fund is not for the timid as a long-term perspective is required to maximize the benefit.

LATIN AMERICAN AND EMERGING MARKETS

LATIN AMERICAN AND EMERGING MARKETS

TEMPLETON EMERGING MARKETS FUND
Mark Mobius (1994-inception)/Templeton Asset Management Ltd.

CONSISTENCY

Performance Trend

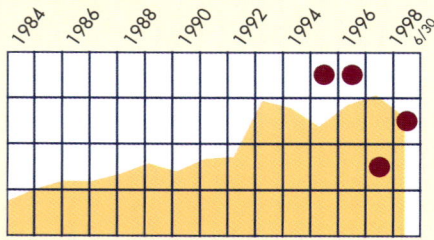

1984 1986 1988 1990 1992 1994 1996 1998 6/30

RISK

How often fund outperformed GICs	**2 years in 6**
How often fund lost money	**4 years in 6**
Worst year's rate of return	**-5.2% (1992)**

REWARD-TO-RISK RELATIONSHIP
SHARPE RATIO QUARTILE RANKINGS

3-Year	**2**
5-Year	**N/A**

EFFICIENCY/MER

Management expense/$100

$3.24

● above average
○ average
○ below average

STYLE

Company Size: Small Medium Big
Value Growth Sector Rotation (SR)

Complementary Fund:
20/20 Latin America Fund

Similar Fund:
Spectrum United Emerging Markets Fund

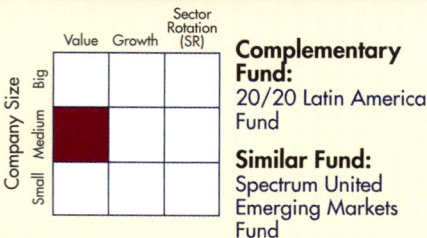

There is no questioning that Templeton is one of the dominant global equity investment managers. Its Emerging Markets Fund, Canada's largest, managed by the eminent Mark Mobius, was somewhat bigger before the Asian contagion decimated emerging markets, prompting the fund to lose approximately 30% over the past year. That is the nature of emerging markets and why it's not such a wise idea to invest next month's mortgage payment in funds like this.

A quick interpretation of the stats indicates that an investor could expect returns from -15% to +25% about two thirds of the time in an emerging market fund.

If you are in this fund or one like it, don't even think of bailing out! We are not saying that there will be a repeat of 1993's 83% return, but market calm and confidence will reign again one day.

If you can afford to wait, Dr. Mobius will likely make an excellent pilot in steering you through the risk/return topography, given his extensive worldwide travel experience in hunting down undervalued stocks in newly liberalized economies.

Mobius has his investments sprayed across a wide number of countries and industries. His current favourites are banking and telecommunications companies that are held up to international standards. The fund also permits investments in stocks on larger bourses, where the company derives greater than 50% of its revenues from emerging economies.

NEW

DYNAMIC FAR EAST FUND
Goodman & Company Investment Counsel (inception)

ASIA-PACIFIC RIM EQUITY

CONSISTENCY

Performance Trend

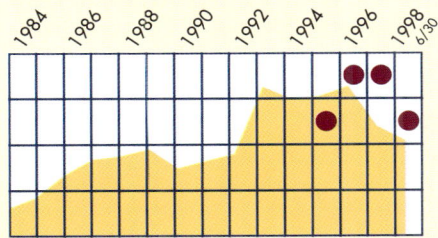

1984 1986 1988 1990 1992 1994 1996 1998 6/30

RISK

How often fund outperformed GICs	**1 year in 3**
How often fund lost money	**1 year in 3**
Worst year's rate of return	**-12.0% (1997)**

REWARD-TO-RISK RELATIONSHIP
SHARPE RATIO QUARTILE RANKINGS

3-Year	**1**
5-Year	**N/A**

EFFICIENCY/MER

Management expense/$100

$2.78

○ above average
● average
○ below average

STYLE

Company Size: Small Medium Big
Value Growth Sector Rotation (SR)

Complementary Fund:
Scotia Excelsior Pacific Rim Fund

Similar Fund:
Fidelity Far East Fund

The key to investment success is to be at the right place at the right time. The key to Far East and Asian investment success is to *not* be at the *wrong* place at the wrong time. The management team at Goodman & Company were smart enough to be underweighted in most of the countries that have melted down over the past year. They have large Australian, New Zealand, and Indian holdings, but apart from a hefty Hong Kong exposure, are generally unexposed to the other "Asian Tigers". This isn't to say that they emerged unscathed, but the fund did hold up relatively well.

The credit can be given to a bottom-up, value investment approach that ignores country weighting and invests solely on a good growth prospect/low price basis. They don't market time or sector rotate, and therefore steered away from some of the lofty valuations evident in some Asian markets. They have no capitalization bias and seek diversification over a wide range of industries.

The largest holding, at 9.4% of the fund, is Pentafour Software & Export, an Indian software consulting firm that exports primarily to the U.S. Not coincidentally, Goodman & Co are high on India and it's burgeoning information technology industry.

The managers are still positive on Asia, despite the recent problems. They feel that the economic reforms and market corrections will ultimately lead to much stronger and more efficient economies.

ASIA-PACIFIC RIM EQUITY

FIDELITY FAR EAST FUND
K.C. Lee (1991-inception)/Fidelity International

CONSISTENCY
Performance Trend

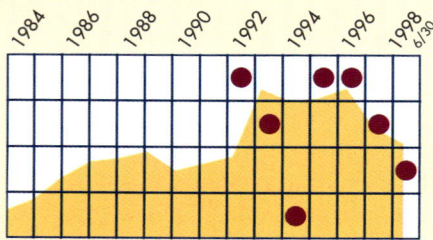

RISK

How often fund outperformed GICs	4 years in 6
How often fund lost money	2 years in 6
Worst year's rate of return	-22.6% (1997)

REWARD-TO-RISK RELATIONSHIP
SHARPE RATIO QUARTILE RANKINGS

3-Year	1
5-Year	1

EFFICIENCY/MER

Management expense/$100

$2.82

● above average
○ average
○ below average

STYLE

Complementary Fund:
Dynamic Far East Fund

Similar Fund:
Navigator Asia-Pacific Fund

No one can accuse fund manager K.C. Lee of being either a closet indexer or indecisive. Before you plunge into this fund, check your portfolio's current Asian exposure. Check it again just to make sure. This fund currently has an 80% exposure to Hong Kong as Lee maintains that compared to the other Asian economies, Hong Kong stocks have sustainable earnings growth and a relatively good track record. Factoring in his other two favourites, Singapore and Taiwan, Lee feels that his concentrated portfolio will outperform others when the economy eventually does turn around.

Once you've gotten over the geographic concentration, there is still the security concentration to consider. Lee's top ten holdings constitute just over 75% of the fund's value. His bottom-up approach is built on two basic pillars: companies with high-quality and consistent earnings growth; and/or companies whose stock trades at a discount to asset value.

These concentrated bets have caused the fund to be quite volatile. How do we preach diversification and risk control but yet include this as a Top Fund? The Fidelity brand name, Lee's investment experience, and the fund's historical returns are the response. If you consider this fund at all, consider it as a long-term play only, since you need to factor in not only the length of time the Asian recovery is likely to take, but also the possibility that Lee is wrong in his concentration, and that you'll have to await his next homerun swing.

NEW

NAVIGATOR ASIA-PACIFIC FUND
Cheah Cheng Hye+V-Nee Yeh (1997)/Value Partners Ltd.

CONSISTENCY

Performance Trend

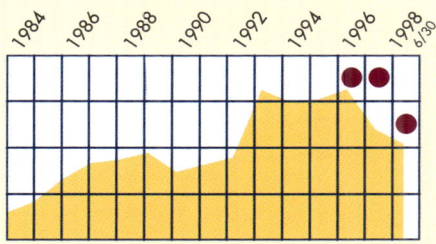

1984 1986 1988 1990 1992 1994 1996 1998 6/30

RISK

How often fund outperformed GICs	**2 years in 2**
How often fund lost money	**0 years in 2**
Worst year's rate of return	**15.0% (1997)**

REWARD-TO-RISK RELATIONSHIP
SHARPE RATIO QUARTILE RANKINGS

3-Year	**1**
5-Year	**N/A**

EFFICIENCY/MER

Management expense/$100

$3.01

● above average
○ average
○ below average

STYLE

Sector Rotation (SR)
Value Growth
Company Size: Big / Medium / Small

Complementary Fund:
Scotia Excelsior Pacific Rim Fund

Similar Fund:
Fidelity Far East Fund

One of the principles behind diversification is that by spreading the investments among different asset classes and different countries, the risk (which is usually defined as volatility of returns), is reduced. Its the old "eggs in one basket" argument. Unfortunately, Asian investments have been the eggs that broke in 1998.

We've chosen Navigator Asia Pacific as a Top Fund, despite its 27% decline over the past 12 months because the diversification approach demands exposure to all markets, including Asia.

Managers Cheah Cheng Hye and V-Nee Yeh of Hong Kong-based Value Partners Ltd. have an enviable record investing in this difficult region. They are primarily small-cap managers, who hold a concentrated number of securities. Cheah and Yeh feel that smaller issues are ignored by the market and that the high valuations that are typical of most Hong Kong securities are not found in the small-cap sector. Their current focus is on Hong Kong and have 65% of their assets deployed there. As Hong Kong residents, they can visit many of their investments in person in order to get a first hand view of operations and management. In a place where only the biggest firms conform to Western accounting standards, this is a real advantage.

NEW

SCOTIA EXCELSIOR PACIFIC RIM FUND
Scotia Investment Management Ltd. (1994)

ASIA-PACIFIC RIM EQUITY

CONSISTENCY

Performance Trend

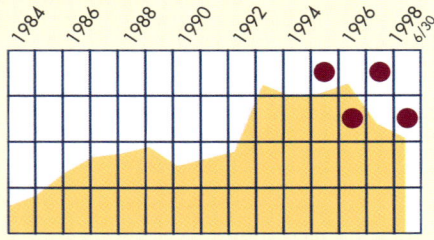

1984 1986 1988 1990 1992 1994 1996 1998 6/30

RISK

How often fund outperformed GICs	**1 year in 3**
How often fund lost money	**1 year in 3**
Worst year's rate of return	**-16.0% (1997)**

REWARD-TO-RISK RELATIONSHIP
SHARPE RATIO QUARTILE RANKINGS

3-Year	**1**
5-Year	**N/A**

EFFICIENCY/MER

Management expense/$100

$2.43

○ above average
○ average
● below average

STYLE

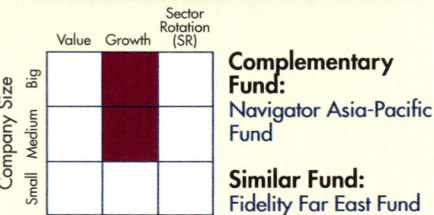

Value Growth Sector Rotation (SR)

Company Size: Big / Medium / Small

Complementary Fund:
Navigator Asia-Pacific Fund

Similar Fund:
Fidelity Far East Fund

This is a great fund for those who feel that export growth in the Far East, and especially in Japan, will be the engine for the region's economic rebirth. Scotia Excelsior Pacific Rim has holdings primarily in Japan and Hong Kong. Its focus is on exporters who will benefit from the weakness of their domestic currencies against the U.S. In fact, the team from Scotia Investment Management Ltd. accept currency risk as a major component of the investment decision, and presently are completely unhedged. They are growth managers with a mid-to-large cap orientation and utilize a process that is 20% top down and 80% bottom up.

They currently favour Japan, especially its consumer and precision electronics industries, as well as China and its long-term growth prospects. They feel that the Japanese economy and currency will remain weak, but that the country's financial market restructuring process will help stabilize the entire region.

NEW

AGF CANADIAN BOND FUND
Warren Goldring (1962)+Clive Coombs (1990)/AGF Funds Inc.

CANADIAN LONG/MID-TERM BONDS

CONSISTENCY

Performance Trend

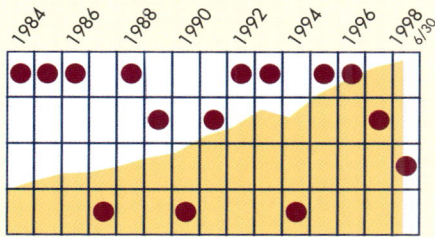

1984 1986 1988 1990 1992 1994 1996 1998 6/30

RISK

How often fund outperformed GICs	**12 years in 21**
How often fund lost money	**1 year in 21**
Worst year's rate of return	**-8.5% (1994)**

REWARD-TO-RISK RELATIONSHIP
SHARPE RATIO QUARTILE RANKINGS

3-Year	**2**
5-Year	**3**

EFFICIENCY/MER

Management expense/$100

$1.93

○ above average
● average
○ below average

STYLE

	Spread Trading (ST)	<Blend>	Rate Anticipation (RA)
Short			
Medium		■	
Long		■	

Term

Complementary Fund:
McLean Budden Fixed Income

Similar Fund:
Phillips, Hager & North Bond Fund

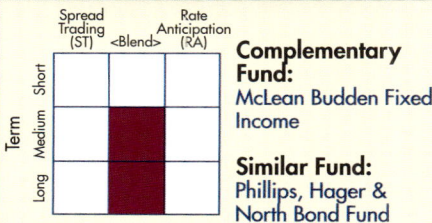

For those investors who wish to confine their risk to their equity investments, this fund invests strictly in quality issues with Government of Canada bonds being its most prevalent holding. But understand that top-notch credit quality does not mean that a bond fund cannot post negative returns, when interest rates increase. In fact, this fund lost 8.5% during the bond market carnage of 1994, like most other bond funds.

While its risk levels have been slightly higher than most bond funds, Coombs and Goldring have demonstrated an ability to provide additional returns over the long haul. The current average time to maturity for the fund's bonds approximates 12 years. This reflects the duo's opinion that the Asian fallout, falling government debt supply, and slower economic growth should preclude any significant hike in interest rates in the near future. By maintaining the longer maturities, they are trying to reap the rewards of the correspondingly higher interest yields (12-year bond rates are currently higher than 5-year bond rates). The offset is that bonds with longer maturities are hit harder, if rates do spike up.

For those funding RRIF payments or living off their portfolio, this fund provides the added convenience of a monthly distribution.

ALTAMIRA BOND FUND
Annette Cappa + Robert Marcus (1991)/Altamira Management

CANADIAN LONG/MID-TERM BONDS

CONSISTENCY

Performance Trend

RISK

How often fund outperformed GICs	**6 years in 10**
How often fund lost money	**1 year in 10**
Worst year's rate of return	**-8.8% (1994)**

REWARD-TO-RISK RELATIONSHIP
SHARPE RATIO QUARTILE RANKINGS

3-Year	**1**
5-Year	**1**

EFFICIENCY/MER

Management expense/$100

$1.30

○ above average
○ average
● below average

STYLE

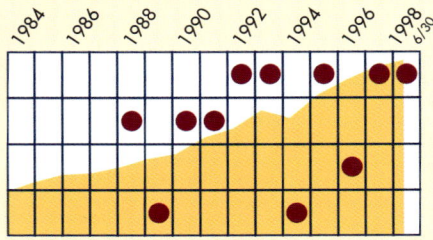

Complementary Fund:
C.I. Canadian Bond Fund

Similar Fund:
Phillips, Hager & North Bond Fund

There is no denying that the Altamira shop has gone through a heap of turmoil over the past two years. Having had to deal with the problems of ownership fights, internal politics, and departing managers, the fund family has faced heavy redemptions and has only this fund left in our Top Fund listing.

The fund has been managed since 1991 by Annette Cappa and Robert Marcus with the latter's responsibility having recently been expanded for the Altamira Income Fund. The fund has excelled and was voted the 1997 Income Fund of the Year at the Canadian Mutual Awards Gala.

A good portion of their superior performance can be attributed to the fund's policy of having a duration of at least six years, which means that the maturity dates of their investments tend to be further out. The result of the long duration is that as rates fall, as they have in Canada over the past few years, the increase in longer-term bond prices exceeds those of shorter-term bonds. This strategy works well when rates fall, but it can result in greater losses if rates back up. In addition, due to Altamira Bond's longer duration, the fund is more volatile than the average Canadian bond fund.

Consider combining this fund with one that focuses on shorter-term bonds, as this will improve your diversification and reduce your risk if rates head north.

NEW

BISSETT BOND FUND
Mike Quinn (inception)/Bissett & Associates Investment Management Ltd.

CANADIAN LONG/MID-TERM BONDS

CONSISTENCY

Performance Trend

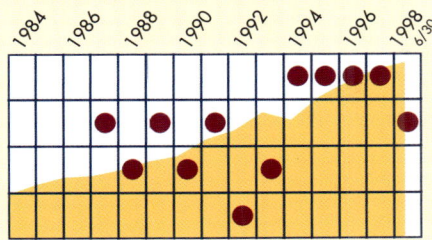

1984 1986 1988 1990 1992 1994 1996 1998 6/30

RISK

How often fund outperformed GICs	**6 years in 11**
How often fund lost money	**1 year in 11**
Worst year's rate of return	**-3.8% (1994)**

REWARD-TO-RISK RELATIONSHIP
SHARPE RATIO QUARTILE RANKINGS

3-Year	**1**
5-Year	**1**

EFFICIENCY/MER

Management expense/$100	○ above average
	○ average
$0.75	● below average

STYLE

	Spread Trading (ST)	<Blend>	Rate Anticipation (RA)
Short			
Medium	■		
Long			

Complementary Fund: Altamira Bond Fund

Similar Fund: Phillips, Hager & North Bond Fund

Another quality offering from Calgary-based Bissett & Associates. Manager Mike Quinn is a yield-spread style investor who focuses on the mid-term section of the bond maturity curve. Currently, over 80% of his holdings are mid-term instruments, i.e., maturing in 5 to 10 years. Quinn also spices up returns with an overweighting to high quality Canadian corporate bonds, which offer higher yields than their government-issued counterparts. Four of the top 10 holdings are federal government issues, three are provincials, and three are corporate bonds.

Quinn is bullish on the prospects for Canadian bonds. He foresees a low interest rate environment, with low inflation, and moderate economic growth.

One of the reasons that this fund has been a consistent top performer over the years has been its rock bottom management expense ratio of only .75%. This gives the fund a leg up over the competition, as the average bond fund MER in Canada is just over 1.6%.

C.I. CANADIAN BOND FUND
John Zechner (1993-inception)/Z. Zechner Associates

CONSISTENCY

Performance Trend

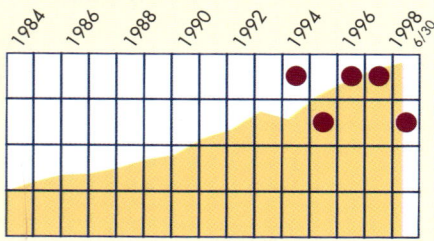

1984 1986 1988 1990 1992 1994 1996 1998 6/30

RISK

How often fund outperformed GICs	**3 years in 4**
How often fund lost money	**1 year in 4**
Worst year's rate of return	**-4.3% (1994)**

REWARD-TO-RISK RELATIONSHIP
SHARPE RATIO QUARTILE RANKINGS

3-Year	**1**
5-Year	**1**

EFFICIENCY/MER

Management expense/$100

$1.65

○ above average
● average
○ below average

STYLE

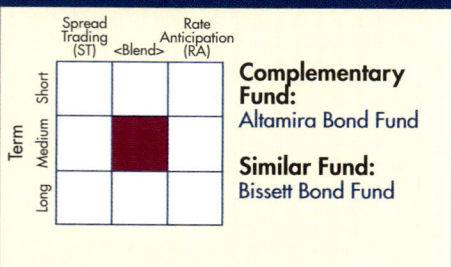

Spread Trading (ST) <Blend> Rate Anticipation (RA)

Term: Short / Medium / Long

Complementary Fund:
Altamira Bond Fund

Similar Fund:
Bissett Bond Fund

John Zechner has been holding the reins of the C.I. Canadian Bond Fund since its inception in 1993. Zechner has been successful in consistently delivering strong risk-adjusted returns. Instead of accomplishing this by buying longer-term bonds that experienced more dramatic gains as rates fell, he has included a healthy component of corporate debentures in his mix. The fund has also reduced the exposure to a hike in interest rates (which would lower the value of the current bond holdings) by moving the cash component up to 15% of the portfolio.

In managing the Triple "A" rated Government of Canada bond component, Zechner concentrates on only a few issues, but maintains a wide spread of maturity dates. Although the corporate bonds invested in are high quality, Zechner has to keep on his toes in order to ensure that the risk of default doesn't creep into the portfolio. The strategy also provides him with some additional latitude as he can maneuver his exposure to the two sectors, government and corporate, as one becomes over- or under-priced relative to the other. Zechner's mandate also allows him to invest a portion of the portfolio in foreign bonds.

NEW

GREEN LINE CANADIAN BOND FUND
Satish Rai (1988)/TD Asset Management Inc.

CONSISTENCY

Performance Trend

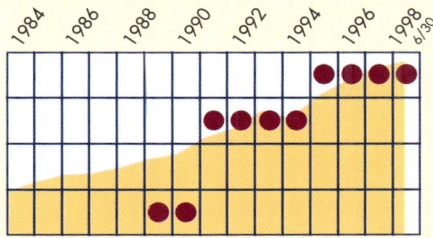

1984 1986 1988 1990 1992 1994 1996 1998 6/30

RISK

How often fund outperformed GICs	**6 years in 9**
How often fund lost money	**1 year in 9**
Worst year's rate of return	**-5.6% (1994)**

REWARD-TO-RISK RELATIONSHIP
SHARPE RATIO QUARTILE RANKINGS

3-Year	**1**
5-Year	**1**

EFFICIENCY/MER

Management expense/$100

$0.94

○ above average
○ average
● below average

STYLE

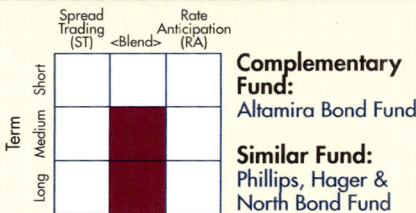

Spread Trading (ST) <Blend> Rate Anticipation (RA)

Term: Short / Medium / Long

Complementary Fund:
Altamira Bond Fund

Similar Fund:
Phillips, Hager & North Bond Fund

Manager Satish Rai of TD Asset Management Inc. is bullish on Canada. He feels that the combination of strong economic growth, low inflation, and a successful deficit fighting campaign by the feds is positive for bonds. Rai also thinks that the lower debt levels will contribute to a diminishing supply of government bonds and Treasury Bills. The result of his thinking is a portfolio with an overweighting to long maturity bonds, which would benefit the most from lower interest rates. A hefty 67% exposure to high quality corporate bonds and debentures helps enhance returns, while the higher than average number of holdings(>80) helps to reduce any default risk. The MER on this no-load fund is among the lowest in the Canadian bond fund universe further increasing investor returns.

CANADIAN LONG/MID-TERM BONDS

CANADIAN LONG/MID-TERM BONDS

1997/1998 RRSP

McLEAN BUDDEN FIXED INCOME FUND
McLean Budden Fixed Income team (1988-inception)

CONSISTENCY

Performance Trend

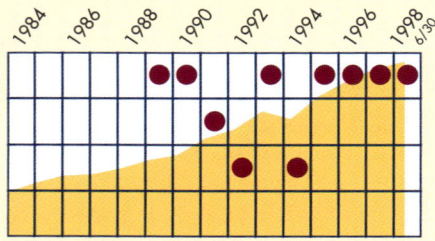

RISK

How often fund outperformed GICs	**7 years in 9**
How often fund lost money	**1 year in 9**
Worst year's rate of return	**-6.2% (1994)**

REWARD-TO-RISK RELATIONSHIP
SHARPE RATIO QUARTILE RANKINGS

3-Year	**1**
5-Year	**1**

EFFICIENCY/MER

Management expense/$100

$1.00

○ above average
○ average
● below average

STYLE

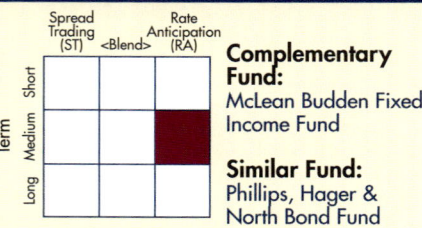

Complementary Fund:
McLean Budden Fixed Income Fund

Similar Fund:
Phillips, Hager & North Bond Fund

Bond investing is a tough game to play as the difference between being on top and on bottom is slim in terms of return percentages. Often one or two suspect trades are enough to throw a fund into the fourth quartile. The spread between the first and fourth quartile for equities is far greater. Despite this, this fund managed by the team of Bill Giblin, Craig Barnard, and Peter Kotsopolous has managed to remain near the top over the past four years.

They use all the strategies in their arsenal in attempting to squeeze out that extra bit of return. They manage the term to bond maturity based on interest rate expectations. They evaluate the various sectors such as federal, provincial, municipal, and corporate, in their hunt for undervalued product. They also try to manage based on credit quality, searching for bonds whose rating is about to increase, which heightens the bond's value.

When purchasing their positions, they consider the level of liquidity, and factor that into the decision as to whether they anticipate holding the bond for the short term (if there is a lot of liquidity) or for the mid-to-long term (upward of five years).

With a relatively low MER and a good track record, this is a bond fund to consider seriously for your portfolio.

PHILLIPS, HAGER & NORTH BOND FUND

P H & N Management team (inception)

CONSISTENCY

Performance Trend

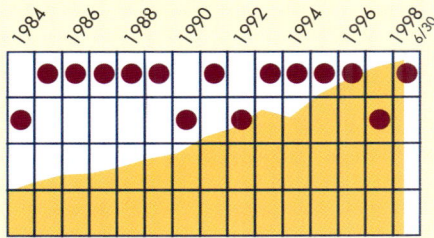

1984 1986 1988 1990 1992 1994 1996 1998 6/30

RISK

How often fund outperformed GICs	**12 years in 21**
How often fund lost money	**2 years in 21**
Worst year's rate of return	**-4.1% (1994)**

REWARD-TO-RISK RELATIONSHIP
SHARPE RATIO QUARTILE RANKINGS

3-Year	**1**
5-Year	**1**

EFFICIENCY/MER

Management expense/$100

$0.57

○ above average
○ average
● below average

STYLE

	Spread Trading (ST)	<Blend>	Rate Anticipation (RA)
Short			
Medium			■
Long			

Term

Complementary Fund:
McLean Budden Fixed Income Fund

Similar Fund:
Bissett Bond Fund

The price of admission, in the form of a $25,000 minimum investment, may be steep but once you are in, you won't be disappointed. Employing a team approach has obviously worked for this shop as the PH & N Bond Fund has ranked within the first quartile in eight of the last ten years. The other two years? Not to worry; their slide left them in the second quartile.

While they have put away the vast majority of the competition, they have closely paralleled the SCM Universe Bond Total Return (interest and capital fluctuations) index over the past ten years. Their tools of the trade include interest rate anticipation, yield enhancement, and security selection strategies.

Contributing to the fund's performance is the ultra-low expense ratio that plays even a greater role in bond funds, where the difference between the winners and losers is scant. While they are permitted to buy corporate and provincial debt, the team has focused their largest holdings on top-quality Canadian government bonds. In fact, all bonds are rated "A" or greater with approximately 60% being accorded a "AAA" (highest possible grade).

CANADIAN LONG/MID-TERM BONDS

NEW

RRSP 🍁

TRIMARK ADVANTAGE BOND FUND

Patrick Farmer (1994)/Trimark Investment Management Inc.

CONSISTENCY

Performance Trend

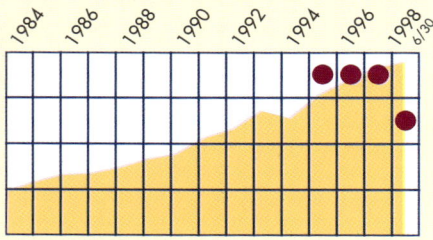

1984 1986 1988 1990 1992 1994 1996 1998 6/30

RISK

How often fund outperformed GICs	**3 years in 3**
How often fund lost money	**1 year in 3**
Worst year's rate of return	**10.5% (1997)**

REWARD-TO-RISK RELATIONSHIP
SHARPE RATIO QUARTILE RANKINGS

3-Year	**1**
5-Year	**N/A**

EFFICIENCY/MER

Management expense/$100

$1.24

○ above average
○ average
● below average

STYLE

Spread Trading (ST) <Blend> Rate Anticipation (RA)

Term: Short / Medium / Long

Complementary Fund:
Altamira Bond Fund

Similar Fund:
Bissett Bond Fund

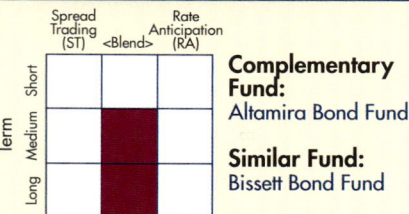

Think of this as a supercharged bond fund. Although primarily a fixed income fund, the investment mandate includes convertible debentures, royalty trusts, mortgage-backed securities, and even preferred shares. The fund can also own foreign-denominated issues and hedge any currency risk if so desired.

The Trimark management team has taken advantage (no pun intended) of this broad mandate and the result is a top-ranked bond fund. Currently, the fund is nearly 55% invested in corporate bonds and only 29% in federal government issues. About 16% of fund assets are U.S. dollar denominated, which has also been a plus as the Canadian currency weakness lingers.

The fund is positioned to take advantage of a rise in short term rates relative to longer maturities. The managers are also watching Asia with interest. Further weakness in those markets would contribute to slower North American economic growth, reduce inflationary pressures, keep interest rates low, and make for happy bond fund managers.

NEW

FIDELITY CANADIAN INCOME FUND
Ford O'Neil (inception)/Fidelity Investments Ltd.

CANADIAN SHORT-TERM BONDS

CONSISTENCY

Performance Trend

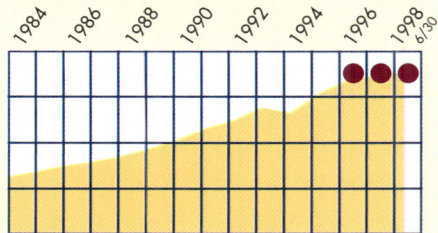

1984 1986 1988 1990 1992 1994 1996 1998 6/30

RISK

How often fund outperformed GICs	**1 year in 2**
How often fund lost money	**0 years in 2**
Worst year's rate of return	**4.5% (1997)**

REWARD-TO-RISK RELATIONSHIP
SHARPE RATIO QUARTILE RANKINGS

3-Year	**N/A**
5-Year	**N/A**

EFFICIENCY/MER

Management expense/$100

$1.25

○ above average
● average
○ below average

STYLE

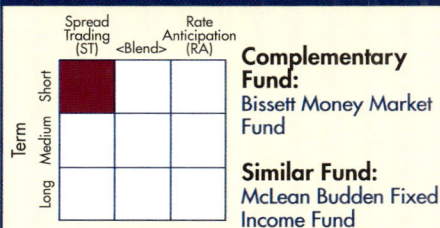

Spread Trading (ST) <Blend> Rate Anticipation (RA)

Term: Short / Medium / Long

Complementary Fund:
Bissett Money Market Fund

Similar Fund:
McLean Budden Fixed Income Fund

It's difficult to assemble a bond fund portfolio that outperforms its peers, especially one that is comprised of bonds that are at the short term end of the maturity spectrum. There are few opportunities to hit investment home runs, and the successful manager must be content to hit lots of singles. Fred O'Neil, manager of Fidelity Canadian Income Fund, definitely is a .300 plus hitter.

Many bond managers use corporate bonds to provide an added kick to portfolio performance. O'Neil has only 25% of his holdings in corporate issues, less than most bond funds. In addition, provincial issues are only 3.7% of total holdings as O'Neil feels that federal bonds are more attractive on risk/reward basis.

Much of the success of this fund can be credited to Fidelity's Targeted Active Management or TAM approach to fixed income investing. Rather than try to anticipate interest rate movements or changes in the term structure of interest rates, the Fidelity analysts emphasis opportunistic trading and individual security research, as well as sector and issuer credit analysis. The goal is reduced volatility and superior portfolio performance

RRSP 🍁

GREAT WEST LIFE MORTGAGE INVESTMENT FUND (G)
DSC Harvé Andres (1987)/GWL Investment Management Ltd.

CANADIAN MORTGAGE

CONSISTENCY

Performance Trend

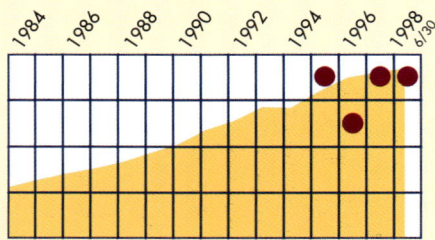

1984 1986 1988 1990 1992 1994 1996 1998 6/30

RISK

How often fund outperformed GICs	**3 years in 3**
How often fund lost money	**0 years in 3**
Worst year's rate of return	**7.2% (1997)**

REWARD-TO-RISK RELATIONSHIP
SHARPE RATIO QUARTILE RANKINGS

3-Year	**1**
5-Year	**N/A**

EFFICIENCY/MER

Management expense/$100

$2.16

● above average
○ average
○ below average

STYLE

Spread Trading (ST) <Blend> Rate Anticipation (RA)

Term: Short / Medium / Long

Complementary Fund:
Hong Kong Bank Mortgage Fund

Similar Fund:
Bissett Bond Fund

This fund, managed by GWL Investment Management Ltd, consists primarily of industrial and commercial mortgages, diversified by both location and sector. This approach provides a big advantage over the competition, which are generally bank-owned mortgage funds. Industrial and commercial mortgages typically have longer terms than their residential counterparts which are the main components of most mortgage funds. For example, the average term to maturity is 8.5 years, which is more typical of a bond fund than a mortgage fund. Yields are therefore higher and there are more opportunities to capture capital gains through trading and interest rate declines. The downside, however, is a more volatile fund.

About 50% of this fund's mortgages are held in Ontario, 21% in B.C., and 13% in Quebec. Apartments represent 44% of the holdings, followed by retail locations at 19%, and office mortgages at 18%. Remarkably, there are no loans in default.

HONG KONG BANK MORTGAGE FUND
Jim Gilliland/M.K. Wong & Associates

CONSISTENCY

Performance Trend

1984 1986 1988 1990 1992 1994 1996 1998 6/30

RISK

How often fund outperformed GICs	**2 years in 4**
How often fund lost money	**0 years in 4**
Worst year's rate of return	**2.6% (1997)**

REWARD-TO-RISK RELATIONSHIP
SHARPE RATIO QUARTILE RANKINGS

3-Year	**2**
5-Year	**1**

EFFICIENCY/MER

Management expense/$100

$1.45

○ above average
○ average
● below average

STYLE

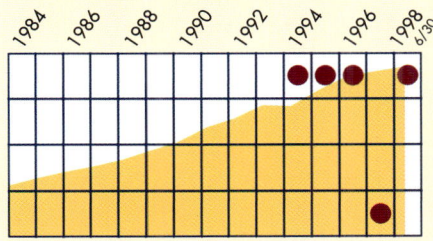

Spread Trading (ST) <Blend> Rate Anticipation (RA)

Term: Short / Medium / Long

Complementary Fund:
Altamira Bond Fund

Similar Fund:
Great West Life Mortgage Inv. Fund (G) DSC

CANADIAN MORTGAGE

As interest rates have fallen over the past few years, bond funds have enjoyed solid returns as bond holdings jumped in price. For mortgage funds, which generally hold shorter-term mortgages, the gains have been watered down. As rates fell and homeowners renewed at lower rates, yields on mortgage funds have declined. While equities and bonds roared ahead, these factors resulted in mortgage funds being viewed as boring and perhaps even unnecessary.

They could, however, enjoy the spotlight again when other asset classes hit the skids. If interest rates do increase, mortgage funds will not be as hard hit as bond or equity funds, and yields will increase over the mid-term as homeowners rush to lock in their mortgages.

A review of the Hong Kong Bank Mortgage Fund's benchmarks and holdings highlights the fact that their mortgages generally mature within three years. Manager Jim Gilliland is also holding 28% of the portfolio in short-term notes boosting the fund's conservatism. The fund's current positions reflect the Bank's view that interest rates are on the upswing as a response to our floundering dollar.

By investing in a diversified portfolio of residential mortgages, Gilliland has posted strong return numbers for a mortgage fund, while maintaining the expected low volatility levels.

From a risk perspective, Hong Kong Bank guarantees all the mortgages invested in by the fund, so any default risk has been eliminated.

BPI GLOBAL RSP BOND FUND
Benedict Cheng (1997)/BPI Capital Management Corporation

INTERNATIONAL BONDS

CONSISTENCY

Performance Trend

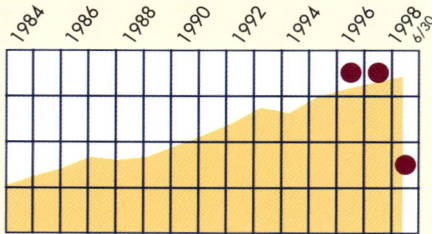

1984 1986 1988 1990 1992 1994 1996 1998 6/30

RISK

How often fund outperformed GICs	**2 years in 2**
How often fund lost money	**0 years in 2**
Worst year's rate of return	**9.9% (1997)**

REWARD-TO-RISK RELATIONSHIP
SHARPE RATIO QUARTILE RANKINGS

3-Year	**1**
5-Year	**N/A**

EFFICIENCY/MER

Management expense/$100

$1.50

○ above average
○ average
● below average

STYLE

Spread Trading (ST)   <Blend>   Rate Anticipation (RA)

Term: Short / Medium / Long

Complementary Fund:
Fidelity Emerging Markets Bond Fund

Similar Fund:
Universal World Income RRSP Fund

One of the challenges for Canadian RRSP investors hoping to diversify internationally is the challenge of getting around the 20% foreign content rule. This fund can be part of the solution. Fully eligible for 100% Canadian content status, it consists of a portfolio of Canadian and foreign bonds denominated in a wide range of currencies.

BPI Global RSP Bond is currently emphasizing North American markets. Manager Benedict Cheng feels that the best value resides there, despite the recent Canadian dollar woes. U.S. and Canadian bonds have the highest yields of the G-7 countries, yet the inflation rates are the 2nd and 3rd lowest (after Japan). As a result, Cheng expects investors to continue to snap up North American bonds.

The fund asset mix is 62% Canadian pay bonds, 34% U.S. pay bonds, and 4% other currencies, and Cheng believes that the U.S. currency's strength will continue thus boosting the U.S. pay portion of the portfolio. A top-down manager, Cheng also actively manages the currency exposure, which can be a large portion of the return component of international bond portfolios.

FIDELITY EMERGING MARKETS BOND FUND
John Carlson (1995)/Fidelity Management & Research

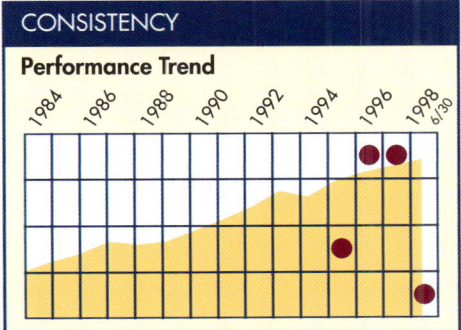

CONSISTENCY

Performance Trend

1984 1986 1988 1990 1992 1994 1996 1998 6/30

RISK

How often fund outperformed GICs	**3 years in 3**
How often fund lost money	**0 years in 3**
Worst year's rate of return	**12.8% (1995)**

REWARD-TO-RISK RELATIONSHIP
SHARPE RATIO QUARTILE RANKINGS

3-Year	**1**
5-Year	**N/A**

EFFICIENCY/MER

Management expense/$100

$2.23

● above average
○ average
○ below average

STYLE

Spread Trading (ST) <Blend> Rate Anticipation (RA)

Term: Short / Medium / Long

Complementary Fund:
Guardian Foreign Income Fund

Similar Fund:
Universal World Income RRSP Fund

As interest rates hit rock bottom, many investors are looking for ways to boost the yields in their fixed income portfolios. This fund certainly fills that need. Our data indicates that it has produced the highest returns of any fixed income fund over the past three years. It is also far and away the most volatile of any fixed income fund over the past three years!

Fund manager John Carlson uses a "mosaic", top-down approach to managing this fund, building an overall picture from smaller bits of information. He looks at economic, social, and political inputs. Corporate holdings are, in addition to the above process, analyzed from the bottom up.

Despite the analytic approach that Carlson employs, this is not a fund for the traditional fixed income investor. It behaves more like an equity fund and should be only part of the diversified portfolio of an aggressive investor.

INTERNATIONAL BONDS

RRSP

GUARDIAN FOREIGN INCOME FUND
Laurence Linklater (inception)/Kleinwort Guardian Overseas Ltd.

INTERNATIONAL BONDS

CONSISTENCY

Performance Trend

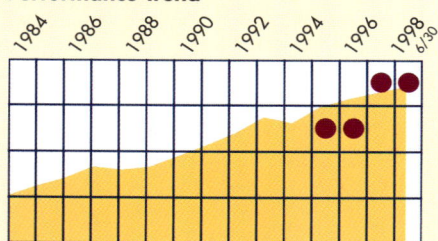

RISK

How often fund outperformed GICs	3 years in 3
How often fund lost money	1 year in 3
Worst year's rate of return	7.4% (1996)

REWARD-TO-RISK RELATIONSHIP
SHARPE RATIO QUARTILE RANKINGS

3-Year	1
5-Year	N/A

EFFICIENCY/MER

Management expense/$100

$1.68

○ above average
○ average
● below average

STYLE

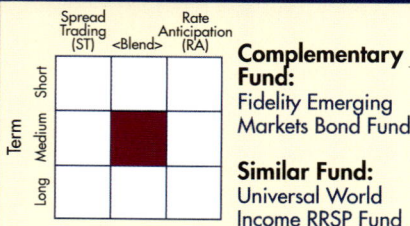

Complementary Fund:
Fidelity Emerging Markets Bond Fund

Similar Fund:
Universal World Income RRSP Fund

Most research indicates that the largest component of the returns of international bonds is the contribution made by currency movements. Guardian Foreign Income Fund explicitly acknowledges the role of currencies in enhancing returns. The portfolio is concentrated in the foreign bond markets and foreign currencies that have the best prospects for long-term success. The fund has the flexibility to fully hedge the currency exposure out of or into any currency, excluding the Canadian dollar. Because 80% of the bonds held are actually issues by Canadian companies or supra nationals, the fund is fully RRSP- and RRIF-eligible.

The fund is currently composed of 36% European currency bonds and 64% U.S. pay securities. Manager Laurence Linklater of Kleinwort Guardian Overseas Ltd. is bullish on Europe, but also feels the U.S. will appreciate against the Euro currencies; hence a 100% hedge back to the greenback. Linklater feels that the Federal Reserve Bank will let interest rates remain where they are and thus provide a favourable background for global bond markets

NEW

UNIVERSAL WORLD INCOME RRSP FUND Brian Barret
+ Michael Borowsky/ Mackenzie Investment Management Inc. (1998)

CONSISTENCY

Performance Trend

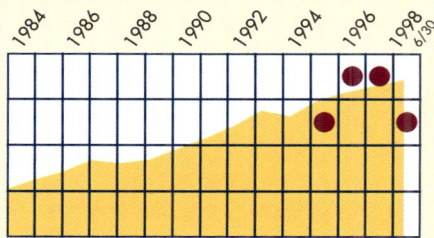

1984 1986 1988 1990 1992 1994 1996 1998 6/30

RISK

How often fund outperformed GICs	**3 years in 3**
How often fund lost money	**0 years in 3**
Worst year's rate of return	**8.8% (1996)**

REWARD-TO-RISK RELATIONSHIP
SHARPE RATIO QUARTILE RANKINGS

3-Year	**1**
5-Year	**N/A**

EFFICIENCY/MER

Management expense/$100

$2.15

○ above average
● average
○ below average

STYLE

	Spread Trading (ST)	<Blend>	Rate Anticipation (RA)
Short			
Medium			
Long		■	

(Term)

Complementary Fund:
Fidelity Emerging Markets Bond Fund

Similar Fund:
Canadian Foreign Income Fund

A fully RRSP-eligible fund, managers Brian Barret and Michael Borowsky use futures contracts to participate in high quality global government issues. They will also invest directly in emerging markets bonds and high yield corporate issues up to 20% of the fund's total assets. The largest holdings are in U.S. bond markets at 33%, followed by continental European issues at 30%, Canadian bonds at 13%, while the U.K., Australia, and New Zealand and emerging markets make up the balance.

Barret and Borowsky feel that two economic scenarios are likely, given the level of interest rates in the U.S. and Europe—either rates will rise slightly in Europe or continue to fall in the U.S. They feel that U.S. interest rates will ease further and are therefore positioned accordingly. Despite some weakness in the global high yield bond sector, the two managers are very bullish on this sector of the market and are continuing to build their positions. Barret and Borowsky's view is that both portfolio yield and diversification are enhanced through owning high yield bonds.

The currency exposure is actively managed. The fund is currently 42% exposed to the U.S. dollar, 29% to the Canadian dollar, and 23% to various European currencies. In their view, the U.S. dollar is fairly valued against its European counterparts, and presently has only partially hedged their currency exposure.

INTERNATIONAL BONDS

NEW

RRSP

C.I. U.S. MONEY MARKET FUND
John Zechner (inception)/J. Zechner & Associates

CONSISTENCY

Performance Trend

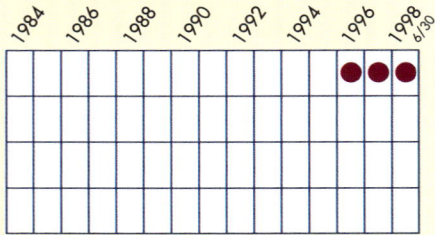

1984	1986	1988	1990	1992	1994	1996	1998 6/30

RISK

How often fund outperformed GICs	**1 year in 2**
How often fund lost money	**0 years in 2**
Worst year's rate of return	**4.7% (1996)**

REWARD-TO-RISK RELATIONSHIP
SHARPE RATIO QUARTILE RANKINGS

3-Year	**1**
5-Year	**N/A**

EFFICIENCY/MER

Management expense/$100	○ above average
$0.51	○ average
	● below average

STYLE

	Spread Trading (ST)	<Blend>	Rate Anticipation (RA)
Short		■	
Medium			
Long			

Term

Complementary Fund:
Fidelity Emerging Markets Bond Fund

Similar Fund:
Phillips, Hager & North $U.S. Money Market

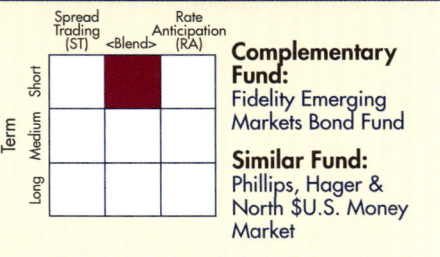

It's no coincidence that the top performing international money market fund also has the lowest management expense ratio at 0.51%. Opportunities for the manager to add value are scant, and offering a low cost management structure is usually the easiest way to do it. The managers at J. Zechner & Associates don't abdicate their investment responsibilities, however. The portfolio consists of mainly Canadian Treasury Bills denominated in U.S.$, with a smattering of U.S. Treasury Bills, and short term discounted notes offered by Canadian issuers.

U.S./INTERNATIONAL MONEY MARKET

PHILLIPS, HAGER & NORTH U.S.$ MONEY MARKET FUND

P H & N Management team

CONSISTENCY

Performance Trend

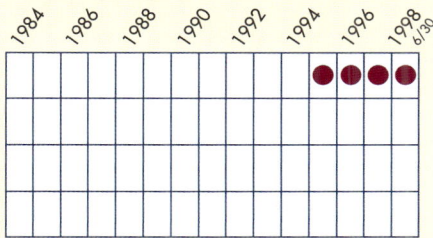

1984 1986 1988 1990 1992 1994 1996 1998 6/30

RISK

How often fund outperformed GICs	**1 year in 7**
How often fund lost money	**0 years in 7**
Worst year's rate of return	**2.7% (1993)**

REWARD-TO-RISK RELATIONSHIP
SHARPE RATIO QUARTILE RANKINGS

3-Year	**1**
5-Year	**N/A**

EFFICIENCY/MER

Management expense/$100

$0.52

○ above average
○ average
● below average

STYLE

	Spread Trading (ST)	<Blend>	Rate Anticipation (RA)
Short		■	
Medium			
Long			

Term

Complementary Fund:
Fidelity Emerging Markets Bond Fund

Similar Fund:
C.I. U.S. Money Market Fund

With inflation abating and short-term interest rates so low, it's hard to get too excited about money market funds when other types of funds have been earning 20%-30% for their owners. On the other hand, some funds have also lost 20%-30% over the past year.

Money market funds can constitute a permanent portion of your portfolio if you have a specific need for liquidity, or if your risk tolerance is particularly low. From a tactical investment strategy perspective, investors can house funds in cash as a protective measure or as a temporary stash awaiting the next correction.

This fund adds another nuance as it permits you to control your portfolio's direct exposure to the U.S. dollar. If you expect the roughshod treatment of the loonie to continue but are wary of the heights scaled by the U.S. equity markets, you may want to consider this fund.

With the exception of 1993, this has been a top-quartile fund since its 1990 inception. Translated, this means that for a nearly riskless investment class (excluding the foreign exchange risk), PH & N has eked out additional annual returns approximating 0.5%. Not a huge difference, but why not take advantage whenever you can.

An added bonus is that it is RRSP/RRIF-eligible.

U.S./INTERNATIONAL MONEY MARKET

RRSP

BISSETT MONEY MARKET FUND
Mike Quinn (1993)/Bissett & Associates Investment Management Inc.

CONSISTENCY

Performance Trend

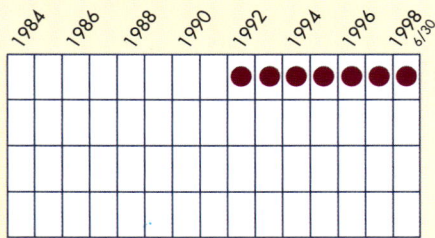

1984 1986 1988 1990 1992 1994 1996 1998 6/30

● ● ● ● ● ● ●

RISK

How often fund outperformed GICs	**0 years in 6**
How often fund lost money	**0 years in 6**
Worst year's rate of return	**3.2% (1997)**

REWARD-TO-RISK RELATIONSHIP
SHARPE RATIO QUARTILE RANKINGS

3-Year	**1**
5-Year	**1**

EFFICIENCY/MER

Management expense/$100

$0.50

○ above average
○ average
● below average

STYLE

	Spread Trading (ST)	\<Blend\>	Rate Anticipation (RA)
Short	■	■	
Medium			
Long			

Term

Complementary Fund:
Fidelity Canadian Income Fund

Similar Fund:
BPI T-Bill Fund

A 36% exposure to short-term corporate paper, provincial T-Bills and bankers acceptances has helped manager Mike Quinn achieve Top Fund status for this fund. A consistent top quartile performer, Quinn uses a yield spread approach to managing this portfolio, which has an average term to maturity of 90 days. The management expense ratio of 0.50% compares very favourably to the Canadian money market fund average of 0.95%.

NEW

BPI T-BILL FUND
Fred Dalley (1994)/BPI Capital Management Corporation

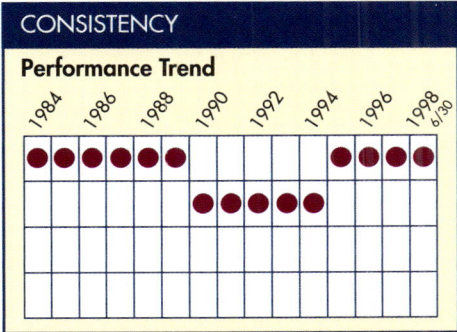

CONSISTENCY

Performance Trend

1984 1986 1988 1990 1992 1994 1996 1998 6/30

RISK

How often fund outperformed GICs	**4 years in 15**
How often fund lost money	**0 years in 15**
Worst year's rate of return	**2.9% (1997)**

REWARD-TO-RISK RELATIONSHIP
SHARPE RATIO QUARTILE RANKINGS

3-Year	**1**
5-Year	**2**

EFFICIENCY/MER

Management expense/$100

$0.65

○ above average
○ average
● below average

STYLE

Spread Trading (ST) — <Blend> — Rate Anticipation (RA)

Term: Short, Medium, Long

Complementary Fund:
Fidelity Canadian Income Fund

Similar Fund:
Talvest Money Fund

A T-Bill fund in name only, BPI T-Bill actually is comprised of 85% short-term corporate paper, bankers acceptances and term deposit receipts (TDRs), and only 15% provincial and federal Treasury Bills. The result is enhanced returns with only an incremental increase in risk, as the corporate and bank holdings are broadly diversified by company and industry.

The management expense ratio is 0.65%, which is below average and goes a long way to helping this fund achieve Top Fund status.

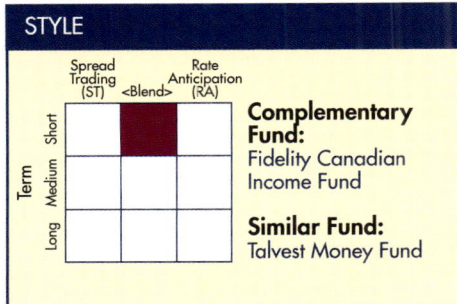

CANADIAN MONEY MARKET

1998 RRSP

TALVEST MONEY FUND
Steven Dubrovsky (1992-inception)/T.A.L. Investment Counsel

CONSISTENCY

Performance Trend

1984 1986 1988 1990 1992 1994 1996 1998 6/30

RISK

How often fund outperformed GICs	**3 years in 10**
How often fund lost money	**0 years in 10**
Worst year's rate of return	**2.8% (1997)**

REWARD-TO-RISK RELATIONSHIP
SHARPE RATIO QUARTILE RANKINGS

3-Year	**1**
5-Year	**1**

EFFICIENCY/MER

Management expense/$100

$0.75

○ above average
○ average
● below average

STYLE

	Spread Trading (ST)	<Blend>	Rate Anticipation (RA)
Short			
Medium			
Long			

Term

Complementary Fund:
Fidelity Canadian Income Fund

Similar Fund:
BPI T-Bill Fund

How different can money market funds be? You're right. The dispersion of performance levels is pretty tight given that they are all basically investing in short-term government securities. But as with every other asset class, you should try to wring every risk-adjusted return dollar possible, as the pennies add up to dollars over the long term. It could represent the difference between a Cadillac and a Chevy on your retirement day.

This fund, managed by Steven Dubrovsky, has managed first and second quartile rankings since 1989. While not the lowest MER (which can chew up a lot of the low yield) in town, Talvest's level is competitive at 0.75%.

The temptation often exists to stretch out the maturity dates to try to grab that little bit of extra yield. But that increases the risk and is not why you put your money into a money market fund to start with. Dubrovsky is certainly not guilty of this but he does squeeze out extra juice by holding an array of provincial and corporate debt, which yield slight premiums to federal debt. Although the additional yield is accompanied theoretically by additional risk, the defacto risk level is negligible.

CANADIAN MONEY MARKET

NEW

AGF CANADIAN TACTICAL ASSET ALLOCATION FUND
Barclay's Global Investors (1996)

CONSISTENCY

Performance Trend

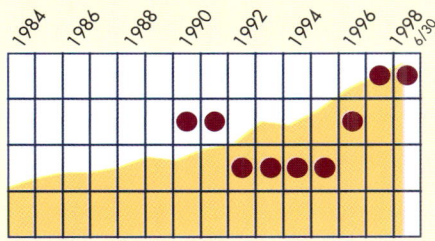

1984 1986 1988 1990 1992 1994 1996 1998 6/30

RISK

How often fund outperformed GICs	**5 years in 8**
How often fund lost money	**1 year in 8**
Worst year's rate of return	**-4.1% (1994)**

REWARD-TO-RISK RELATIONSHIP
SHARPE RATIO QUARTILE RANKINGS

3-Year	**2**
5-Year	**2**

EFFICIENCY/MER

Management expense/$100

$2.42

● above average
○ average
○ below average

STYLE

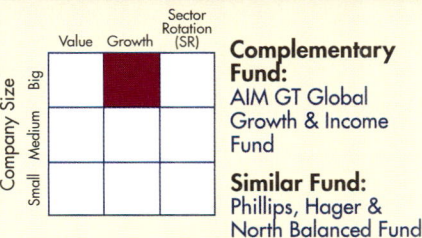

Value Growth Sector Rotation (SR)

Company Size: Big / Medium / Small

Complementary Fund:
AIM GT Global Growth & Income Fund

Similar Fund:
Phillips, Hager & North Balanced Fund

Barclays Global Investors, the managers of this fund, use a quantitative value model to determine the appropriate mix of stocks, bonds, and cash. Tactical asset allocation practitioners are essentially market timers and while some experts dispute whether market timing can be consistently successful, there is no doubt that this fund is a top performer.

The management view is less than bullish on equities. From an equity exposure of 91% in September of 1997, the current mix is 60% stocks, 35% bonds, and 5% cash. Their comparative bench mark is 60% TSE 100 and 40% SCM Long Bond Index, which implies that the weighting is neutral on stocks and slightly underweight to bonds. Barclays feels that the weak Canadian dollar will prompt a rate hike by the Bank of Canada, a move that will adversely affect bonds.

The stock holdings are TSE 100 companies—the large blue-chip issues that are consistent dividend payers. The top four equity positions are BCE, Royal Bank, Northern Telecom, and Bank of Montreal—all household names.

CANADIAN TACTICAL BALANCED

CALDWELL ASSOCIATE FUND
Thomas Caldwell (1990)/Caldwell Investment Management

CONSISTENCY

Performance Trend

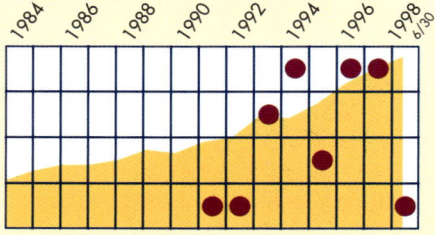

RISK

How often fund outperformed GICs	**6 years in 7**
How often fund lost money	**1 year in 7**
Worst year's rate of return	**-3.4% (1990)**

REWARD-TO-RISK RELATIONSHIP
SHARPE RATIO QUARTILE RANKINGS

3-Year	**4**
5-Year	**2**

EFFICIENCY/MER

Management expense/$100

$2.36

○ above average
● average
○ below average

STYLE

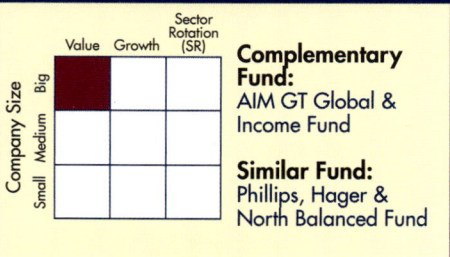

Complementary Fund:
AIM GT Global & Income Fund

Similar Fund:
Phillips, Hager & North Balanced Fund

CANADIAN TACTICAL BALANCED

Caldwell Investment Management uses a team approach to managing their funds. While a team approach generally protects a fund against the risk of a single manger leaving, Caldwell has had little to worry about given the long tenure of its eight-member team. The team's experienced members have a variety of backgrounds and skill sets that lead to interesting consensus building. The success of this approach has paved the way to a record of consistently good results.

The fund's objectives, as are those of most balanced funds, is capital appreciation while stressing the overall preservation of capital. The balanced fund is currently slanted toward equities with a particular focus on the metals and minerals and industrial product sectors.

The fund's largest exposure is in a Canadian Housing and Mortgage Corporation bond due in 2003 that constitutes a hefty 23.4% of the portfolio's value. The investment emphasis is on holding their investments longer term, which helps to reduce trading charges and defer capital gains taxes for taxable unitholders.

Caldwell feels confident in its current portfolio allocations. They contend that the economy will continue to grow, markets will flourish, and that commodities will make a comeback. The basis for the prediction is the belief that Asia will restructure and emerge as a stronger, more open economy, and that the overvalued U.S. dollar will prevent the U.S. economy from growing too strongly, thus avoiding the need for higher interest rates.

NEW

CLEAN ENVIRONMENT BALANCED FUND
Ian Ihnatowycz (inception)/Acuity Investment Management Inc.

CONSISTENCY

Performance Trend

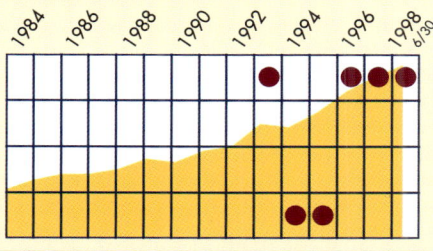

1984 1986 1988 1990 1992 1994 1996 1998 6/30

RISK

How often fund outperformed GICs	**4 years in 5**
How often fund lost money	**1 year in 5**
Worst year's rate of return	**-8.0% (1994)**

REWARD-TO-RISK RELATIONSHIP
SHARPE RATIO QUARTILE RANKINGS

3-Year	**1**
5-Year	**1**

EFFICIENCY/MER

Management expense/$100

$2.60

● above average
○ average
○ below average

STYLE

	Value	Growth	Sector Rotation (SR)

Company Size: Big / Medium / Small

Complementary Fund:
AGF American Tactical Asset Allocation Fund

Similar Fund:
Bissett Retirement Fund

The Clean Environment approach to investing is unique. To start with, the fund follows the Warren Buffet style, i.e., long-term, value investing. Beyond that, manager Ian Ihnatowycz has embraced the environmental concept of sustainable growth, which is "development that meets the needs of the present without compromising the ability of future generations to meet their own needs". Companies which develop the new technologies and processes that will provide solutions to the world's environmental problems will also provide, not coincidentally, excellent investment opportunities.

The asset mix is 47% equities, 24% cash, and 29% royalty trusts. We find this royalty trust weighting a little disconcerting. Despite what investors think, royalty trusts are not bond substitutes. In fact, they are not debt instruments at all, and the recent downturn in trust prices has acted as a reminder of this rather important fact. Thus, we think that calling this a balanced fund, in the traditional and generally accepted sense, is inaccurate and misleading.

CANADIAN TACTICAL BALANCED

BISSETT RETIREMENT FUND
Michael Quinn (1991-inception)/Bissett & Associates

CONSISTENCY

Performance Trend

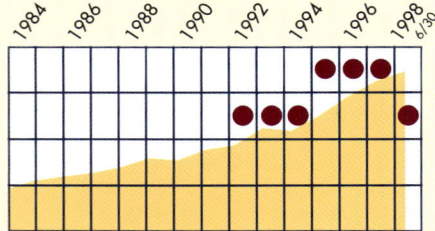

RISK

How often fund outperformed GICs	**4 years in 6**
How often fund lost money	**1 year in 6**
Worst year's rate of return	**-1.8% (1994)**

REWARD-TO-RISK RELATIONSHIP
SHARPE RATIO QUARTILE RANKINGS

3-Year	**1**
5-Year	**1**

EFFICIENCY/MER

Management expense/$100	○ above average
$0.44	○ average
	● below average

STYLE

Complementary Fund:
AIM GT Global Growth & Income Fund

Similar Fund:
McLean Budden Balanced Fund

Recognizing that a minimum of $10,000 per fund may be a little steep for some investors hoping to obtain a balanced portfolio, Bissett launched a "fund of funds" in 1991 which in turn invests in eight of its own funds. This approach allows an investor to gain access to a quality management team that has historically served up good results while incurring low fund fees. While widely diversified, its main investment is in the Bond Fund (40%) and Canadian Equity Funds (32%) allowing it to qualify as an RRSP-eligible fund. Factoring in the foreign component of the underlying Canadian funds boosts the foreign exposure of the Retirement Fund to 28%.

Mike Quinn, coincidentally, also manages the Bond Fund and the Canadian Equity Fund. In the former, the focus is on quality and government issues. In the equity fund, Quinn uses a company-by-company approach to selecting reasonably priced stocks that can demonstrate good earnings growth and returns on equity numbers.

The holdings reflect Quinn's opinion that we are in for a spell of stable interest rates and that the equity markets are fully valued. Quinn currently views the bond component as having less downside risk while contributing to the safety of capital and income; accordingly he has increased the Retirement Fund's exposure to the fixed income side.

The strong performance of the underlying funds with a successful asset allocation overlay has served up excess returns to investors without increasing the fund's volatility over that of competitive products.

CANADIAN STRATEGIC BALANCED

GLOBAL STRATEGY INCOME PLUS FUND
Tony Massie (1992-inception)/Global Strategy Financial

CONSISTENCY

Performance Trend

RISK

How often fund outperformed GICs	**4 years in 5**
How often fund lost money	**1 year in 5**
Worst year's rate of return	**-3.0% (1994)**

REWARD-TO-RISK RELATIONSHIP
SHARPE RATIO QUARTILE RANKINGS

3-Year	**1**
5-Year	**1**

EFFICIENCY/MER

Management expense/$100

$2.40

○ above average
● average
○ below average

STYLE

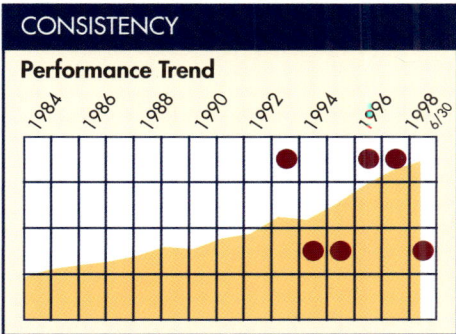

Complementary Fund:
C.I. International Balanced Fund

Similar Fund:
Phillips, Hager & North Balanced Fund

Massie's Global Strategy Income Plus Fund has been a solid first quartile performer over the past two years. He has convinced the critics by delivering returns, while maintaining the volatility of his portfolio below those of his peers.

Part of the fund's low volatility is Massie's willingness to sit on cash, currently at 20%, until he finds investment opportunities that meet his criteria for strong cash flows and prices that reflect low price-to-earnings and price-to-book value valuations. His approach differs from many that have merely mirrored the indices and gunned for the fast-moving targets like the banks. This different sense of value can only help the diversification within your portfolio, assuming you hold some standard funds.

The fund varies its allocations between cash, bonds, common and preferred shares based on economic indicators. Interestingly, they state the TSE 300 as being their benchmark but we don't agree given the fund's latitude (currently bonds at 30%), and suggest that an easy way to determine if Tony is adding value is to compare the returns to the average balanced fund. He does.

Another plus for the fund has been the reduction of the MER from last year's 2.63% to the current 2.40%, as assets under management have grown.

Yet another plus for some is the quarterly distribution of $0.35/unit which often comes in the tax-advantaged form of dividends and capital gains versus income or even a return of capital.

CANADIAN STRATEGIC BALANCED

INDUSTRIAL PENSION FUND
Bill Proctor (1994)/Mackenzie Financial Corporation

CONSISTENCY

Performance Trend

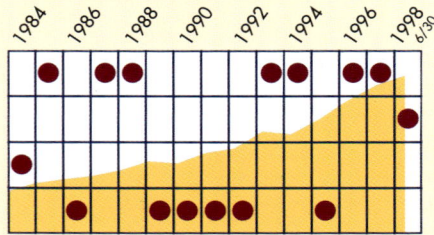

1984 1986 1988 1990 1992 1994 1996 1998 6/30

RISK

How often fund outperformed GICs	**11 years in 12**
How often fund lost money	**5 years in 12**
Worst year's rate of return	**-20.4% (1990)**

REWARD-TO-RISK RELATIONSHIP
SHARPE RATIO QUARTILE RANKINGS

3-Year	**1**
5-Year	**1**

EFFICIENCY/MER

Management expense/$100

$2.40

○ above average
● average
○ below average

STYLE

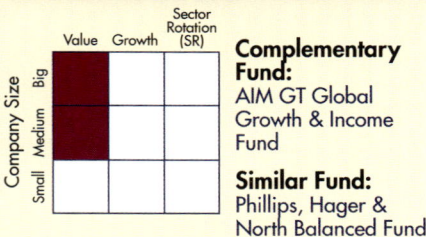

Value Growth / Sector Rotation (SR)

Company Size: Big / Medium / Small

Complementary Fund: AIM GT Global Growth & Income Fund

Similar Fund: Phillips, Hager & North Balanced Fund

Latte? Decaf? Regular or Grande? The dilemma of choice. Aggressive stocks because over the long haul they maximize wealth? A balanced fund to maximize sleep? Bill Proctor has come to your rescue. He's a little bit bonds (25%) and a lot of equity (75%). Compared to the more common mix within balanced funds that are generally around 60%, Mackenzie Financial predicted that there would be a market for this niche product.

And what do you know? The extra layer of cream in the form of returns resulting from soaring markets has beckoned balanced fund investors to ante up $320 million to the fund. And Proctor hasn't failed them.

Relying on his ability to pick stocks, the fund has handily beat the averages and benchmarks. Wary of the high valuations, Proctor has ramped up the cash allocation to 16%. He has also attempted to scale back the risk level of his equity component. Proctor is heavily weighted in financial services stocks as he contends that despite their huge run up in prices, they remain a value buy.

For those of you looking for a pre-packaged investment portfolio, be cognizant of the different allocation parameters permitted, as well as how much and how frequently shifts take place. For those who can tolerate a little more volatility, this fund may fit the bill.

IVY GROWTH & INCOME FUND
Jerry Javasky (1997)/Mackenzie Financial Corporation

CONSISTENCY

Performance Trend

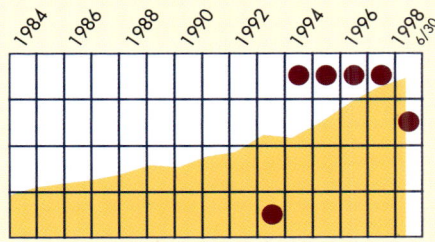

1984 1986 1988 1990 1992 1994 1996 1998 6/30

RISK

How often fund outperformed GICs	**4 years in 5**
How often fund lost money	**1 year in 5**
Worst year's rate of return	**-0.7% (1994)**

REWARD-TO-RISK RELATIONSHIP
SHARPE RATIO QUARTILE RANKINGS

3-Year	**1**
5-Year	**1**

EFFICIENCY/MER

Management expense/$100

$2.12

○ above average
● average
○ below average

STYLE

	Value	Growth	Sector Rotation (SR)
Big			
Medium			
Small			

Company Size

Complementary Fund:
AGF American Tactical Asset Allocation Fund

Similar Fund:
Standard Life Balanced Mutual Fund

If you're after a smooth ride and want quality and reputation, this fund could be the ticket. Everything about this fund smacks of conservatism without leaving all the upside on the table. Manager Jerry Javasky has the fund currently allocated 36% in bonds, 33% in Canadian equities, 5% in U.S. equities, 1% in U.K. equities, and 25% in cash equivalents. Although the percentages have changed over time (from December 31, 1997 to June 30, 1998, the equity allocation was reduced from 56% to 39%), Javasky's ability to post solid numbers while maintaining below-average volatility has helped ensconce the fund as a solid performer.

For this fund, Javasky compares himself to similar funds and only considers it a success if he attains higher returns at lower risk levels.

Within the fund's well-diversified equity component, Javasky searches for opportunities on a company-by-company basis and only makes the investment, if his strict value criteria are met. While searching for companies that have long-term growth potential, thoughts of capital preservation are never far away.

The bond strategy used by Javasky is not based on expectations of where interest rates are heading, but on whether the current fixed income environment rewards investors appropriately for the risks assumed. He also sticks to the quality stuff.

There is no doubt that the heavy allocation in cash will reduce return levels going forward until the next shift in allocation, but the accompanying reduced risk levels may just be what the good doctor ordered.

CANADIAN STRATEGIC BALANCED

MCLEAN BUDDEN BALANCED FUND
McLean Budden Asset Mix Group (inception)

CONSISTENCY

Performance Trend

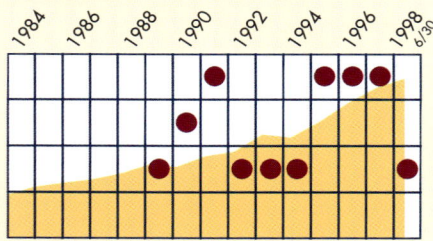

1984 1986 1988 1990 1992 1994 1996 1998 6/30

RISK

How often fund outperformed GICs	**6 years in 9**
How often fund lost money	**2 years in 9**
Worst year's rate of return	**-4.2% (1994)**

REWARD-TO-RISK RELATIONSHIP
SHARPE RATIO QUARTILE RANKINGS

3-Year	**1**
5-Year	**2**

EFFICIENCY/MER

Management expense/$100

$1.75

○ above average
○ average
● below average

STYLE

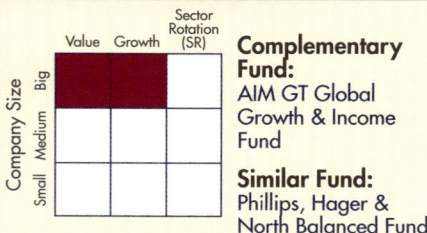

Company Size: Big, Medium, Small
Value, Growth, Sector Rotation (SR)

Complementary Fund:
AIM GT Global Growth & Income Fund

Similar Fund:
Phillips, Hager & North Balanced Fund

This is another winning fund from the McLean Budden group. Consistent with their general approach to management, the fund is managed by a team of five. This approach keeps the dynamics of asset allocation and security selection relatively consistent over time.

Within the classification, this fund is relatively conservative; its current asset allocation is 51% in equities, 41% in bonds with the balance in cash. Most balanced funds are currently pushing 60% or more in equities. Despite its relative under-weighting in equities, which have experienced superior returns, it has still kept pace return-wise.

The equity component is based on stock picking with the target being growth companies. Diversification is achieved by maintaining a wide exposure to the various sectors. Its foreign content is focused mainly in the U.S. If the management team does find any attractively priced international equities, they generally buy the corresponding American Depository Receipt (ADR). These are trust receipts traded on an American exchange that represent ownership in the underlying non-American company—just an easier way to buy international stocks.

PHILLIPS, HAGER & NORTH BALANCED FUND

P H & N Management team (inception)

CONSISTENCY

Performance Trend

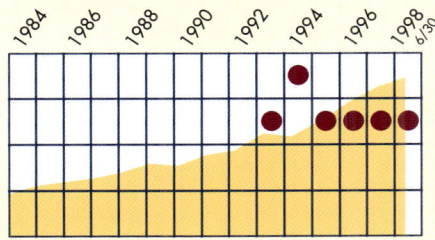

1984 1986 1988 1990 1992 1994 1996 1998 6/30

RISK

How often fund outperformed GICs	**4 years in 5**
How often fund lost money	**0 years in 5**
Worst year's rate of return	**0.4% (1994)**

REWARD-TO-RISK RELATIONSHIP
SHARPE RATIO QUARTILE RANKINGS

3-Year	**2**
5-Year	**1**

EFFICIENCY/MER

Management expense/$100

$0.91

○ above average
○ average
● below average

STYLE

Company Size: Big / Medium / Small
Value / Growth / Sector Rotation (SR)

Complementary Fund:
AIM GT Global Growth & Income Fund

Similar Fund:
McLean Budden Balanced Fund

As you would expect from a strong and consistently performing fund family, PH & N has delivered a historically solid balanced fund.

PH & N Balanced, managed by a team, invests both directly in securities and in its family of funds. Compared to a number of its peers, it has a relatively low allocation toward equities (approximately 52%) while maintaining a healthy cash balance of 9%. With the stock markets' amazing run over the last couple of years, this conservatism has kept the fund from hitting the first quartile but it has also never ranked lower than the second quartile.

Within its equity component, once past the heavier allocation to financial services and industrial products, the fund is nicely diversified across the various sectors. There is also a decent foreign equity component adding further diversification.

The end result is a solid, conservative fund that shouldn't turn you into an insomniac. While the returns have not reached the stratosphere, investors have not had to pay a high-risk penalty.

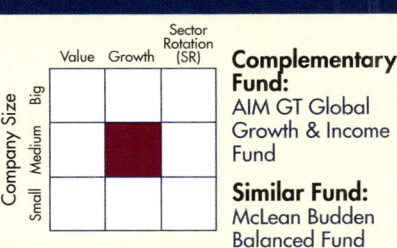

CANADIAN STRATEGIC BALANCED

SAXON BALANCED FUND
Richard Howson (1991)/Howson Tattersall Investment Counsel

CONSISTENCY

Performance Trend

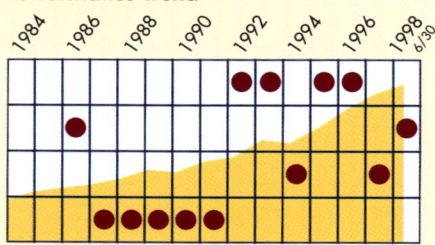

1984 1986 1988 1990 1992 1994 1996 1998 6/30

RISK

How often fund outperformed GICs	**7 years in 12**
How often fund lost money	**3 years in 12**
Worst year's rate of return	**-15.8% (1987)**

REWARD-TO-RISK RELATIONSHIP
SHARPE RATIO QUARTILE RANKINGS

3-Year	**3**
5-Year	**2**

EFFICIENCY/MER

Management expense/$100

$1.75

○ above average
○ average
● below average

STYLE

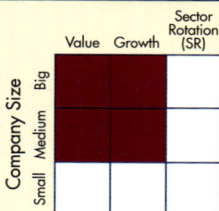

Complementary Fund:
AGF American Tactical Asset Allocation Fund

Similar Fund:
Industrial Pension Fund

Small can be beautiful. And if not beautiful, at least different. Saxon's Balanced Fund managed by Richard Howson only has $11 million in net assets, likely because its performance hasn't shot the lights out. A terrible fund shortly after it was launched, it has settled down over the past four years to become a more mature, solid performer.

Howson manages the fund by concentrating on excess returns after inflation. The focus on real returns (actual returns less inflation) dovetails well with investors, who are concerned with combating inflation leading up to and during their retirement.

One added benefit of this fund is that it is not like every other fund. Its top ten equity holdings are quite different from others showing Howson's experience, confidence, and refusal to partake in consensus investing.

The fund's normalized allocation is 55% in stock, 40% in bonds, and 5% in cash equivalents. However, Howson is currently running at 64% in stock, 29% in bonds, and 7% in cash , as he believes that the moderate growth and low inflation environment is here for a while. He is particularly keen on retail and food services, given the accelerating job creation and the re-emergence of the Canadian consumer. He also likes the low valuations currently found in the oil patch, as well as the widening yields over government treasuries offered by income trusts.

This is not the only fund that you would want to own, but due to its uniqueness it may be an appropriate addition to an overall portfolio.

SCEPTRE BALANCED GROWTH FUND
Lyle Stein (1993)/Sceptre Investment Counsel

CONSISTENCY

Performance Trend

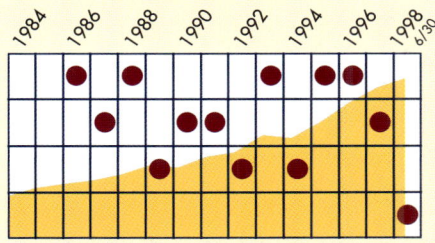

RISK

How often fund outperformed GICs	**8 years in 12**
How often fund lost money	**2 years in 12**
Worst year's rate of return	**-4.2% (1994)**

REWARD-TO-RISK RELATIONSHIP
SHARPE RATIO QUARTILE RANKINGS

3-Year	**2**
5-Year	**1**

EFFICIENCY/MER

Management expense/$100

$1.44

○ above average
○ average
● below average

STYLE

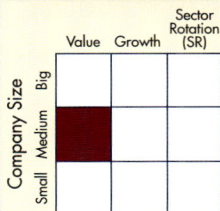

Complementary Fund:
AIM GT Global Growth & Income Fund

Similar Fund:
Bissett Retirement Fund

Lyle Stein exudes a sense of loyalty toward his investment policy, his investment selections, and the fund's unitholders.

Recognizing that the asset class decisions within a balanced fund are critical to a balanced fund's performance, he currently has the Balanced Growth Fund at equal equity and bond weightings as he is in a defensive mode.

Stein generally holds his stocks for an average of three years and adds to his long-term bond positions on unjustified price dips. Part of his bottom-up value style dictates that there is relative value in industrials, transportation, and oil and gas stocks. He recognizes that the market's hunt for liquidity has propelled financials ahead, hurting his relative performance in the process. Stein is not about to jump on the bandwagon, but he is scaling back his small-cap exposure due to continuing negative market sentiment.

With regards to his bosses, the unitholders, his attitude is that they will stick with him and that it is his responsibility to see them through thick and thin. Accordingly, thinking more of investors that have enjoyed his success instead of trying to attract new ones, he is more concerned with protecting the winnings on the table instead of lunging ahead during what he perceives as one of the final stages of the bull. His mantra is to focus on the return **of** capital instead of the return **on** capital. If this conservatism causes his ranking to suffer somewhat, he can live with it.

Those readers seeking further comfort may find it in the fact that this fund was the Balanced Fund of the Year in 1996 and 1997 at the Canadian Mutual Fund Awards.

CANADIAN STRATEGIC BALANCED

RRSP 🍁

STANDARD LIFE BALANCED MUTUAL FUND
Standard Life Portfolio Management (inception)

CONSISTENCY

Performance Trend

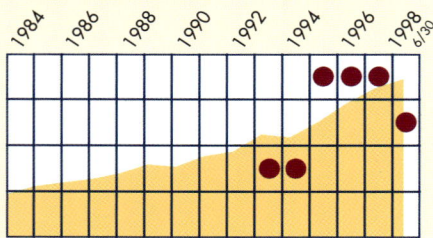

1984 1986 1988 1990 1992 1994 1996 1998 6/30

RISK

How often fund outperformed GICs	**4 years in 5**
How often fund lost money	**1 year in 5**
Worst year's rate of return	**-3.6% (1994)**

REWARD-TO-RISK RELATIONSHIP
SHARPE RATIO QUARTILE RANKINGS

3-Year	**1**
5-Year	**1**

EFFICIENCY/MER

Management expense/$100

$2.00

○ above average
● average
○ below average

STYLE

	Value	Growth	Sector Rotation (SR)
Big			
Medium			
Small			

Company Size

Complementary Fund:
AIM GT Global Growth & Income Fund

Similar Fund:
Phillips, Hager & North Balanced Fund

With 78% of the portfolio committed to bonds and cash, the managers at Standard Life Portfolio Management don't need to tell us their views on the equity markets or their thoughts on the prospects for interest rates. As recently as May of 1998, the fund had only 47% of the portfolio invested in fixed income and cash. The balance was in Canadian and U.S. equities. Clearly, they believe that bonds offer more value at this time.

The mandate is to provide superior capital appreciation and a steady income stream while limiting short-term risk . Investments are selected with an emphasis on quality and liquidity. Investors expect a degree of conservatism in a balanced fund, but not at the expense of performance. Standard Life Balanced has been a top quartile performer over the past three years, while still exhibiting low volatility.

U.S. securities make up the 20% foreign content limit because the managers feel North American markets will still benefit from the continuing low interest rate environment.

CANADIAN STRATEGIC BALANCED

AGF AMERICAN TACTICAL ASSET ALLOCATION FUND
Kathy Taylor (1996)/Barclays Global Investors (inception)

CONSISTENCY

Performance Trend

1984 1986 1988 1990 1992 1994 1996 1998 6/30

RISK

How often fund outperformed GICs	**6 years in 9**
How often fund lost money	**0 years in 9**
Worst year's rate of return	**0.6% (1994)**

REWARD-TO-RISK RELATIONSHIP
SHARPE RATIO QUARTILE RANKINGS

3-Year	**1**
5-Year	**1**

EFFICIENCY/MER

Management expense/$100

$2.56

○ above average
● average
○ below average

STYLE

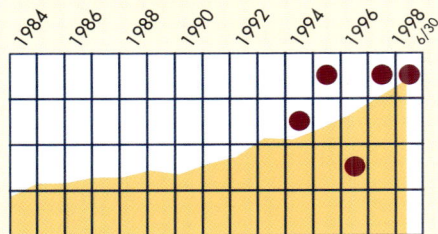

Company Size: Big / Medium / Small
Value / Growth / Sector Rotation (SR)

Complementary Fund:
Clean Environment Balanced Fund

Similar Fund:
Fidelity Global Asset Allocation Fund

Making a return appearance as a Top Fund, this U.S. asset allocation fund has yet to have a losing calendar year since its inception in 1988. AGF's sub-advisor, San Francisco-based Barclays Global Investors, utilizes a proprietary quantitative approach to security selection. The manager, Kathy Taylor, has been at the helm since 1996. The fund's current split between asset classes, 65% in equities and 35% in bonds, approximates the allocation adopted by most of the competing funds.

This fund has beaten the U.S. and international balanced fund average by focusing on large-cap U.S. stocks and risk-free Treasury Bills to produce both capital growth and income. Helping performance in this long-lasting bull market has been the maintenance of a minimal cash balance, a reasonable management fee expense ratio, and an increasing allocation toward equities.

Being an asset allocation fund as opposed to a balanced fund, allows greater latitude in adjusting the fund's exposure between asset classes. Compared to the fund's benchmark of the S&P 500 (60%) and the Lehman Brothers 20+ Year Treasury Bond (40%) indices, Taylor is currently over-weighted in equities at 65%, given her view that inflation fears will dominate the bond market in the second half of 1998. Taylor has deftly managed to complete the various market timing re-balancings without creating huge tax liabilities for investors holding the fund outside their RRSPs.

GLOBAL BALANCED

NEW

1997/1998 RRSP

AIM GT GLOBAL GROWTH & INCOME FUND
Nick Train (inception)/LGT Asset Management Inc.

CONSISTENCY

Performance Trend

1984 1986 1988 1990 1992 1994 1996 1998 6/30

RISK

How often fund outperformed GICs	**3 years in 3**
How often fund lost money	**0 years in 3**
Worst year's rate of return	**11.9% (1996)**

REWARD-TO-RISK RELATIONSHIP
SHARPE RATIO QUARTILE RANKINGS

3-Year	**1**
5-Year	**N/A**

EFFICIENCY/MER

Management expense/$100	● above average
$2.87	○ average
	○ below average

STYLE

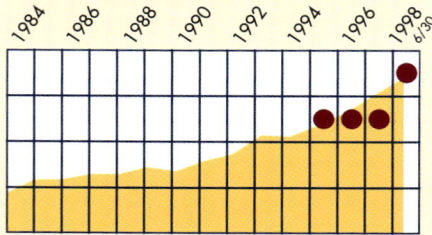

Company Size: Big, Medium, Small
Value, Growth, Sector Rotation (SR)

Complementary Fund:
Saxon Balanced fund

Similar Fund:
C.I. International Balanced Fund

Perhaps more than any other fund category, global balanced funds truly have the world as their oyster. For example, the mandate of AIM GT Global Growth & Income Fund is to invest in blue-chip securities and high quality government bonds of issuers in Canada, the U.S., and throughout the world. From this wide array of choices, managers Nick Train and Paul Griffiths of LGT Asset Management Inc. have created a portfolio that consists of 58 stocks and 11 bonds. The stocks represent 68% of the portfolio, bonds 20%, and cash holdings 12%.

Currently, Europe is favoured with 52% of total assets, while North American securities total 32% of the portfolio, and Asia-Pacific an insignificant 4%. Union Bank of Switzerland shares and a seven-year U.S. Treasury bond share top billing with 6.3% of the assets each. Eight of the top ten equity positions are financial issues, a portfolio mix that reflects the management view about interest rates and the effect of the world-wide financial sector merger mania on share prices.

C.I. INTERNATIONAL BALANCED FUND
William Sterling (1994)/BEA Associates

CONSISTENCY

Performance Trend

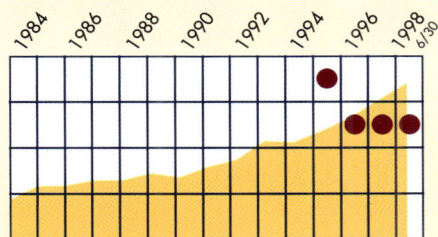

1984 1986 1988 1990 1992 1994 1996 1998 6/30

RISK

How often fund outperformed GICs	3 years in 3
How often fund lost money	0 years in 3
Worst year's rate of return	13.0% (1996)

REWARD-TO-RISK RELATIONSHIP
SHARPE RATIO QUARTILE RANKINGS

3-Year	1
5-Year	N/A

EFFICIENCY/MER

Management expense/$100

$2.41

○ above average
○ average
● below average

STYLE

Complementary Fund:
Saxon Balanced Fund

Similar Fund:
Fidelity Global Asset Allocation Fund

This fund could also be called the C.I. U.S. and Europe Balanced Fund. Manager Bill Sterling of New York-based BEA Associates is concerned about Asia and favours the U.S. and Europe almost exclusively. His geographic allocation is 62% to those two regions and 28% to cash, with a tiny 3.2% exposure to Latin America, 2.5% to Japan, and a microscopic 0.6% weighting to other Asian markets. He doesn't ignore the risks involved with the U.S. market, however, as his large cash position implies. Sterling has also reduced his equity weighting to 55% from 60%. He is less confident that equities will outperform bonds over the next 12 months. Sterling still has confidence in Europe, which is earlier in its economic cycle and has increased his holdings there.

GLOBAL BALANCED

NEW

RRSP

FIDELITY GLOBAL ASSET ALLOCATION FUND

Dick Habermann (1996)+Steve Snider+Charles Morrison (1997)/Fidelity Investments Ltd.

CONSISTENCY

Performance Trend

1984 1986 1988 1990 1992 1994 1996 1998 6/30

RISK

How often fund outperformed GICs	**3 years in 4**
How often fund lost money	**1 year in 4**
Worst year's rate of return	**-4.1% (1994)**

REWARD-TO-RISK RELATIONSHIP
SHARPE RATIO QUARTILE RANKINGS

3-Year	**1**
5-Year	**2**

EFFICIENCY/MER

Management expense/$100

$2.70

○ above average
● average
○ below average

STYLE

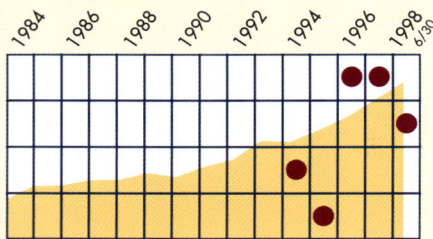

Company Size: Small / Medium / Big
Value / Growth / Sector Rotation (SR)

Complementary Fund:
Clean Environment Balanced Fund

Similar Fund:
AGF Canadian Tactical Asset Allocation Fund

GLOBAL BALANCED

Fidelity's traditional strength and world-wide research capabilities are fully utilized in this fund. Their asset allocation style is to assign each sub-portfolio to a dedicated manager who is then overseen by a lead manager, who has the asset allocation responsibility. The asset allocation decision is determined by a combination of fundamental, bottom-up research, and a computer model that helps determine the optimal weightings. Risk reduction is an important issue and reducing the volatility of returns is an important consideration.

Lead manager Dick Habermann, along with the equity managers, Steve Snider and Charles Morrison, who look after the fixed income side, have currently a "neutral" asset mix, i.e., 70% equities, 25% fixed income, and 5% cash. They feel that the previous asset mix, which was overweighted in equities, is no longer justified as market volatility and the Asian situation make a cautious approach necessary.

They like the U.S. markets, despite the lofty valuations. About 59% of the assets are U.S. investments, with many other countries also represented. In fact, the total holdings add up to a staggering 989. These guys take diversification seriously!

NEW

MACKENZIE STAR INVESTMENT CONSERVATIVE INCOME AND GROWTH PORTFOLIO
Gordon Garmaise (inception)/
Garmaise Investment Technologies

CONSISTENCY

Performance Trend

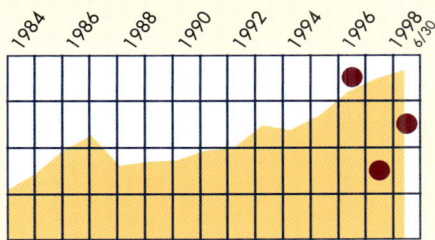

1984 1986 1988 1990 1992 1994 1996 1998 6/30

RISK

How often fund outperformed GICs	**2 years in 2**
How often fund lost money	**0 years in 2**
Worst year's rate of return	**7.8% (1997)**

REWARD-TO-RISK RELATIONSHIP
SHARPE RATIO QUARTILE RANKINGS

3-Year	**N/A**
5-Year	**N/A**

EFFICIENCY/MER

Management expense/$100

$N/A

○ above average
○ average
○ below average

STYLE

	Value	Growth	Sector Rotation (SR)
Big			
Medium			
Small			

Company Size

Complementary Fund:
AGF American Tactical Asset Allocation Fund

Similar Fund:
Saxon Balanced Fund

We admit that we've broken the rules a little bit here. Mackenzie STAR is not a single mutual fund, but an asset allocation/asset optimization program that has been a pioneer in bringing investment technology to the world of retail investing. Gordon Garmaise, creator of the STAR program, has designed 17 portfolios* that combine various members of the Mackenzie fund family into semi-custom "optimal" portfolios. Investor risk tolerances are determined by a questionnaire, with a scoring system that recommends an appropriate portfolio. The process is dynamic; portfolios are rebalanced and reallocated when the expected risk/return characteristics of the portfolios change. Since 1995, three rebalances have occurred, the latest in July, 1998.

We are advocates of asset allocation, and especially like systemized approaches that utilize technology and sound, research-based investment principles. We like Garmaise's methodology and we like his results. He was the first to popularize the "optimal" portfolio approach and for that he deserves inclusion in Top Funds.

We've chosen STAR Investment Conservative Income and Growth to represent the program. The investment policy for this portfolio is to invest approximately 60% of fund assets in three fixed income funds, with the balance allocated across Canadian, U.S., European and precious metals funds. The geographic weighting is currently 55% Canada, 19% U.S., 21% Europe, and 5% the rest of the world. In other words, a global balanced fund. Volatility is remarkably low, and in fact only one other global balanced fund sold in Canada is less volatile, based on the three-year standard deviation of returns.

ASSET ALLOCATION SERVICES

*See Monster Tables, page 300.

167

TOP FUNDS
FUND COMPANY OF THE YEAR: AGF

It was a close race this year as AGF nosed out both Fidelity Canada and 1998's champ, Mackenzie Financial.

In Chinese folklore, 1998 is the Year of the Tiger. AGF, with its well-known orange and black tiger logo, may have had more in its favour than most. The underlying theme of the Year of the Tiger is "breathing in new life and vitality", which is what AGF has had to accomplish over the past few years. After limping along for a number of years with modest returns, AGF, one of Canada's oldest mutual funds with $15 billion under management, had to re-establish itself with Canadian investors.

Its 1996 takeover of the 20/20 family of funds underscored the seriousness with which AGF applied itself to the challenge. It has updated and revamped its product line. It has attempted to foster more open communication within the firm so that good ideas know no boundaries. It has recognized the limitations of its own investment management skills and accordingly, has hired well-established sub-managers to do the job in markets where AGF lacks the presence or expertise. A good long hard look in the mirror can often inspire a change for the better; it seems to have happened at AGF. The naysayers may not believe that the tiger's stripes have changed, but a review of the company's fund returns indicates that they have improved dramatically.

AGF can boast **nine** Top Funds this year. That's the same number that Mackenzie posted last year, and ties for the largest number of Top Funds by a fund company since our first edition in 1995.

1. AGF Dividend Fund
2. AGF American Growth Class Fund
3. AGF International Value Fund
4. AGF International Group Germany Class Fund
5. AGF Canadian Tactical Asset Allocation Fund
6. AGF American Tactical Asset Allocation Fund
7. AGF Canadian Bond
8. 20/20 Canadian Resources Fund
9. 20/20 Latin American Fund

From a Canadian perspective, AGF has always had an international bent as it offered American (1957) and Japanese (1969) funds early in the game. In fact, five out of its nine Top Funds are international in nature

Using the overriding principle of long-term investing, AGF is building a research platform and infrastructure which it hopes will allow it to replicate its recent successes well into the future, in both bull and bear markets.

RUNNER UP: MACKENZIE FINANCIAL CORPORATION

Another strong performance was turned in this year by Mackenzie Financial, which was last year's Fund Company of the Year. A wide array of Mackenzie funds continue to perform exceptionally well and fulfill client expectations. Of particular note in this year's book is the inclusion of Mackenzie's STAR program as a Top Fund. This asset allocation service, which invests in other Mackenzie funds, has not only been hugely popular with Canadians, but has also registered solid numbers. Within the industry, Mackenzie is recognized as a proactive force with enough diversity in its fund line-up to not only appeal to a wide spectrum of different investors, but to the same investors over time as their needs and objectives change.

Among its eight Top Funds, Mackenzie received representation from its Ivy (bottom-up, value and growth), Industrial (top-down, value), and Universal group of funds. For next year, we expect good things to come from its recent alliance with Peter Cundill & Associates. This will form their fourth fund family and will significantly bolster the diversity of management style available under the Mackenzie umbrella.

Mackenzie contributed **eight** funds to the 100 Top Funds this year:

1. Ivy Canadian
2. Industrial Dividend Growth Fund
3. Universal Canadian Resources
4. Universal European Opportunities Fund
5. Universal World Income RSP Fund
6. Industrial Pension
7. Ivy Growth & Income
8. STAR Investment Conservative Income & Growth Portfolio

RUNNER UP: FIDELITY

Although Fidelity's Canadian operations only started in late 1987, its $17 billion in investor money under management makes it Canada's sixth largest mutual fund company already. Fidelity did not start from ground zero in Canada; its American parent has been in business since 1946 and has amassed $750 billion in funds under management, making it among the largest in the world. While it is the combination of investment performance, client service, and savvy marketing that has driven Fidelity ahead so quickly, it is the performance where it earns its kudos from us.

Acknowledged as the leader in investment research, its Boston-based investment management style has allowed it to develop its global brand. But it has not been without adversity, as Fidelity has been forced on occasion to change managers and methods to achieve its success To date, they have been successful due to their ability to focus. And what Fidelity continually focuses on is your long-term investment returns, knowing that this is the only way to keep your money under management. While size alone does not dictate better investment performance, Fidelity's formula of dedicating huge resources toward their global managers has obviously borne fruit.

Fidelity has **eight** funds on our Top Funds roster this year:

① Fidelity Canadian Growth Company Fund

② Fidelity Growth America Fund

③ Fidelity International Portfolio Fund

④ Fidelity European Growth Fund

⑤ Fidelity Far East Fund

⑥ Fidelity Canadian Income Fund

⑦ Fidelity Emerging Markets Bond Fund

⑧ Fidelity Global Asset Allocation Fund

HONOURABLE MENTIONS

Following the leaders closely was **Bissett** with 6 funds, and **Phillips, Hager & North** with 5.

AIC, BPI, C.I., and **Templeton** all placed 4 Top Funds on our list.

Former Fund Companies of the Year fell on tougher times this year. **Dynamic**, which won the award in 1995, placed 3 funds; **Trimark**, which won in 1997, placed 2; and **Altamira**, which won in 1996, placed only 1. How the mighty have fallen!

UP AND COMERS

Our methodology excludes any fund with less than a three-year track record. Why? Well, because we feel that luck, and not management skill, could easily produce a fund with wonderful performance over the short term. Focusing on short term performance also runs counter to our deeply held belief that investing is a long process.

So we're going out on a limb here and are picking four newcomers that we feel have the potential to be Top Funds in the future. They're great performers, but more importantly, have unique approaches and management styles or are exposed to sectors that we feel hold great promise. We believe that these attributes will bode well for these funds in both bull and bear markets.

Scudder Canadian Equity

The Scudder family of mutual funds opened up shop in Canada to much fanfare in 1995. The oldest investment counsel firm in North America, Boston-based Scudder felt that their achievements in the U.S. marketplace would translate to equal success north of the border. Unfortunately, they underestimated the strength of Canada's existing distribution networks and sales were dismal. Investor interest in the Scudder offerings has picked up, however. The reason? Good returns and low fees.

Scudder Canadian Equity is the company's flagship fund. Managed out of San Francisco by Phil Fortuna, this fund has been one of the top five Canadian equity funds over the past two years. Taking advantage of Scudder's prodigious research capabilities, Fortuna has crafted a low volatility portfolio of stocks that is well diversified across sector and industry. He is a value manager who uses computerized model techniques to root out undervalued investment opportunities.

A no-load fund, Scudder Canadian Equity's MER is a rock bottom 1.3%. That compares favourably with the Canadian equity fund's average MER of 2.13%, and goes a long way to explain why this fund is a top performer and is likely to remain so.

CIBC U.S. Index RRSP

The goal of manager Bich Pham of T.A.L. Investment Counsel is to duplicate the performance of the S & P 500 Index. Research indicates that most active fund managers have a very difficult time beating that index, so if you can't beat 'em, join 'em. The advantage of this approach is that the research and transaction costs are low, which translates to a low MER of only 0.9%.

Pham's approach is to invest in options and futures contracts on the S & P 500 Index. The bulk of the remaining cash is invested in high quality short-term bonds, debentures, and corporate paper. The result is a portfolio that only slightly underperforms the S & P, but at a lower level of volatility. As an added bonus, CIBC U.S. Index RRSP, as the name implies, is 100% eligible as Canadian content for RRSP purposes.

The fund has been a first quartile performer from the very beginning. It would be an excellent choice as a core holding in a diversified portfolio, especially if matched with an actively-managed, value type U.S. equity fund.

Altamira High Yield Bond Fund

Altamira Investment Services has been in the news a lot this year. Unfortunately, not for the right reasons. The publicity surrounding the company ownership battles, the high profile resignations, and the poor performance of the Altamira Equity Fund should not disguise the fact that the company still has some excellent fund offerings. The High Yield Bond Fund is one of them.

Manager Barry Allan's challenge is to manage a portfolio of high yield bonds that are high yield for a reason: investors wouldn't touch them unless the high yield incentive was there. Also known as "junk bonds", they do have the risk of default and it takes a savvy manager like Allan to manage that risk. Unlike most fixed income funds, where the analysis of the default risk is an almost perfunctory process, Allan must use an equity analysis approach to his security selection.

This fund should not be a core holding in a portfolio, but it certainly does provide yield enhancement. The fund has had a stellar 16.0% return over the past two years.

C.I. Global Telecommunications Sector Shares

As economists and market analysts scratch their heads over how the world's developed nations have achieved the seemingly incongruous combination of strong economic growth and low inflation, the success of this fund provides a clue. The credit can be attributed to the role of technology, especially telecommunications and computers in creating business efficiencies and productivity advances. This fund has tapped into this phenomenon, and indeed, its performance has been phenomenal! Returning 51.4% over the past two years, the fund mandate is to invest in companies throughout the world that specialize in the development, manufacture or sale of telecommunications services or equipment, or that supply goods and services to such companies.

Manager Stephen Waite of BEA Associates has holdings which are widely diversified around the globe. His largest holdings are in the U.S., but he has representation in Hong Kong, Canada, France, Germany, and the U.K., as well as other parts of Europe and Central and South America.

This is certainly a niche fund, but it's one that is appropriate for aggressive investors wishing to be exposed to a sector of the economy that holds great promise going into the new millennium.

HOW TO BUILD A TOP FUNDS PORTFOLIO

We believe that the research findings presented in the *Top Funds* listings can be valuable to individual investors, but only if they are applied. Knowledge is **not** power; *applied* knowledge is.

So let's get started on building your Top Funds portfolio.

THE IMPORTANCE OF ASSET ALLOCATION

What is the most critical factor in successful mutual fund investing? Like many people, you may believe that it all depends on picking the "right" fund — the one with the best numbers. But as most fund managers know, consistently high returns do not depend on putting money into specific securities; rather, they depend on putting money into the right *types* of securities. The same rule applies to mutual fund investing: put your money into the right fund categories, and chances are you'll be further ahead in the long run.

The categories of funds you choose — and the weighting of each category relative to the portfolio as a whole — is known as asset allocation. And research has shown that it accounts for between 85% and 92% of the difference in total returns in a broadly diversified portfolio. (By contrast, the same research puts the contribution of security selection — that is, choice of specific investments — at only about 2%!)

Clearly, the overriding decision in the development of any investment portfolio is the mix of assets within it. Traditionally, however, individual investors have given the **least** consideration to this **most important** decision.

Conversely, the selection of individual components (securities) is of relatively little importance. Yet investors usually spend the most time and energy in making this **least significant** decision.

WHAT ASSET CATEGORIES SHOULD BE INCLUDED?

A well-balanced portfolio should include the following:

Fixed income investments, such as

- Cash or cash equivalents (CSBs, term deposits, Treasury Bills) to provide liquidity for an emergency or an opportunity

- Canadian bonds for stability and high income

- International bonds for protection against Canadian interest-rate risk

Equity (stock) investments, such as

- Canadian equities, to participate in our growth via a number of world-class Canadian success stories

- International equities, to hedge the "Canada risk" and for the broadest possible range of investment choices

- Real estate, for inflation protection with tax benefits and income

- Precious metals, including gold, for protection from inflation and crisis

- Oil and gas, for inflation protection with tax benefits and income

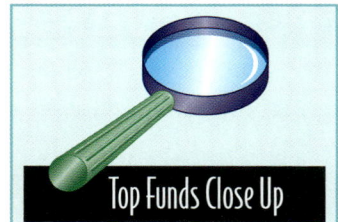

Top Funds Close Up

Why some investors do worse than their own funds

It's not how the funds do that matters. It's how the investors do! U.S. data confirm what we've long suspected in Canada; many people trade funds like they trade stocks — badly! The ease of entry and exit to and from no-load, direct-purchase funds makes them the perfect vehicle for trading, but a study by Boston-based Dalbar Inc. shows that investors in no-load funds do trade more, and earn less overall — even though no-load funds' performance is equal to load funds.

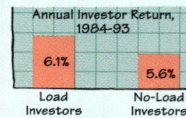

Annual Investor Return, 1984-93

6.1%	5.6%
Load Investors	No-Load Investors

How come?
No-load investors hold for just 12 months.

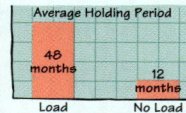

Average Holding Period

48 months	12 months
Load	No Load

And do-it-yourselfers buy high! They had twice the relative buying activity of load investors during the January '87 peak rally of 13.4% in the S&P 500; three times in the August '87 peak; and boy, did they sell en masse after the October '87

Buy	Buy	Sell
		No Load
	No Load	
No Load		
Load	Load	Load

Source: *1995 Qualitative Analysis of Investor Behaviour, DALBAR Financial Services Inc.*

WHAT'S THE RIGHT BALANCE FOR ME?

There is no "perfect" asset mix that's right for every investor. It will vary from person to person, depending on factors such as *time horizon*, *investment objectives*, and *risk tolerance*.

Here are some super-simplified guidelines that will help you approximate the mix that's right for you:

● 1. Start with your age

The total percentage of your portfolio held in fixed income investments (that is, cash and cash equivalents, as well as government and corporate bonds) should approximately match your age. So if you have a $100,000 portfolio and you are 40 years old, about $40,000 should be in fixed income. This is a very rough rule of thumb, but without a questionnaire or interview, this is the best way for you to start on your own.

● 2. Assess your risk tolerance

Imagine a scale ranging from 1 to 10, where a "1" represents the most pathologically cautious, nervous type of investor — the sort of person who keeps his money under the mattress because he's certain the banks will collapse. A "10" is (or would like to be) a professional gambler.

Which number are you? Our experience is that nearly everyone has an intuitive sense of where they fall on the scale.

● 3. Adjust your fixed income percentage

Here we combine the previous two factors: **age** and **risk tolerance**.

If your risk tolerance is in the middle of the scale at "5," then make no adjustment to the fixed income component of your portfolio based on your age.

For every number **higher** than 5, reduce the fixed income component by 5%. For example, if you are 40 years old and rate yourself a "7" on the risk tolerance scale, reduce your fixed income component by 10% — in this case, from 40% to 30%.

MODIFYING THE "AGE RULE"										
Percentage variation to the Fixed Income/Equity Split										
Tolerance Risk *(1-10)* Investment Split	1	2	3	4	5	6	7	8	9	10
Fixed Income	+20	+15	+10	+5	age	-5	-10	-15	-20	-25
Equity	-20	-15	-10	-5	only	+5	+10	+15	+20	+25

For every number **lower** than 5, add 5% to the fixed income component. For example, if you are 40 years old and rate yourself a "2" on the risk tolerance scale, **increase** your fixed income component by 15% — in this case, from 40% to 55%.

Notice that the effect of these guidelines is to increase the conservative component of your portfolio as you become less aggressive.

WHAT ABOUT THE OTHER ASSET WEIGHTINGS?

Again, this will vary from person to person. But let's continue with the example of our 40-year-old investor who ranks a "5" on the risk-tolerance scale.

For this individual, a reasonable balance might look like this:

How do we know that this balance will work? Well, history is on our side, as you'll see — just study the table shown below. It outlines the portfolio that's been developed for our 40-year-old

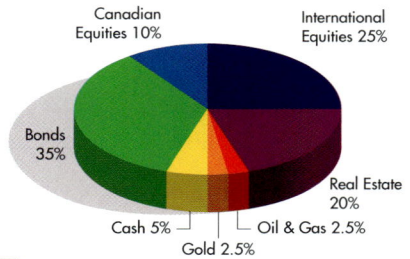

investor. As you'll see, it shows that a balanced portfolio has offered a number of major advantages over this period.

RETURNS BY ASSET TYPE

Asset Allocation Year	5% Cash	35% Bonds	10% Canadian Equities	25% International Equities	20% Real Estate	2.50% Oil & Gas	2.50% Gold	100% Balanced Portfolio
1978	9	4	30	21	12	16	8	13
1979	12	-3	45	14	13	82	91	15
1980	13	7	30	33	23	46	43	21
1981	18	4	-10	-5	26	-29	-38	4
1982	14	35	6	21	1	-14	39	20
1983	9	12	36	25	7	19	-2	16
1984	11	15	-2	16	12	-19	-20	11
1985	10	21	25	40	10	11	33	24
1986	9	15	9	29	13	-2	29	17
1987	8	4	6	5	14	18	17	7
1988	9	10	11	10	17	-8	-28	10
1989	12	13	21	21	20	25	5	17
1990	13	8	-15	-12	5	-10	1	0
1991	9	22	12	22	0	-9	-12	14
1992	7	10	-1	6	-6	23	2	5
1993	6	18	33	22	-4	68	83	18
1994	5	-4	0	10	2	-12	-3	1
1995	8	21	15	26	5	13	-17	17
1996	5	12	28	19	6	51	22	15
1997	3	10	15	30	8	-9	-34	13
Average	10	12	15	18	9	14	11	13
Variation high to low	13	39	60	52	32	111	129	24
# of years of positive rates	19	17	15	17	17	11	13	19
# of years of negative rates	0	2	4	2	2	8	6	0

Courtesy of The Equion Group

Sources

Cash	91-day Canada T-Bill
Bonds	Scotia McLeod Universe Bond Index prior to 1985 - Scotia McLeod Long Bond Index
Cdn. Equities	TSE 300 Return Index
Int'l Equities	50% Morgan Stanley World Total Return Index, 50% S&P 500
Real Estate	Russell Property Index prior to 1990 - Morguard Property Index
Oil & Gas	20/20 Canadian Resource Fund
Gold	Gold Trust Mutual Fund

The bottom line for the balanced portfolio is that it can provide **above-average returns** with **reduced risk**, and offer **preferred tax treatment** at the same time. (See pages 199–200 for more on tax-advantaged mutual fund investing.) Our experience is that investors who can obtain all three of these advantages are very happy indeed.

Clearly, there's a lot to be said for developing the right balance among asset categories.

THE IMPORTANCE OF DIVERSIFICATION

A Nobel Prize was awarded for research related to investments. The prizewinning conclusion: it's better not to put "all your eggs in one basket"!

Sounds simple, and it is. But what does it mean for individuals and why is it so important?

We've already discussed the concept of a balanced portfolio — where that balance is achieved by weighting your holdings across various asset categories. There are other ways to diversify, some of which were discussed earlier in the book.

DIVERSIFICATION TYPE	EXAMPLES
Geography	Canada, U.S., Pacific Rim, Latin America
Investment Style	value, growth
Investment Objective	growth, income
Management Team	Fidelity, Mackenzie, Templeton, Trimark

As our portfolio becomes appropriately balanced, it becomes more diversified, and there are major advantages to this diversification.

The accompanying chart shows how diversifying across asset categories helps to reduce risk. Notice that with one asset category in a portfolio (that is, "all your eggs in one basket"), the risk (measured by standard deviation) is about 15%. With each additional asset category, the risk declines, so that with representation in eight asset categories (and there really aren't many more) it's cut almost in half to 9%.

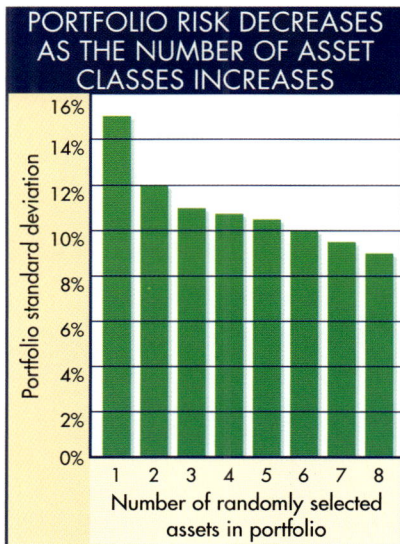

PORTFOLIO RISK DECREASES AS THE NUMBER OF ASSET CLASSES INCREASES

Portfolio standard deviation — Number of randomly selected assets in portfolio

Source: Ibbotson Assoc.

Similarly, when dealing with stocks only, unsystematic risk is substantially reduced by going from owning one stock to owning 128 (although research shows that after 50 stocks are in a portfolio, subsequent additions reduce risk only minimally).

Top Funds Close Up

Can you be overdiversified?

Our rule on diversification is this: Don't buy two things that do the same thing. That is, you don't need three small-cap Canadian equity value funds. They're just too similar. If you're going to buy three Canadian equity funds you should get three of legitimately different styles. We would argue that such a strategy could lower the risk to your portfolio through diversification. In his introduction to *Bogle on Mutual Funds*, Paul Samuelson shows that returns by underdiversified managers are lower. And Morningstar has proven that such managers do have higher risk. Those are two arguments that over-diversification is a myth. So the real enemy is over-duplication!

HOW MANY STOCKS TO HOLD

PORTFOLIO RISK DECREASES AS THE NUMBER OF STOCKS INCREASES

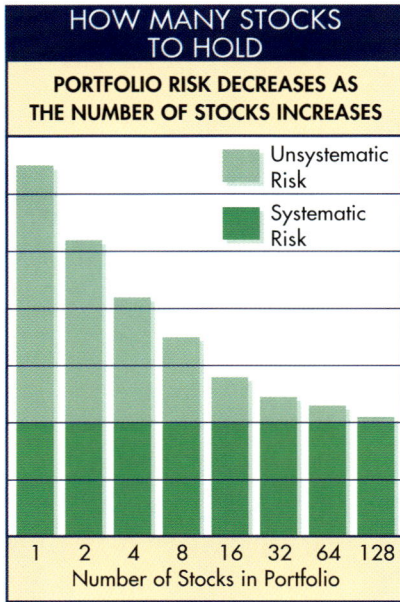

Legend: Unsystematic Risk, Systematic Risk

Number of Stocks in Portfolio: 1 2 4 8 16 32 64 128

Source: Ibbotson Assoc.

Essentially, diversification is a conservative strategy which acknowledges that we will not always be right in our selection of securities, geographic location, or manager. By not overweighting our position in any one of these, the negative impact of being wrong is reduced. Once we acknowledge that we will not be right all the time, we are able to adjust our thinking to achieve more consistent (if less spectacular) growth and avoid big (and potentially) devastating losses.

PORTFOLIOS AND MUTUAL FUND CLASSIFICATIONS

You blink twice and the number of mutual funds available to Canadians balloons to over 1800. Along with the proliferation of funds, the number of classifications has expanded in order to accommodate the wider spectrum of fund types. While finding your funds in the newspaper has become more of a challenge, the narrower classifications do facilitate making more meaningful comparisons between funds and against benchmarks. Standardization is on the way as the industry has determined fixed classifications to be used by fund companies, fund dealers, and media sources. Also being determined is the investment holding criteria that funds have to meet in order to qualify for inclusion in a particular classification.

Most retail portfolio management systems accomplish their diversification objectives by using broad asset classifications. This is not bad, as it is easier to understand for investors and does the job. But as an investor accumulates a larger portfolio and has covered the basic classifications, there are asset classes that are more focused, or are managed in different styles, and which allow the investor to further tailor their portfolio to their desired risk level. The additional classes tend to be somewhat riskier on a stand-alone basis but they add some further diversification to an already-established portfolio. Remember to cover the basics first before scampering off into the more specialized classes.

Investors can also take their investment decisions to an even more basic level by selecting funds or "funds of funds" where a company manages the re-balancing and allocation between various funds.

PORTFOLIO CLASSIFICATIONS	THE BASICS FOR PORTFOLIOS LESS THAN $100,000	FINE TUNING FOR PORTFOLIOS GREATER THAN $100,000
Money Market	Canadian Money Market	U.S. and International Money Market
Short-Term Bond	Canadian Short-Term Bond	
Canadian Fixed Income	Canadian Long/Mid-Term Bond	Canadian Mortgage
Global Fixed Income	International Bonds	
Canadian Equity	Canadian Large Cap/Diversified Blend	Canadian Large Cap/Diversified Value
		Canadian Large Cap/Diversified Growth
		Canadian Small/Mid Cap
		Canadian Dividend
		Canadian Sector
		Canadian Resources & Precious Metals
U.S. Equity	U.S. Large Cap/Diversified	U.S. Small Cap
International Equity	International	Global
		Global Sector
		European
		North American
		Latin American & Emerging Markets
		Asia & Pacific Rim
Balanced	Canadian Tactical Balanced	
	Canadian Strategic Balanced	
	Global Balanced	
	Asset Allocation Services	
Other		

A FUND FAMILY APPROACH TO INVESTING

Good fund families have all or most of these characteristics:

- broad choice of consistent funds

- reasonable expenses

- easy availability (i.e., not available only to civil servants in P.E.I.)

- good administration/service/communication

- deep stable of talented analysts on staff or on contract

- sufficient resources to hire the best, promote their funds and keep from being acquired (when your fund company gets bought, the new owners often bring their own team in, even if they're not always better)

Let's explore the merit of the fund family approach to investing.

Try to pick a great family (or a couple of them if you've got lots of dough), a family that's strong all around — great stock funds in Canada and abroad, and great bond and specialty funds. Since few fund families actually possess all these attributes, here's a subjective listing of some of the major fund families and best/worst characteristics of each. Decide which are best for you by leaning towards those that are strong in areas you favour:

	Strength	Weakness
Templeton	International equities	Domestic stocks & bonds
AGF 20/20	Bonds, specialty/ regional funds	Canadian equity
Mackenzie	Broad selection, STAR program	Equity funds in the Industrial Group have lagged due to cyclical overweighting
Investors	Asia (Carlson), training	No unbiased intermediary
Trimark	International equity	Canadian equity
Fidelity	U.S./Europe/Far East	Canadian equity
Dynamic	Precious metals, Global bonds	Canadian equity

CAUTION: DYSFUNCTIONAL FAMILIES

Avoid fund families with:
- few strong, consistent funds
- high likelihood of a takeover to mess up your plans
- high, unjustified MERs
- inability to hire or keep good managers
- organization not conducive to talent (poor pay, structure, prestige)

BUILDING YOUR PERSONALIZED PORTFOLIO

Now we get down to the business of building a portfolio that is customized to your needs and goals. We're going to provide you with 24 specific portfolios here — 12 are RRSP, and 12 are non-RRSP or non-registered. We have distinguished six *types* of portfolios:

① very conservative

② very to moderately conservative

③ middle of the road (moderately conservative)

④ moderate to high growth

⑤ high growth

⑥ aggressive

These portfolios have been developed in consultation with experts in the field of modern portfolio theory and strategic asset allocation. We hope you'll find them helpful as you put together your own personalized portfolio.

Remember two key things as you read on. **First**, these are examples intended as a guide; for your personal needs, you should seek assistance from an experienced, professional financial advisor. It's too big and important a decision to be making without some experienced professional help. **Second**, this asset mix decision is the **most important decision you make**. It will account for about 90% of the returns of your portfolio. So, take time here, get assistance, and do it right.

Earlier, we identified two key factors that you can use in deciding the right allocation between the two major asset categories of equities and fixed income: your age and risk tolerance, identified on a scale from 1 to 10.

A more sophisticated method of determining the asset mix that's right for you is to complete one or more of the Client Profile Questionnaires that have been produced in the last few years by various fund companies and brokerage houses. The one we like best was developed by Garmaise Investment Technologies in support of Mackenzie's STAR Strategic Asset Allocation Program. By completing the STAR Investor Profile, investors will learn the appropriate asset mix for them based on their response to about 15 questions. While the appropriate asset mix will be identified within STAR's 17 portfolio offerings, the data can also be used to put your own portfolio together, based on our guidelines for the creation of 24 personalized portfolios.

Here are **six** model **RRSP/RRIF** portfolios. Note that they all contain 20% foreign content and **no real estate**:

REGISTERED ACCOUNTS (RRSP/RRIF)

ASSET CATEGORY	TYPE OF PORTFOLIO					
	VERY CONSERVATIVE	VERY TO MODERATELY CONSERVATIVE	MIDDLE OF THE ROAD	MODERATE TO HIGH GROWTH	HIGH GROWTH	AGGRESSIVE
Short-Term	25%	25%	19%	0%	0%	0%
Canadian Fixed Income	37%	33%	29%	33%	24%	0%
Global Fixed Income	20%	19%	12%	10%	0%	0%
Canadian Equity	18%	22%	32%	47%	56%	80%
U.S. Equity	0%	0%	0%	6%	5%	0%
International Equity	0%	1%	8%	4%	15%	20%
Real Estate	0%	0%	0%	0%	0%	0%
Total	100%	100%	100%	100%	100%	100%
Foreign Content	20%	20%	20%	20%	20%	20%

For our **six** model non-registered accounts shown on page 183, we are guided by long-term research studies indicating that in very conservative portfolios, the ideal overall mix of Canadian to foreign content at about 55% Canadian and 45% foreign. This appears to be the ideal "trade off" between risk and reward. More growth-oriented portfolios incorporate more foreign content, and correspondingly more short-term volatility.

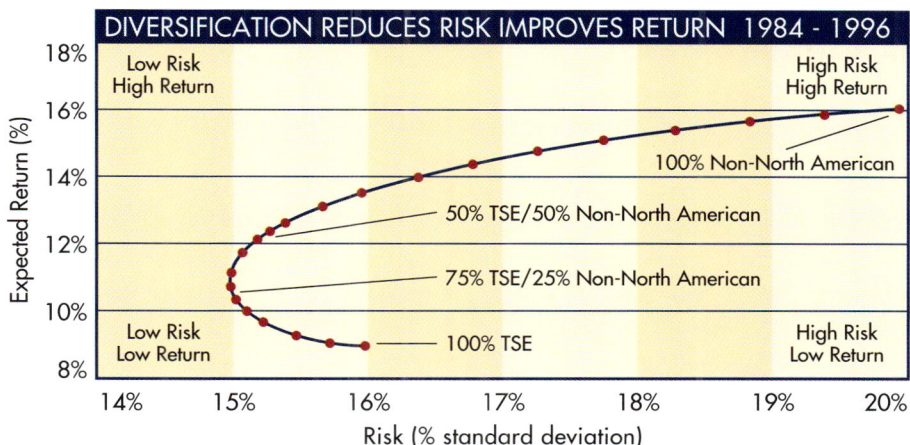

DIVERSIFICATION REDUCES RISK IMPROVES RETURN 1984 - 1996

Low Risk High Return

High Risk High Return

100% Non-North American

50% TSE/50% Non-North American

75% TSE/25% Non-North American

Low Risk Low Return

100% TSE

High Risk Low Return

Expected Return (%)

Risk (% standard deviation)

Source: Loring Ward Investment Counsel

Following are six non-RRSP/RRIF portfolios with **no real estate weighting.**

NON-REGISTERED ACCOUNTS (NON-RRSP/RRIF)

ASSET CATEGORY	TYPE OF PORTFOLIO					
	VERY CONSERVATIVE	VERY TO MODERATELY CONSERVATIVE	MIDDLE OF THE ROAD	MODERATE TO HIGH GROWTH	HIGH GROWTH	AGGRESSIVE
Short-Term	25%	20%	16%	4%	1%	0%
Canadian Fixed Income	21%	17%	16%	17%	9%	0%
Global Fixed Income	24%	19%	16%	13%	8%	0%
Canadian Equity	11%	9%	10%	11%	10%	7%
U.S. Equity	14%	21%	25%	33%	41%	51%
International Equity	5%	14%	17%	22%	31%	42%
Real Estate	0%	0%	0%	0%	0%	0%
Total	**100%**	**100%**	**100%**	**100%**	**100%**	**100%**
Foreign Content	43%	54%	58%	68%	80%	93%

The practical limitation to including real estate in the ideal portfolio is that there are so few real estate funds currently available in Canada. Having said that, we know that research suggests the inclusion of real estate in a well-balanced portfolio. One reason for doing so is its correlation with stocks and bonds. Generally speaking real estate tends to do well during times of higher inflation, while stocks and bonds tend to suffer during periods of inflation.

Another reason for including real estate is that as another asset category it distributes the "eggs" into another "basket " and helps to reduce risk in a portfolio.

Therefore, we include the 12 portfolios presented earlier, this time modified **to include real estate.**

Real estate can be included by adding some of the few real estate funds in Canada (Dynamic, Investors, and Royal Lepage are all players in this field), real estate limited partnerships, commercial property or rental property. While the choice of real estate funds is currently quite limited, and while many real estate limited partnerships have struggled, and commercial or rental real estate has not always been as liquid or ideal, real estate is the world's largest asset category and there should be consideration given to including it in a well-diversified portfolio.

Here are our six model RRSP/RRIF portfolios **including real estate.**

REGISTERED ACCOUNTS (RRSP/RRIF)						
ASSET CATEGORY	**TYPE OF PORTFOLIO**					
	VERY CONSERVATIVE	**VERY TO MODERATELY CONSERVATIVE**	**MIDDLE OF THE ROAD**	**MODERATE TO HIGH GROWTH**	**HIGH GROWTH**	**AGGRESSIVE**
Short-Term	25%	24%	20%	4%	0%	0%
Canadian Fixed Income	38%	35%	26%	28%	13%	0%
Global Fixed Income	12%	7%	4%	2%	2%	0%
Canadian Equity	17%	21%	34%	48%	67%	80%
U.S. Equity	4%	5%	7%	9%	9%	10%
International Equity	1%	3%	4%	4%	4%	5%
Real Estate	3%	5%	5%	5%	5%	5%
Total	**100%**	**100%**	**100%**	**100%**	**100%**	**100%**
Foreign Content	20%	20%	20%	20%	20%	20%

With these portfolio models before you, you can now select some of the Top Funds that you wish to use to build your own personalized portfolio. Again though, we urge you to see these as guidelines and to enlist the help of a full-time professional advisor to assist in making the decisions that are best for you. Remember, this asset mix decision is the most important investment decision you will make, so it's vital to get it right, and then to monitor and rebalance it when necessary to keep it right!

Finally, here are our six model non-RRSP/RRIF portfolios **including real estate**.

ASSET CATEGORY	TYPE OF PORTFOLIO					
	VERY CONSERVATIVE	VERY TO MODERATELY CONSERVATIVE	MIDDLE OF THE ROAD	MODERATE TO HIGH GROWTH	HIGH GROWTH	AGGRESSIVE
Short-Term	24%	19%	13%	6%	0%	0%
Canadian Fixed Income	21%	14%	10%	9%	3%	0%
Global Fixed Income	21%	21%	16%	11%	7%	0%
Canadian Equity	10%	7%	9%	4%	1%	1%
U.S. Equity	14%	21%	28%	36%	48%	55%
International Equity	6%	12%	15%	22%	26%	39%
Real Estate	4%	6%	9%	12%	15%	5%
Total	**100%**	**100%**	**100%**	**100%**	**100%**	**100%**
Foreign Content	50%	63%	70%	83%	96%	99%

Table title: **NON-REGISTERED ACCOUNTS (NON-RRSP/RRIF)**

MUTUAL FUND CHECKUP

Is your fund portfolio a mess? Many are. Many investors acquire funds like groceries; they buy whatever strikes their fancy at that moment. They end up with too many funds, too much paperwork, and no real plan. Here's a quiz to identify whether you're making some of the more common mistakes:

● *Is your asset allocation off-balance?*

This is by far the most important determinant of how you do over time, so don't ignore it. Some investors hope that great funds in a random mix will help them prosper. But even owning great funds (in the wrong asset categories) could sink you. Achieving a balanced portfolio is critical to reducing risk and making more money. Use the simple "Age Rule" guide on page 175 or an asset-allocation questionnaire such as Mackenzie's STAR to determine your optimal asset allocation. Re-jig within the same families you already own to achieve a more appropriate mix if necessary.

● *Are you using too much leverage?*

One financial-planning firm in Ontario advocates a ton of leverage for most client accounts. That's worked well as funds have risen and interest rates have fallen. The tax deductibility of investment borrowing adds to the appeal of the leveraging strategy (see page 198, "The Leveraging Strategy," for more details). But going forward, excessive leverage can be dangerous. Use the one-third rule (even if you're aggressive): be certain

to borrow no more than one-third of the value of your total investment portfolio. And don't allow debt payments from your own income (not income on the funds) to exceed one-third of your total income.

● *Do you own too many funds?*

While there's no magic number of funds investors should own, here's a sensible guideline that can help you keep your records simple and your wallet fat. Never own two funds that do the same thing. Just because you're uncomfortable with a big chunk going into, say, one broad Asian fund doesn't mean that you should buy four to mitigate risk. Better to buy a Japanese fund — they've proven to have actually shown a negative correlation to Asian funds historically — a real risk-reducer. More than a dozen funds creates a mess for most people. We try to keep positions to no less than $10,000 per fund.

● *Are you tax-backwards?*

Too many investors hold GICs outside their RRSP where they get the full tax whack. Then those same investors hold equities inside their RRSP, considering them a long-term investment, naturally suited for the retirement account. It's better to reverse this situation, holding equities (which are so tax advantaged by nature) in an open account where the tax benefits can be realized. Then hold the bonds or GICs inside the RRSP — where they'll grow tax-free until retirement. (See page 200 for further information.)

How Well Are Your Assets Protected?

Most people who invest in mutual funds are concerned primarily about the returns they obtain on their investments, and have very little knowledge or even interest in the type of protection they may be afforded if the firm they invest with collapses.

Providing the highest level of protection are firms that qualify as members of self-regulatory organizations (SROs) such as the Investment Dealers Association of Canada or a Canadian Stock Exchange.

Members of such groups include the large brokerage firms that trade stocks on the Toronto Stock Exchange as well as some smaller planning firms who qualify because they own a seat on a recognized stock exchange. For example, Equion Securities Canada Limited belongs to the TSE while Fortune Financial Corporation belongs to the Montreal Exchange.

SROs require member firms to meet strict requirements of capital, monitoring of client accounts, and protection and compliance rules. If a member firm goes bankrupt, clients are insured by the Canadian Investor Protection Fund (CIPF) which compensates for losses up to $500,000 per account, including $60,000 in cash. The fund ensures that clients of an SRO will be protected against insolvency, fraud or theft, but not from market correction that could reduce the value of investments. The CIPF has a cushion of about $130 million which is increased every quarter by contributions of member firms.

A lower lever of protection is provided by the Ontario Contingency Trust Fund (OCTF) run by the Ontario Securities Commission. Interestingly, most mutual fund dealers are not members of an SRO or the CIPF. They belong instead to the OCTF and are required only to make one contribution of $10,000. The maximum client protection is $5,000 per client. Currently the OCTF's assets are less than $3 million.

Clearly there are two distinct levels of compliance, service and protection in the marketplace and it's a problem which is receiving attention.

Ontario Securities Commissioner Glorianne Stromberg has said that "Participation in an adequately-funded national contingency fund should be mandatory for all dealers." Tom Hocken, President of the Investment Funds Institute of Canada said: "Our view is that the contingency fund for mutual fund dealers is inadequate."

Although the level of protection is lower under the Ontario Contingency Trust Fund, clients have no immediate cause for concern. Money given to these companies to invest in mutual funds must be placed immediately in trust accounts. As soon as the money is transferred to a mutual fund company, the fund company must also segregate the investment in a trust account. A client's money would only be at risk if it were in transit between trust accounts, when a firm went bankrupt or in the case of fraudulent dipping into trust accounts. In fact, no one in Canada has ever lost a nickel due to fraud, theft or bankruptcy in Canadian mutual funds.

Still, as Stromberg has warned, "If a disaster happens, people will realize the inadequacy of their coverage if they are dealing with a firm that is not a member of a self-regulatory body."

MORE ON... SEGREGATED FUNDS

Q. What investment vehicle has been around since the '60s, has spent 30 years in relative obscurity and is now suddenly "hot"?

A. Segregated funds, which depending on who you speak to, are either mutual funds with a twist or a high-octane form of life insurance. In fact, they are the insurance industry's version of a mutual fund. Segregated funds assets are held separate (or segregated) from the assets of the life insurance company, hence the term.

Like mutual funds, segregated funds represent the pooled assets of thousands of investors, managed by professionals to achieve a range of investment objectives. Historically, they have been marketed by Canadian insurance companies. More recently mutual fund companies have created alliances with insurance companies and have begun to market their own segregated funds, along side their traditional offerings. Segregated funds can be purchased on a front-load, no-load or deferred sales charge basis, just like mutual funds.

While there are notable similarities between segregated funds and mutual funds, there are some key differences too.

Difference #1: Guarantee of Principal

Segregated funds guarantee that, except for withdrawals and fees, the investment will be worth at least 75%, and sometimes 100% of the original investment, after either a period of 10 years from the deposit date, or on the death of the owner. This feature of course is of interest to people for whom security of principal is an overriding consideration.

Difference #2: The "Reset" Opportunity

Some segregated funds carry an option allowing the investor to "reset"or "lock in" the guaranteed amount periodically, without triggering capital gains. The caveat is that the investor must be prepared to begin a new 10-year holding period. If the value of the segregated fund increases, the reset feature will increase the investor's guarantee.

For example, assume Sandra invests $100,000 in a segregated fund, which guarantees a minimum $100,000 in ten years or earlier if she dies. After 4 years, the market value has increased to $132,000. Sandra could take advantage of the reset opportunity to ensure that she'll get a minimum of $132,000 back if she's prepared to lock in the investment for an additional 10 years, or until she dies, whichever comes first.

Difference #3: Fund Withdrawals

Despite the fact that you have locked in for 10 years, you may need some money before the period is up. Several segregated funds allow for a 10% free withdrawal each year without incurring a redemption fee. In such a situation, the guaranteed amount is reduced proportionally.

David invested $100,000 in a segregated fund. After a year or two, the market value has grown to $110,000 and he decides he will withdraw $10,000 free as he is allowed to do. The contract guarantees $100,000 after 10 years (or at death, whichever comes first). The $10,000 withdrawal reduces the guaranteed amount, in proportion to the percentage redeemed from the guaranteed amount and the increase in market value. In this case, David has withdrawn $10,000 or 10% of the original amount. The new guaranteed amount is $90,900; the withdrawal has reduced the guaranteed amount by $9,100.

Difference #4: Higher Management Fees

Segregated funds generally carry higher management fees than mutual funds; in some cases it's up to 25% higher. To a large degree, these higher fees are used to fund the guarantee of the principal.

Additional Differences from Regular Mutual Funds

Under certain conditions, segregated funds offer creditor protection.

Beneficiaries can be names on non-registered accounts as well as on RRSP/RRIF accounts, thus reducing probate fees. As well, insurance contract payouts are received tax-free.

Depending on your needs, circumstances and priorities, segregated funds may be worthy of your consideration.

TOP FUNDS INVESTMENT STRATEGIES

• • • • • • • • • • •

Depending on your investment style, your level of expertise, and the amount of time you feel you can afford to devote to managing your portfolio personally, several investment strategies may be of interest and of help.

THE "DOLLAR COST AVERAGING" STRATEGY

This is probably the best and simplest way for people to invest in mutual funds.

Ideally, every investor seeks to buy at a low price and sell at a higher price at a later date. The question is how to do that, given the fact that there are market fluctuations. Nobody seems to mind the upward trends; it's those slides that upset us so much. However, by using a simple strategy called "dollar cost averaging," even the downside fluctuations can actually work to your advantage! It's as close as one can get to infallible investing — and most people don't even know about it.

Psychologically, if you are committed to regular investments and if you are prepared to invest over the long term, then downward trends (which are bound to come along) are simply opportunities to buy additional shares at lower-than-usual prices. As always, of course, the upward trends will continue to be rewarding and satisfying.

Let's see how it actually works by using the following three examples. We're going to invest $100 a month for nine years (i.e., $12,000 will be invested).

Fund Fact

Dollar cost averaging is a system of buying mutual funds (or stocks) on a regular basis (usually monthly) with a fixed amount of money (usually $100 to $300). That's it!

● Scenario 1

Because the unit prices constantly increase, the number of shares purchased each year actually declines, as the chart shows. For example, in Year 1, the unit price is $6.00 and therefore $1,200 per year ($100 per month) buys 200 units. By the end of Year 6, the unit price has increased to $8.50, and therefore $1,200 buys only 141 units. At the end of nine years, at $10 per unit, the value of the portfolio is $13,869 — a 28% increase.

● Scenario 2

Notice here that for the first five years, the unit price declines. Imagine how happy you'd be in that situation! But patience is rewarded. The result of lower unit prices is that a larger number of units are purchased while you

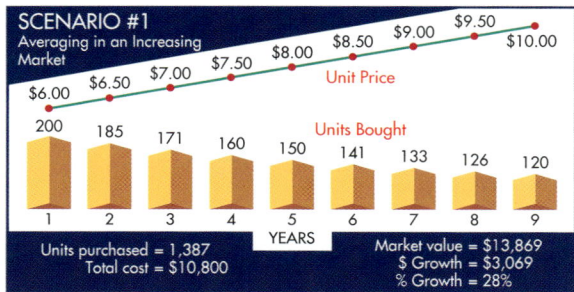

SCENARIO #1
Averaging in an Increasing Market
Unit Price: $6.00 $6.50 $7.00 $7.50 $8.00 $8.50 $9.00 $9.50 $10.00
Units Bought: 200 185 171 160 150 141 133 126 120
YEARS 1–9
Units purchased = 1,387
Total cost = $10,800
Market value = $13,869
$ Growth = $3,069
% Growth = 28%

continue to invest $100 per month. Note that in Scenario 2 the original purchase price and the final purchase price are the same ($6), so there is no market rise at all.

Despite this, 2,150 units have been acquired in this scenario. And even at a $6 unit price at the end of nine years, the value of the portfolio is $12,898 — a 19% increase. Significant growth in the value of your investment actually occurs in a declining and recovering market. You get the benefit of purchasing more mutual fund units when prices are at a reduced value.

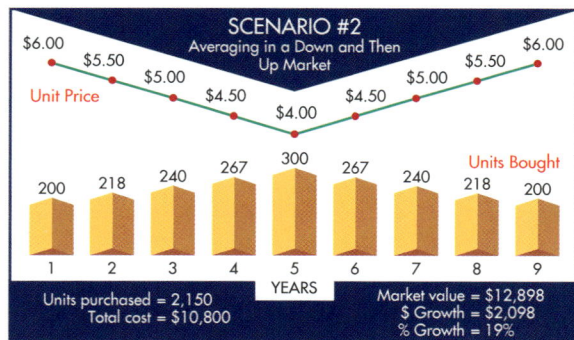

SCENARIO #2
Averaging in a Down and Then Up Market
Unit Price: $6.00 $5.50 $5.00 $4.50 $4.00 $4.50 $5.00 $5.50 $6.00
Units Bought: 200 218 240 267 300 267 240 218 200
YEARS 1–9
Units purchased = 2,150
Total cost = $10,800
Market value = $12,898
$ Growth = $2,098
% Growth = 19%

● *Scenario 3*

Here the unit price increases and decreases over time. Therefore, in some years more units are bought, and in others, fewer. This example is probably the most realistic in reflecting actual conditions. After nine years, the number of units purchased is greater than in Scenario 1 — 1,479 to be exact. At $10 per unit at the end of Year 9, the investment is worth $14,787 — a 37% increase in value.

Dollar cost averaging can thus remove the psychological barrier of purchasing more shares when prices are low and that's the very best time to buy. (Remember the goal: buy low, sell high.) It also removes the problem of timing from investment management. By investing regularly, we don't get hung up on timing, for we've now got a logical comprehensive investment strategy based on confidence in the long-term health of the Canadian and international economies.

It's true! For most people, dollar cost averaging is the best way to invest.

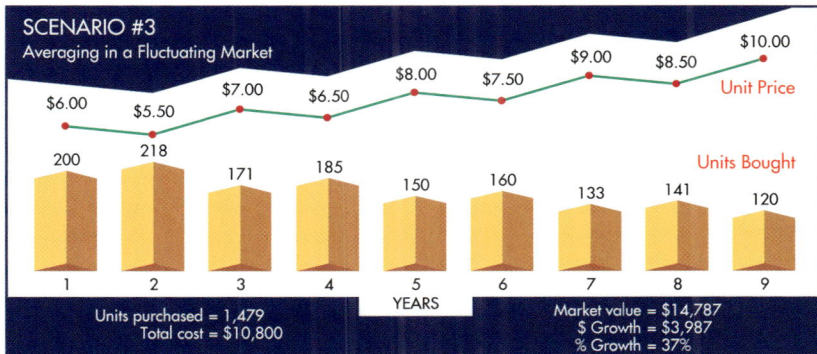

SCENARIO #3
Averaging in a Fluctuating Market

Unit Price: $6.00, $5.50, $7.00, $6.50, $8.00, $7.50, $9.00, $8.50, $10.00

Units Bought: 200, 218, 171, 185, 150, 160, 133, 141, 120

YEARS: 1, 2, 3, 4, 5, 6, 7, 8, 9

Units purchased = 1,479
Total cost = $10,800

Market value = $14,787
$ Growth = $3,987
% Growth = 37%

THE "BUY AND HOLD" STRATEGY

This approach is similar to dollar cost averaging except that in this strategy, the investment may not be made as regularly.

Assuming you've done your research or had the benefit of the advice of a financial advisor, there's a strong argument for picking a fund, investing the money, and getting on with your life.

Templeton Growth Fund is a classic example of a buy-and-hold fund. A $10,000 investment in this fund in November 1954 — with no subsequent contributions or withdrawals — was worth over $5.0 million at July 31, 1998. You could have been Rip Van Winkle and slept for 40 years and done very well with Templeton Growth.

The Temptation To Time

Like a dieter mesmerized by a piece of chocolate cake, investors in volatile markets are often gripped by the irresistible impulse to try timing the market.

Who can blame them? On the surface, the case for market timing is deceptively appealing. By shifting out of equities into T-bills when markets are pricey, you can avoid losses in down markets, and then by simply shifting back in near the bottom, you capture most of the gains in the up markets. Better returns with less risk—who doesn't want that?

So if the recent market fluctuations have sent a spasm of fear through your belly, while a seemingly endless parade of financial gurus are claiming that stocks are now overpriced, isn't it about time to market time? Well, before you nibble on that cake, consider the following:

First, virtually every significant study of market timing has concluded that it generally results in reduced returns.

Gary Brinson's landmark study in 1986 entitled "Determinants of Portfolio Performance" evaluated 91 pension funds over a 10-year period. On average, they lost 66 basis points (i.e., nearly two thirds of 1%) per year by market timing. As a group, the pension funds would have been better off to just stick with their long-term strategy and asset mix.

Further, the range in returns for the individual plan managers were from a meagre plus 0.25% to minus 2.54% per year. So not only were they poor on average, but even the most skilled did not materially add to return.

In his classic work, *Investment Policy*, Charles Ellis reviewed a study of 100 large pension funds. He determined that not one of the funds had improved its returns as a result of market timing, and 89 of the 100 pension funds reduced their expected returns by 0.9% per year.

Second, even if market timing has worked previously, it is not a reliable methodology. A study published in the Fall 1996 issue of the Journal of Portfolio Management looked at the results of 11 tactical asset allocation managers (i.e., market timers) who collectively managed close to 95% of the domestic tactical asset allocation assets in the U.S.

The authors concluded that although the managers did add value prior to 1988, they underperformed in the post-1988 period. They also concluded that the managers failed to detect fundamental changes in the relationship between fixed income and equity returns, and consequently performed poorly.

Another study, published in the Winter issue, which analyzed the prediction skills of market timers also concluded that they are not reliable. The article stated that "luck and style variation tend to be just as important as the timer's skill in the determination of portfolio performance". Do you really want your retirement monies managed by a methodology, where luck is as important as skill?

Third, individual investors are the worst market timers. Dalbar Inc., a Boston consulting firm, completed a study which compared the performance of actual investors in funds to market returns. They concluded that ==investors, on average, lost a staggering 4% to 5% annually by failed attempts to time the market.==

Many would-be timers don't realize that you have to be right **twice** to be right. You have to know when to leave and when to re-enter the market. The first decision to avoid a down market is difficult enough. Even in a typical bear market, stock prices advance 30% to 40% of the time. Most bears are only apparent to everyone near their end.

Then, you have to be right a second time by getting back in at the proper time. Yet, market gains tend to occur in short, unpredictable bursts. Missing these bursts is catastrophic for long-term returns.

In a recent review of the Equion U.S. Equity Fund subindex for the 20-year period from January 1977 to December 1996, the Managed Money Research Group determined that had you been out of the market for the six best months (i.e., 2.5% of the time) your returns would have collapsed to 8.9% annually from 15.2% for the "buy and hold" investor. If you missed the best 12 months (i.e., only 5% of the time) you earned a meagre 6.4%.

However, just because market timing doesn't work, it doesn't mean that you just grit your teeth and hold on. There are three steps to follow to ensure long-term success:

• You should have a long-term plan with a customized asset mix which meets your needs in terms of liquidity, risk tolerance, income and capital requirements. You should have target percentages for all the major asset groups: short-term Canadian bonds; Canadian and International bonds; Canadian, U.S. and International equities; real estate investment trusts, and tangible assets.

• You should be automatically rebalancing back to these target mixes whenever differential asset class performance throws your portfolio off target. Typically, given the last two years of bull market performance, many investors would have been rebalancing back to targeted mixes by selling rising equities and buying the underperforming asset groups.

No, this isn't market timing! This is simply ensuring that the portfolio stays on the right road for the long run based on your personal plan. It is primarily a risk management device but during volatile markets such as in 1987, rebalancing actually added to return.

• If you are investing substantial dollars in the market today, you may want to dollar cost average. Invest equivalent monthly or quarterly payments over a 12- to 18-month period. Dollar cost averaging tends to reduce the volatility of a portfolio during the start-up period and hence builds more comfort.

So, quit worrying about market timing. Stick with this advice and you'll even get to enjoy the chocolate cake!

But even if your interest is to "buy and hold," we're generally not comfortable ignoring the investment completely. So to monitor, we suggest you look for changes in the fund's management or for changes to its investment philosophy and, of course, continue to be aware of its performance compared to others in its category.

The buy-and-hold strategy isn't as exciting as some others, but if you can find a true "buy and hold" fund, you'll be a happy investor.

THE "BOB AND WEAVE" STRATEGY

This approach is quite the opposite of "buy and hold" and "dollar cost averaging." It's based on a belief that we, as individuals, can anticipate certain trends, developments, or events, and can "bob and weave," or switch among funds and asset categories to take advantage of them.

Most fund companies now allow you to switch from one of their funds to another — generally at no cost, although a fund's prospectus often provides for a fee of up to 2%. Some of the no-load funds charge an administration fee each time you do so after a certain number of "free" switches.

Now it's true that certain asset categories tend to do better at different times in the economic cycle. For example, when interest rates are falling, government bonds will tend to do well; when interest rates are low, equities will likely do well; and, when rates are rising, a cash-type investment may perform best.

But we believe very strongly that you should hold a balanced portfolio. So we urge that the "bob and weave" approach not be taken too far. Sure, there could be strategic times to rebalance; but those who attempt to be "market timers" do not consistently come out on top. It's a risky strategy and one that we urge be used with caution — probably as part of ongoing discussions with your financial advisor.

THE ASSET ALLOCATION STRATEGY

The asset allocation approach is a much more disciplined and more effective strategy than the "bob and weave." In this strategy, the overall mix between fixed income and equities is determined by your age and aggressiveness as an investor. (For more about asset allocation, see pages 173-176.) Then the specific components of the portfolio are selected and "plugged in" to the overall framework.

Remember, the research shows very clearly that the overall mix between equities and fixed income is the single most important decision. All other variables, including market timing, are of very little importance.

Of course, it will be necessary to rebalance your portfolio from time to time, particularly if one asset category has done extremely well in the past year. If it has, it may have grown to a larger-than-appropriate percentage of the portfolio.

● *Rebalancing Your Portfolio*

Rebalancing is the process of adjusting a portfolio in order to maintain a target asset mix. The discipline of rebalancing serves to maintain the portfolio risk that is appropriate for you, by reducing overweighted positions.

In addition to managing portfolio risk, an effective rebalancing program will "force" a methodical and disciplined process of buying low and selling high. When your asset mix moves away from the target mix it is very often due to one or two asset classes outperforming the others. In order to correct the portfolio, it is necessary to sell off some of the asset classes which have outperformed, using the proceeds to buy the asset classes that have performed less well.

Research Tidbits

Important to Rebalance Your Portfolio

A study published in Benefits Canada by Michael Gallimore showed the effects of rebalancing a $100 million portfolio split equally between the TSE 300 Index and Canadian Bonds represented in the Scotia McLeod 40 Index. Between 1974 and 1990, bringing back the portfolio to a 50/50 basis on an annual basis increased the annual returns by 47 basis points. Over 17 years, this translated to additional returns of over $40 million!

A recent research study tracked the market value of two portfolios from January 1, 1987 to December 1, 1996. Both portfolios began with $500,000 invested in the same asset mix, which is representative of a moderate risk tolerance. However, after the initial investment, one portfolio was **not** monitored or rebalanced to the target asset mix, whereas the other portfolio was rebalanced according to the desired mix. (See chart on page 198).

Over the ten-year period, the market value of the rebalanced portfolio **never fell below** the market value of the portfolio in which no rebalancing occurred. At the end of the period, the market value of the rebalanced portfolio was **$42,000 higher, or 8.4% of the original capital of** the portfolio. Well worth the effort!

Another reason to adjust your portfolio may be advancing age. We believe that as you age (and all other things being equal), the relative weighting of fixed-income assets in your portfolio should grow. As well, some investors become more (or less) aggressive over the years—for a whole variety of reasons—and this change must be reflected in the overall holdings.

Finally, certain economic conditions lend themselves to shifts in the weighting of certain asset categories that may not otherwise be appropriate.

The main point here is that changes made to a balanced portfolio should be the result of a well-considered set of plans and have little to do with an attempt to time the market—which is more a part of the "bob and weave" approach.

THE EFFECTS OF REBALANCING

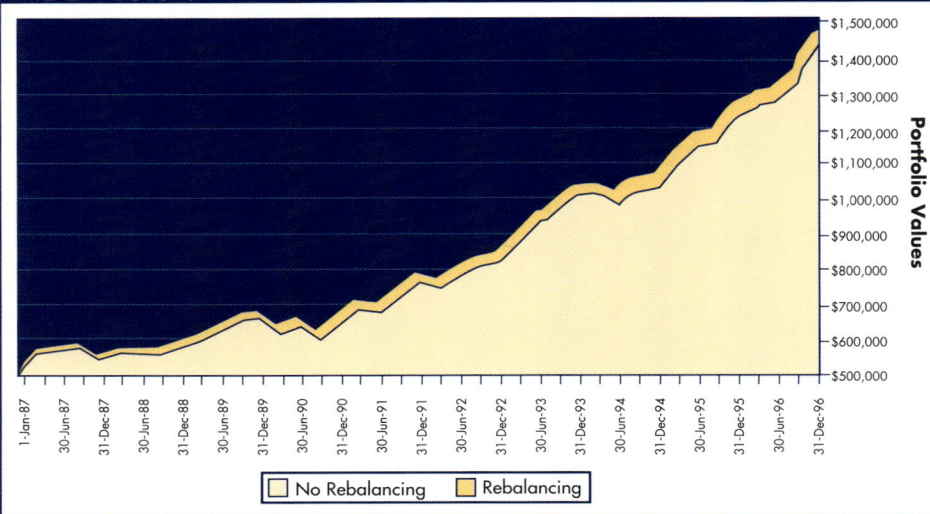

Legend: No Rebalancing | Rebalancing

* Source: Loring Ward Investment Counsel

THE LEVERAGING STRATEGY

This is an aggressive strategy with great upside potential — as well as some significant risk. The theory is to use other people's money — usually a bank loan — adding it to yours and investing the entire amount. What you owe remains constant, or may be reduced by monthly payments, while the overall investment grows in value.

Let's assume you take $20,000 of your own money and borrow another $80,000 to make a $100,000 investment. Let's assume your investment grows by 20% to $120,000. You still owe $80,000, so you "own" $40,000 of the investment. Although the value of the portfolio grew by only 20%, your "stake" actually doubled from $20,000 to $40,000 — a 100% increase!

It can get even better. Assuming you borrowed the money to invest outside your RRSP, the interest you pay the bank to finance the loan will be tax deductible. (Interest on RRSP loans is no longer deductible.) And assuming that you selected investments that generate tax-advantaged dividends or capital gains, your after-tax returns will be better still. (Even though the $100,000 capital gains exemption has been abolished, capital gains are still taxed at only 75% of the amount charged on, say, interest income.)

So far, we've seen only the rosy side of leveraging. But there's another side that must be considered. Let's assume our $100,000 declines in value by 20% to $80,000. That represents the entire amount of your contribution to the total investment. So your original $20,000 will have been wiped out — for a pretty frightening loss of 100%!

Given the potential dangers inherent in leveraging strategies, we suggest that you adhere to the following guidelines:

● Borrow to a maximum of one-third of the total investment.

● Be sure cash flow will allow ongoing loan payments; don't expect to pay the loan back from profits.

● Try to avoid "securing" the loan with other assets, especially your home; unsecured loans are widely available at slightly higher rates.

THE INCOME-SPLITTING STRATEGY

For those who want to reduce their income tax burden, income splitting is very effective.

This simple strategy attempts to take a portion of the earnings attributed to a high-income earner, and place it in the hands of the lower-income spouse. By doing so, many thousands of tax dollars can be saved annually.

Take a look at the chart below.

SAVE TAXES THROUGH INCOME SPLITTING

THE USUAL SITUATION

	Jim	Peggy
Annual Retirement Income	$100,000	$0.00
Marginal Tax Rate*	53.2%	0.00%
Tax Liability	$40,509	$0.00

THE INCOME-SPLITTING STRATEGY

	Jim	Peggy
Annual Retirement Income	$60,000	$40,000
Marginal Tax Rate*	50.1%	42.7%
Tax Liability	$19,377	$10,688
Total Tax Liability		$30,065
Tax Savings: $10,443 after-tax per year		

* Basic personal exemption only

In most cases, as shown in the first example, retirement income is concentrated (if not placed exclusively) in the hands of the higher-income earner. By creating and contributing to a spousal RRSP over a number of years, Jim has achieved the same level of retirement income, but it is more evenly split between Jim and Peggy, as the second example shows.

Notice that in the first example, the tax bill is over $40,000, but that in the income-splitting example, the combined tax bill is just over $30,000. This has been achieved by moving Jim to a lower tax bracket so he pays only about $20,000 in tax instead of $40,000. Peggy now pays tax too, but at a lower rate, so she pays about $10,000.

That's an after-tax saving of over $10,000 per year! By repeating the scene over and over again, Jim and Peggy can likely save well over $100,000 in taxes over 10 years.

THE TAX-EFFICIENT STRATEGY

● *Tax-Efficient/Inefficient Portfolio*

Examine the tax-**inefficient** portfolio. Notice that the bonds are held outside the RRSP and are, therefore, fully taxed. The stocks held in an equity fund are inside the RRSP and therefore tax-free. Because the bonds are taxed, the after-tax return is 11.25%.

Now look at the tax-**efficient** portfolio and notice that now, the bonds are held inside the RRSP and are, therefore, tax-free. The equities are held outside the RRSP and even though they are subject to tax, capital gains or dividends are taxed more favourably than interest generated by fixed-income vehicles. The after-tax return in this situation is 12.2%, and while that 1% may not sound like a lot, it becomes very significant as it compounds over the years.

The message is that, where possible, hold assets which are fully taxed (fixed income) inside the RRSP and more favourably taxed assets (equities) **outside** the RRSP.

TAX-INEFFICIENT PORTFOLIO

ASSET CLASS	RRSP	NON-RRSP	TOTAL
Bonds ($100,000 @ 15%)	0	$15,000	$15,000
Stocks ($100,000 @ 15%)	$15,000	0	$15,000
Taxes payable (@ 50%)	0	-$7,500	-$7,500
Total	$15,000	$7,500	$22,500
After-tax return: $22,500/$200,000 = 11.25%			

TAX-EFFICIENT PORTFOLIO

ASSET CLASS	RRSP	NON-RRSP	TOTAL
Bonds ($100,000 @ 15%)	$15,000	0	$15,000
Stocks ($100,000 @ 15%)	0	$15,000	$15,000
Taxes payable (@ 50%)	0	-5,625	-5,625
Total	$15,000	$9,375	$24,375
After-tax return: $24,375/$200,000 = 12.20%			

Monitor "Drift" In Your Mutual Fund Portfolio

Why do we need to monitor fund "drift"? Simply stated, mutual funds are not static. Portfolio managers come and go, philosophies evolve and client goals change over time. A perfect match between an investor and funds in one year may be wildly inappropriate three years later. Investing is a means to an end—not an end in itself. It's imperative that you know which path you are on, and that your investments reflect the goals you hold dear.

What happens when you buy a Canadian equity fund which you expect will be invested in Canadian equities and only discover later that it holds 30% in cash? This is exactly the situation currently with the Ivy Canadian fund. It's not necessarily bad to be holding 30% in cash and it is not difficult to understand how this has happened (Tons of cash being thrown at Jerry Javasky more quickly than he can find a good home for it!). But if, using this example, you want a 100% Canadian equity portfolio, because that fits with your goals, you probably won't be pleased to learn that your portfolio is only 70% in equities and 30% in cash during a period of low interest rates.

And it can get worse! Increasingly people aren't looking at just one fund, but at a portfolio of funds; this makes the asset allocation analysis that much harder, especially if you hold a large number of funds. Not only do you have to know what's going on in each individual fund, but you have to understand how these funds play off against one another. All of this complexity increases the likelihood that the portfolios investors have don't make sense.

It's no longer enough to simply look at an individual fund and understand that it has had good returns and good risk relative to its category. It's vital to look "under the hood" and understand what each fund is actually invested in. It's also important to think about how the funds combine and to determine whether that combination is actually helping investors achieve their goals. It's essential that we look at residual cash, bonds and foreign positions in funds that are labelled simply as "growth" or "equity" funds. It's important, too, to check the sectors of the economy in which funds are being invested so the investor can be satisfied that the actual sector exposure which is being achieved is the appropriate exposure for his/her goals.

Finally there's the issue of a well-balanced portfolio becoming badly imbalanced as a result of the extraordinary growth of a portion of the portfolio. Recently, for example, if one had not been watchful, it would have been easy to allow one's Canadian equity weighting to become far greater than may be desired, simply because of the unusually strong growth in Canadian equities.

All the research shows that it's vital not only to begin with an appropriately balanced portfolio, but that it must be continually fine tuned, rebalanced or optimized to retain the ideal mix.

It's not that normal "drift" in a fund or portfolio is good or bad. But it's important to be aware of the fact that if it's ignored, the fund or portfolio you thought you owned may be quite different from the one you own today.

FIND YOUR OWN PERSONAL "MONEY COACH"

You are **forced** to play the "money game" from the time you begin to earn a living until you die, and many of us will play it for 40, 50, 60 years or more. Don't you agree that when you're going to play a game for that length of time, it makes sense to be able to play it as well as possible? There are rules to the game and there are strategies you can use to play more effectively and successfully.

In this game, it's important to know who your teammates are and who's the "opposition." Revenue Canada makes the rules, interprets the rules, and enforces the rules of the game — Revenue Canada is not on your "team."

To learn the rules and the strategies of the money game, you need a "money coach" to work with you over the long term, and more and more people are coming to this conclusion.

If, like many others, you are too busy to take the time to learn all the rules and strategies, or if you don't have the interest, the ability or the inclination to learn them, then you need to find expert advice.

It's true that books like this one can provide some useful assistance, but your personal situation is unlikely to be covered in any book. You really need an individual to coach you, over the long term, in all aspects of your financial life. It's my heartfelt belief that an experienced professional advisor can help you save thousands of dollars in taxes over time and can increase the value of your portfolio over what you can do yourself by many thousands of dollars.

Why would you not use the expertise of someone who can help you achieve those results? Well, more and more people are recognizing the advantages of seeking a "money coach." But where do you look to find one?

Some people use bank managers, but their expertise is generally limited to loans or mortgages. Accountants are often thought to be good money coaches and no doubt many are. Again, we suggest you look for someone with a broader overview. Tax considerations are significant, but there are many others that need to be taken into account in creating an overall financial strategy. Lawyers are often relied upon for general financial and investment advice, but they are not trained in investment theory and may have no expertise in the area of asset allocation or in personal taxation.

We recommend you seek out someone whose professional career is completely focused on providing expert, pertinent, and timely financial advice.

WHAT QUALIFICATIONS SHOULD YOUR MONEY COACH HOLD?

Generally, someone in the field will have at least completed the Investment Funds course which (along with being registered by the appropriate Securities Commission) allows one to sell mutual funds to the public. The Canadian Securities Course (along with the appropriate registration) allows one to sell a full range of securities (including stocks and bonds as well as mutual funds). Stockbrokers have all completed the Canadian Securities Course.

But those are minimum qualifications — both prerequisites for anyone registered to sell securities. You should also look for an advisor who has completed (or is enrolled in) the Certified Financial Planner (CFP) program. It's offered by the Financial Planners Standards Council of Canada (FPSCC) as part of their ongoing educational programs and covers many pertinent topics such as taxation, personal financial planning, asset management, estate planning, etc.

Some people take advanced programs offered by the Canadian Securities Institute, including the FCSI designation (Fellow of the Canadian Securities Institute) or the new Certified Investment Manager (CIM) designation.

Any of these programs ensure that your advisor has a commitment to ongoing professional development, which will likely be beneficial to you.

As well, you should probably expect that your advisor would be a member of the Canadian Association of Financial Planners and adhere to its Code of Ethics.

HOW DO YOU FIND THE RIGHT ADVISOR?

Many advisors provide an ongoing series of educational seminars which are intended to provide up-to-the-moment information on trends in the economy, which funds are "hot," methods of tax reduction, and so on. You may find it worthwhile to attend some of these and get a sense of whether you could work with that individual.

THE MONSTER FUND TABLES

In this section, you'll find information on the over 1800 funds available in Canada, arranged by *category* and in *alphabetical order* within each category.

THE MONSTER FUND TABLES LEGEND

The Monster Table has been sorted first by fund category.

● 27 categories have been used, 25 of which comprise the Equion All-Fund Index. The two Money Market categories (U.S./ International Money Market and Canadian Money Market) are excluded from the All-Fund Index since they do not really represent "managed money".

● The categories are:

① Canadian Large Cap/Diversified Blend

② Canadian Large Cap/Diversified Value

③ Canadian Large Cap/Diversified Growth

④ Canadian Small/Mid Cap Equity

⑤ Canadian Dividend

⑥ Canadian Sector Equity

⑦ Canadian Resources & Precious Metals

⑧ U.S. Large Cap/Diversified Equity

⑨ U.S. Small Cap Equity

⑩ International Equity

⑪ Global Equity

⑫ Global Sector

⑬ North American Equity

⑭ European Equity

⑮ Latin American & Emerging Markets

⑯ Asia-Pacific Rim Equity

⑰ Canadian Long/Mid-Term Bonds

⑱ Canadian Short-Term Bonds

⑲ Canadian Mortgage

⑳ International Bonds

㉑ U.S./International Money Market

㉒ Canadian Money Market

㉓ Canadian Tactical Balanced

㉔ Canadian Strategic Balanced

㉕ Global Balanced

㉖ Asset Allocation Services

㉗ Other

CONSISTENCY

Performance Trend/Quartile Rankings

- Quartile Rankings were calculated for the 20 years from 1977 to 1997 (June 30), and are shown for the 15 years from 1984 to 1998 (June 30).

- They represent performance compared to their peer group (i.e., category) to achieve a true "apples to apples" comparison.

- The methodology used was as follows: Assume there were 100 funds in a category. These funds were sorted by annual calendar-year performance, calculated to four decimals. The top 25 funds were assigned a top quartile ranking; the next were assigned a second quartile ranking, and so on. If the total number of funds included in the rating was odd, the fund quartile may include a slightly larger or smaller number than the previous three.

- If a fund did not have data for a full calendar year, the square will be empty. For 1998, only funds with a full six months of data were included. If a fund did have data but there were fewer than 20 funds within the classification, quartile ratings were not assigned.

RISK

Fund Beats GICs (%)

This column is stated in **percentage** terms, and indicates the percentage of time that the fund's monthly performance beat the monthly performance of GICs.

Fund Beats GICs (Yr)

- This column indicates the number of years that the fund (since its inception) outperformed GICs. For example, 11/14 indicates that the fund outperformed GICs for 11 of its 14-year history.

The range of years considered is from 1977 to 1997.

Worst 12 Months

- This section includes **two** components:

① The month and year which ends the worst 12 months of fund performance, for example, 9/90 indicates that the worst 12 months ended in September, 1990.

② The percentage amount lost during that worst 12-month period.

Worst Calendar Year

This section includes two components:

● The calendar year in which the fund suffered its worst loss.

● The percentage loss suffered in that worst year.

The range of years considered is from 1977 to 1997.

Years Fund Lost $

● This column indicates the number of years the fund lost money. For example, 3/12 indicates the fund lost money in 3 of its 12 complete years of existence.

The range of years considered is from 1977 to 1997.

REWARD-TO-RISK

Risk-Adjusted Returns (Sharpe Ratio: 3-Year and 5-Year Quartile Ratings)

● Named after Dr. William Sharpe, the Nobel prize winner who invented it, the Sharpe Ratio is a means of measuring risk-adjusted returns for a fund and can be effectively used as a measure of risk.

● To calculate, the annual average 91-Day T-Bill rate is subtracted from the annual average performance of the fund. The resulting value is then divided by the fund's standard deviation.

● Finally the fund was assigned a quartile ranking (measured against its category peers) for a three- and five-year period. If a fund did not have data for the full three- or five-year period, "N/A" was used.

● As you'd probably expect, the higher the quartile ranking the better the fund on a risk-adjusted return basis. Stated differently, the higher the quartile ranking, the more likely the fund will do well in the up markets, and the less likely it will lose in down markets.

EFFICIENCY

MER (Management Expense Ratio)

This section also includes **two** components:

① The MER as obtained by Fund Data and supplemented with information from Pal Track.

② The use of a "stop light" model to indicate how the fund's MER compares to others in its category.

If it's **above average**, the **red** light symbol is used.

If it's **average**, the **orange** light symbol is used.

If it's **below average**, the **green** light symbol is used.

If it's a **dash** (–), this means that it is **not applicable**.

1 CANADIAN LARGE CAP/DIVERSIFIED-BLEND

Fund Name	Performance Trend by Quartiles (84–98/June)	Fund Beats GICs %	Fund Beats GICs(Yr)	Worst 12 mo. End	Chng (%)	Worst Calendar Year	Worst Calendar Year %	Years Fund Lost $	Sharpe 3-Yr	Sharpe 5-Yr	MER	Efficiency
Acadia Canadian Equity Fund		N/A	0|0	N/A	0.00	N/A	N/A	0|0	N/A	N/A	0.00	—
Acker Finley QSA Canadian Equity Fund		N/A	0|0	N/A	0.00	N/A	N/A	0|0	N/A	N/A	1.00	green
Acuity Pooled Canadian Equity Fund	4 1 1 1 1	48%	3|4	01/95	-16.25	1994	-12.7%	1|4	1.00	1.00	0.00	—
AGF Canada Class	4	56%	0|0	01/98	-3.81	N/A	N/A	0|0	N/A	N/A	2.63	red
AGF Canadian Equity Fund Limited	1 1 3 3 4 4 3 2 2 4 3 3 4 4	55%	12|21	06/82	-31.48	1990	-20.0%	4|21	4.00	4.00	2.95	red
AGF Canadian Growth Fund	1 2 4 2 2 4 4 2 3	50%	5|8	01/95	-9.51	1990	-6.9%	3|8	4.00	3.00	2.46	orange
AIC Advantage Fund II	1 1	67%	1|1	06/98	28.21	1997	41.3%	0|1	N/A	N/A	2.63	red
AIM Canadian Premier Fund	4 3 3 4 3 4 3 1	52%	4|7	01/95	-12.93	1994	-5.2%	2|7	3.00	3.00	2.80	red
All-Canadian CapitalFund	2 4 2 2 4 4 1 1 4 4 4 4 4	52%	11|21	07/88	-14.60	1992	-2.7%	2|21	4.00	4.00	2.00	orange
All-Canadian Compound Fund	2 4 2 2 4 4 1 4 3 2 1 4 4 4	53%	11|21	07/88	-13.18	1990	-2.6%	2|21	4.00	4.00	0.00	green
Allstar AIG Canadian Equity Fund	3 3 2	56%	2|2	07/96	7.21	1997	13.0%	0|2	2.00	N/A	2.68	red
AltaFund Investment Corp.	1 1 3 3 1 4 4	57%	4|6	05/98	-19.01	1997	-12.6%	2|6	4.00	4.00	2.32	orange
Altamira Equity Fund	1 1 1 1 1 2 4 4	60%	6|9	01/95	-7.56	1990	-1.8%	1|9	4.00	4.00	2.28	orange
S Apex Canadian Growth Fund (AGF)	4 4 1 1 2 1 4 2 4 3 2 3 4 3	51%	11|21	11/81	-14.60	1981	-9.8%	4|21	4.00	4.00	3.00	red
S Apex Canadian Stock Fund	3 3	53%	1|1	01/98	9.70	1997	11.1%	0|1	N/A	N/A	2.54	red
Argentum Canadian Equity Portfolio		N/A	0|0	N/A	0.00	N/A	N/A	0|0	N/A	N/A	0.00	—
Atlas Canadian Large Cap Growth Fund	3 4 2 3 2 2 4 4 2 2 1 1 2	48%	7|12	08/88	-15.89	1990	-10.7%	3|12	1.00	1.00	2.45	red
Atlas Canadian Large Cap Value Fund	4 4 3 2	49%	3|3	07/96	1.60	1995	8.7%	0|3	3.00	N/A	2.55	red
Azura RSP Aggressive Growth Pooled Fund		N/A	0|0	N/A	0.00	N/A	N/A	0|0	N/A	N/A	2.28	orange
S Bell Group RRSP Equity	2 4 4 4	59%	2|3	01/98	-0.99	1997	4.1%	0|3	4.00	N/A	2.65	orange
Beutel Goodman Canadian Equity Fund	4 3 1 4 3 2 3	52%	4|6	01/93	-8.41	1992	-4.7%	1|6	3.00	2.00	2.08	orange
Bissett Canadian Equity Fund	2 4 1 3 2 1 1 2 3 1 1 1 1	57%	9|14	08/88	-14.97	1990	-8.5%	3|14	1.00	1.00	1.33	green

S = Seg Funds

1 CANADIAN LARGE CAP/DIVERSIFIED-BLEND

Fund Name	Performance Trend by Quartiles (84–98 | June)	Fund Beats GICs %	Fund Beats GICs (Yr)	Worst 12 mo. End	Worst 12 mo. Chng (%)	Worst Calendar Year	Worst Calendar %	Years Fund Lost $	Sharpe 3-Yr	Sharpe 5-Yr	MER	Efficiency
BNP (Canada) Equity Fund	92:2 93:4 94:2 95:2 96:2 97:1 98:2 | Jun:2	56%	4|6	01/95	-6.99	1994	-2.1%	1|6	1.00	2.00	2.35	orange
BPI Canadian Mid-Cap Fund	98:4 | Jun:4	46%	0|0	06/98	3.50	N/A		0|0	N/A	N/A	2.85	red
S BPI Canadian Mid-Cap Segregated Fund		N/A	0|0	N/A	0.00	N/A	N/A	0|0	N/A	N/A	0.00	—
BPI Canadian Opportunities II Fund	98:4 | Jun:4	N/A	0|0	N/A	0.00	N/A	N/A	0|0	N/A	N/A	1.96	green
BPI Canadian Opportunities RSP Fund	97:1 98:4 | Jun:4	56%	1|2	02/98	-22.16	1997	-16.2%	1|2	3.00	N/A	2.49	orange
BPI Dividend Equity Fund		N/A	0|0	N/A	0.00	N/A	N/A	0|0	N/A	N/A	0.00	—
C.I. Canadian Growth Fund	95:2 96:3 97:4 98:4 | Jun:1	55%	3|4	01/95	-7.55	1994	0.4%	0|4	4.00	3.00	2.35	orange
C.I Sector Canadian Shares	89:1 90:4 91:4 92:4 93:1 94:2 95:3 96:4 97:4 98:2 | Jun:2	47%	5|10	10/90	-20.20	1990	-18.3%	3|10	4.00	4.00	2.40	orange
C.I. Sector Monarch Canadian Shares	98:4	39%	0|0	01/98	-1.79	N/A	N/A	0|0	N/A	N/A	2.40	orange
S C.U. Canadian TSE 35 Total Return Index Fund		N/A	0|0	N/A	0.00	N/A	N/A	0|0	N/A	N/A	2.63	red
Caldwell Canadian Equity Fund	98:4 | Jun:4	54%	0|0	06/98	2.50	N/A	N/A	0|0	N/A	N/A	0.50	green
Camaf (Cdn. Anaesthetists Mut. Accumulating Fund)	84:3 85:3 86:2 87:2 88:2 89:2 90:2 91:4 92:3 93:3 94:3 95:3 96:2 97:3 98:2 | Jun:2	54%	13|21	06/82	-25.25	1990	-8.9%	4|21	3.00	3.00	1.52	orange
S Canada Life Canadian Equity S-9	84:1 85:2 86:2 87:2 88:1 89:3 90:4 91:1 92:2 93:3 94:2 95:2 96:3 97:3 98:2 | Jun:2	54%	14|21	06/82	-26.84	1990	-16.4%	3|21	2.00	2.00	2.25	orange
Canada Trust Canadian Equity Index Fund	98:1	N/A	0|0	N/A	0.00	N/A	N/A	0|0	N/A	N/A	0.75	green
Canada Trust Stock Fund	89:3 90:1 91:1 92:1 93:2 94:4 95:4 96:3 97:1 98:2 | Jun:2	53%	6|9	01/95	-12.22	1990	-7.7%	2|9	3.00	3.00	1.87	green
Canso Canadian Equity Fund	98:2	N/A	0|0	N/A	0.00	N/A	N/A	0|0	N/A	N/A	2.00	green
S CCPE Growth Fund	88:2 89:2 90:3 91:2 92:2 93:4 94:1 95:2 96:2 97:3 98:2 | Jun:2	51%	7|11	10/90	-13.41	1990	-11.0%	2|11	2.00	1.00	1.35	orange
S CDA Canadian Equity Fund (Trimark)	98:3 | Jun:3	39%	0|0	06/98	1.40	N/A	N/A	0|0	N/A	N/A	1.45	green
S CDA Common Stock Fund (Altamira)	87:2 88:1 89:1 90:2 91:1 92:3 93:2 94:3 95:3 96:4 97:4 98:1 | Jun:1	52%	13|21	06/82	-21.47	1990	-8.7%	3|21	4.00	4.00	0.96	green
CentrePost Canadian Equity Fund	94:1 95:4 96:4 97:1 98:3	57%	3|5	01/95	-16.11	1994	-8.2%	1|5	4.00	4.00	1.00	green
CIBC Canadian Equity Fund	89:3 90:1 91:4 92:4 93:3 94:4 95:4 96:2 97:1 98:1	50%	5|9	01/95	-14.11	1994	-7.3%	3|9	2.00	3.00	2.20	orange
CIBC Canadian Index Fund	97:2 98:1 | Jun:1	63%	1|1	11/97	9.13	1997	14.0%	0|1	N/A	N/A	0.90	green

S = Seg Funds

1 CANADIAN LARGE CAP/DIVERSIFIED-BLEND

CONSISTENCY — Performance Trend by Quartiles

Fund Name	84	85	86	87	88	89	90	91	92	93	94	95	96	97	98	June
CIBC Capital Appreciation Fund								1	2	4	4	4	4	3		1
Clarington Canadian Equity Fund														3		3
Colonia Equity Fund(s)										4	4	3	2	1		2
S Co-operators Life Canadian Equity Fund									2	2	4	3	1			1
Cornerstone Canadian Growth Fund				4	4	3	4	1	2	4	3	1	3	4		2
COTE 100 REER								1	4	1	1	1	1			2
S CUMIS Life Memberfunds Canadian Growth Equity														4		3
Desjardins Environment Fund							3	4	4	2	2	2	1			1
Desjardins Equity Fund						3	3	3	3	3	2	3	2	3		3
S Desjardins Life Equity Fund	3	1	1	3	3	4	2	1	2	2	2	2	3	1		2
Dynamic Canadian Growth Fund			1	4	4	2	3	1	1	4	1	1	4	4		4
Dynamic Fund of Canada Ltd.	4	2	3	1	3	1	2	2	1	1	4	4	3	3		3
Dynamic Quebec Fund																1
Elliott & Page Equity Fund					1	3	1	1	2	2	1	3	4	2		2
Empire Elite Equity Fund(s)	2	1	3	4	2	1	3	3	2	3	2	2	3	2		2
S Empire Premier Equity Fund	3	1	3	2	1	2	3	3	1	3	3	2	1	3		2
S Equitable Life Canadian Stock Fund									4	1	3	2	3	4		4
S Equitable Life Segregated Common Stock Fund	4	2	2	4	3	3	2	4	1	1	1	1	2	4		4
Ethical Growth Fund				1	2	1	1	3	3	2	1	2	2	2		2
Ficadre Equity Fund					4	4	4	3	3	4	1	1	4	4		4
Fidelity True North Fund														1		2
First Canadian Equity Index Fund					2	4	3	3	2	2	2	2	2	2		1

RISK / REWARD-TO-RISK / EFFICIENCY

Fund Name	Fund Beats GICs %	Fund Beats GICs(Yr)	Worst 12 mo. End	Chng (%)	Worst Calendar Year		Years Fund Lost $	Sharpe Ratio 3-Yr	5-Yr	MER
CIBC Capital Appreciation Fund	60%	5|6	01/95	-18.53	1994	-13.0%	1|6	4.00	4.00	2.40
Clarington Canadian Equity Fund	59%	1|1	06/98	8.00	1997	11.9%	0|1	N/A	N/A	2.75
Colonia Equity Fund(s)	52%	4|5	01/95	-15.12	1994	-10.5%	1|5	2.00	3.00	2.27
Co-operators Life Canadian Equity Fund	56%	4|5	01/95	-7.04	1994	-0.1%	1|5	2.00	1.00	2.06
Cornerstone Canadian Growth Fund	55%	5|11	09/90	-20.48	1990	-15.0%	4|11	4.00	4.00	2.21
COTE 100 REER	59%	4|5	01/95	-18.70	1994	-14.9%	1|5	1.00	1.00	1.41
CUMIS Life Memberfunds Canadian Growth Equity	53%	1|1	01/98	1.57	1997	6.2%	0|1	N/A	N/A	3.00
Desjardins Environment Fund	51%	4|7	01/95	-11.41	1992	-3.5%	2|7	1.00	1.00	2.14
Desjardins Equity Fund	52%	13|21	06/82	-29.03	1990	-12.7%	6|21	3.00	3.00	1.93
Desjardins Life Equity Fund	53%	9|14	08/88	-17.81	1990	-9.0%	4|14	2.00	2.00	1.93
Dynamic Canadian Growth Fund	51%	6|12	05/88	-32.10	1987	-18.8%	4|12	4.00	4.00	2.31
Dynamic Fund of Canada Ltd.	55%	12|21	06/82	-31.07	1994	-11.6%	4|21	3.00	4.00	2.24
Dynamic Quebec Fund	47%	0|0	06/98	11.63	N/A		0|0	N/A	N/A	2.49
Elliott & Page Equity Fund	55%	6|9	10/90	-17.23	1990	-12.5%	3|9	4.00	3.00	1.94
Empire Elite Equity Fund(s)	57%	12|19	07/82	-27.57	1990	-18.2%	4|19	1.00	3.00	2.42
Empire Premier Equity Fund	55%	15|21	06/82	-25.99	1990	-12.8%	4|21	1.00	2.00	1.44
Equitable Life Canadian Stock Fund	55%	4|5	01/95	-5.70	1994	2.7%	0|5	3.00	2.00	2.25
Equitable Life Segregated Common Stock Fund	52%	8|17	06/82	-39.13	1981	-15.2%	3|17	2.00	1.00	1.04
Ethical Growth Fund	48%	7|11	01/95	-7.82	1992	-4.3%	3|11	1.00	1.00	2.10
Ficadre Equity Fund	46%	4|10	08/88	-29.14	1990	-17.2%	4|10	3.00	3.00	2.17
Fidelity True North Fund	64%	1|1	01/98	15.00	1997	24.1%	0|1	N/A	N/A	2.50
First Canadian Equity Index Fund	52%	6|9	10/90	-19.44	1990	-15.8%	3|9	2.00	2.00	1.21

S = Seg Funds

1 CANADIAN LARGE CAP/DIVERSIFIED-BLEND

Fund Name	Fund Beats GICs %	Fund Beats GICs(Yr)	Worst 12 mo. End	Worst 12 mo. Chng (%)	Worst Calendar Year	Worst Calendar %	Years Fund Lost $	Sharpe Ratio 3-Yr	Sharpe Ratio 5-Yr	MER
First Canadian Growth Fund	54%	3|4	01/95	-12.17	1994	-5.4%	1|4	1.00	N/A	2.20
FMOQ Canadian Equity Fund	65%	3|3	10/95	3.34	1995	12.1%	0|3	1.00	N/A	0.75
S Fonds Astra - Actions canadiennes	N/A	0|0	N/A	0.00	N/A		0|0	N/A	N/A	2.40
S Forester Growth Funds - Equity	56%	6|8	11/90	-10.42	1990	-8.1%	2|8	3.00	2.00	2.00
General Trust of Cda - Canadian Equity	53%	11|21	06/82	-36.15	1990	-16.4%	4|21	4.00	3.00	2.13
Global Strategy Canadian Opportunities Fund	47%	1|1	01/98	13.39	1997	19.6%	0|1	N/A	N/A	2.57
S Great-West Life Canadian Equity Investment (G)DSC	55%	3|3	08/95	0.79	1995	10.9%	0|3	3.00	N/A	2.40
S Great-West Life Canadian Equity Investment (G) NL	54%	6|11	07/88	-17.42	1990	-8.7%	3|11	4.00	4.00	2.64
S Great-West Life Equity Fund (M) DSC	60%	1|1	01/98	11.42	1997	14.9%	0|1	N/A	N/A	2.63
S Great-West Life Equity Fund (M) NL	60%	1|1	01/98	11.13	1997	14.6%	0|1	N/A	N/A	2.87
S Great-West Life Equity Index Investment (G) DSC	60%	3|3	09/96	-21.86	1995	11.6%	0|3	4.00	N/A	2.33
Great-West Life Equity Index Investment (G) NL	50%	7|14	10/90	-19.51	1990	-15.9%	4|14	3.00	3.00	2.57
S Great-West Life Larger Company Fund (M) DSC	53%	1|1	11/97	5.28	1997	9.5%	0|1	N/A	N/A	2.69
S Great-West Life Larger Company Fund (M) NL	53%	1|1	11/97	5.01	1997	9.2%	0|1	N/A	N/A	2.94
S Great-West Life Smaller Company Fund (M) DSC	67%	1|1	06/98	12.53	1997	19.8%	0|1	N/A	N/A	2.66
S Great-West Life Smaller Company Fund (M) NL	67%	1|1	06/98	12.24	1997	19.5%	0|1	N/A	N/A	2.91
Green Line Blue Chip Equity Fund	53%	6|10	10/90	-13.88	1990	-10.6%	3|10	2.00	3.00	2.25
Green Line Canadian Equity Fund	51%	6|9	10/90	-19.60	1990	-14.7%	3|9	2.00	2.00	2.10
Green Line Canadian Index Fund	52%	6|12	10/90	-19.40	1990	-15.8%	3|12	2.00	2.00	1.08
Guardian Growth Equity Fund	56%	6|8	01/95	-11.74	1994	-4.4%	2|8	1.00	2.00	2.15
Guardian Monthly High Income Fund	48%	1|1	06/98	-5.60	1997	6.8%	0|1	N/A	N/A	1.50
S Hartford Canadian Equity Fund	N/A	0|0	N/A	0.00	N/A		0|0	N/A	N/A	2.75

S = Seg Funds

1 CANADIAN LARGE CAP/DIVERSIFIED-BLEND

CONSISTENCY — Performance Trend by Quartiles

Fund Name	84	85	86	87	88	89	90	91	92	93	94	95	96	97	98	June
Hirsch Canadian Growth Fund																4
Hongkong Bank Equity Fund						3	3	2	1	4	4	1		2	2	2
I.G. Beutel Goodman Canadian Equity Fund														2	3	3
I.G. Sceptre Canadian Equity Fund														2	2	2
ICM Equity Fund					3	3	3	2	2	2	2	1	2	4	4	2
S Imperial Growth Canadian Equity Fund	3	3	1	1	1	3	2	2	2	3	2	3	4	2	3	3
S Industrial Alliance Canadian Advantage Fund N																
S Industrial Alliance Ecoflex Investment Fund N																
S Industrial Alliance Ecoflex Investment Fund S																1
S Industrial Alliance Ecoflex Investment Fund T																
S Industrial Alliance Ecoflex Investment Fund U																
S Industrial Alliance Ecoflex Investment Fund V																
S Industrial Alliance Stock Fund Series 2																4
Industrial Growth Fund	1	2	3	1	1	4	4	4	4	1	2	4	4	4	4	4
Industrial Horizon Fund						4	3	4	4	1	1	4	4	2	2	2
InvesNat Canadian Equity Fund							4	1	2	3	3	2	1	2	4	2
InvesNat Canadian Index Plus Fund																1
InvesNat Protected Canadian Equity Fund																
Investors Canadian Enterprise Fund																
Investors Canadian Equity Fund	4	3	1	3	2	3	1	2	1	2	2	3	2	3	4	
Investors Retirement Growth Portfolio						1	2	2	3	1	3	3	3	3	3	3
Investors Retirement Mutual Fund	2	2	4	1	1	4	3	2	3	3	1	3	3	3	4	

RISK / REWARD-TO-RISK / EFFICIENCY

Fund Name	Fund Beats GICs %	Fund Beats GICs (Yr)	Worst 12 mo. End	Worst 12 mo. Chng (%)	Worst Calendar Year	Worst Calendar Value	Years Fund Lost $	Sharpe Ratio Quartile 3-Yr	Sharpe Ratio Quartile 5-Yr	MER
Hirsch Canadian Growth Fund	N/A	0|0	N/A	0.00	N/A		0|0	N/A	N/A	2.80
Hongkong Bank Equity Fund	53%	4|8	10/90	-16.16	1990	-12.1%	2|8	1.00	3.00	1.87
I.G. Beutel Goodman Canadian Equity Fund	63%	1|1	11/97	10.93	1997	16.5%	0|1	N/A	N/A	2.79
I.G. Sceptre Canadian Equity Fund	63%	1|1	01/98	10.19	1997	13.8%	0|1	N/A	N/A	2.77
ICM Equity Fund	51%	6|10	05/92	-36.77	1990	-12.5%	1|10	3.00	1.00	0.11
S Imperial Growth Canadian Equity Fund	56%	15|21	06/82	-27.43	1990	-10.9%	3|21	3.00	3.00	1.96
S Industrial Alliance Canadian Advantage Fund N	N/A	0|0	N/A	0.00			0|0	N/A	N/A	1.50
S Industrial Alliance Ecoflex Investment Fund N	N/A	0|0	N/A	0.00			0|0	N/A	N/A	2.41
S Industrial Alliance Ecoflex Investment Fund S	61%	0|0	01/98	27.02	N/A		0|0	N/A	N/A	2.99
S Industrial Alliance Ecoflex Investment Fund T	N/A	0|0	N/A	0.00	N/A		0|0	N/A	N/A	2.41
S Industrial Alliance Ecoflex Investment Fund U	N/A	0|0	N/A	0.00	N/A		0|0	N/A	N/A	2.41
S Industrial Alliance Ecoflex Investment Fund V	N/A	0|0	N/A	0.00	N/A		0|0	N/A	N/A	1.86
S Industrial Alliance Stock Fund Series 2	44%	0|0	06/98	4.13	N/A		0|0	N/A	N/A	2.77
Industrial Growth Fund	51%	12|21	06/82	-17.09	1990	-15.0%	5|21	4.00	4.00	2.37
Industrial Horizon Fund	48%	5|10	10/90	-14.84	1990	-11.9%	2|10	2.00	2.00	2.37
InvesNat Canadian Equity Fund	48%	5|9	10/90	-10.47	1990	-5.7%	2|9	4.00	3.00	2.11
InvesNat Canadian Index Plus Fund	N/A	0|0	N/A	0.00	N/A		0|0	N/A	N/A	1.21
InvesNat Protected Canadian Equity Fund	N/A	0|0	N/A	0.00	N/A		0|0	N/A	N/A	3.00
Investors Canadian Enterprise Fund	N/A	0|0	N/A	0.00	N/A		0|0	N/A	N/A	2.60
Investors Canadian Equity Fund	51%	9|14	03/88	-14.99	1990	-7.7%	3|14	4.00	3.00	2.46
Investors Retirement Growth Portfolio	51%	5|8	09/90	-12.72	1990	-8.8%	1|8	3.00	2.00	2.62
Investors Retirement Mutual Fund	53%	12|21	06/82	-26.99	1990	-12.3%	3|21	3.00	3.00	2.42

S = Seg Funds

1 CANADIAN LARGE CAP/DIVERSIFIED-BLEND

Fund Name	Performance Trend by Quartiles (84–98, June)	Fund Beats GICs %	Fund Beats GICs(Yr)	Worst 12 mo. End	Chng (%)	Worst Calendar Year	Worst Cal. Chng	Years Fund Lost $	Sharpe 3-Yr	Sharpe 5-Yr	MER
Investors Summa Fund Ltd.	4 2 3 4 1 2 4 3 2 1 1 1	55%	7|11	10/90	-23.53	1990	-15.5%	3|11	1.00	1.00	2.48
Jones Heward Fund Ltd.	3 2 1 4 1 3 4 1 1 1 4 4 2 2 3	54%	14|21	06/82	-34.74	1990	-16.2%	5|21	4.00	4.00	2.50
Lasalle Equity Fund	3 2	54%	1|1	03/97	5.62	1997	11.2%	0|1	N/A	N/A	3.09
S London Life Canadian Equity Fund	4 2 2 1 1 2 4 1 1 2 3 3 1 2 3	53%	13|21	09/90	-23.10	1990	-21.5%	4|21	2.00	3.00	2.00
Mackenzie Sentinel Canada Equity Fund Limited	3 4 3 4 4 3 1 1 4 2 4 4	48%	4|11	11/90	-22.17	1990	-21.3%	3|11	4.00	4.00	1.99
S Manulife AGF Canadian Equity GIF	4	56%	0|0	06/98	0.50	N/A		0|0	N/A	N/A	3.20
S Manulife Cabot Blue Chip Fund	1 4 2 1	64%	3|3	02/95	4.33	1997	13.7%	0|3	1.00	N/A	2.50
S Manulife Cabot Canadian Equity Fund	1 3 3 1	60%	3|3	02/95	4.63	1997	12.5%	0|3	2.00	N/A	2.50
S Manulife Canadian Equity Index GIF		N/A	0|0	N/A		N/A		0|0	N/A	N/A	1.75
S Manulife Elliott & Page Equity GIF	3	N/A	0|0	N/A		N/A		0|0	N/A	N/A	2.75
S Manulife Fidelity Capital Builder GIF	3	56%	0|0	06/98	4.70	N/A		0|0	N/A	N/A	3.00
S Manulife Fidelity True North GIF(s)	2	63%	0|0	06/98	15.46	N/A		0|0	N/A	N/A	3.00
S Manulife GT Global Canada Fund Canada Growth GIF	1	56%	0|0	06/98	24.38	N/A		0|0	N/A	N/A	3.00
S Manulife O'Donnell Canadian GIF		N/A	0|0	N/A		N/A		0|0	N/A	N/A	3.00
S Manulife O'Donnell Select GIF		N/A	0|0	N/A		N/A		0|0	N/A	N/A	3.00
S Manulife Trimark Select Canadian Growth GIF	4	56%	0|0	06/98	0.28	N/A		0|0	N/A	N/A	2.85
S Manulife VistaFund Capital Gains Growth 1	3 4 1 2 1 3 2 1 2 3 2 4 4 4 4	52%	8|13	08/88	-16.19	1990	-13.5%	3|13	4.00	4.00	1.63
S Manulife VistaFund Equity 1	3 4 4 2 3 2 3 1 2 4 4 4 1	52%	9|17	09/88	-19.55	1990	-13.7%	3|17	4.00	4.00	1.63
Marathon Performance Large Cap Canadian Fund		N/A	0|0	N/A		N/A		0|0	N/A	N/A	2.15
S Maritime Life Canadian Equity Fund (A&C)	3 4 1	55%	1|2	11/97	-0.94	1997	4.4%	0|2	3.00	N/A	2.55
S Maritime Life Canadian Equity Fund Series B	4 1	45%	0|1	11/97	-1.13	1997	4.2%	0|1	N/A	N/A	2.55
S Maritime Life Diversified Equity Fund (A&C)	1	N/A	0|0	N/A		N/A		0|0	N/A	N/A	2.55

S = Seg Funds

1 CANADIAN LARGE CAP/DIVERSIFIED-BLEND

	Fund Name	Performance Trend by Quartiles (84–98, June)	Fund Beats GICs %	Fund Beats GICs(Yr)	Worst 12 mo. End / Chng (%)	Worst Calendar Year	Years Fund Last $	Sharpe 3-Yr	Sharpe 5-Yr	MER
S	Maritime Life Diversified Equity Fund Series - B	June:1	N/A	0|0	N/A / 0.00	N/A	0|0	N/A	N/A	2.55
S	Maritime Life Growth Fund (A&C)	1 3 2 3 4 1 4 4 2 2 4 2 1 2 3	52%	12|21	06/82 / -30.94	1990 -15.5%	3|21	2.00	3.00	2.55
S	Maritime Life Growth Fund Series B	2 3 3 4 1 2	45%	1|1	01/98 / 9.61	1997 15.7%	0|1	N/A	N/A	2.55
	Mawer Canadian Equity Fund	4 2 3 3 4 1 2	56%	4|6	01/95 / -10.61	1992 -5.9%	2|6	2.00	2.00	1.30
	Maxxum Canadian Equity Growth Fund	4 4 1 3 4 1 4 2 1 1 4 1 3 4 2	56%	12|21	06/82 / -35.48	1990 -15.6%	4|21	4.00	4.00	2.13
	McLean Budden Canadian Equity - Pooled	2 2 1 3 1 1 3 1 1 2 3 1 1 1 3	51%	10|16	06/82 / -22.60	1990 -12.4%	3|16	1.00	1.00	1.00
	McLean Budden Equity Growth Fund	2 3 1 2 3 3 2 1 2 3	54%	6|9	10/90 / -18.01	1990 -12.5%	2|9	1.00	2.00	1.75
	MD Equity Fund	1 1 3 1 1 4 2 4 2 1 2 4 3 2 1	55%	12|21	10/90 / -12.58	1990 -11.8%	3|21	2.00	2.00	1.27
	MD Select Fund	3 4 1 3 2	59%	3|4	01/95 / -9.61	1994 -4.6%	1|4	1.00	N/A	1.31
	Merrill Lynch Canadian Equity Fund	3 4	57%	1|1	06/98 / -1.22	1997 10.0%	0|1	N/A	N/A	2.78
S	MetLife MVP Equity Fund	3 2 3 4 3 4 3 4 4 1 2	50%	5|10	08/88 / -20.80	1990 -13.4%	3|10	3.00	3.00	2.19
S	Millennia III Canadian Equity Fund Series 1	4 2 3	59%	2|2	06/98 / 9.08	1997 14.9%	0|2	N/A	N/A	2.75
	Monarch Canadian Fund	4 4 4	43%	0|1	01/98 / -1.46	1997 3.8%	0|1	N/A	N/A	2.35
	Montrusco Select Canadian Equity Fund	2 1 1 2 2 3 1 1 2 3 3	55%	7|10	09/90 / -14.27	1990 -7.5%	1|10	3.00	1.00	0.00
	Montrusco Select Growth Fund	4 1 2 1 1 4 4 1 1 4	59%	7|10	09/90 / -20.17	1990 -9.6%	2|10	3.00	2.00	0.00
	Mutual Alpine Equity Fund	4	46%	0|0	06/98 / 0.60	N/A	0|0	N/A	N/A	0.00
	Mutual Equifund	4 3 1 2 4 2 4 4 2 1 2 3 3	52%	7|12	10/90 / -24.18	1990 -19.0%	4|12	2.00	2.00	1.86
	Mutual Premier Blue Chip Fund	4 2 2 2 2 3 1	56%	4|5	01/95 / -8.61	1994 -0.1%	1|5	2.00	2.00	2.36
	Mutual Summit Equity Fund	2	54%	0|0	06/98 / 14.11	N/A	0|0	N/A	N/A	0.00
S	NAL-Investor Canadian Equity Fund	3 2 2 4 3 3 2 1 2 4 3	52%	4|10	08/88 / -15.66	1990 -10.1%	3|10	4.00	4.00	1.75
S	NAL-Investor Equity Growth Fund	2 1 2 3	54%	3|3	10/95 / 5.70	1995 12.9%	0|3	1.00	N/A	2.00
S	National Life Equities Fund	2 3 3 1 4 3 1 2 2 3 2 2 3 1 1 2	55%	11|21	06/82 / -30.96	1990 -7.8%	4|21	1.00	1.00	2.25

S = Seg Funds

1 CANADIAN LARGE CAP/DIVERSIFIED-BLEND

Risk / Reward-to-Risk / Efficiency

Fund Name	Fund Beats GICs %	Fund Beats GICs (Yr)	Worst 12 mo. End	Worst 12 mo. Chng (%)	Worst Calendar Year	Worst Calendar %	Years Fund Lost $	Sharpe 3-Yr	Sharpe 5-Yr	MER
National Trust Canadian Equity Fund	53%	11|21	06/82	-20.52	1990	-9.2%	4|21	2.00	3.00	1.55 (green)
National Trust Canadian Index Fund	56%	0|0	01/98	10.78	N/A	N/A	0|0	N/A	N/A	0.87 (green)
S NN Canadian 35 Index Fund	49%	4|8	10/90	-16.38	1990	-12.9%	2|8	2.00	1.00	2.00 (green)
S NN Canadian Growth Fund	54%	13|21	03/88	-21.60	1990	-10.7%	5|21	2.00	3.00	2.80 (red)
S North West Life Ecoflex Investment Fund A	56%	0|0	06/98	2.18	N/A	N/A	0|0	N/A	N/A	2.48 (green)
S North West Life Ecoflex Investment Fund N	N/A	0|0	N/A	0.00	N/A	N/A	0|0	N/A	N/A	2.41 (orange)
S North West Life Ecoflex Investment Fund T	N/A	0|0	N/A	0.00	N/A	N/A	0|0	N/A	N/A	2.41 (orange)
Northwest Growth Fund	57%	3|5	01/95	-7.47	1994	-1.0%	1|5	3.00	2.00	2.00 (green)
O.I.Q. FERIQUE Growth Fund	54%	0|1	01/98	-5.33	1997	0.8%	0|1	N/A	N/A	0.76 (green)
O'Donnell Canadian Fund	N/A	0|0	N/A	0.00	N/A	N/A	0|0	N/A	N/A	2.75 (red)
O'Donnell Select Fund	N/A	0|0	N/A	0.00	N/A	N/A	0|0	N/A	N/A	2.75 (red)
Optimum Fonds d'actions	54%	3|3	01/95	-13.62	1995	12.7%	0|3	1.00	N/A	1.62 (green)
Pacific Total Return Fund	12%	0|0	02/98	-14.04	N/A	N/A	0|0	N/A	N/A	2.90 (red)
Phillips, Hager & North Canadian Equity Fund	56%	13|21	06/82	-40.93	1990	-10.4%	4|21	2.00	1.00	1.09 (green)
Phillips, Hager & North Canadian Equity Plus Fund	58%	14|21	06/82	-38.93	1990	-10.9%	3|21	2.00	1.00	1.18 (green)
Phillips, Hager & North Cdn Equity Plus Pension Tr	54%	14|21	06/82	-34.57	1990	-10.8%	2|21	1.00	1.00	0.54 (green)
Quebec Professionals' Canadian Equity Fund	53%	7|10	09/90	-16.04	1990	-11.3%	3|10	2.00	2.00	0.95 (green)
REA Inc. Fonds d'Investissement IDEM	55%	4|5	01/95	-15.74	1994	-12.8%	1|5	1.00	2.00	2.66 (green)
Rothschild Canadian Equity Fund	64%	1|1	06/98	6.55	1997	15.9%	0|1	N/A	N/A	2.79 (red)
Royal Canadian Strategic Index Fund	N/A	0|0	N/A	0.00	N/A	N/A	0|0	N/A	N/A	1.50 (green)
Saxon Stock Fund	50%	6|12	03/88	-18.52	1990	-14.8%	3|12	1.00	1.00	1.75 (red)
Sceptre Equity Growth Fund	55%	7|11	10/90	-13.22	1990	-9.6%	2|11	2.00	1.00	1.42 (green)

S = Seg Funds

1 CANADIAN LARGE CAP/DIVERSIFIED-BLEND

CONSISTENCY — Performance Trend by Quartiles

Fund Name	84	85	86	87	88	89	90	91	92	93	94	95	96	97	98	June
Scotia Excelsior Canadian Blue Chip Fund				4	3	4	2	1	2	4	4	4	4	3	4	2
Scotia Excelsior Canadian Growth Fund	4	4	3	1	3	3	2	3	2	2	1	1	4	3		3
Spectrum United Canadian Equity Fund	1	1	2	4	1	2	1	2	1	2	3	2	2	3		3
Spectrum United Canadian Maximum Growth Portfolio																3
Spectrum United Canadian Stock Fund					3	4	3	3	4	4	1	3	3	1		2
Standard Life Equity Mutual Fund									3	1	2	3	1	1		1
Standard Life Ideal Equity Fund(s)						4	4	3	4	1	1	2	1			1
Stone & Co Flagship Stock Fund Canada												3	1	3		3
Strategic Value Canadian Equity Fund	1	3	4	3	1	4	4	2	3	4	4	2	1			1
Strategic Value Canadian Equity Value Fund															1	4
Strategic Value RSP Fund																3
Synergy Canadian Fund Inc. - Canadian Momentum Cl																
Synergy Canadian Fund Inc. - Cdn Style Mgmt																1
Talvest Canadian Equity Value Fund	3	2	3	1	2	4	1	1	4	1	3	4	3			2
Templeton Canadian Stock Fund						3	4	4	1	2	4	3	1	3		3
The McElvaine Investment Trust													3	1		1
Tradex Canadian Growth Fund																4
Tradex Equity Fund Limited	3	3	2	2	3	2	2	4	2	3	1	1	1	1		3
Trimark Canadian Fund	1	1	4	1	1	2	3	1	1	1	3	2	4	4		4
Trust Pret et Revenu Canadian Fund	4	4	3	4	4	2	3	1	2	3	3	2	4	3		3
Universal Canadian Growth Fund											3	1	3	2		3
Universal Future Fund				3	4	4	4	4	1	1	1	4	2	2		2

RISK / REWARD-TO-RISK / EFFICIENCY

Fund Name	Fund Beats GICs %	Fund Beats GICs (Yr)	Worst 12 mo. End	Worst 12 mo. Chng (%)	Worst Calendar Year	Worst Calendar Year %	Years Fund Lost $	Sharpe Ratio 3-Yr	Sharpe Ratio 5-Yr	MER
Scotia Excelsior Canadian Blue Chip Fund	47%	7|11	08/88	-19.71	1987	-15.4%	3|11	3.00	4.00	1.93
Scotia Excelsior Canadian Growth Fund	55%	12|21	06/82	-30.17	1990	-8.9%	4|21	2.00	1.00	2.09
Spectrum United Canadian Equity Fund	55%	15|21	06/82	-29.04	1990	-9.3%	5|21	2.00	1.00	2.35
Spectrum United Canadian Maximum Growth Portfolio	N/A	0|0	N/A	0.00	N/A		0|0	N/A	N/A	2.33
Spectrum United Canadian Stock Fund	49%	6|10	10/90	-16.70	1990	-12.5%	2|10	1.00	2.00	2.33
Standard Life Equity Mutual Fund	57%	4|5	01/95	-6.44	1994	0.6%	0|5	1.00	1.00	2.00
Standard Life Ideal Equity Fund(s)	55%	6|11	08/88	-18.22	1990	-6.8%	2|11	1.00	1.00	2.00
Stone & Co Flagship Stock Fund Canada	59%	2|2	01/98	10.23	1997	18.1%	0|2	N/A	N/A	2.88
Strategic Value Canadian Equity Fund	53%	12|21	06/82	-27.17	1990	-17.5%	3|21	3.00	3.00	2.70
Strategic Value Canadian Equity Value Fund	60%	1|1	06/98	4.45	1997	27.6%	0|1	N/A	N/A	2.70
Strategic Value RSP Fund	N/A	0|0	N/A	0.00	N/A		0|0	N/A	N/A	4.15
Synergy Canadian Fund Inc. - Canadian Momentum Cl	N/A	0|0	N/A	0.00	N/A		0|0	N/A	N/A	0.00
Synergy Canadian Fund Inc. - Cdn Style Mgmt	N/A	0|0	N/A	0.00	N/A		0|0	N/A	N/A	0.00
Talvest Canadian Equity Value Fund	49%	12|21	06/82	-29.82	1990	-7.4%	4|21	3.00	3.00	2.40
Templeton Canadian Stock Fund	47%	4|8	09/90	-16.38	1990	-13.0%	2|8	1.00	1.00	2.44
The McElvaine Investment Trust	64%	1|1	12/97	12.88	1997	12.9%	0|1	N/A	N/A	0.00
Tradex Canadian Growth Fund	50%	0|0	06/98	7.49	N/A		0|0	N/A	N/A	1.50
Tradex Equity Fund Limited	56%	13|21	06/82	-26.24	1990	-9.4%	2|21	1.00	1.00	1.35
Trimark Canadian Fund	53%	8|16	10/90	-16.48	1990	-12.1%	1|16	3.00	2.00	1.52
Trust Pret et Revenu Canadian Fund	48%	12|21	06/82	-35.63	1981	-13.5%	5|21	3.00	2.00	1.93
Universal Canadian Growth Fund	63%	2|2	08/96	11.34	1996	22.8%	0|2	N/A	N/A	2.39
Universal Future Fund	53%	5|10	10/90	-17.20	1990	-15.0%	2|10	3.00	2.00	2.38

S = Seg Funds

217

1 CANADIAN LARGE CAP/DIVERSIFIED-BLEND

Fund Name	CONSISTENCY — Performance Trend by Quartiles (84 85 86 87 88 89 90 91 92 93 94 95 96 97 98 / June)	RISK — Fund Beats GICs %	Fund Beats GICs(Yr)	Worst 12 mo. End Chng (%)	Worst Calendar Year	Years Fund Lost $	REWARD-TO-RISK — Sharpe Ratio Quartile Rankings 3-Yr	5-Yr	EFFICIENCY — MER
University Avenue Canadian Fund	1 1 1 4 4 4 4 4 / 4	54%	4|7	01/95 -18.59	1994 -9.5%	2|7	4.00	4.00	2.40 ●
Valorem Canadian Equity-Value Fund	/ 3	47%	0|0	06/98 9.22	N/A	0|0	N/A	N/A	2.45 ●
Value Contrarian Canadian Equity	/ 1	61%	0|0	06/98 26.98	N/A	0|0	N/A	N/A	2.00 ●
YMG Growth Fund	4 3 1 4 1 4 4 1 4 4 3 1 4 / 4	49%	6|12	01/95 -20.05	1994 -14.9%	4|12	3.00	4.00	2.02 ●

S = Seg Funds

2 CANADIAN LARGE CAP/DIVERSIFIED-VALUE

Fund Name	Performance Trend by Quartiles (84–98)	Fund Beats GICs %	Fund Beats GICs(Yr)	Worst 12 mo. End	Chng (%)	Worst Calendar Year	Worst Calendar %	Years Fund Lost $	Sharpe 3-Yr	Sharpe 5-Yr	Efficiency	MER
ABC Fundamental-Value Fund	1 3 1 2 4	57%	5|8	01/95	-8.10	1990	-2.0%	1|8	2.00	1.00	green	2.00
AIM GT Canada Value Class	1	N/A	0|0	N/A	0.00	N/A		0|0	N/A	N/A	red	2.87
Associate Investors Limited	4 3 3 1 1 1	55%	13|21	06/82	-32.29	1981	-9.9%	4|21	1.00	1.00	green	1.83
Batirente Equity Fund	2 2 2 1	58%	3|3	03/95	-1.52	1995	13.3%	0|3	2.00	N/A	green	1.50
S BPI Canadian Bond Segregated Fund		N/A	0|0	N/A	0.00	N/A		0|0	N/A	N/A	—	0.00
BPI Canadian Equity Value Fund	3 4 1 2 3 3	49%	6|8	01/95	-15.42	1994	-9.4%	2|8	3.00	4.00	red	2.49
S BPI Canadian Equity Value Segregated Fund		N/A	0|0	N/A	0.00	N/A		0|0	N/A	N/A	—	0.00
S C.I. Harbour Segregated Fund	3	N/A	0|0	N/A	0.00	N/A		0|0	N/A	N/A	red	3.05
Elliott & Page Value Equity Fund	2	N/A	0|0	N/A	0.00	N/A		0|0	N/A	N/A	orange	2.09
Global Strategy Canada Growth Fund	1 4 3 3 3 4	61%	4|5	01/95	-12.12	1994	-8.5%	1|5	3.00	3.00	red	2.57
S Great-West Life Equity Fund DSC	2 2	57%	1|1	06/98	10.47	1997	15.2%	0|1	N/A	N/A	red	2.61
S Great-West Life Equity Fund NL	3 2	57%	1|1	06/98	10.19	1997	14.9%	0|1	N/A	N/A	red	2.85
Green Line Value Fund	3 3 1 2 4	55%	3|4	01/95	-13.88	1994	-6.1%	1|4	2.00	N/A	green	2.09
S Growsafe Canadian Equity Fund	2 3 3 4	57%	3|3	01/98	2.75	1997	6.5%	0|3	3.00	N/A	red	2.45
Harbour Fund	2	46%	0|0	06/98	5.20	N/A		0|0	N/A	N/A	orange	2.33
Harbour Sector Shares	3	38%	0|0	06/98	4.10	N/A		0|0	N/A	N/A	green	2.33
S Industrial Alliance Ecoflex Investment Fund A	2 1 4 4 3	58%	2|4	01/95	-5.17	1994	1.6%	0|4	4.00	3.00	red	2.48
S Industrial Alliance Ecoflex Stock Fund "ANL"		N/A	0|0	N/A	0.00	N/A		0|0	N/A	N/A	orange	2.40
S Industrial Alliance Stock Fund "ANL"		N/A	0|0	N/A	0.00	N/A		0|0	N/A	N/A	green	1.50
S Industrial Alliance Stock Fund	2 2 1 4 3 3	52%	8|14	08/88	-14.20	1990	-8.7%	2|14	3.00	2.00	green	1.57
Ivy Canadian Fund	4 1 1 2 2 1	60%	4|5	01/95	0.09	1994	5.0%	0|5	1.00	1.00	orange	2.38
Leith Wheeler Canadian Equity Fund	4 1 1 1	60%	2|3	09/95	0.80	1995	6.7%	0|3	1.00	N/A	green	1.50

S = Seg Funds

2 CANADIAN LARGE CAP/DIVERSIFIED-VALUE

Fund Name	84	85	86	87	88	89	90	91	92	93	94	95	96	97	98	June	Fund Beats GICs %	Fund Beats GICs(Yr)	Worst 12 mo. End	Chng (%)	Worst Calendar Year		Years Fund Lost $	Sharpe Ratio 3-Yr	Sharpe Ratio 5-Yr	MER	Efficiency
S Manulife Elliott & Page Value Equity GIF																	N/A	0|0	N/A	0.00	N/A		0|0	N/A	N/A	2.80	● red
S Manulife Harbour GIF																	N/A	0|0	N/A	0.00	N/A		0|0	N/A	N/A	3.00	● red
S North West Life Ecoflex Stock Fund "ANL"																3	N/A	0|0	N/A	0.00	N/A		0|0	N/A	N/A	2.40	● orange
S Royal & SunAlliance Equity Fund											4	2	2	3	1	2	50%	5|7	01/91	-9.29	1994	-0.1%	1|7	1.00	2.00	2.37	● orange
Royal Canadian Equity Fund											2	2	2	4	3	2	55%	11|21	06/82	-40.69	1990	-14.7%	5|21	2.00	2.00	1.95	● green
Royal Canadian Value Fund														1	1	3	N/A	0|0	N/A	0.00	N/A		0|0	N/A	N/A	2.00	● green
Scudder Canadian Equity Fund																	64%	2|2	06/98	26.21	1996	33.4%	0|2	N/A	N/A	1.35	● green
Spectrum United Canadian Investment Fund											4	3	1	2	1	2	54%	11|21	06/82	-22.68	1990	-12.9%	4|21	1.00	1.00	2.33	● orange
Synergy Canadian Fund Inc. - Canadian Value Class																3	N/A	0|0	N/A	0.00	N/A		0|0	N/A	N/A	0.00	—
The Goodwood Fund															1	1	52%	1|1	01/98	31.30	1997	41.1%	0|1	N/A	N/A	1.49	● green
Trans-Canada Value Fund												1	4	4	4	4	51%	12|21	05/82	-26.52	1981	-16.3%	4|21	4.00	4.00	3.52	● red
Trimark RSP Equity Fund											3	1	3	3	4	4	52%	5|9	09/90	-15.21	1990	-11.2%	1|9	4.00	3.00	2.00	● green
Trimark Select Canadian Growth Fund											3	1	2	3	4	4	60%	3|5	01/95	-4.83	1997	3.3%	0|5	3.00	2.00	2.30	● orange
S Westbury Canadian Life - Equity Growth Fund											2	3	4	2	2	1	51%	4|8	01/95	-11.03	1992	-4.8%	3|8	2.00	3.00	2.40	● orange

S = Seg Funds

3 CANADIAN LARGE CAP/DIVERSIFIED-GROWTH

Fund Name	CONSISTENCY — Performance Trend by Quartiles															June	RISK — Fund Beats GICs %	Fund Beats GICs(Yr)	Worst 12 mo. End	Worst 12 mo. Chng (%)	Worst Calendar Year	Worst Calendar %	Years Fund Lost $	REWARD-TO-RISK Sharpe Ratio Quartile Rankings 3-Yr	5-Yr	EFFICIENCY MER
	84	85	86	87	88	89	90	91	92	93	94	95	96	97	98											
20/20 RSP Aggressive Equity Fund												1	1	4	2	2	56%	2|4	01/95	-18.02	1994	-14.1%	2|4	3.00	N/A	2.47
20/20 RSP Aggressive Smaller Companies Fund														3	3	3	52%	0|1	05/97	-7.39	1997	3.7%	0|1	N/A	N/A	2.73
AGF Growth Equity Fund Limited											3	3	3	2	4		57%	14|21	06/82	-49.84	1981	-25.6%	6|21	4.00	N/A	2.80
AIC Diversified Canada Fund													1	1	1	1	79%	2|2	01/98	28.44	1997	32.1%	0|2	1.00	N/A	2.39
Altamira Capital Growth Fund Limited											4	4	3	2			53%	15|21	05/88	-17.56	1987	-6.6%	3|21	4.00	N/A	2.00
Azura Growth RRSP Pooled Funds														3	4		57%	1|1	01/98	3.48	1997	8.7%	0|1	N/A	N/A	2.23
Clean Environment Equity Fund											1	2	1	3		3	64%	4|5	01/95	-18.13	1994	-13.7%	1|5	1.00	N/A	2.60
Desjardins Growth Fund												3	4	2	3		54%	3|3	01/95	-10.41	1995	10.5%	0|3	3.00	N/A	1.95
S Empire Equity Growth Fund											3	3	3	3	3		55%	12|17	06/82	-22.27	1990	-15.0%	5|17	2.00	N/A	1.24
Fidelity Capital Builder Fund											2	4	4	4	3		54%	5|9	01/95	-16.11	1994	-7.5%	2|9	4.00	N/A	2.45
S Great-West Life Growth Equity Fund (A) DSC														2	4		60%	1|1	01/98	4.68	1997	14.3%	0|1	N/A	N/A	3.00
S Great-West Life Growth Equity Fund (A) NL														2	4		60%	1|1	01/98	4.41	1997	14.0%	0|1	N/A	N/A	3.24
S Great-West Life Mid Cap Canada Fund (G) DSC															1		N/A	0|0	N/A	0.00	N/A		0|0	N/A	N/A	2.40
S Great-West Life Mid Cap Canada Fund (G) NL															1		N/A	0|0	N/A	0.00	N/A		0|0	N/A	N/A	2.64
Infinity Canadian Fund															1		61%	0|0	01/98	23.26	N/A		0|0	N/A	N/A	2.95
Lotus Canadian Equity Fund												4	1	1	4		51%	3|4	01/95	-22.69	1994	-13.4%	1|4	3.00	N/A	2.12
S Maritime Life Aggressive Equity (A&C)														4	2		35%	0|1	01/98	-3.90	1997	0.9%	0|1	N/A	N/A	2.55
S Maritime Life Aggressive Equity Series B														4	2		35%	0|1	01/98	-3.86	1997	1.0%	0|1	N/A	N/A	2.55
Navigator Canadian Growth Fund															4		N/A	0|0	N/A	0.00	N/A		0|0	N/A	N/A	2.75
Phillips, Hager & North Vintage Fund											1	2	2	2	3		62%	8|11	08/88	-18.44	1990	-5.1%	2|11	2.00	N/A	1.76
Pursuit Canadian Equity Fund												2	3	1	2		53%	7|14	08/88	-25.90	1987	-14.3%	3|14	2.00	N/A	2.00
Quebec Growth Fund Inc.												4	2	1	1		50%	6|10	08/88	-51.76	1990	-38.0%	3|10	1.00	N/A	2.00

S = Seg Funds

3 CANADIAN LARGE CAP/DIVERSIFIED-GROWTH

Fund Name	CONSISTENCY — Performance Trend by Quartiles (84 85 86 87 88 89 90 91 92 93 94 95 96 97 98 June)	RISK — Fund Beats GICs %	Fund Beats GICs(Yr)	Worst 12 mo. End	Chng (%)	Worst Calendar Year	Years Fund Lost $	Sharpe Ratio Quartile Rankings 3-Yr	5-Yr	MER	EFFICIENCY
Royal Balanced Growth Fund		N/A	0|0	N/A	0.00	N/A	0|0	N/A	N/A	2.25	●
Synergy Canadian Fund Inc. - Canadian Growth Class	1	N/A	0|0	N/A	0.00	N/A	0|0	N/A	N/A	0.00	–
Talvest Hyperion Canadian Equity Growth Fund	2	56%	0|0	01/98	16.60	N/A	0|0	N/A	N/A	2.10	●
Talvest New Economy Fund	2 4 3 4	50%	3|4	11/94	-10.40	1994 -8.2%	1|4	4.00	N/A	2.50	●

S = Seg Funds

4 CANADIAN SMALL/ MID-CAP EQUITY

	Fund Name	CONSISTENCY: Performance Trend by Quartiles 84	85	86	87	88	89	90	91	92	93	94	95	96	97	June 98	RISK: Fund Beats GICs %	Fund Beats GICs(Yr)	Worst 12 mo. End	Worst 12 mo. Chng (%)	Worst Calendar Year	Worst Calendar Year (%)	Years Fund Lost $	REWARD-TO-RISK: Sharpe Ratio Quartile Rankings 3-Yr	5-Yr	EFFICIENCY: MER
	Altamira Special Growth Fund				4	4	1	1	1	1	2	4	3	3	2	3	53%	8|12	01/95	-25.62	1994	-19.6%	3|12	3.00	3.00	1.60
	Argentum Canadian Small Company Portfolio																N/A	0|0	N/A	0.00	N/A		0|0	N/A	N/A	0.00 –
	Atlas Canadian Emerging Growth Fund												1	2	4	4	58%	2|3	06/98	-22.15	1997	-8.0%	1|3	4.00	N/A	2.47
	Atlas Canadian Small Cap Growth Fund														2	3	57%	1|1	06/98	5.03	1997	22.8%	0|1	N/A	N/A	2.74
	Atlas Canadian Small Cap Value Fund												4	2	2	4	64%	2|3	10/95	-4.12	1995	4.4%	0|3	3.00	N/A	2.56
	Beutel Goodman Small Cap Fund													1	3	1	60%	2|2	06/98	3.38	1997	6.1%	0|2	2.00	N/A	2.39
	Bissett Microcap Fund															1	N/A	0|0	N/A	0.00	N/A		0|0	N/A	N/A	2.00
	Bissett Small Cap Fund										1	3	2	1	1	3	63%	4|5	01/95	-16.43	1994	-8.6%	1|5	1.00	1.00	1.90
	BPI Canadian Small Companies Fund					4	3	3	1	2	3	2	2	1	4	4	47%	6|10	01/98	-24.86	1997	-18.6%	4|10	4.00	4.00	2.92
	Cambridge Growth Fund				2	2	2	1	2	3	2	4	4	4	4	4	51%	12|21	11/97	-38.55	1997	-31.5%	4|21	4.00	4.00	3.46
	Cambridge Special Equity Fund					1	2	4	4	4	1	4	2	4	4	4	46%	4|10	05/97	-52.38	1997	-43.9%	5|10	4.00	4.00	3.46
	Canada Trust Special Equity Fund				3	3	3	2	1	2	2	4	4	4	2	3	54%	7|11	07/88	-25.04	1994	-18.5%	2|11	3.00	3.00	2.15
S	CDA Aggressive Equity Fund (Altamira)												4	3	2	3	53%	2|3	04/95	-12.50	1995	7.1%	0|3	3.00	N/A	1.00
S	CDA Special Equity Fund (KBSH)														1	3	65%	1|1	06/98	14.96	1997	46.1%	0|1	N/A	N/A	1.44
	Chou RRSP Fund				2	2	2	2	3	2	4	3	2	3	1	1	52%	7|11	10/90	-15.71	1990	-11.4%	2|11	1.00	1.00	2.02
	Clarington Canadian Micro-Cap Fund															2	N/A	0|0	N/A	0.00	N/A		0|0	N/A	N/A	2.95
	Clarington Canadian Small Cap Fund															2	56%	0|0	06/98	3.18	N/A		0|0	N/A	N/A	2.75
S	Colonia Special Growth Fund											2	2	1	1	4	55%	3|4	01/95	-9.36	1994	-5.0%	1|4	1.00	N/A	2.27
	COTE 100 EXP												1	2	3	1	65%	3|3	04/95	7.18	1997	13.3%	0|3	1.00	N/A	2.60
	COTE 100 REA-action													2	3	2	59%	1|2	01/98	-5.55	1997	-0.2%	1|2	N/A	N/A	2.60
	Cundill Security Fund Series A				2	3	3	3	4	4	3	1	3	4	2	1	49%	10|17	06/82	-24.15	1990	-14.0%	3|17	1.00	1.00	2.04
	Cundill Security Fund Series B															1	62%	0|0	06/98	17.26	N/A		0|0	N/A	N/A	2.39

S = Seg Funds

4 CANADIAN SMALL/MID-CAP EQUITY

Performance Trend by Quartiles (quartile rank per year, 84–98 | June 98)

Fund Name	Performance Trend (year: quartile)	June 98
Dynamic Small Cap Fund	98:1	1
Empire Elite Small Cap Equity Fund (S)	—	3
Ethical Special Equity Fund	96:3, 97:2, 98:2	2
Fidelity Canadian Growth Company Fund	94:1, 95:4, 96:1, 97:1, 98:1	1
GBC Canadian Growth Fund	88:1, 89:3, 90:1, 91:1, 92:4, 93:2, 94:2, 95:2, 96:1, 97:1, 98:1	1
General Trust of Cda - Growth Fund	88:1, 89:3, 90:1, 91:1, 92:3, 93:4, 94:4, 95:3, 96:1, 97:2	2
Global Strategy Canadian Small Cap Fund	95:2, 96:1, 97:2, 98:4	4
Green Line Canadian Small-Cap Equity Fund	98:4	
GTS Canadian Protected Fund	87:1, 88:3, 89:4, 90:1, 91:3, 92:3, 93:4, 94:1, 95:4, 96:4, 97:3	1
Guardian Enterprise Fund	86:3, 87:3, 88:2, 89:2, 90:3, 91:3, 92:3, 93:4, 94:3, 95:1, 96:1, 97:3	3
Harbour Explorer Fund	—	1
Harbour Explorer Sector Shares	—	1
Harbour Explorer Sector Shares US	98:2	
Hartford Aggressive Growth Fund (S)	98:3	
Hongkong Bank Small Cap Growth Fund	96:2, 97:2, 98:2	2
I.G. Beutel Goodman Canadian Small Cap	97:3	1
Industrial Equity Fund Limited	88:1, 89:2, 90:4, 91:4, 92:4, 93:1, 94:3, 95:4, 96:4, 97:4, 98:4	4
Investors Canadian Small Cap Fund	97:1	2
Investors Canadian Small Cap Fund II	—	
Ivy Enterprise Fund	94:3, 95:3, 96:3, 97:1, 98:2	2
Lion Knowledge Industries Fund	93:4, 94:1, 95:1, 96:2, 97:4, 98:2	2
Manulife Cabot Canadian Growth Fund	94:4, 95:1, 96:2, 97:4	4

Risk / Reward-to-Risk / Efficiency

Fund Name	Fund Beats GICs %	Fund Beats GICs (Yr)	Worst 12 mo. End	Worst 12 mo. Chng (%)	Worst Calendar Year	Worst Calendar Year %	Years Fund Lost $ (Lost $)	Sharpe 3-Yr	Sharpe 5-Yr	MER	Efficiency
Dynamic Small Cap Fund	47%	0|0	06/98	17.00	N/A		0|0	N/A	N/A	2.99	●
Empire Elite Small Cap Equity Fund (S)	N/A	0|0	N/A	0.00	N/A		0|0	N/A	N/A	2.40	●
Ethical Special Equity Fund	64%	2|2	06/98	4.47	1997	16.3%	0|2	2.00	N/A	2.71	●
Fidelity Canadian Growth Company Fund	71%	3|3	04/97	14.28	1996	20.5%	0|3	1.00	1.00	2.47	●
GBC Canadian Growth Fund	60%	7|9	01/95	-14.73	1990	-13.6%	2|9	1.00	1.00	1.90	●
General Trust of Cda - Growth Fund	55%	6|9	10/90	-23.30	1990	-20.8%	2|9	2.00	3.00	2.15	●
Global Strategy Canadian Small Cap Fund	58%	3|3	06/98	-0.97	1995	14.9%	0|3	2.00	N/A	2.71	●
Green Line Canadian Small-Cap Equity Fund	N/A	0|0	N/A	0.00	N/A		0|0	N/A	N/A	2.35	●
GTS Canadian Protected Fund	35%	3|13	08/94	-5.15	1994	-1.5%	1|13	4.00	4.00	2.40	●
Guardian Enterprise Fund	52%	12|21	06/82	-24.56	1990	-10.2%	4|21	2.00	2.00	2.10	●
Harbour Explorer Fund	N/A	0|0	N/A	0.00	N/A		0|0	N/A	N/A	2.32	●
Harbour Explorer Sector Shares	N/A	0|0	N/A	0.00	N/A		0|0	N/A	N/A	2.32	●
Harbour Explorer Sector Shares US	N/A	0|0	N/A	0.00	N/A		0|0	N/A	N/A	2.32	●
Hartford Aggressive Growth Fund (S)	N/A	0|0	N/A	0.00	N/A		0|0	N/A	N/A	2.80	●
Hongkong Bank Small Cap Growth Fund	60%	2|2	01/98	4.43	1997	15.5%	0|2	2.00	N/A	2.15	●
I.G. Beutel Goodman Canadian Small Cap	63%	0|1	06/98	1.80	1997	4.1%	0|1	N/A	N/A	2.78	●
Industrial Equity Fund Limited	51%	12|21	06/98	-29.71	1990	-28.1%	6|21	4.00	4.00	2.42	●
Investors Canadian Small Cap Fund	63%	1|1	06/98	14.57	1997	29.1%	0|1	N/A	N/A	2.51	●
Investors Canadian Small Cap Fund II	N/A	0|0	N/A	0.00	N/A		0|0	N/A	N/A	2.61	●
Ivy Enterprise Fund	65%	3|3	09/95	7.18	1995	14.6%	0|3	1.00	N/A	2.39	●
Lion Knowledge Industries Fund	54%	2|4	01/98	-26.88	1997	-23.6%	2|4	4.00	3.00	2.90	●
Manulife Cabot Canadian Growth Fund	55%	3|3	02/95	-20.54	1995	8.5%	0|3	2.00	N/A	2.50	●

S = Seg Funds

224

4 CANADIAN SMALL/MID-CAP EQUITY

CONSISTENCY: Performance Trend by Quartiles (years 84 85 86 87 88 89 90 91 92 93 94 95 96 97 98, June 98)

Fund Name	Performance Trend (quartiles, reading L→R toward June '98)	Fund Beats GICs %	Fund Beats GICs (Yr)	Worst 12 mo. End	Worst 12 mo. Chng (%)	Worst Calendar Year	Worst Cal. Yr %	Years Fund Lost $	Sharpe 3-Yr	Sharpe 5-Yr	MER
Manulife Cabot Emerging Growth Fund	3 2 3 3 · 3	51%	3|3	02/95	-17.60	1997	6.4%	0|3	2.00	N/A	2.50
Marathon Equity Fund	4 1 1 3 2 1 1 2 1 1 4 · 4	52%	7|11	03/88	-39.99	1987	-31.4%	4|11	4.00	3.00	2.51
Mawer New Canada Fund	3 1 2 2 2 2 1 4 1 2 3 · 3	57%	6|9	01/95	-10.17	1994	-3.1%	1|9	2.00	1.00	1.46
S MetLife MVP Growth Fund	2 2 3 1 1 2 · 2	67%	3|4	01/95	-13.71	1994	-5.9%	1|4	1.00	1.00	2.17
Millennium Next Generation Fund	2 1 2 1 2 · 2	56%	3|4	01/95	-8.00	1994	-5.9%	1|4	1.00	N/A	2.50
Multiple Opportunities Fund	1 4 2 2 4 3 1 4 1 1 1 4 · 4	53%	7|12	09/88	-51.37	1988	-37.5%	5|12	4.00	2.00	2.50
Mutual Premier Growth Fund	3 1 2 3 3 4 · 4	63%	4|5	01/95	-8.31	1994	-0.9%	1|5	3.00	2.00	2.38
National Trust Special Equity Fund	3 4 3 3 3 3 · 3	52%	4|5	01/95	-22.61	1994	-14.9%	1|5	3.00	3.00	2.50
Navigator Value Investment Retirement Fund	1 1 1 1 4 · 4	61%	3|5	06/98	-21.87	1997	-4.1%	2|5	4.00	2.00	2.99
O'Donnell Canadian Emerging Growth Fund	2 4 4 · 4	55%	1|2	06/98	-21.11	1997	-8.1%	1|2	N/A	N/A	2.75
O'Donnell Growth Fund	2 3 3 · 3	61%	2|2	01/98	0.98	1997	8.3%	0|2	N/A	N/A	2.75
OTG Investment Fund - Growth Section	3 1 1 2 3 4 4 2 3 3 3 1 · 1	54%	12|21	06/82	-28.85	1990	-12.9%	4|21	2.00	2.00	1.00
Resolute Growth Fund	4 1 4 1 · 1	54%	2|3	06/97	-17.67	1997	-5.4%	1|3	3.00	N/A	2.00
S Royal & SunAlliance Canadian Growth Fund	2 3 2 4 · 4	64%	3|3	06/98	-1.12	1997	14.9%	0|3	3.00	N/A	2.35
Royal Canadian Growth Fund	3 3 4 3 2 · 2	58%	3|4	01/95	-16.82	1994	-10.1%	1|4	3.00	3.00	2.23
Royal Canadian Small Cap Fund	4 3 3 4 4 3 · 3	57%	3|5	01/95	-19.24	1994	-11.9%	2|5	4.00	4.00	2.23
Saxon Small Cap	4 2 4 2 2 2 3 3 3 1 1 · 1	52%	9|12	10/90	-25.88	1990	-25.3%	3|12	1.00	1.00	1.75
Spectrum United Canadian Growth Fund	4 1 3 4 2 3 2 1 1 4 3 4 · 4	56%	15|21	06/82	-40.52	1981	-26.3%	5|21	3.00	2.00	2.35
Spectrum United Canadian Small-Mid Cap Fund	2 · 2	N/A	0|0	N/A	0.00	N/A		0|0	N/A	N/A	2.35
Strategic Value Canadian Small Companies Fund	1 3 4 3 1 4 4 2 2 · 2	53%	5|8	01/95	-11.86	1990	-3.6%	2|8	3.00	2.00	2.70
Synergy Canadian Fund Inc. - Cdn Small Cap Class	2 · 2	N/A	0|0	N/A	0.00	N/A	N/A	0|0	N/A	N/A	0.00
Talvest/Hyperion Small Cap Canadian Equity Fund	3 2 1 3 · 3	59%	3|3	01/95	-19.60	1995	14.6%	0|3	2.00	N/A	2.54

S = Seg Funds

4 CANADIAN SMALL/MID-CAP EQUITY

Fund Name	CONSISTENCY — Performance Trend by Quartiles (84 85 86 87 88 89 90 91 92 93 94 95 96 97 98 / June)	RISK — Fund Beats GICs %	Fund Beats GICs(Yr)	Worst 12 mo. End	Chng (%)	Worst Calendar Year	Years Fund Lost $	REWARD-TO-RISK — Sharpe Ratio Quartile Rankings 3-Yr	5-Yr	EFFICIENCY — MER
Trimark Canadian Small Companies Fund		N/A	0|0	N/A	0.00	N/A	0|0	N/A	N/A	● 2.40
University Avenue Canadian Small Cap Fund		N/A	0|0	N/A	0.00	N/A	0|0	N/A	N/A	● 2.40
YMG Emerging Companies Fund	3	61%	0|0	06/98	6.20	N/A	0|0	N/A	N/A	● 2.00

S = Seg Funds

5 CANADIAN DIVIDEND

Performance Trend by Quartiles (Consistency)

Fund Name	84	85	86	87	88	89	90	91	92	93	94	95	96	97	98	June
Acuity Pooled High Income Fund											1	4	2	2	3	
AGF Dividend Fund				3		1	1	3	3	3	1	2	1	1	2	1
AGF High Income Fund									1	4	1	4	3	2	4	4
Altamira Dividend Fund Inc.												1	3	2	1	
Argentum Income Portfolio																
Atlas Canadian Dividend Growth Fund														3	3	
Atlas Canadian Income Trust Fund															4	
Bissett Dividend Income Fund						2	3	2	2	2	2	1	1	2	2	2
Bissett Income Trust Fund															4	4
BPI Dividend Income Fund					4	3	3	1	3	4	2	1	3	3	3	
BPI Dividend Income Segregated Fund														2	4	
BPI High Income Fund																
BPI High Income Segregated Fund														3	3	
C.I. Dividend Fund														3	3	
Canada Life Enhanced Dividend Fund S-39												1	2	3	1	
Canada Trust Dividend Income Fund										3	1	4	4	3	4	2
CIBC Dividend Fund																1
CIBC International Small Companies Fund												2	3	1	2	
Desjardins Dividend Fund					2	2	3	2	2	1	3	3	2	4	3	
Dynamic Dividend Fund									2	3	1	2	3	2	4	
Dynamic Dividend Growth Fund				4	4	3	1	2	3	4	2	2	4			
Elliott & Page Monthly High Income Fund															4	

Risk / Reward-to-Risk / Efficiency

Fund Name	Fund Beats GICs %	Fund Beats GICs (Yr)	Worst 12 mo. End	Chng (%)	Worst Calendar Year		Years Fund Lost $	Sharpe Ratio Quartile 3-Yr	5-Yr	MER	Efficiency
Acuity Pooled High Income Fund	63%	2|4	10/94	3.74	1995	5.9%	0|4	4.00	2.00	0.00	—
AGF Dividend Fund	53%	7|11	09/90	-7.25	1990	-5.1%	1|11	4.00	3.00	1.87	●
AGF High Income Fund	59%	5|8	01/95	-3.50	1994	-1.3%	1|8	4.00	4.00	1.68	●
Altamira Dividend Fund Inc.	65%	3|3	10/95	12.66	1995	16.1%	0|3	2.00	N/A	1.56	●
Argentum Income Portfolio	N/A	0|0	N/A	0.00	N/A		0|0	N/A	N/A	0.00	—
Atlas Canadian Dividend Growth Fund	71%	1|1	06/98	15.01	1997	18.6%	0|1	N/A	N/A	2.25	●
Atlas Canadian Income Trust Fund	N/A	0|0	N/A	0.00	N/A		0|0	N/A	N/A	1.86	●
Bissett Dividend Income Fund	55%	6|9	09/90	-12.17	1990	-7.2%	1|9	1.00	1.00	1.50	●
Bissett Income Trust Fund	56%	1|1	06/98	-1.07	1997	12.9%	0|1	N/A	N/A	1.25	●
BPI Dividend Income Fund	51%	10|21	10/90	-4.41	1987	-1.9%	4|21	1.00	1.00	1.21	●
BPI Dividend Income Segregated Fund	N/A	0|0	N/A	0.00	N/A		0|0	N/A	N/A	0.00	—
BPI High Income Fund	63%	1|1	06/98	10.73	1997	22.4%	0|1	N/A	N/A	1.48	●
BPI High Income Segregated Fund	N/A	0|0	N/A	0.00	N/A		0|0	N/A	N/A	0.00	—
C.I. Dividend Fund	62%	1|1	10/97	16.56	1997	17.9%	0|1	N/A	N/A	1.85	●
Canada Life Enhanced Dividend Fund S-39	N/A	0|0	N/A	0.00	N/A		0|0	N/A	N/A	2.00	●
Canada Trust Dividend Income Fund	71%	3|3	11/97	13.56	1995	15.9%	0|3	2.00	N/A	1.90	●
CIBC Dividend Fund	60%	4|6	01/95	-13.69	1994	-6.8%	2|6	3.00	4.00	1.88	●
CIBC International Small Companies Fund	N/A	0|0	N/A	0.00	N/A		0|0	N/A	N/A	2.80	●
Desjardins Dividend Fund	61%	3|3	01/95	-6.76	1995	14.2%	0|3	2.00	N/A	1.94	●
Dynamic Dividend Fund	57%	7|12	01/95	-6.57	1994	-2.6%	2|12	1.00	2.00	1.51	●
Dynamic Dividend Growth Fund	50%	6|12	11/90	-10.96	1990	-8.7%	3|12	3.00	2.00	1.57	●
Elliott & Page Monthly High Income Fund	N/A	0|0	N/A	0.00	N/A		0|0	N/A	N/A	1.55	●

S = Seg Funds

5 CANADIAN DIVIDEND

Fund Name	Fund Beats GICs %	Fund Beats GICs(Yr)	Worst 12 mo. End	Worst 12 mo. Chng (%)	Worst Calendar Year	Worst Calendar (%)	Years Fund Lost $	Sharpe Ratio Quartile 3-Yr	Sharpe Ratio Quartile 5-Yr	MER
S Empire Elite Dividend Growth Fund	N/A	0|0	N/A	0.00	N/A		0|0	N/A	N/A	2.40
First Canadian Dividend Income Fund	69%	3|3	10/95	9.56	1995	13.2%	0|3	2.00	N/A	1.65
S Fonds Astra - Dividendes	N/A	0|0	N/A	0.00	N/A		0|0	N/A	N/A	2.40
S Great-West Life Dividend Fund (G) DSC	N/A	0|0	N/A	0.00	N/A		0|0	N/A	N/A	2.28
S Great-West Life Dividend Fund (G) NL	N/A	0|0	N/A	0.00	N/A		0|0	N/A	N/A	2.52
S Great-West Life Dividend/Growth Fund (M) DSC	N/A	0|0	N/A	0.00	N/A		0|0	N/A	N/A	2.46
S Great-West Life Dividend/Growth Fund (M) NL	N/A	0|0	N/A	0.00	N/A		0|0	N/A	N/A	2.70
Green Line Dividend Fund	55%	5|10	09/90	-8.54	1990	-4.4%	2|10	4.00	3.00	2.00
S Growsafe Canadian Dividend & Income Fund	N/A	0|0	N/A	0.00	N/A		0|0	N/A	N/A	2.25
Guardian Monthly Dividend Fund Ltd.	48%	4|12	01/95	-4.98	1990	-4.1%	2|12	4.00	4.00	1.25
Hongkong Bank Dividend Income Fund	69%	2|2	02/96	14.13	1997	23.2%	0|2	1.00	N/A	1.85
S Industrial Alliance Dividend Fund V	N/A	0|0	N/A	0.00	N/A		0|0	N/A	N/A	1.50
Industrial Dividend Growth Fund	51%	12|21	10/90	-21.96	1990	-19.7%	5|21	3.00	3.00	2.38
Infinity Income Fund	31%	0|0	06/98	-0.02	N/A		0|0	N/A	N/A	2.24
InvesNat Dividend Fund	63%	4|5	01/95	-3.28	1994	-0.5%	1|5	3.00	3.00	1.63
Investors Dividend Fund Ltd.	54%	12|21	06/82	-14.92	1981	-8.4%	2|21	2.00	2.00	2.36
S Manulife AGF Dividend GIF	N/A	0|0	N/A	0.00	N/A		0|0	N/A	N/A	2.80
S Manulife AGF High Income GIF	N/A	0|0	N/A	0.00	N/A		0|0	N/A	N/A	2.35
S Manulife Dynamic Dividend Growth GIF	N/A	0|0	N/A	0.00	N/A		0|0	N/A	N/A	2.94
S Maritime Life Dividend Income Fund (A)	69%	2|2	06/96	8.93	1996	18.4%	0|2	3.00	N/A	2.10
S Maritime Life Dividend Income Fund (C)	69%	2|2	06/96	8.93	1996	18.4%	0|2	3.00	N/A	2.25
S Maritime Life Dividend Income Fund Series B	65%	1|1	11/97	18.51	1997	24.5%	0|1	N/A	N/A	2.10

S = Seg Funds

5 CANADIAN DIVIDEND

Performance Trend by Quartiles (CONSISTENCY) with RISK, REWARD-TO-RISK and EFFICIENCY columns.

Fund Name	84	85	86	87	88	89	90	91	92	93	94	95	96	97	98	June	Fund Beats GICs %	Fund Beats GICs (Yr)	Worst 12 mo. End	Worst 12 mo. Chng (%)	Worst Calendar Year	Worst Calendar %	Years Fund Lost $	Sharpe 3-Yr	Sharpe 5-Yr	MER
Maxxum Dividend Fund of Canada				2	1	4	4	1	1	1	1	1	2	1	3	2	55%	6|11	09/90	-17.47	1990	-9.3%	1|11	3.00	1.00	1.73
MD Dividend Fund										4	2	3	4	3	2		64%	4|5	01/95	-4.53	1994	-0.2%	1|5	1.00	2.00	1.29
S MetLife - AGF Dividend Fund														3	2		N/A	0|0	N/A	0.00	N/A		0|0	N/A	N/A	2.69
S Middlefield High Income Trust (MINT)																	N/A	0|0	N/A	0.00	N/A		0|0	N/A	N/A	0.00
S Millennia III Canadian Dividend Series 1															3	4	N/A	0|0	N/A	0.00	N/A		0|0	N/A	N/A	2.25
S Millennia III Canadian Dividend Series 2																	N/A	0|0	N/A	0.00	N/A		0|0	N/A	N/A	2.43
Millennium Income Fund																4	41%	0|0	06/98	-4.72	N/A		0|0	N/A	N/A	2.50
Mutual Summit Dividend Growth Fund																2	38%	0|0	06/98	19.58	N/A		0|0	N/A	N/A	0.00
National Trust Dividend Fund											2	4	4	2	1	1	67%	4|5	01/95	-8.78	1994	-4.4%	1|5	1.00	2.00	1.75
S NN Dividend Fund													1	3	4	3	68%	3|3	05/95	9.41	1997	13.8%	0|3	1.00	N/A	2.60
S North West Life Ecoflex Investment Fund V																	N/A	0|0	N/A	0.00	N/A		0|0	N/A	N/A	1.86
Northwest Dividend Fund														1	3	4	74%	2|2	06/98	7.85	1997	21.0%	0|2	3.00	N/A	1.75
OTG Investment Fund - Diversified Section		2	2	1	4	4	4	2	3	1	1		2	2	3	1	54%	12|21	06/82	-26.56	1990	-13.3%	4|21	4.00	4.00	1.00
Phillips, Hager & North Dividend Income Fund		1	3	1	3	2	3	1	1	1	3	1	1	1	1	1	56%	12|20	03/82	-13.56	1981	-7.2%	3|20	1.00	1.00	1.21
S Royal & SunAlliance Dividend Fund																	N/A	0|0	N/A	0.00	N/A		0|0	N/A	N/A	0.00
Royal Dividend Fund												2	3	1	1	1	68%	3|4	01/95	-6.90	1994	-0.7%	1|4	2.00	1.00	1.77
Royal Monthly Income Fund															3		N/A	0|0	N/A	0.00	N/A		0|0	N/A	N/A	1.12
Saxon High Income Fund															4		N/A	0|0	N/A	0.00	N/A		0|0	N/A	N/A	1.25
Scotia Excelsior Dividend Fund					4	3	3	2	1	2	4	3	2	2	1	1	59%	7|11	01/95	-6.40	1987	-3.5%	3|11	2.00	1.00	1.09
Spectrum United Dividend Fund						2	2	1	3	3	2	4	4	3	3	3	53%	7|10	01/95	-9.09	1994	-3.0%	3|10	2.00	3.00	1.61
Standard Life Canadian Dividend Mutual Fund												2	1	1	1	1	73%	3|3	11/95	14.22	1995	14.7%	0|3	1.00	N/A	1.50
Strategic Value Dividend Fund Ltd.	3	1	1	2	2	2	3	4	4	3	4	3	3	3	3	3	53%	11|19	06/82	-14.35	1981	-5.3%	3|19	3.00	3.00	2.70

S = Seg Funds

5 CANADIAN DIVIDEND

Fund Name	CONSISTENCY — Performance Trend by Quartiles (84–98, June)	RISK — Fund Beats GICs %	Fund Beats GICs(Yr)	Worst 12 mo. End	Chng (%)	Worst Calendar Year		Years Fund Lost $	REWARD-TO-RISK — Sharpe Ratio Quartile Rankings 3-Yr	5-Yr	EFFICIENCY — MER
Talvest Dividend Fund	3 4 3	69%	2|2	11/97	7.99	1997	11.6%	0|2	N/A	N/A	1.99 ●
Trans-Canada Dividend Fund	1 3 4 4 4 3 1 3 3 4 4	48%	10|21	09/90	-11.97	1990	-7.7%	2|21	4.00	4.00	3.51 ●
Trust Pret et Revenu Dividend Fund	1 3 4	79%	2|2	06/98	8.59	1997	20.9%	0|2	2.00	N/A	1.62 ●

S = Seg Funds

6 CANADIAN SECTOR EQUITY

Fund Name	Performance Trend by Quartiles (84–98) / June	Fund Beats GICs %	Fund Beats GICs(Yr)	Worst 12 mo. End Chng (%)	Worst Calendar Year	Years Fund Lost $	Sharpe Ratio 3-Yr	Sharpe Ratio 5-Yr	MER
AIC Advantage Fund	1	56%	8|12	09/90 -26.16	1990 -18.6%	3|12	N/A	N/A	2.31 ●
All-Canadian Consumer Fund	3	48%	3|5	01/95 -2.26	1995 1.0%	0|5	N/A	N/A	2.00 ●
Altamira Science and Technology Fund	1	56%	2|2	04/97 -8.53	1996 13.0%	0|2	N/A	N/A	2.31 ●
CIBC Canadian Real Estate Fund	4	N/A	0|0	N/A		0|0	N/A	N/A	2.25 ●
CIBC Financial Companies Fund	1	N/A	0|0	N/A		0|0	N/A	N/A	2.45 ●
Dynamic Canadian Real Estate Fund	4	29%	0|0	06/98 6.10	N/A	0|0	N/A	N/A	2.73 ●
First Trust Financial Institutions Tr 1997 Ser	1	N/A	0|0	N/A	N/A	0|0	N/A	N/A	0.00 –
First Trust REIT & Real Estate Growth Trust 1998		N/A	0|0	N/A	N/A	0|0	N/A	N/A	0.00 –
First Trust Wealth Management Trust 1997 Series	3	N/A	0|0	N/A	N/A	0|0	N/A	N/A	0.00 –
S Great-West Life Canadian Opportunity Fund (M) DSC	2	N/A	0|0	N/A	N/A	0|0	N/A	N/A	2.58 ●
S Great-West Life Canadian Opportunity Fund (M) NL	2	N/A	0|0	N/A	N/A	0|0	N/A	N/A	2.82 ●
S Great-West Life Canadian Real Estate 1 (G) DSC	3	40%	1|3	08/95 -1.21	1995 0.1%	0|3	N/A	N/A	2.70 ●
S Great-West Life Canadian Real Estate 1 (G) NL	3	23%	1|8	06/93 -13.35	1993 -9.9%	5|8	N/A	N/A	2.94 ●
Green Line Science & Technology Fund	1	61%	4|4	04/97 -9.56	1997 5.9%	0|4	N/A	N/A	2.58 ●
S Hartford Canadian Advanced Technology Fund	2	N/A	0|0	N/A	N/A	0|0	N/A	N/A	2.50 ●
S Hartford Real Estate Income Fund	4	N/A	0|0	N/A	N/A	0|0	N/A	N/A	2.75 ●
Infinity Wealth Management	2	63%	0|0	06/98 25.31	N/A	0|0	N/A	N/A	2.95 ●
Investors Real Property Fund	3	26%	3|13	09/93 -3.37	1992 -1.6%	2|13	N/A	N/A	2.39 ●
Middlefield Canadian Realty Fund	4	33%	0|0	N/A	N/A	0|0	N/A	N/A	2.65 ●
Navigator Canadian Technology Fund	4	N/A	0|0	N/A	N/A	0|0	N/A	N/A	2.85 ●
Royal LePage Commercial Real Estate Fund	4	20%	1|8	12/93 -5.73	1993 -5.7%	2|8	N/A	N/A	3.40 ●
Royal Life Science and Technology Fund	2	58%	2|2	04/97 6.38	1996 17.5%	0|2	N/A	N/A	2.81 ●

S = Seg Funds

7 CANADIAN RESOURCES & PRECIOUS METALS

Fund Name	Performance Trend by Quartiles (84–98, June)	Fund Beats GICs %	Fund Beats GICs (Yr)	Worst 12 mo. End	Worst 12 mo. Chng (%)	Worst Calendar Year	Worst Calendar Year %	Years Fund Lost $	Sharpe Ratio 3-Yr	Sharpe Ratio 5-Yr	MER	Efficiency
20/20 Canadian Resources Fund Limited	2 2 3 2 2 4 2 4 2 1 1 3	53%	12|21	06/82	-52.40	1981	-29.4%	9|21	1.00	2.00	2.88	● red
All-Canadian Resources Corporation	4 4 2 4 2 1 4 4 2 1	47%	8|21	01/91	-36.05	1990	-28.8%	8|21	4.00	3.00	2.00	● green
Altamira Precious and Strategic Metal Fund	1 3 4 3 3 3 2	54%	2|3	11/97	-45.77	1997	-41.3%	1|3	4.00	N/A	2.30	● green
Altamira Resource Fund	1 1 1 3 4 3 3 3 2	60%	4|8	06/98	-33.65	1997	-27.0%	3|8	4.00	4.00	2.27	● green
BPI Canadian Resource Fund Inc.	3 2 1 1 3 4 4 3 3 3	50%	11|21	02/98	-33.92	1997	-30.3%	6|21	4.00	4.00	2.99	● red
C.I. Canadian Resource Fund	2	33%	0|0	05/98	-29.48	N/A		0|0	N/A	N/A	2.35	● orange
C.I. Sector Global Resource Shares	2 3	50%	0|1	06/98	-21.57	1997	-10.7%	1|1	N/A	N/A	2.42	● orange
Cambridge Precious Metals Fund	4	38%	0|1	08/97	-56.09	1997	-46.0%	1|1	N/A	N/A	3.49	● red
Cambridge Resource Fund	4 4 3 2 1 2 2 4 4	49%	12|21	02/98	-51.13	1997	-42.3%	6|21	3.00	4.00	3.42	● orange
CIBC Canadian Resources Fund	4 2 3 1 3	49%	1|2	06/98	-28.01	1997	-18.1%	1|2	N/A	N/A	2.30	● orange
CIBC Energy Fund	1 3	58%	1|1	06/98	-16.63	1997	15.0%	0|1	N/A	N/A	2.30	● green
CIBC Precious Metals Fund	4 2	38%	0|1	11/97	-47.77	1997	-43.3%	1|1	N/A	N/A	2.20	● red
Desjardins High Potential Sectors Fund		N/A	0|0	N/A	0.00	N/A		0|0	N/A	N/A	0.00	–
Dominion Equity Resource Fund Inc.	2 2 3 2 2 4 2 4 2 2 2	52%	4|12	09/88	-55.21	1988	-36.9%	7|12	1.00	4.00	2.30	● orange
Dynamic Precious Metals Fund	3 3 2 3 1 1 4 3 4 1	49%	6|13	11/97	-48.04	1997	-45.9%	4|13	4.00	3.00	2.47	● orange
FCMI Double Gold Plus Fund	4 2 4 4 1 4 4 1 1	29%	2|9	04/91	-28.48	1991	-20.0%	5|9	4.00	3.00	0.00	–
FCMI Precious Metals Fund Inc.	4 2 1 4 1 1	45%	3|5	03/95	-18.34	1994	-7.9%	1|5	1.00	1.00	3.84	● red
First Canadian Precious Metals Fund	3	39%	0|0	02/98	-49.84	N/A		0|0	N/A	N/A	2.07	● green
First Canadian Resource Fund	3 3 3 2 4	51%	2|4	06/98	-32.49	1997	-18.2%	2|4	3.00	N/A	2.30	● orange
First Heritage Fund	2 3 3 4 3 2 3 4 2 1	46%	4|10	07/88	-23.52	1997	-19.4%	5|10	3.00	3.00	4.66	● red
Global Strategy Gold Plus Fund	1 2 1 4 4	50%	2|4	02/98	-49.47	1997	-48.2%	1|4	4.00	N/A	2.75	● red
Great-West Life Canadian Resources Fund (A) DSC	2 4	53%	0|1	06/98	-23.48	1997	-12.0%	1|1	N/A	N/A	3.05	● red

S = Seg Funds

7 CANADIAN RESOURCES & PRECIOUS METALS

Fund Name	Fund Beats GICs %	Fund Beats GICs(Yr)	Worst 12 mo. End Chng (%)	Worst Calendar Year	Years Fund Lost $	Sharpe Ratio 3-Yr	Sharpe Ratio 5-Yr	MER
S Great-West Life Canadian Resources Fund (A) NL	53%	0|1	06/98 -23.68	1997 -12.2%	1|1	N/A	N/A	3.30
Green Line Energy Fund	45%	2|3	06/98 -38.53	1997 -2.7%	1|3	2.00	N/A	2.10
Green Line Precious Metals Fund	52%	2|3	02/98 -44.10	1997 -41.0%	1|3	2.00	N/A	2.12
Green Line Resource Fund	48%	2|4	06/98 -35.50	1997 -24.1%	2|4	3.00	N/A	2.12
Hirsch Natural Resource Fund	N/A	0|0	N/A 0.00	N/A	0|0	N/A	N/A	2.95
Investors Canadian Natural Resources Fund	54%	0|1	06/98 -8.20	1997 -5.0%	1|1	N/A	N/A	2.48
Lion Natural Resource Fund	N/A	0|0	N/A 0.00	N/A	0|0	N/A	N/A	0.00
Marathon Resource Fund	44%	0|0	06/98 -38.43	N/A	0|0	N/A	N/A	3.09
Maxxum Natural Resource Fund	55%	5|9	02/98 -43.85	1997 -39.2%	3|9	2.00	2.00	2.23
Maxxum Precious Metals Fund	48%	4|9	02/98 -46.79	1997 -44.2%	4|9	2.00	1.00	2.23
Middlefield Growth Fund Limited	45%	5|7	01/95 -15.46	1994 -10.7%	1|7	1.00	2.00	2.56
Mutual Alpine Resources Fund	38%	0|0	06/98 -25.60	N/A	0|0	N/A	N/A	0.00
Royal Energy Fund	50%	8|17	06/82 -41.76	1982 -18.1%	7|17	1.00	1.00	2.28
Royal Precious Metals Fund	50%	3|9	11/97 -38.77	1997 -33.7%	4|9	1.00	1.00	2.41
Scotia Excelsior Precious Metals Fund	51%	1|4	02/98 -45.96	1997 -39.4%	2|4	3.00	N/A	2.19
Spectrum United Canadian Resource Fund	40%	0|1	01/98 -35.08	1997 -32.8%	1|1	N/A	N/A	2.35
Standard Life Natural Resource Mutual Fund	57%	2|3	05/98 -21.32	1997 -15.8%	1|3	2.00	N/A	2.00
Talvest/Hyperion Canadian Resource Fund	N/A	0|0	N/A 0.00	N/A	0|0	N/A	N/A	2.50
Trimark Canadian Resources Fund	N/A	0|0	N/A 0.00	N/A	0|0	N/A	N/A	2.40
Universal Canadian Resource Fund	52%	9|19	06/82 -39.24	1981 -24.5%	8|19	2.00	2.00	2.39
Universal Precious Metals Fund	44%	1|3	11/97 -41.46	1997 -35.2%	1|3	3.00	N/A	2.42

S = Seg Funds

8 U.S. LARGE CAP/DIVERSIFIED EQUITY

Fund Name	84	85	86	87	88	89	90	91	92	93	94	95	96	97	98	June	Fund Beats GICs %	Fund Beats GICs (Yr)	Worst 12 mo. End	Chng (%)	Worst Calendar Year	(%)	Years Fund Lost $	Sharpe 3-Yr	Sharpe 5-Yr	MER	Efficiency
20/20 Aggressive Growth Fund											3	1	4	4	3	3	61%	2|4	04/97	-10.90	1994	-0.6%	1|4	4.00	4.00	2.55	● red
AGF American Growth Class	1	3	4	2	3	2	4	3	2	2	2	2	2	3	1	1	53%	13|21	08/88	-21.78	1990	-9.3%	4|21	3.00	2.00	2.78	● red
AGF Special U.S. Class	3	1	3	2	2	2	3	1	3	3	3	4	4	4	4	2	53%	14|21	05/82	-17.92	1981	-11.4%	5|21	4.00	4.00	2.86	● red
AIC American Advantage Fund																2	N/A	0|0	N/A	0.00	N/A		0|0	N/A	N/A	2.72	● red
AIC Value Fund							2	1	1	4	1	1	1	1	1	2	62%	6|7	11/94	-7.16	1994	-4.2%	1|7	1.00	1.00	2.44	● orange
AIM American Aggressive Growth Fund																4	N/A	0|0	N/A	0.00	N/A		0|0	N/A	N/A	2.74	● red
AIM American Premier Fund										4	4	1	4	4	2	1	44%	2|6	07/96	-10.57	1995	1.3%	0|6	4.00	4.00	2.78	● red
AIM GT America Growth Class												3	3	4	3	1	60%	3|3	04/97	-8.68	1997	11.2%	0|3	4.00	N/A	2.86	● red
AIM GT Canada Growth Class													1	4	3	2	60%	2|2	04/97	1.82	1997	12.4%	0|2	4.00	N/A	2.47	● orange
Altamira U.S. Larger Company Fund											2	1	4	3	2	3	59%	3|4	01/95	-1.76	1994	3.2%	0|4	3.00	N/A	2.30	● orange
S Apex U.S. Equity Fund														3	1	1	79%	1|1	12/97	24.35	1997	24.3%	0|1	N/A	N/A	2.79	● red
Argentum Market Neutral Portfolio CS																	N/A	0|0	N/A	0.00	N/A		0|0	N/A	N/A	0.00	–
Argentum U.S. Master Portfolio CS																	N/A	0|0	N/A	0.00	N/A		0|0	N/A	N/A	0.00	–
Atlas American Advantage Fund												1	2	3	4		69%	3|3	07/96	11.46	1996	21.4%	0|3	1.00	N/A	2.53	● red
Atlas American Large Cap Growth Fund				3	4	1	3	3	4	2	2	2	2	3		3	56%	6|12	08/88	-21.17	1987	-6.5%	2|12	1.00	2.00	2.55	● red
Atlas American RSP Index Fund														3	2	2	67%	1|1	01/98	19.73	1997	25.2%	0|1	N/A	N/A	1.52	● green
Beutel Goodman American Equity Fund										1	3	4	3	2	4	4	63%	5|6	01/95	-4.28	1994	0.5%	0|6	4.00	3.00	2.46	● orange
Bissett American Equity Fund			1	4	4	1	3	2	2	3	1	2	4	3	3	3	55%	9|13	08/88	-21.91	1987	-13.9%	2|13	3.00	3.00	1.50	● green
BPI American Equity Value Fund							1	3	3	3	2	2	3	2	1	1	53%	6|8	10/90	-4.55	1990	0.3%	0|8	1.00	2.00	2.36	● orange
S BPI American Equity Value Segregated Fund																	N/A	0|0	N/A	0.00	N/A		0|0	N/A	N/A	0.00	–
C.I. American Fund										1	1	2	3	3	3	3	69%	5|5	01/95	6.25	1994	8.1%	0|5	3.00	1.00	2.38	● orange
C.I. American RSP Fund													2	3	2	2	69%	2|2	03/97	11.78	1996	20.3%	0|2	N/A	N/A	2.35	● orange

Column group headings: CONSISTENCY — Performance Trend by Quartiles (84 – 98, June); RISK — Fund Beats GICs %, Fund Beats GICs (Yr), Worst 12 mo. End / Chng (%), Worst Calendar Year, Years Fund Lost $; REWARD-TO-RISK — Sharpe Ratio Quartile Rankings (3-Yr, 5-Yr); EFFICIENCY — MER.

S = Seg Funds

8 U.S. LARGE CAP/DIVERSIFIED EQUITY

Fund Name	June (Quartile)	RISK: Fund Beats GICs %	Fund Beats GICs (Yr)	Worst 12 mo. End Chng (%)	Worst Calendar Year	Years Fund Lost $	REWARD-TO-RISK: Sharpe Ratio Quartile 3-Yr	Sharpe Ratio Quartile 5-Yr	EFFICIENCY: MER
S C.I. American Segregated Fund	2	N/A	0|0	N/A 0.00	N/A	0|0	N/A	N/A	3.16
C.I. Sector American Shares	3	69%	5|5	02/95 6.37	1994 8.3%	0|5	3.00	1.00	2.43
S C.U. U.S. Equity Index Fund		N/A	0|0	N/A 0.00	N/A	0|0	N/A	N/A	2.59
Caldwell American Equity Fund	4	62%	0|0	06/98 15.98	N/A	0|0	N/A	N/A	0.50
Canada Trust AmeriGrowth Fund	2	69%	3|4	01/95 -0.67	1994 0.1%	0|4	2.00	2.00	1.39
Canada Trust U.S. Equity Fund	4	60%	6|7	09/94 -4.68	1994 -1.0%	1|7	4.00	4.00	2.34
Canada Trust U.S. Equity Index Fund	1	N/A	0|0	N/A 0.00	N/A	0|0	N/A	N/A	0.85
S CCPE U.S. Equity Fund	1	67%	2|2	08/96 7.24	1996 19.9%	0|2	2.00	N/A	1.75
S CDA U.S. Equity Fund (KBSH)	3	65%	1|1	05/98 22.02	1997 22.6%	0|1	N/A	N/A	1.20
CIBC North American Demographics Fund	2	68%	1|1	01/98 40.29	1997 43.2%	0|1	N/A	N/A	2.50
CIBC U.S. Equity Fund	1	60%	4|6	11/94 1.59	1993 2.6%	0|6	2.00	3.00	0.90
CIBC U.S. Index RRSP Fund	1	79%	1|1	11/97 32.78	1997 36.8%	0|1	N/A	N/A	0.90
Clarington U.S. Equity Fund	3	73%	1|1	06/98 36.14	1997 40.4%	0|1	N/A	N/A	2.95
Clarington U.S. Smaller Company Growth Fund	2	64%	1|1	01/98 30.41	1997 30.9%	0|1	N/A	N/A	2.95
S Co-operators Life U.S. Equity Fund	4	65%	3|3	07/96 8.26	1996 27.8%	0|3	4.00	N/A	2.12
Cornerstone U.S. Fund	2	55%	12|21	08/88 -31.16	1987 -16.4%	4|21	1.00	1.00	2.23
COTE 100 U.S. Fund	4	45%	1|1	06/98 -6.49	1997 5.3%	0|1	N/A	N/A	2.00
Desjardins American Market Fund	2	67%	1|1	03/97 13.54	1997 28.0%	0|1	N/A	N/A	2.13
Dynamic Americas Fund	3	56%	12|18	07/82 -15.91	1990 -5.1%	3|18	1.00	3.00	2.37
Elliott & Page American Growth Fund Ltd.	1	55%	14|21	08/88 -29.50	1984 -8.7%	4|21	1.00	1.00	1.41
Elliott & Page U.S. Mid-Cap Fund	4	N/A	0|0	N/A 0.00	N/A	0|0	N/A	N/A	3.44
S Empire Elite S&P 500 Index Fund	4	N/A	0|0	N/A 0.00	N/A	0|0	N/A	N/A	2.40

Consistency section: Performance Trend by Quartiles (columns 84 85 86 87 88 89 90 91 92 93 94 95 96 97 98). The June column quartile values are listed above.

S = Seg Funds

8 U.S. LARGE CAP/DIVERSIFIED EQUITY

Fund Name	CONSISTENCY: Performance Trend by Quartiles 84	85	86	87	88	89	90	91	92	93	94	95	96	97	June 98	RISK: Fund Beats GICs %	Fund Beats GICs(Yr)	Worst 12 mo. End	Worst 12 mo. Chng (%)	Worst Calendar Year	Worst Calendar Year %	Years Fund Lost $	REWARD-TO-RISK: Sharpe Ratio Quartile Rankings 3-Yr	5-Yr	EFFICIENCY: MER	
Ethical North American Equity Fund	3	4	2	3	2	3	4	4	4	1	4	2	2	1	1	54%	9|15	08/88	-19.82	1990	-14.0%	4|15	2.00	2.00	2.47	●
Fidelity Focus Consumer Industries Fund															1	69%	0|0	06/98	43.70	N/A		0|0	N/A	N/A	2.50	●
Fidelity Focus Financial Services Fund															1	77%	0|0	06/98	49.47	N/A		0|0	N/A	N/A	2.50	●
Fidelity Growth America Fund								1	1	2	1	2	2	2	2	63%	6|7	09/94	-1.17	1994	6.2%	0|7	2.00	2.00	2.34	●
First Canadian Special Growth Fund											4	4	1	4	4	54%	3|4	01/95	-24.22	1994	-17.9%	1|4	4.00	N/A	2.22	●
First Canadian U.S. Equity Index Fund															2	67%	0|0	01/98	22.30	N/A		0|0	N/A	N/A	1.23	●
First Canadian U.S. Growth Fund											2	4	4	1	2	64%	3|4	07/96	-9.42	1994	3.4%	0|4	3.00	N/A	2.18	●
First Canadian U.S. Special Growth Fund															3	67%	0|0	01/98	24.77	N/A		0|0	N/A	N/A	1.90	●
First Canadian U.S. Value Fund															3	67%	0|0	01/98	33.58	N/A		0|0	N/A	N/A	2.06	●
S First Trust DJIA Target 10 Trust 1998 Series C$																N/A	0|0	N/A	0.00	N/A		0|0	N/A	N/A	0.00	–
S First Trust Target 10 Trust 1996 Series C$													1	4	4	71%	2|2	06/98	15.20	1997	20.0%	0|2	N/A	N/A	1.00	●
S First Trust Target 10 Trust 1997 Series C$															4	56%	0|0	01/98	18.67	N/A		0|0	N/A	N/A	1.00	●
S Fonds Astra - Actions americaines															3	N/A	0|0	N/A	0.00	N/A		0|0	N/A	N/A	2.50	●
Fonds de Croissance Select											2	3	1	2	2	54%	3|4	12/94	3.52	1994	3.5%	0|4	1.00	1.00	1.00	●
Global Manager U.S. Bear Fund												4	4	4	4	13%	0|3	07/97	-28.66	1995	-22.7%	3|3	4.00	N/A	1.82	●
Global Manager U.S. Geared Fund												1	1	1	1	74%	3|3	07/96	17.09	1996	36.2%	0|3	3.00	N/A	1.82	●
Global Manager U.S. Index Fund												1	1	3	2	72%	3|3	07/96	12.24	1996	22.6%	0|3	1.00	N/A	1.82	●
Global Strategy U.S. Equity Fund												2	3	2	3	70%	3|3	07/96	10.03	1996	17.7%	0|3	2.00	N/A	2.59	●
S Great-West Life American Growth Fund (A) DSC															1	N/A	0|0	N/A	0.00	N/A		0|0	N/A	N/A	2.73	●
S Great-West Life American Growth Fund (A) NL															1	N/A	0|0	N/A	0.00	N/A		0|0	N/A	N/A	2.97	●
S Great-West Life U.S. Equity Investment (G) DSC												4	3	1	3	66%	3|3	07/96	5.33	1996	14.1%	0|3	2.00	N/A	2.55	●
S Great-West Life U.S. Equity Investment Fund (G) NL												4	3	2	3	68%	3|3	07/96	5.11	1996	13.8%	0|3	2.00	N/A	2.79	●

S = Seg Funds

8 U.S. LARGE CAP/DIVERSIFIED EQUITY

Fund Name	RISK: Fund Beats GICs %	Fund Beats GICs(Yr)	Worst 12 mo. End	Chng (%)	Worst Calendar Year		Years Fund Lost $	Sharpe Ratio Quartile 3-Yr	5-Yr	MER	Efficiency
Green Line Dow Jones Industrial Average Index C$	N/A	0|0	N/A	0.00		N/A	0|0	N/A	N/A	0.00	—
Green Line Dow Jones Industrial Average Index US	N/A	0|0	N/A	0.00		N/A	0|0	N/A	N/A	0.80	green
Green Line U.S. Blue Chip Equity Fund	71%	1|1	11/97	27.33	30.5%	1997	0|1	N/A	N/A	2.34	orange
Green Line U.S. Index Fund C$	N/A	0|0	N/A	0.00		N/A	0|0	N/A	N/A	0.00	—
Green Line U.S. Index Fund US	63%	7|11	08/88	-19.13	-4.2%	1990	1|11	2.00	2.00	0.66	green
Green Line U.S. Mid-Cap Growth Fund	66%	3|4	01/95	1.25	4.4%	1994	0|4	2.00	N/A	2.33	orange
Green Line U.S. RSP Index Fund	N/A	0|0	N/A	0.00		N/A	0|0	N/A	N/A	0.80	green
Growsafe U.S. 21st Century Index Fund	57%	1|1	12/97	22.71	22.7%	1997	0|1	N/A	N/A	2.13	orange
Growsafe US 500 Index Fund	71%	2|2	03/97	17.45	18.7%	1996	0|2	N/A	N/A	2.13	orange
GTS First American Fund	41%	1|6	08/94	-8.46	-3.4%	1994	3|6	4.00	4.00	2.80	red
GTS Protected American Fund	40%	3|12	02/97	-7.56	-2.3%	1996	2|12	4.00	4.00	2.30	orange
Guardian American Equity Fund Ltd.	55%	14|21	08/88	-20.30	-8.1%	1990	4|21	4.00	4.00	2.19	orange
Guardian American Large Cap Fund	N/A	0|0	N/A	0.00		N/A	0|0	N/A	N/A	2.19	orange
Guardian American Large Cap Fund	N/A	0|0	N/A	0.00		N/A	0|0	N/A	N/A	2.79	red
Hongkong Bank U.S. Equity Fund	68%	3|3	11/95	7.81	13.5%	1995	0|3	1.00	1.00	2.17	orange
Industrial Alliance U.S. Stock Fund	61%	0|0	01/98	27.92		N/A	0|0	N/A	N/A	2.23	orange
Industrial Alliance US Advantage Fund U	N/A	0|0	N/A	0.00		N/A	0|0	N/A	N/A	1.50	green
Industrial American Fund	55%	15|21	09/90	-16.91	-11.0%	1990	1|21	4.00	4.00	2.38	orange
Infinity International Fund	67%	0|0	01/98	22.57		N/A	0|0	N/A	N/A	2.95	red
InvesNat American Index Plus Fund	N/A	0|0	N/A	0.00		N/A	0|0	N/A	N/A	1.23	green
Investors U.S. Growth Fund Ltd.	56%	14|21	08/88	-20.49	-14.5%	1981	3|21	1.00	1.00	2.41	orange
Investors U.S. Opportunities Fund	67%	1|1	06/98	27.65	41.1%	1997	0|1	N/A	N/A	2.49	orange

S = Seg Funds

237

8 U.S. LARGE CAP/DIVERSIFIED EQUITY

Fund Name	Fund Beats GICs %	Fund Beats GICs (Yr)	Worst 12 mo. End	Worst 12 mo. Chng (%)	Worst Calendar Year	Worst Calendar %	Years Fund Lost $	Sharpe Ratio Quartile 3-Yr	Sharpe Ratio Quartile 5-Yr	MER
Jones Heward American Fund	54%	8|14	08/88	-25.57	1994	-12.9%	3|14	3.00	4.00	2.50
Leith Wheeler U.S. Equity Fund	62%	3|3	07/96	9.28	1996	14.3%	0|3	3.00	N/A	1.34
S London Life U.S. Equity Fund	57%	7|9	09/90	-29.31	1990	-15.2%	2|9	1.00	3.00	2.00
S Manulife AGF International American Growth GIF	69%	0|0	05/98	35.69	N/A		0|0	N/A	N/A	0.00
S Manulife Elliott & Page American Growth GIF	N/A	0|0	N/A	0.00	N/A		0|0	N/A	N/A	3.05
S Manulife Fidelity Growth America GIF	75%	0|0	06/98	33.06	N/A		0|0	N/A	N/A	3.15
S Manulife GT Global America Growth Class GIF	63%	0|0	05/98	24.84	N/A		0|0	N/A	N/A	3.15
S Manulife Hyperion Value Line U.S. Equity GIF	N/A	0|0	N/A	0.00	N/A		0|0	N/A	N/A	3.15
S Manulife U.S. Equity Index GIF	N/A	0|0	N/A	0.00	N/A		0|0	N/A	N/A	1.80
S Manulife VistaFund American Stock 1	64%	2|2	07/96	2.12	1996	11.1%	0|2	4.00	N/A	1.63
Marathon Performance Large Cap U.S. Fund	N/A	0|0	N/A	0.00	N/A		0|0	N/A	N/A	2.15
Margin of Safety Fund	53%	7|9	10/90	-18.42	1990	-3.5%	2|9	1.00	1.00	1.88
S Maritime Life American Growth & Income Fund (A&C)	71%	3|3	08/95	7.63	1996	15.9%	0|3	1.00	N/A	2.55
S Maritime Life American Growth & Income Series B	70%	1|1	06/98	26.23	1997	33.4%	0|1	N/A	N/A	2.55
S Maritime Life S&P 500 Fund (A&C)	74%	3|3	07/96	14.32	1996	18.8%	0|3	3.00	N/A	2.20
S Maritime Life S&P 500 Fund Series B	65%	1|1	01/98	21.40	1997	26.4%	0|1	N/A	N/A	2.20
Mawer U.S. Equity Fund	63%	4|5	09/94	1.34	1994	3.8%	0|5	1.00	1.00	1.27
Maxxum American Equity Fund	62%	2|2	07/96	13.42	1997	19.1%	0|2	2.00	N/A	2.48
McDonald New America Fund	59%	1|1	03/97	4.45	1997	23.1%	0|1	N/A	N/A	2.00
McLean Budden American Equity - Pooled	58%	8|14	08/88	-28.76	1987	-1.4%	2|14	2.00	1.00	1.00
McLean Budden American Growth Fund	62%	6|9	09/90	-1.91	1993	2.8%	0|9	3.00	2.00	1.75
MD U.S. Equity Fund	68%	4|5	09/94	-0.76	1994	2.0%	0|5	2.00	2.00	1.29

S = Seg Funds

8 U.S. LARGE CAP/DIVERSIFIED EQUITY

Fund Name	Fund Beats GICs %	Fund Beats GICs(Yr)	Worst 12 mo. End	Chng (%)	Worst Calendar Year	Worst Calendar %	Years Fund Lost $	Sharpe 3-Yr	Sharpe 5-Yr	MER	Efficiency
S MetLife MVP U.S. Equity Fund	62%	3|4	01/95	-4.05	1994	-1.0%	1|4	2.00	2.00	2.16	yellow
S Millennia III American Equity Fund Series 1	66%	2|2	03/97	5.20	1996	8.4%	0|2	N/A	N/A	2.80	red
Montrusco Select Non-Taxable U.S. Equity Fund	64%	7|9	09/90	-12.46	1990	-6.5%	2|9	2.00	3.00	0.00	–
Montrusco Select Strategic U.S. Equity Fund	62%	1|1	06/98	18.85	1997	30.8%	0|1	N/A	N/A	0.00	–
Montrusco Select Taxable U.S. Equity Fund	61%	8|10	09/90	-13.26	1990	-6.1%	2|10	3.00	3.00	0.00	–
Montrusco Select U.S. Growth Fund	52%	1|1	06/98	0.96	1997	18.1%	0|1	N/A	N/A	0.00	–
Mutual Amerifund	60%	8|11	10/90	-25.25	1990	-14.3%	2|11	2.00	2.00	2.07	green
Mutual Beacon Fund CS	71%	0|0	06/98	21.98	N/A		0|4	2.00	2.00	2.50	yellow
Mutual Premier American Fund	67%	3|4	09/94	-1.32	1994	0.3%	0|4	2.00	2.00	2.40	yellow
S NAL-Investor U.S. Equity Fund	61%	3|3	01/95	0.08	1996	19.4%	0|3	2.00	N/A	2.25	green
National Trust American Equity Fund	56%	4|5	01/95	-7.36	1994	-2.1%	1|5	2.00	3.00	2.25	red
National Trust U.S. Index Fund	72%	0|0	01/98	35.87	N/A		0|0	N/A	N/A	0.89	green
Navigator American Growth Fund	64%	2|2	01/97	18.49	1996	26.6%	0|2	4.00	N/A	2.99	red
Navigator American Value Fund	65%	2|2	01/97	15.10	1996	19.0%	0|2	1.00	N/A	2.99	red
S NN Can-Am Fund	68%	4|5	01/95	-0.52	1994	0.2%	0|5	3.00	3.00	2.65	red
NN Can-Daq 100 Fund	55%	1|1	01/98	11.01	1997	14.2%	0|1	N/A	N/A	2.65	yellow
S North West Life Ecoflex Investment Fund S	61%	0|0	01/96	27.02	N/A		0|0	N/A	N/A	2.99	red
S North West Life Ecoflex Investment Fund U	N/A	0|0	N/A	0.00	N/A		0|0	N/A	N/A	2.41	yellow
O.I.Q. FERIQUE American Fund	68%	1|1	03/97	18.46	1997	36.4%	0|1	N/A	N/A	0.39	green
O'Donnell American Sector Growth Fund	55%	1|2	03/97	-4.84	1996	3.3%	0|2	N/A	N/A	2.90	red
O'Donnell U.S. Mid-Cap Fund	74%	1|2	04/97	3.63	1996	5.4%	0|2	N/A	N/A	2.90	red
Phillips, Hager & North U.S. Equity Fund	61%	14|21	08/88	-21.95	1981	-5.5%	3|21	1.00	1.00	1.10	green

S = Seg Funds

8 U.S. LARGE CAP/DIVERSIFIED EQUITY

Performance Trend by Quartiles (84 85 86 87 88 89 90 91 92 93 94 95 96 97 98 | June)

Fund Name	Performance Trend (84 → 98 | June)
Phillips, Hager & North U.S. Pooled Pension Fund	2 2 3 3 2 1 2 2 1 2 2 2 1 2 2 | 3
Principal Growth Fund Inc.	3 1 1 3 4 2 2 4 3 2 |
Rothschild American Equity Fund (S)	1 | 3
Royal & SunAlliance U.S. Equity Fund	1 1 | 1
Royal U.S. Equity Fund CS	3 3 1 1 4 1 2 3 1 3 2 2 3 2 4
Royal U.S. Growth Strategic Index Fund	| 2
Royal U.S. Value Strategic Index Fund	| 4
Scotia CanAm Growth Fund	3 1 2 3 | 2
Scotia Excelsior American Growth Fund	4 4 4 3 2 2 1 3 4 3 | 3
Scudder U.S. Growth & Income Fund	2 2 | 3
Spectrum United American Equity Fund	1 1 1 3 2 2 4 4 1 1 3 | 1
Spectrum United American Growth Fund CS	1 2 4 1 3 3 1 1 1 1 1 3 4 | 1
Spectrum United Optimax USA Fund	3 4 4 3 | 2
Standard Life U.S. Equity Mutual Fund	3 3 2 | 1
Strategic Value American Equity Fund	2 3 1 3 1 4 3 4 3 1 3 4 3 | 2
Talvest/Hyperion Value Line U.S. Equity Fund CS	2 2 3 1 2 4 | 3
Trust Pret et Revenu American Fund	2 2 1 4 3 3 2 2 2 4 3 1 3 4 | 3
University Avenue U.S. Growth Fund	4 1 4 1 4 4 4 4 3 4 3 | 3
University Avenue U.S. Small Cap Fund	| 4
Valorem U.S. Equity-Value Fund	| 3
Zweig Strategic Growth Fund	1 2 3 3 3 | 4

Fund Name	Fund Beats GICs %	Fund Beats GICs (Yr)	Worst 12 mo. End	Worst 12 mo. Chng (%)	Worst Calendar Year	Worst Calendar %	Years Fund Lost $	Sharpe 3-Yr	Sharpe 5-Yr	MER	Efficiency
Phillips, Hager & North U.S. Pooled Pension Fund	60%	14|21	08/88	-20.60	1987	-2.9%	3|21	1.00	1.00	0.03	green
Principal Growth Fund Inc.	59%	6|9	09/90	-10.98	1990	-1.4%	1|9	3.00	3.00	0.50	green
Rothschild American Equity Fund	57%	1|1	03/97	14.76	1997	37.1%	0|1	N/A	N/A	2.80	red
Royal & SunAlliance U.S. Equity Fund	69%	2|2	04/97	17.34	1996	26.8%	0|2	N/A	N/A	0.00	–
Royal U.S. Equity Fund CS	55%	14|21	08/88	-23.86	1981	-10.2%	4|21	3.00	3.00	2.11	orange
Royal U.S. Growth Strategic Index Fund	N/A	0|0	N/A	0.00	N/A		0|0	N/A	N/A	1.50	green
Royal U.S. Value Strategic Index Fund	N/A	0|0	N/A	0.00	N/A		0|0	N/A	N/A	1.50	green
Scotia CanAm Growth Fund	72%	3|4	01/95	-0.18	1994	0.5%	0|4	3.00	N/A	1.34	green
Scotia Excelsior American Growth Fund	52%	7|11	08/88	-34.37	1987	-20.1%	3|11	4.00	4.00	2.19	orange
Scudder U.S. Growth & Income Fund	71%	1|1	06/98	26.78	1997	33.5%	0|1	N/A	N/A	1.25	green
Spectrum United American Equity Fund	60%	13|21	07/82	-19.54	1990	-6.6%	5|21	1.00	2.00	2.30	orange
Spectrum United American Growth Fund CS	57%	15|21	10/90	-22.46	1987	-14.4%	3|21	3.00	3.00	2.35	orange
Spectrum United Optimax USA Fund	64%	3|4	11/94	-0.13	1994	1.7%	0|4	3.00	N/A	2.35	orange
Standard Life U.S. Equity Mutual Fund	68%	3|3	07/96	11.47	1996	17.3%	0|3	2.00	N/A	2.00	green
Strategic Value American Equity Fund	59%	16|21	07/82	-19.61	1990	-12.4%	2|21	3.00	3.00	2.70	red
Talvest/Hyperion Value Line U.S. Equity Fund CS	60%	5|6	09/94	-6.78	1994	0.6%	0|6	3.00	4.00	3.01	red
Trust Pret et Revenu American Fund	52%	12|21	08/88	-29.31	1987	-8.3%	5|21	4.00	4.00	2.02	green
University Avenue U.S. Growth Fund	46%	4|12	08/88	-30.49	1990	-20.3%	5|12	4.00	4.00	2.40	orange
University Avenue U.S. Small Cap Fund	54%	0|0	06/98	29.00	N/A		0|0	N/A	N/A	2.40	orange
Valorem U.S. Equity-Value Fund	53%	0|0	01/98	18.68	N/A		0|0	N/A	N/A	3.30	red
Zweig Strategic Growth Fund	59%	4|5	09/94	-0.17	1994	3.7%	0|5	1.00	1.00	2.49	orange

S = Seg Funds

9 U.S. SMALL-CAP EQUITY

Fund Name	Performance Trend by Quartiles (84–98) / June	Fund Beats % GICs	Fund Beats GICs(Yr)	Worst 12 mo. End / Chng (%)	Worst Calendar Year	Years Fund Lost $	Sharpe Ratio 3-Yr	Sharpe Ratio 5-Yr	MER
Altamira Select American Fund		61%	5|6	04/97 -2.43	1994 2.1%	0|6	N/A	N/A	2.28
BPI American Small Companies Fund		54%	7|9	06/89 -17.89	1990 -0.3%	1|9	N/A	N/A	2.56
Cambridge American Growth Fund		45%	2|5	07/96 -19.43	1994 -16.9%	2|5	N/A	N/A	3.56
CIBC U.S. Small Companies Fund		61%	2|2	04/97 -13.05	1996 10.0%	0|2	N/A	N/A	2.45
Fidelity Small Cap America Fund		61%	3|3	07/96 -6.35	1996 17.0%	0|3	N/A	N/A	2.51
S Forester Growth Funds - Money Market		12%	1|8	11/97 0.81	1997 1.0%	0|8	N/A	N/A	2.00
Franklin U.S. Small Cap Growth Fund CS		60%	0|0	06/98 24.60	N/A	0|0	N/A	N/A	2.50
Green Line U.S. Small-Cap Equity Fund		N/A	0|0	N/A 0.00	N/A	0|0	N/A	N/A	2.35
S Maritime Life Discovery Fund (A&C)		55%	1|1	01/98 10.86	1997 12.7%	0|1	N/A	N/A	2.55
S Maritime Life Discovery Fund Series B		55%	1|1	01/98 10.96	1997 12.7%	0|1	N/A	N/A	2.55
S MetLife - Fidelity Small Cap America Fund		N/A	0|0	N/A 0.00	N/A	0|0	N/A	N/A	2.69
Universal U.S. Emerging Growth Fund		62%	3|5	04/97 -25.43	1997 4.7%	0|5	N/A	N/A	2.40

S = Seg Funds

241

10 INTERNATIONAL EQUITY

Fund Name	Performance Trend by Quartiles (84–98 / June)	RISK: Fund Beats GICs %	Fund Beats GICs (Yr)	Worst 12 mo. End	Chng (%)	Worst Calendar Year	Years Fund Lost $	Sharpe Ratio 3-Yr	Sharpe Ratio 5-Yr	MER	Efficiency
Acadia International Equity Fund		N/A	0|0	N/A	0.00	N/A	0|0	N/A	N/A	0.00	–
AGF International Stock Class	3	54%	0|0	06/98	15.44	N/A	0|0	N/A	N/A	2.98	●
AIC World Equity Fund	4 4 1 1 1 | 1	55%	2|4	12/94	-6.97	1994 -7.0%	1|4	1.00	N/A	2.70	●
Argentum International Master Portfolio CS		N/A	0|0	N/A	0.00	N/A	0|0	N/A	N/A	0.00	–
Artisan International Equity Fund	1 1 | 1	N/A	0|0	N/A	0.00	N/A	0|0	N/A	N/A	2.99	●
Atlas International Large Cap Growth Fund	1 1 | 1	81%	1|1	12/97	13.57	1997 13.6%	0|1	N/A	N/A	2.84	●
Atlas International RSP Index Fund	1 3	71%	1|1	06/98	11.88	1997 16.3%	0|1	N/A	N/A	2.01	●
Beutel Goodman International Equity Fund	4 4 2 2 4 | 2 4	59%	3|5	02/95	-14.29	1994 0.9%	0|5	4.00	3.00	2.60	●
Bissett International Equity Fund	3 2 3 | 2 3	62%	2|2	07/96	-0.28	1996 7.6%	0|2	3.00	N/A	2.50	●
BPI International Equity Value Fund	1	69%	0|0	06/98	37.30	N/A	0|0	N/A	N/A	2.35	●
S BPI International Equity Value Segregated Fund		N/A	0|0	N/A	0.00	N/A	0|0	N/A	N/A	0.00	–
C.I. Sector Hansberger International Shares	4 4 | 4	54%	0|1	06/98	-8.70	1997 1.1%	0|1	N/A	N/A	2.50	●
S C.U. International G7 Index Fund		N/A	0|0	N/A	0.00	N/A	0|0	N/A	N/A	2.84	●
Canada Trust International Equity Fund	4 4 2 2 1 | 2 1	59%	5|10	02/95	-12.66	1995 -0.5%	2|10	1.00	2.00	2.62	●
Canada Trust International Equity Index Fund	2 | 2	N/A	0|0	N/A	0.00	N/A	0|0	N/A	N/A	0.53	●
S CDA International Equity Fund (KBSH)	2 4 2 | 2	62%	1|2	12/97	-0.05	1997 -0.1%	1|2	4.00	N/A	1.45	●
CIBC International Index Fund		N/A	0|0	N/A	0.00	N/A	0|0	N/A	N/A	0.90	●
CIBC International Index RRSP Fund	3 2 | 3 2	68%	0|1	11/97	2.38	1997 3.6%	0|1	N/A	N/A	0.90	●
First Canadian International Growth Fund	1 3 4 3 2 | 3 2	61%	3|5	06/95	-5.62	1995 2.7%	0|5	3.00	3.00	2.01	●
S First Trust Global Target 15 Trust 1997 CS	4 | 4	50%	0|0	06/98	-4.17	N/A	0|0	N/A	N/A	0.00	–
S Fonds Astra - Actions internationales	4 | 4	N/A	0|0	N/A	0.00	N/A	0|0	N/A	N/A	2.85	●
GBC International Growth Fund	4 4 3 3 3 | 3 3	54%	3|8	02/95	-17.77	1990 -10.1%	4|8	4.00	4.00	1.91	●

S = Seg Funds

10 INTERNATIONAL EQUITY

	Fund Name	Performance Trend by Quartiles (94–98)	June	Fund Bears GICs %	Fund Bears GICs(Yr)	Worst 12 mo. End	Chng (%)	Worst Calendar %	Year	Years Fund Lost $	Sharpe 3-Yr	Sharpe 5-Yr	MER	Eff.
S	Great-West Life International Equity Inv (P) DSC	2 2 1 2	2	68%	3|3	11/95	6.00	8.1%	1995	0|3	1.00	N/A	2.69	●
S	Great-West Life International Equity Invest (P) NL	2 2 1 2	2	68%	3|3	11/95	5.87	8.0%	1995	0|3	1.00	N/A	2.93	●
S	Great-West Life Int'l Opportunity Fund (P) DSC		1	N/A	0|0	N/A	0.00		N/A	0|0	N/A	N/A	2.52	●
S	Great-West Life Int'l Opportunity Fund (P) NL		1	N/A	0|0	N/A	0.00		N/A	0|0	N/A	N/A	2.76	●
	Green Line International Equity Fund	2 4 3 3 3	3	63%	3|5	08/95	-7.47	0.6%	1995	0|5	4.00	4.00	2.32	●
	Green Line International RSP Index Fund		2	N/A	0|0	N/A	0.00		N/A	0|0	N/A	N/A	1.25	●
	Hansberger International Fund	4 4	4	56%	0|1	06/98	-8.06	2.2%	1997	0|1	N/A	N/A	2.45	●
	ICM International Equity Fund	1 1 2 2 2	2	59%	4|4	02/95	-0.40	6.5%	1997	0|4	2.00	1.00	0.35	●
S	Industrial Alliance Ecoflex Investment Fund I	2 4	4	63%	1|1	06/98	8.96	12.9%	1997	0|1	N/A	N/A	2.98	●
S	Industrial Alliance International Fund	1 4	4	63%	1|1	06/98	9.78	13.7%	1997	0|1	N/A	N/A	2.22	●
	InvesNat Protected International Fund			N/A	0|0	N/A	0.00		N/A	0|0	N/A	N/A	3.17	●
S	London Life International Equity Fund	4 4 2	2	51%	0|2	04/97	-6.48	-1.6%	1997	1|2	4.00	N/A	2.50	●
S	Mackenzie Sentinel Global Fund	2 3 4 4 1	1	51%	2|11	08/88	-29.79	-13.7%	1990	4|11	3.00	3.00	0.51	●
S	Manulife Fidelity International Portfolio GIF	3	3	75%	0|0	06/98	23.12		N/A	0|0	N/A	N/A	3.38	●
S	Manulife VistaFund Global Equity 1	3 3 2	2	57%	2|2	01/97	2.93	5.6%	1997	0|2	3.00	N/A	1.63	●
S	Maritime Life EurAsia Fund (A&C)	2 2	2	65%	1|1	11/97	7.26	8.9%	1997	0|1	N/A	N/A	2.40	●
S	Maritime Life EurAsia Fund Series B	2 2	2	65%	1|1	11/97	7.29	8.8%	1997	0|1	N/A	N/A	2.40	●
	Mawer World Investment Fund	3 2 1 1 3	3	52%	5|10	11/89	-6.98	-2.1%	1988	2|10	2.00	1.00	1.42	●
	Montrusco Select E.A.F.E. Fund	1 1 4 4 1	1	54%	7|10	09/90	-17.82	-15.2%	1990	2|10	4.00	2.00	0.00	–
	Mutual Premier International Fund	3 3 1 3 1	1	62%	1|4	01/95	-6.25	3.0%	1994	0|4	2.00	1.00	2.43	●
	National Trust International Equity Fund	3 4 4 1	1	58%	1|3	08/95	-4.63	1.3%	1997	0|3	3.00	N/A	2.36	●
S	North West Life Ecoflex Investment Fund E	4	4	50%	0|0	06/98	-36.71		N/A	0|0	N/A	N/A	3.82	●

S = Seg Funds

10 INTERNATIONAL EQUITY

Performance Trend by Quartiles columns: 84 85 86 87 88 89 90 91 92 93 94 95 96 97 98

Fund Name	Performance Trend (recent quartiles)	Fund Beats GICs %	Fund Beats GICs (Yr)	Worst 12 mo. End	Worst 12 mo. Chng (%)	Worst Calendar Year	Worst Calendar %	Years Fund Lost $	Sharpe 3-Yr	Sharpe 5-Yr	MER
S North West Life Ecoflex Investment Fund I	98:4	61%	0|0	06/98	8.96	N/A		0|0	N/A	N/A	2.98 ●
O.I.Q. FERIQUE International Fund	95:3 96:4 97:3 98:1	56%	2|4	08/95	-7.72	1995	1.0%	0|4	1.00	N/A	0.63 ●
Optimum Funds international	95:1 96:4 97:1 98:3	61%	2|3	04/97	-2.36	1996	4.0%	0|3	1.00	N/A	1.96 ●
Phillips, Hager & North International Equity Fund	95:2 96:2 97:4 98:4	57%	2|3	08/95	-2.12	1997	3.1%	0|3	4.00	N/A	1.49 ●
Pursuit Global Equity Fund	96:1 97:2 98:3	71%	2|2	12/97	7.81	1997	7.8%	0|2	N/A	N/A	2.50 ●
S Royal & SunAlliance International Equity Fund	95:2 96:3 97:3 98:1	56%	2|3	10/95	-2.65	1997	4.1%	0|3	3.00	N/A	2.60 ●
Royal International Equity Fund	94:2 95:3 96:1 97:3 98:3	61%	2|4	01/95	-3.72	1997	5.5%	0|4	2.00	2.00	2.68 ●
Spectrum United Global Growth Portfolio	98:3	N/A	0|0	N/A	0.00	N/A		0|0	N/A	N/A	2.43 ●
Standard Life International Equity Mutual Fund	95:1 96:4 97:2 98:2	59%	3|3	01/97	3.93	1996	6.4%	0|3	2.00	N/A	2.00 ●
Templeton International Stock Fund	94:3 95:1 96:1 97:1 98:3	54%	6|8	09/90	-13.70	1990	-11.5%	1|8	1.00	1.00	2.49 ●
Universal International Stock Fund	94:1 95:2 96:4 97:3 98:1	54%	6|12	09/90	-14.52	1990	-13.9%	2|12	2.00	2.00	2.41 ●
Universal World Growth RRSP Fund	95:1 96:1 97:3 98:4	59%	3|3	06/98	0.87	1997	6.2%	0|3	2.00	N/A	2.44 ●
YMG International Fund	94:2 95:3 96:3 97:2 98:3	60%	2|4	02/95	-8.93	1995	2.7%	0|4	3.00	3.00	1.78 ●

S = Seg Funds

11 GLOBAL EQUITY

Fund Name	CONSISTENCY — Performance Trend by Quartiles (84–98, June)	RISK: Fund Beats GICs %	Fund Beats GICs (Yr)	Worst 12 mo. End	Worst 12 mo. Chng (%)	Worst Calendar Year	Years Fund Lost $	Sharpe 3-Yr	Sharpe 5-Yr	MER
20/20 Aggressive Global Stock Fund	95:4, Jun:1	66%	1|1	05/97	-1.91	1997 6.4%	0|1	N/A	N/A	3.64
Acuity Pooled Global Equity Fund	94:4, 95:1, 96:1, 97:1, 98:1, Jun:1	55%	3|4	10/94	-11.25	1994 -7.8%	1|4	3.00	3.00	0.00
AGF International Value Fund	90:1, 91:2, 92:1, 93:4, 94:3, 95:1, 96:1, 97:1, Jun:3	56%	6|8	02/95	-5.14	1990 -2.8%	1|8	1.00	1.00	2.77
AGF RSP International Equity Allocation Fund	94:3, 95:2, 96:3, 97:3, 98:2, Jun:2	58%	3|4	01/95	-8.13	1994 -1.2%	1|4	2.00	N/A	2.45
AGF World Equity Class	96:3, 97:3, Jun:2	59%	2|2	07/96	4.97	1996 9.2%	0|2	2.00	N/A	3.07
AIM Global RSP Index Fund	98:2, Jun:3	74%	1|1	01/98	14.39	1997 14.6%	0|1	N/A	N/A	1.94
AIM International Fund	88:4, 89:2, 90:4, 91:4, 92:3, 93:1, 94:2, 95:4, 96:4, 97:1, 98:2, Jun:3	51%	3|10	09/90	-18.69	1990 -15.2%	3|10	3.00	4.00	2.97
Altamira Global Small Company Fund	98:2, Jun:3	65%	1|1	06/98	10.08	1997 14.9%	0|1	N/A	N/A	2.36
S Apex Global Equity Fund	98:2, Jun:1	74%	1|1	12/97	14.95	1997 14.9%	0|1	N/A	N/A	2.79
Atlas Global Value Fund	91:3, 92:1, 93:2, 94:3, 95:3, 96:3, 97:4, Jun:3	50%	6|7	06/91	-7.29	1994 1.6%	0|7	4.00	3.00	2.75
Azura Growth Fund	96:2, 97:3, Jun:4	61%	2|2	07/96	6.08	1997 8.9%	0|2	4.00	N/A	2.28
Bissett Multinational Growth Fund	95:1, 96:1, 97:1, Jun:2	71%	3|3	08/95	10.82	1995 22.0%	0|3	1.00	N/A	1.50
S BPI Global Equity Value Fund	88:4, 89:1, 90:4, 91:1, 92:1, 93:3, 94:4, 95:3, 96:2, 97:2, 98:2, Jun:1	54%	6|12	08/88	-23.92	1988 -11.4%	1|12	1.00	1.00	2.43
S BPI Global Equity Value Segregated Fund	Jun:1	N/A	0|0	N/A	0.00	N/A	0|0	N/A	N/A	0.00
BPI Global Opportunities Fund	97:1, 98:1, Jun:1	64%	2|2	07/96	9.29	1996 32.7%	0|2	1.00	N/A	2.55
BPI Global Small Companies Fund	94:1, 95:4, 96:1, 97:3, Jun:4	54%	3|4	10/95	-5.60	1995 -4.5%	1|4	4.00	3.00	2.45
C.I. Global Equity RSP Fund	94:4, 95:4, 96:2, 97:3, Jun:3	59%	2|4	02/95	-12.41	1994 -4.6%	1|4	3.00	N/A	2.44
C.I. Global Fund	88:2, 89:3, 90:3, 91:3, 92:1, 93:2, 94:2, 95:3, 96:4, 97:2, 98:1, Jun:1	56%	6|11	08/88	-18.73	1990 -11.2%	2|11	1.00	2.00	2.48
S C.I. Global Segregated Fund	Jun:1	N/A	0|0	N/A	0.00	N/A	0|0	N/A	N/A	3.30
S C.I. Hansberger Value Segregated Fund	Jun:4	N/A	0|0	N/A	0.00	N/A	0|0	N/A	N/A	3.30
C.I. Sector Global Shares	88:3, 89:3, 90:3, 91:1, 92:2, 93:2, 94:3, 95:4, 96:2, 97:1, 98:1, Jun:1	55%	6|10	09/90	-12.62	1990 -10.9%	2|10	2.00	3.00	2.51
C.I. Sector Hansberger Global Small Cap Shares	98:4, Jun:4	50%	0|1	06/98	-7.54	1997 4.4%	0|1	N/A	N/A	2.74

S = Seg Funds

11 GLOBAL EQUITY

Performance Trend by Quartiles columns span years: 84 85 86 87 88 89 90 91 92 93 94 95 96 97 98 June

Fund Name	Performance Trend by Quartiles (84–June)	Fund Beats GICs %	Fund Beats GICs (Yr)	Worst 12 mo. End	Worst 12 mo. Chng (%)	Worst Calendar Year	Worst Calendar %	Years Fund Lost $	Sharpe Ratio 3-Yr	Sharpe Ratio 5-Yr	MER
C.I. Sector Hansberger Value Shares	4 4 4	56%	0|1	06/98	-10.26	1997	0.8%	0|1	N/A	N/A	2.50
Cambridge Global Fund	1 3 1 1 2 4 4 2 1 4 4 4 4 4 4 4	50%	11|21	01/98	-57.71	1997	-52.0%	6|21	4.00	4.00	3.54
S Canada Life U.S. & Int'l. Equity Fund S-34	4 3 3 1 1 2 1 1 3 2 1 1 2 2	58%	10|13	08/88	-14.01	1990	-6.1%	2|13	1.00	1.00	2.40
Canada Trust GlobalGrowth Fund	4 2	59%	1|1	11/97	6.40	1997	8.0%	0|1	N/A	N/A	2.05
Capstone Balanced Fund	4 4 4 3 3 3 1 4 3 4 4 2 1 2 1 2	51%	10|17	08/88	-16.56	1994	-4.8%	2|17	1.00	2.00	2.00
S CCPE Global Equity Fund	4 3 2 3	55%	2|2	01/97	2.97	1996	8.5%	0|2	4.00	N/A	1.75
S CDA Global Fund (Trimark)	3	61%	0|0	06/98	7.44	N/A	12.3%	0|0	N/A	N/A	1.45
CentrePost Foreign Equity Fund	4 1 2 2 1 2	60%	5|5	07/96	0.63	1994	-4.9%	0|5	2.00	1.00	1.75
CIBC Global Equity Fund	3 2 3 3 3 3 3 1 1 1	51%	7|9	09/90	-11.25	1990	18.4%	2|9	1.00	2.00	2.50
Clarington Global Opportunities Fund	2 1	68%	1|1	01/98	18.29	1997	-4.1%	0|1	N/A	N/A	2.95
S Colonia Bond Fund	4 4 1 4 4 4	53%	4|5	01/95	-5.91	1994	-9.3%	1|5	4.00	4.00	1.63
Cornerstone Global Fund	2 1 4 1 1 2 2 4 2 1 2 2 3	58%	9|12	08/88	-30.93	1988	N/A	1|12	2.00	2.00	2.37
COTE 100 Excel		N/A	0|0	N/A	0.00	N/A	-9.3%	0|0	N/A	N/A	2.60
Cundill Value Fund Series A	1 4 4 1 4 3 4 3 1 1 3 3 4 4	55%	14|21	12/90	-9.30	1990	N/A	1|21	4.00	2.00	2.01
Cundill Value Fund Series B	4	31%	0|0	06/98	-6.15	N/A	-9.8%	0|0	N/A	N/A	2.36
Desjardins International Fund	2 3 3 2 4 3 1 2 3 3 1 2 4 4 1	53%	12|21	08/88	-25.41	1981	-18.6%	1|21	3.00	3.00	2.29
Dynamic Global Millennia Fund	3 3 4 3 4 4 1 4 3 1 3 4	49%	5|11	01/95	-23.98	1994	-24.3%	5|11	4.00	4.00	2.41
Dynamic International Fund	1 4 4 4 2 3 3 2 4 3 1 1 1 3	54%	7|12	09/88	-38.36	1987	11.8%	4|12	3.00	3.00	2.57
Elliott & Page Global Equity Fund	2 2 2 3 1	65%	3|3	08/95	1.85	1997	-2.9%	0|3	2.00	N/A	2.00
S Empire Elite International Growth Fund	1 2 2 3 2 1 3 3	55%	6|8	01/95	-11.38	1990	7.2%	2|8	3.00	3.00	2.45
Equitable Life International Fund	3 3 3 3 2	62%	3|3	10/95	-0.51	1995	-8.8%	0|3	1.00	N/A	2.75
S Fidelity International Portfolio Fund	3 1 2 2 4 2 2 1 2 1 2	58%	6|10	09/90	-14.18	1990	N/A	1|10	1.00	1.00	2.69

S = Seg Funds

11 GLOBAL EQUITY

Fund Name	Performance Trend by Quartiles (84–98)	June	Fund Beats GICs %	Fund Beats GICs (Yr)	Worst 12 mo. End	Chng (%)	Worst Calendar Year	Worst Cal. %	Years Fund Lost $	Sharpe 3-Yr	Sharpe 5-Yr	MER	Efficiency
FMOQ International Equity Fund	4 4 1	1	55%	2|3	08/95	-11.30	1995	1.5%	0|3	2.00	N/A	0.81	● green
S Fonds Astra - Tendances demographiques	2	2	N/A	0|0	N/A	0.00	N/A		0|0	N/A	N/A	2.50	● orange
Global Strategy Diversified World Equity Fund	4 3 2 1	1	60%	2|3	12/95	4.80	1995	4.8%	0|3	2.00	N/A	2.37	● orange
Global Strategy World Companies Fund	1 1 4 1	1	72%	3|3	12/97	6.68	1997	6.7%	0|3	1.00	N/A	2.79	● red
Global Strategy World Equity Fund	3 3 2 2	2	65%	3|3	04/97	5.93	1995	10.6%	0|3	2.00	N/A	2.79	● red
Green Line Global Select Fund	1 2 3 2 3	3	61%	4|4	02/95	0.49	1996	13.2%	0|4	3.00	N/A	2.34	● orange
Guardian Global Equity Fund	3 1 1 4 2 2 2 4 4 2 2 3 2 4 1	1	58%	10|21	09/90	-27.24	1990	-24.7%	3|21	3.00	2.00	1.35	● green
Hansberger Global Small Cap Fund	4 4	4	52%	1|1	06/98	-6.70	1997	5.6%	0|1	N/A	N/A	2.69	● red
Hansberger Value Fund	4 4	4	56%	0|1	06/98	-9.67	1997	2.0%	0|1	N/A	N/A	2.45	● orange
S Hartford Select World Economies Fund			N/A	0|0	N/A	0.00	N/A		0|0	N/A	N/A	0.00	–
Hillsdale LS American Equity Fund	1 4	4	63%	1|1	05/98	15.27	1997	19.2%	0|1	N/A	N/A	1.00	● green
Hongkong Bank Global Equity Fund			N/A	0|0	N/A	0.00	N/A		0|0	N/A	N/A	0.00	–
Investors Global Fund Ltd.	2 4 2 1 3 4 4 2 2 3 2 2	2	58%	6|11	08/88	-22.88	1990	-4.2%	2|11	1.00	1.00	2.36	● orange
Investors Growth Portfolio	3 2 4 3 2 1 1 1 1	3	59%	5|8	09/90	-15.74	1990	-10.2%	1|8	1.00	1.00	2.61	● orange
Ivy Foreign Equity Fund	4 1 1 1 2 1 3	3	63%	5|5	09/94	6.80	1993	9.9%	0|5	1.00	1.00	2.39	● orange
Manulife Cabot Global Equity Fund	2 4 3 3	3	53%	3|3	02/95	-0.53	1996	9.1%	0|3	2.00	N/A	2.50	● orange
S Manulife Trimark Select Growth GIF	4	4	56%	0|0	06/98	4.19	N/A		0|0	N/A	N/A	3.25	● red
S Maritime Life Global Equities Fund (A&C)	4 4 3 2	2	60%	2|3	07/96	1.18	1995	4.5%	0|3	4.00	N/A	2.75	● red
S Maritime Life Global Equities Fund Series B	3 2	2	75%	1|1	11/97	9.06	1997	12.5%	0|1	N/A	N/A	2.75	● red
Maxxum Global Equity Fund	3 2 1	1	69%	2|2	07/96	0.57	1996	11.5%	0|2	2.00	N/A	2.48	● orange
MB Global Equity Fund - Pooled	1 1	1	67%	1|1	04/97	13.37	1997	20.9%	0|1	N/A	N/A	0.00	–
McDonald Enhanced Global Fund	1 1	1	74%	1|1	02/98	18.37	1997	19.0%	0|1	N/A	N/A	2.75	● red

S = Seg Funds

11 GLOBAL EQUITY

Fund Name	84	85	86	87	88	89	90	91	92	93	94	95	96	97	98	June	Fund Beats GICs %	Fund Beats GICs(Yr)	Worst 12 mo. End Chng (%)		Worst Calendar Year		Years Fund Lost $	Sharpe Ratio Quartile Rankings 3-Yr	5-Yr	MER	Efficiency
MD Growth Investment Limited	2	1	2	2	2	4	2	2	1	3	1	1	1	1	1	3	60%	16|21	09/90	-17.87	1990	-15.7%	3|21	1.00	1.00	1.29	● green
MetLife MVP Global Equity Fund (S)																2	67%	0|0	01/98	12.06	N/A		0|0	N/A	N/A	2.69	● red
Millennia III International Equity Fund Series 1 (S)														4	4	2	53%	1|2	01/97	-1.38	1996	2.8%	0|2	N/A	N/A	2.90	● red
Mutual Summit Foreign Equity Fund																3	62%	0|0	06/98	18.78	N/A		0|0	N/A	N/A	0.00	—
NAL-Investor Global Equity Fund (S)										4	2	1	4	4	3	3	52%	4|6	02/93	-6.44	1992	-1.1%	1|6	4.00	4.00	2.50	● orange
National Life Global Equities Fund (S)								1	2	2	1	2	2	3	4	4	58%	7|9	02/95	-6.55	1990	-6.5%	1|9	3.00	3.00	2.65	● red
Northwest International Fund													3	3	1	1	65%	2|2	04/97	0.60	1997	10.0%	0|2	3.00	N/A	2.25	● green
O'Donnell World Equity Fund															4	4	32%	0|1	12/97	1.90	1997	1.9%	0|1	N/A	N/A	2.75	● red
Orbit World Fund							4	4	3	1	4	4	1	1	1	1	55%	4|7	12/95	-11.61	1995	-11.6%	1|7	2.00	3.00	2.65	● red
OTG Investment Fund - Global Value Section								4	4	1	3	2	3			3	59%	4|5	01/95	-3.68	1994	-3.1%	1|5	2.00	2.00	1.00	● green
Phillips, Hager & North Global Equity Trust															3	3	73%	0|0	06/98	13.54	N/A		0|0	N/A	N/A	0.00	—
Principal International Fund					3	3	3	4	1	4	4	1	3	2		2	56%	5|9	01/95	-14.48	1990	-10.2%	2|9	3.00	4.00	0.75	● green
Pursuit Growth Fund														2	1	1	73%	1|1	11/97	15.25	1997	17.0%	0|1	N/A	N/A	1.75	● green
Quebec Professionals' International Equity Fund								2	4	2	3	2	4	2		2	62%	4|6	02/95	0.22	1997	2.0%	0|6	3.00	2.00	1.25	● green
Rothschild International Equity Fund													2	3		3	61%	1|1	04/97	6.94	1997	16.1%	0|1	N/A	N/A	2.78	● red
Saxon World Growth			3	3	1	4	1	2	1	1	2	2	2	3	4	4	58%	10|12	09/90	-26.64	1990	-21.8%	2|12	4.00	1.00	1.75	● green
Sceptre International Fund			1	2	1	1	3	1	1	4	4	3	4	4	4	4	59%	6|11	08/88	-16.08	1994	-5.6%	2|11	4.00	4.00	2.07	● green
Scotia Excelsior International Fund			1	4	3	1	3	2	3	2	3	4	2	2		2	55%	14|21	08/88	-23.28	1990	-12.7%	2|21	3.00	3.00	2.23	● red
Scudder Global Fund													1	1	2	2	79%	2|2	10/96	13.32	1996	17.6%	0|2	4.00	N/A	1.75	● green
Spectrum United Global Equity Fund							4	3	3	3	3	3	3	3	1	1	55%	4|7	02/95	-10.82	1994	-0.7%	1|7	2.00	4.00	2.30	● green
Spectrum United Global Growth Fund	4	2	4	4	4	1	4	1	1	1	3	4	4	4	3	3	52%	11|21	10/90	-33.98	1990	-26.4%	7|21	4.00	4.00	2.30	● green
Strategic Value Commonwealth Fund Ltd.	2	3	2	2	2	2	3	3	3	2	3	4	2			2	56%	12|21	07/82	-11.02	1990	-5.5%	1|21	4.00	4.00	2.70	● red

S = Seg Funds

11 GLOBAL EQUITY

Fund Name	Performance Trend by Quartiles (84 85 86 87 88 89 90 91 92 93 94 95 96 97 98 · June)	Fund Beats GICs %	Fund Beats GICs (Yr)	Worst 12 mo. End Chng (%)	Worst Calendar Year	Years Fund Lost $	Sharpe Ratio 3-Yr	Sharpe Ratio 5-Yr	MER
Strategic Value Fund	2 4 · 4	41%	1|1	06/98 -22.26	1997 16.9%	0|1	N/A	N/A	3.13
Strategic Value International Fund Ltd.	3 4 3 4 1 3 2 3 4 3 1 3 4 4 2 · 2	59%	15|21	07/82 -18.58	1990 -7.3%	2|21	4.00	4.00	2.70
Talvest Global RRSP Fund	3 4 3 2 2 1 · 1	58%	4|5	02/95 -10.64	1994 -2.7%	1|5	1.00	2.00	2.50
Talvest/Hyperion Global Small Cap Fund		N/A	0|0	N/A 0.00	N/A	0|0	N/A	N/A	2.75
Templeton Global Smaller Companies Fund	4 1 1 2 3 1 1 1 4 4 · 4	53%	6|8	09/90 -20.76	1990 -17.1%	1|8	3.00	2.00	2.61
Templeton Growth Fund Ltd.	1 2 2 4 2 2 4 1 1 2 2 1 1 2 4 · 4	58%	16|21	07/82 -17.53	1990 -13.6%	3|21	4.00	3.00	2.00
Trimark Fund	4 2 4 3 1 2 3 1 1 1 2 1 2 2 4 · 4	59%	13|16	09/90 -21.97	1990 -9.9%	2|16	3.00	1.00	1.52
Trimark Select Growth Fund	2 1 1 3 1 2 2 3 4 · 4	59%	7|8	09/90 -17.92	1990 -7.2%	1|8	3.00	2.00	2.32
Trust Pret et Revenu International Fund	2 3 2 · 2	62%	2|2	07/96 6.22	1997 13.1%	0|2	2.00	N/A	1.32
Universal Growth Fund	3 1 3 · 3	63%	2|2	07/96 3.59	1996 9.6%	0|2	2.00	N/A	2.39
Universal World Value Fund	3 · 3	N/A	0|0	N/A 0.00	N/A	0|0	N/A	N/A	0.00
University Avenue World Fund	3 · 3	N/A	0|0	N/A 0.00	N/A	0|0	N/A	N/A	2.40

S = Seg Funds

12 GLOBAL SECTOR

Fund Name	June (97|98)	Fund Beats GICs %	Fund Beats GICs(Yr)	Worst 12 mo. End	Chng (%)	Worst Calendar Year	(Year %)	Years Fund Lost $	Sharpe 3-Yr	Sharpe 5-Yr	MER
Acuity Pooled Environment, Science & Technology	2 2	48%	2|4	01/95	-5.00	1994	-1.8%	1|4	N/A	N/A	0.00
AGF Global Real Estate Equity Class		N/A	0|0	N/A	0.00	N/A		0|0	N/A	N/A	0.00
AIM Global Health Sciences Fund	2 2	65%	4|5	04/97	-2.47	1994	4.2%	0|5	N/A	N/A	2.94
AIM Global Technology Fund	1 3	63%	1|1	05/98	29.35	1997	37.9%	0|1	N/A	N/A	2.94
AIM GT Global Health Care Class	4 3	50%	1|1	01/98	5.83	1997	8.6%	0|1	N/A	N/A	2.78
AIM GT Global Infrastructure Class	3 3	53%	3|3	10/95	0.84	1997	9.8%	0|3	N/A	N/A	2.76
AIM GT Global Natural Resources Class	4 4	53%	2|3	01/98	-9.50	1997	1.6%	0|3	N/A	N/A	2.95
AIM GT Global Telecommunications Class	3 2	64%	2|3	04/97	-17.08	1996	3.1%	0|3	N/A	N/A	2.82
AIM GT Global Theme Class	3 2	62%	1|1	01/98	9.87	1997	13.6%	0|1	N/A	N/A	2.89
Allstar Adrian Day Gold Plus Fund	4	17%	0|0	06/98	-54.18	N/A		0|0	N/A	N/A	5.28
C.I. Sector Global Consumer Products Shares	3	73%	0|0	06/98	23.96	N/A		0|0	N/A	N/A	2.42
C.I. Sector Global Financial Services Shares	1 3	67%	1|1	11/97	32.81	1997	38.6%	0|1	N/A	N/A	2.43
C.I. Sector Global Health Sciences Shares	1 3	63%	1|1	06/98	17.62	1997	29.5%	0|1	N/A	N/A	2.42
C.I. Sector Global Technology Shares	2 2	50%	1|1	01/98	20.15	1997	20.3%	0|1	N/A	N/A	2.42
C.I. Sector Global Telecommunications Shares	1 1	75%	1|1	08/97	23.83	1997	28.8%	0|1	N/A	N/A	2.42
CIBC Global Technology Fund	3 2	65%	2|2	04/97	-5.50	1997	16.7%	0|2	N/A	N/A	2.60
Clarington Global Communications Fund	1 1	79%	1|1	12/97	31.35	1997	31.3%	0|1	N/A	N/A	2.95
Dynamic Global Precious Metals Fund	4 4	43%	0|1	11/97	-46.59	1997	-44.4%	1|1	N/A	N/A	2.85
Dynamic Global Resource Fund	4 4	58%	1|3	06/98	-17.82	1997	-12.1%	1|3	N/A	N/A	2.63
Dynamic Real Estate Equity Fund	1 4	68%	2|2	06/98	12.97	1997	38.5%	0|2	N/A	N/A	2.72
Fidelity Focus Health Care Fund	2	85%	0|0	06/98	34.33	N/A		0|0	N/A	N/A	2.50
Fidelity Focus Technology Fund	1	54%	0|0	06/98	22.90	N/A		0|0	N/A	N/A	2.50

S = Seg Funds

12 GLOBAL SECTOR

Fund Name	Performance Trend by Quartiles (June)	Fund Beats GICs %	Fund Beats GICs(Yr)	Worst 12 mo. End	Chng (%)	Worst Calendar Year	Years Fund Lost $	Sharpe Ratio 3-Yr	Sharpe Ratio 5-Yr	MER
First Canadian Global Science & Technology Fund	1	56%	0|0	05/98	36.92	N/A	0|0	N/A	N/A	2.01 ●
S First Trust Pharmaceutical 1996 Series CS	1 1	79%	1|1	08/97	32.80	1997 41.7%	0|1	N/A	N/A	1.00 ●
S First Trust Pharmaceutical 1997 Series CS	1	77%	0|0	06/98	44.84	N/A	0|0	N/A	N/A	1.15 ●
S First Trust Pharmaceutical 1998 Series CS		N/A	0|0	N/A	0.00	N/A	0|0	N/A	N/A	0.00 –
Goldfund Ltd.	4 4	47%	9|21	09/88	-40.37	1981 -38.7%	10|21	N/A	N/A	1.03 ●
Green Line Entertainment & Communications Fund	2	N/A	0|0	N/A	0.00	N/A	0|0	N/A	N/A	2.57 ●
Green Line Health Sciences Fund	2 3	71%	1|1	12/97	22.42	1997 22.4%	0|1	N/A	N/A	2.58 ●
Greystone Managed Global Fund	2 2	66%	3|3	05/95	-1.49	1995 17.4%	0|3	N/A	N/A	2.50 ●
O'Donnell World Precious Metals Fund	4 4	37%	0|1	05/98	-42.50	1997 -39.2%	1|1	N/A	N/A	2.90 ●
Spectrum United Global Telecommunications Fund	3 1	63%	3|3	04/97	-8.64	1996 6.1%	0|3	N/A	N/A	2.55 ●
Talvest/Hyperion Global Health Care Fund	2 4	65%	1|1	01/98	12.09	1997 18.5%	0|1	N/A	N/A	3.30 ●
Talvest/Hyperion Global Science & Technology CS	2 1	67%	1|1	01/98	20.08	1997 21.7%	0|1	N/A	N/A	2.25 ●
Trimark Discovery Fund	3 3	50%	1|1	01/98	6.15	1997 9.3%	0|1	N/A	N/A	2.65 ●
Universal World Real Estate Fund	3	N/A	0|0	N/A	0.00	N/A	0|0	N/A	N/A	0.00 –
Universal World Science & Technology Fund	3 1	59%	1|1	12/97	16.67	1997 16.7%	0|1	N/A	N/A	2.41 ●
Valorem Global Equity-Value Fund		N/A	0|0	N/A	0.00	N/A	0|0	N/A	N/A	3.15 ●

S = Seg Funds

13 NORTH AMERICAN EQUITY

Fund Name	Consistency: Perf. Trend by Quartiles (84–98, June)	Risk: Fund Beats GICs %	Fund Beats GICs(Yr)	Worst 12 mo. End	Worst 12 mo. Chng (%)	Worst Calendar Year	Worst Calendar Year %	Years Fund Last $	Sharpe Ratio 3-Yr	Sharpe Ratio 5-Yr	MER	Efficiency
ABC American-Value Fund	1 (June)	58%	1|1	05/97	23.87	1997	38.8%	0|1	N/A	N/A	2.00	green
Altamira North American Recovery Fund	2 4 1 2 3	61%	2|4	01/95	-11.27	1994	-1.7%	1|4	2.00	N/A	2.30	orange
Cambridge Americas Fund	3 3 2 4 1	49%	5|10	08/88	-22.12	1990	-7.7%	2|10	4.00	4.00	3.50	red
Canada Trust North American Fund	3 3 4 4 2	53%	13|21	06/82	-28.04	1990	-11.7%	4|21	2.00	3.00	2.34	orange
Chou Associates Fund	2 1 2 1 2	59%	8|11	10/90	-17.06	1990	-10.7%	2|11	1.00	1.00	1.86	green
Clean Environment International Equity Fund	3 3 2 1 1	54%	3|4	01/95	-9.69	1994	-6.7%	1|4	1.00	N/A	2.62	red
COTE 100 Amerique	4 1 1 4 3	59%	4|5	01/95	-17.67	1994	-14.7%	1|5	2.00	2.00	1.38	green
Fidelity Focus Natural Resources Fund	3	54%	0|0	06/98	6.90	N/A		0|0	N/A	N/A	2.50	orange
First Canadian NAFTA Advantage Fund	2 3 1 4	60%	3|3	10/95	-0.24	1995	12.2%	0|3	3.00	N/A	2.07	orange
S First Trust N.A. Technology Trust 1997 Series CS	1	46%	0|0	06/98	19.70	N/A		0|0	N/A	N/A	0.00	—
GBC North American Growth Fund Inc.	2 1 4 2 4	60%	15|21	06/82	-28.64	1990	-23.5%	5|21	4.00	2.00	1.95	green
S Great-West Life North American Equity Fund (B) DSC	3 2	57%	1|1	11/97	12.54	1997	17.6%	0|1	N/A	N/A	2.56	red
S Great-West Life North American Equity Fund (B) NL	3 2	57%	1|1	11/97	12.25	1997	17.3%	0|1	N/A	N/A	2.80	orange
S Imperial Growth North American Equity Fund	1 1 4 2 1	57%	15|21	06/82	-28.92	1990	-20.7%	3|21	1.00	1.00	1.59	green
Investors North American Growth Fund	1 2 3 4 3	54%	14|21	06/82	-23.68	1990	-6.2%	3|21	2.00	1.00	2.38	orange
Investors Special Fund Ltd.	1 2 3 3 3	53%	13|21	05/82	-32.09	1981	-18.1%	4|21	3.00	2.00	2.39	orange
Marathon Performance N.A. Long-Short Fund		N/A	0|0	N/A	0.00	N/A		0|0	N/A	N/A	1.50	green
Millennia III North American Small Co Series 1		N/A	0|0	N/A	0.00	N/A		0|0	N/A	N/A	2.90	red
S Millennia III North American Small Co Series 2		N/A	0|0	N/A	0.00	N/A		0|0	N/A	N/A	3.08	red
Orbit North American Equity Fund	1 2	67%	1|1	06/98	20.13	1997	28.7%	0|1	1.00	N/A	2.65	green
Phillips, Hager & North North American Equity Fund	3 4 1 2 4	56%	3|5	02/95	-19.69	1994	-10.3%	1|5	3.00	3.00	1.18	green
Special Opportunities Fund Ltd.	4 2 2 2 4	42%	4|10	08/90	-24.35	1990	-18.0%	3|10	4.00	4.00	2.14	orange

S = Seg Funds

13 NORTH AMERICAN EQUITY

Fund Name	Performance Trend by Quartiles (84–98, June)	Fund Beats GICs %	Fund Beats GICs(Yr)	Worst 12 mo. End	Chng (%)	Worst Calendar Year	Worst Calendar %	Years Fund Lost $	Sharpe 3-Yr	Sharpe 5-Yr	MER
Standard Life Growth Equity Mutual Fund	3 1 | 4 2	64%	3|3	07/96	9.94	1995	11.3%	0|3	1.00	N/A	● 2.00
Trimark - The Americas Fund	1 4 3 | 3 4	59%	2|4	02/95	-11.55	1995	-0.6%	1|4	4.00	4.00	● 2.65
Universal Americas Fund	2 4 4 | 3 3	53%	11|18	02/95	-19.09	1990	-9.1%	2|18	3.00	3.00	● 2.55
Valorem Demographic Trends Fund	1	65%	0|0	01/98	25.71	N/A		0|0	N/A	N/A	● 3.15

Column group headers: CONSISTENCY | RISK | REWARD-TO-RISK (Sharpe Ratio Quartile Rankings) | EFFICIENCY

S = Seg Funds

14 EUROPEAN EQUITY

Fund Name	Performance Trend by Quartiles (84–98)	June	Fund Beats GICs %	Fund Beats GICs(Yr)	Worst 12 mo. End	Chng (%)	Worst Calendar Year	(%)	Years Fund Lost $	Sharpe 3-Yr	Sharpe 5-Yr	MER	Efficiency
AGF European Growth Class	3 4 1 1	1	59%	3|3	10/95	3.48	1995	10.1%	0|3	2.00	N/A	3.03	red
AGF International Group Germany Class	1 2 1	1	69%	2|2	07/96	6.12	1997	24.2%	0|2	3.00	N/A	2.99	red
AIM Europa Fund	4 3 4 4 2 1	1	58%	2|5	01/95	-4.97	1993	0.1%	0|5	2.00	3.00	2.91	red
Altamira European Equity Fund	1 2 2 2 2	2	66%	4|4	04/95	1.03	1994	8.5%	0|4	1.00	N/A	2.32	orange
Atlas European Value Fund	2 3 3 2 2	2	67%	3|4	01/95	1.16	1994	6.8%	0|4	1.00	N/A	2.65	red
C.I. Sector Hansberger European Shares	4 3 4 2 3 4	4	61%	3|5	01/95	-8.95	1994	-1.9%	1|5	4.00	4.00	2.49	red
S Canada Life European Equity Fund S-37	1 3 3	3	74%	2|2	12/97	17.29	1997	17.3%	0|2	N/A	N/A	2.40	green
Canada Trust EuroGrowth Fund	3 3 1 3	3	63%	3|3	01/95	-15.70	1995	10.4%	0|3	4.00	N/A	2.20	green
S CDA European Fund (KBSH)	2 4 1	1	67%	2|2	07/96	8.64	1997	13.5%	0|2	3.00	N/A	1.45	green
CIBC European Equity Fund	4 3 4	4	71%	2|2	01/97	8.46	1996	11.2%	0|2	N/A	N/A	2.50	orange
Dynamic Europe Fund	1 3 4 1 3 1	1	52%	3|8	06/91	-17.42	1990	-9.6%	3|8	3.00	3.00	2.50	orange
Fidelity European Growth Fund	1 1 2 2 1 2	2	64%	5|5	01/95	2.28	1994	10.1%	0|5	1.00	1.00	2.72	orange
First Canadian European Growth Fund	4 3 2 3	3	62%	3|3	10/95	4.90	1995	8.6%	0|3	3.00	N/A	2.08	green
Global Manager German Bear Fund	4 4 4 4	4	17%	0|3	07/97	-53.68	1997	-39.9%	2|3	4.00	N/A	1.82	green
Global Manager German Geared Fund	2 1 1 1	1	72%	3|3	10/95	2.75	1995	11.0%	0|3	4.00	N/A	1.82	green
Global Manager German Index Fund	2 4 1 1	1	67%	3|3	07/96	1.52	1995	13.0%	0|3	4.00	N/A	1.82	green
Global Manager U.K. Bear Fund	4 4 4 4	4	35%	0|3	02/98	-22.93	1997	-18.9%	2|3	4.00	N/A	1.82	green
Global Manager U.K. Geared Fund	1 1 1 3	3	63%	3|3	07/96	7.10	1996	32.7%	0|3	3.00	N/A	1.82	green
Global Manager U.K. Index Fund	1 2 1 4	4	65%	3|3	07/96	4.41	1995	18.8%	0|3	2.00	N/A	1.82	orange
Global Strategy Diversified Europe Fund	4 4 2 3 2 3	3	66%	4|5	01/95	-8.06	1994	-4.6%	1|5	2.00	3.00	2.51	orange
Global Strategy Europe Plus Fund	2 2 2 3 4	4	72%	3|3	07/96	9.84	1995	11.6%	0|3	1.00	N/A	2.79	red
S Great-West Life European Equity Fund (S) NL		3	N/A	0|0	N/A	0.00	N/A		0|0	N/A	N/A	2.88	red

S = Seg Funds

14 EUROPEAN EQUITY

Fund Name	Performance Trend by Quartiles (recent, → June '98)	Fund Beats GICs %	Fund Beats GICs (Yr)	Worst 12 mo. End	Worst 12 mo. Chng (%)	Worst Calendar Year	Worst Calendar %	Years Fund Lost $	Sharpe 3-Yr	Sharpe 5-Yr	MER
Great-West Life European Equity Fund (S) NL	3	N/A	0|0	N/A	0.00	N/A	—	0|0	N/A	N/A	2.64
Green Line European Growth Fund	1 1 3 2	80%	3|3	07/96	13.88	1995	18.7%	0|3	1.00	N/A	2.58
Green Line European Index Fund	3	N/A	0|0	N/A	0.00	N/A	—	0|0	N/A	N/A	0.90
Growsafe European 100 Index Fund	3 3	81%	1|1	12/97	30.02	1997	30.0%	0|1	N/A	N/A	2.13
Hansberger European Fund	3 4 4 2 3 4	59%	3|6	01/95	-9.34	1992	-4.0%	2|6	4.00	4.00	2.44
Hongkong Bank European Growth Fund	1 3 2 2	75%	3|3	07/96	9.22	1995	15.3%	0|3	1.00	N/A	2.16
InvesNat European Equity Fund	2 1 3 3 3 2	64%	4|5	06/93	-7.90	1994	7.2%	0|5	2.00	1.00	2.26
Investors European Growth Fund	2 2 1 3 4 2	60%	5|7	02/93	-4.34	1992	1.3%	0|7	3.00	1.00	2.45
Maritime Life Europe Fund (A&C)	4	N/A	0|0	N/A	0.00	N/A	—	0|0	N/A	N/A	2.40
Maritime Life Europe Fund Series - B	4	N/A	0|0	N/A	0.00	N/A	—	0|0	N/A	N/A	2.40
McDonald Euro Plus Fund	4 3	66%	1|1	02/97	10.44	1997	10.7%	0|1	N/A	N/A	2.20
MetLife - Fidelity European Growth Fund	1	N/A	0|0	N/A	0.00	N/A	—	0|0	N/A	N/A	2.94
Montrusco Select Continental Europe Equity Fund	3	75%	0|0	N/A	0.00	N/A	—	0|0	N/A	N/A	0.00
Montrusco Select United Kingdom Equity Fund	3	58%	0|0	N/A	0.00	N/A	—	0|0	N/A	N/A	0.00
NN Can-Euro Fund	3 1 3	70%	2|2	07/96	11.36	1996	19.3%	0|2	2.00	N/A	2.65
RCC Euro Fund	3 2 1 4 4 4	54%	3|5	06/93	-5.13	1994	3.2%	0|5	4.00	4.00	9.79
Royal European Growth Fund	1 1 3 3 2 2	55%	6|10	08/88	-24.37	1990	-12.7%	3|10	3.00	2.00	2.51
Scotia Excelsior European Growth Fund	4 1	76%	1|1	12/97	14.42	1997	14.4%	0|1	N/A	N/A	2.26
Scudder Greater Europe Fund	1 2 1	79%	2|2	05/97	18.88	1997	22.4%	0|2	N/A	N/A	1.92
Spectrum United European Growth Fund	1 4 1	68%	2|2	12/97	16.89	1997	16.9%	0|2	1.00	N/A	2.60
Strategic Value Europe Fund	3 4 3 2	72%	3|3	07/96	5.03	1995	10.3%	0|3	2.00	N/A	2.70
Talvest/Hyperion European Fund	2 3 3 3 1 4	56%	4|7	07/91	-13.59	1994	3.0%	0|7	2.00	2.00	3.03

S = Seg Funds

14 EUROPEAN EQUITY

Fund Name	CONSISTENCY — Performance Trend by Quartiles (84–98)	June	RISK — Fund Beats GICs %	Fund Beats GICs (Yr)	Worst 12 mo. End Chng (%)		Worst Calendar Year		Years Fund Lost $	REWARD-TO-RISK — Sharpe Ratio Quartile Rankings 3-Yr	5-Yr	EFFICIENCY MER	
Trimark Europlus Fund C$		4	N/A	0|0	N/A	0.00	N/A		0|0	N/A	N/A	2.50	●
Universal European Opportunities Fund	1 1 3	2	72%	3|3	12/97	20.00	1997	20.0%	0|3	1.00	N/A	2.48	●
Vision Europe Fonds	3 2 2 2 2 2	2	61%	5|6	06/93	-2.15	1994	3.1%	0|6	3.00	2.00	1.67	●

$ = Seg Funds

15 LATIN AMERICAN & EMERGING MARKETS

Fund Name	Perf. Trend (quartiles, recent)	Fund Beats GICs %	Fund Beats GICs(Yr)	Worst 12 mo. End / Chng (%)	Worst Calendar Year	Years Fund Lost $	Sharpe 3-Yr	Sharpe 5-Yr	MER	Eff.
20/20 Emerging Markets Value Fund	3 4 3	43%	0|3	06/98 -43.80	1997 -15.7%	2|3	4.00	N/A	3.57	● red
20/20 Latin America Fund	4 1 1 4	55%	2|3	06/98 -35.94	1995 -29.4%	1|3	2.00	N/A	3.24	● orange
AIM GT Latin America Growth Class	1 1 1 4	62%	2|3	06/98 -21.07	1995 4.0%	0|3	1.00	N/A	2.86	● orange
Altamira Global Discovery Fund	2 2 3 1	54%	1|3	06/98 -30.36	1995 -12.6%	2|3	3.00	N/A	2.95	● orange
Atlas International Emerging Market Growth Fund	2 1	67%	1|1	06/98 -10.69	1997 16.4%	0|1	N/A	N/A	3.50	● red
Atlas Latin American Fund	4 1 1 2	47%	2|4	02/95 -44.23	1995 -24.3%	2|4	1.00	N/A	2.95	● orange
BPI Emerging Markets Fund	2 1	64%	1|1	06/98 -15.92	1997 9.5%	0|1	N/A	N/A	3.01	● orange
C.I. Emerging Markets Fund	3 3 1 1	56%	4|6	10/95 -28.77	1995 -15.6%	2|6	2.00	N/A	2.72	● orange
C.I. Latin American Fund	4 2 2 3	57%	2|4	02/95 -37.07	1995 -20.9%	2|4	2.00	N/A	2.81	● orange
C.I. Sector Emerging Markets Shares	3 3 2 1	55%	3|5	10/95 -28.93	1995 -16.0%	2|5	2.00	N/A	2.77	● orange
C.I. Sector Hsbgr Developing Markets Shares	4 4	46%	0|1	06/98 -42.37	1997 -20.8%	1|1	N/A	N/A	2.85	● orange
C.I. Sector Latin American Shares	4 2 2 4	56%	2|3	10/95 -34.36	1995 -20.8%	1|3	2.00	N/A	2.86	● orange
Canada Trust Emerging Markets Fund	3 3 4	52%	1|2	06/98 -38.25	1997 -1.4%	1|2	4.00	N/A	3.22	● red
CDA Emerging Markets Fund (KBSH)	4 4 1	33%	0|2	06/98 -35.77	1997 -24.6%	2|2	4.00	N/A	1.45	● green
CIBC Emerging Economies Fund	4 2 1	55%	1|2	06/98 -12.55	1996 0.8%	0|2	N/A	N/A	2.70	● orange
CIBC Latin American Fund	1 2	64%	1|1	06/98 -19.38	1997 22.2%	0|1	N/A	N/A	2.70	● orange
Dynamic Israel Growth Fund US		N/A	0|0	N/A 0.00	N/A	0|0	N/A	N/A	0.00	—
Dynamic Latin American Fund	3	47%	0|0	06/98 -17.13	N/A	0|0	N/A	N/A	3.48	● red
Elliott & Page Emerging Markets Fund	3 4 2 1	46%	1|3	06/98 -27.30	1995 -15.1%	1|3	3.00	N/A	4.69	● red
Fidelity Emerging Markets Portfolio Fund	1 1 4 3	51%	2|3	02/98 -51.73	1997 -44.9%	1|3	4.00	N/A	3.55	● red
Fidelity Latin American Growth Fund	4 1 1 3	60%	2|3	02/95 -43.91	1995 -22.3%	1|3	1.00	N/A	3.12	● red
First Canadian Emerging Markets Fund	2 4 2 2	44%	0|3	06/98 -28.24	1995 -9.0%	1|3	3.00	N/A	2.21	● green

S = Seg Funds

257

15 LATIN AMERICAN & EMERGING MARKETS

Fund Name	Fund Beats GICs %	Fund Beats GICs(Yr)	Worst 12 mo. End	Chng (%)	Worst Calendar Year	Years Fund Lost $	Sharpe 3-Yr	Sharpe 5-Yr	MER
First Canadian Latin American Fund	61%	0|0	06/98	-28.61	N/A	0|0	N/A	N/A	2.08
GFM Emerging Markets Country Fund	47%	1|2	06/98	-29.95	1997 -1.0%	1|2	3.00	N/A	1.50
Global Strategy Diversified Latin America Fund	53%	2|3	10/95	-34.32	1995 -20.4%	1|3	1.00	N/A	2.95
Global Strategy Latin America Fund	55%	2|3	10/95	-24.94	1995 -14.8%	1|3	1.00	N/A	2.95
Globalinvest Emerging Markets Country Fund	43%	0|2	06/98	-30.78	1997 -4.2%	1|2	N/A	N/A	2.70
Green Line Emerging Markets Fund	52%	2|5	06/98	-31.27	1995 -15.1%	3|5	3.00	N/A	2.69
Green Line Latin American Growth Fund	57%	2|3	11/95	-34.43	1995 -16.7%	1|3	1.00	N/A	2.66
Guardian Emerging Markets Fund	43%	1|3	06/98	-28.74	1997 -6.7%	1|3	3.00	N/A	0.80
Hansberger Developing Markets Fund	44%	0|1	06/98	-41.72	1997 -20.0%	1|1	N/A	N/A	2.80
Hongkong Bank Emerging Markets Fund	50%	1|3	06/98	-32.81	1995 -10.3%	2|3	4.00	N/A	2.61
S Industrial Alliance Ecoflex Investment Fund E	50%	0|0	06/98	-36.71	N/A	0|0	N/A	N/A	3.82
S Industrial Alliance Emerging Markets Fund	50%	0|0	06/98	-36.23	N/A	0|0	N/A	N/A	3.06
Investors Latin American Growth Fund	67%	1|1	06/98	-27.13	1997 22.7%	0|1	N/A	N/A	2.94
McDonald Emerging Economies Fund	48%	0|1	06/98	-21.88	1997 -8.1%	1|1	N/A	N/A	2.50
MD Emerging Markets Fund	45%	1|3	06/98	-48.02	1997 -17.4%	2|3	4.00	N/A	3.01
Merrill Lynch Emerging Markets Fund	57%	0|1	06/98	-30.76	1997 0.1%	0|1	N/A	N/A	3.02
Montrusco Select Emerging Markets Fund	54%	0|4	06/98	-41.09	1997 -9.3%	1|4	4.00	N/A	0.26
Mutual Premier Emerging Markets Fund	50%	1|2	06/98	-31.39	1997 -8.1%	1|2	N/A	N/A	3.37
National Trust Emerging Markets Fund	40%	1|3	06/98	-37.59	1995 -16.1%	2|3	3.00	N/A	2.72
S NN Can-Emerge Fund	36%	0|1	06/98	-38.25	1997 -22.0%	1|1	N/A	N/A	2.65
S Royal & SunAlliance Glo Emerging Markets Fund	58%	0|1	06/98	-31.15	1997 -3.0%	1|1	N/A	N/A	0.00
S Royal Latin American Fund	61%	2|2	06/98	-9.52	1996 14.4%	0|2	1.00	N/A	2.99

S = Seg Funds

15 LATIN AMERICAN & EMERGING MARKETS

Fund Name	CONSISTENCY — Performance Trend by Quartiles (84 85 86 87 88 89 90 91 92 93 94 95 96 97 / June 98)	RISK — Fund Beats GICs %	Fund Beats GICs(Yr)	Worst 12 mo. End Chng (%)	Worst Calendar Year	Years Fund Lost $	REWARD-TO-RISK — Sharpe Ratio Quartile Rankings 3-Yr	5-Yr	EFFICIENCY — MER
Scotia Excelsior Latin American Fund	1 1 1 3	58%	2|3	06/98 -17.91	1995 3.7%	0|3	1.00	N/A	2.39 ●
Scudder Emerging Markets Fund	1 2 1	67%	2|2	06/98 -15.60	1997 10.0%	0|2	N/A	N/A	2.11 ●
Spectrum United Emerging Markets Fund	1 1 2 4	57%	2|4	06/98 -31.09	1994 -14.0%	2|4	2.00	N/A	2.66 ●
Strategic Value Emerging Markets Fund	1 4 3 2	47%	0|3	06/98 -35.05	1997 -6.5%	1|3	4.00	N/A	2.95 ●
Templeton Emerging Markets Fund	2 2 3 2	53%	2|6	06/98 -30.92	1992 -5.2%	4|6	2.00	N/A	3.24 ●
Tradex Emerging Markets Country Fund	4 3 1	43%	0|2	06/98 -26.37	1997 -1.7%	1|2	3.00	N/A	2.50 ●
Universal World Emerging Growth Fund	2 3 2 1	57%	2|4	06/98 -24.06	1995 -7.5%	2|4	2.00	N/A	2.54 ●

S = Seg Funds

16 ASIA-PACIFIC RIM EQUITY

Fund Name	Fund Beats GICs %	Fund Beats GICs(Yr)	Worst 12 mo. End	Chng (%)	Worst Calendar Year	(Worst Cal %)	Years Fund Lost $	Sharpe 3-Yr	Sharpe 5-Yr	MER
20/20 India Fund	36%	0|3	11/95	-49.00	1995	-46.2%	2|3	3.00	N/A	3.74
AGF Asian Growth Class	44%	4|6	06/98	-53.56	1997	-41.5%	2|6	4.00	2.00	3.03
AGF China Focus Class	35%	1|3	06/98	-47.35	1997	-20.5%	2|3	2.00	N/A	3.49
AGF Japan Class	50%	11|21	07/82	-26.30	1990	-20.0%	5|21	1.00	1.00	3.07
AIM GT Pacific Growth Class	38%	2|3	06/98	-48.24	1997	-37.3%	1|3	1.00	N/A	2.95
AIM Korea Fund	37%	2|6	06/98	-66.20	1997	-61.9%	3|6	4.00	4.00	3.25
AIM Nippon Fund	43%	1|5	06/98	-29.51	1997	-21.5%	2|5	1.00	3.00	3.26
AIM Tiger Fund	48%	3|7	06/98	-55.56	1997	-33.7%	3|7	4.00	4.00	3.36
Allstar AIG Asian Fund	28%	0|0	06/98	-53.73	N/A		0|0	N/A	N/A	3.46
Altamira Asia Pacific Fund	41%	2|5	06/98	-38.49	1997	-20.6%	3|5	4.00	4.00	2.34
Altamira Japanese Opportunity Fund	37%	0|3	06/98	-26.90	1997	-17.9%	3|3	1.00	N/A	2.37
Apex Asian Pacific Fund	33%	0|3	06/98	-39.41	1997	-30.4%	1|3	4.00	N/A	2.80
Atlas Pacific Basin Value Fund	40%	0|4	04/97	-21.81	1997	-13.5%	3|4	2.00	N/A	2.90
BPI Asia Pacific Fund	27%	0|1	06/98	-44.47	1997	-29.2%	1|1	N/A	N/A	3.25
C.I. Pacific Fund	52%	9|16	06/98	-49.34	1997	-29.5%	4|16	2.00	1.00	2.54
C.I. Sector Hansberger Asian Shares	38%	1|3	06/98	-60.14	1997	-46.9%	2|3	4.00	N/A	2.83
C.I. Sector Pacific Shares	49%	6|10	06/98	-49.72	1997	-29.8%	4|10	3.00	2.00	2.59
Cambridge China Fund	44%	0|3	05/97	-31.79	1997	-14.3%	3|3	2.00	N/A	3.51
Cambridge Pacific Fund	44%	5|14	02/98	-54.99	1988	-50.0%	6|14	4.00	4.00	3.68
Canada Life Asia Pacific Equity Fund S-38	39%	0|2	06/98	-28.25	1997	-20.9%	2|2	N/A	N/A	2.40
Canada Trust AsiaGrowth Fund	46%	1|3	06/98	-35.07	1997	-28.8%	1|3	2.00	N/A	2.48
CDA Pacific Basin Fund (KBSH)	48%	0|2	06/98	-24.93	1997	-8.2%	1|2	1.00	N/A	1.45

S = Seg Funds

16 ASIA-PACIFIC RIM EQUITY

Fund Name	Performance Trend by Quartiles (recent → June 98)	Fund Beats GICs %	Fund Beats GICs(Yr)	Worst 12 mo. End Chng (%)	(date)	Worst Calendar Year	Year	Years Fund Lost $	Sharpe 3-Yr	Sharpe 5-Yr	MER	Efficiency
CIBC Far East Prosperity Fund	3 3 2 2 2	41%	1|4	-34.98	06/98	-24.9%	1997	3|4	2.00	N/A	2.69	orange
CIBC Japanese Equity Fund	3 1 1	49%	1|2	-5.43	06/98	-0.8%	1996	1|2	N/A	N/A	2.50	green
Clarington Asia Pacific Fund	4	N/A	0|0	0.00	N/A	N/A	N/A	0|0	N/A	N/A	2.95	red
Dynamic Far East Fund	2 1 1 1 2	48%	1|3	-28.86	06/98	-12.0%	1997	1|3	1.00	N/A	2.78	orange
Elliott & Page Asian Growth Fund	1 3 2 2	38%	1|3	-30.99	06/98	-21.5%	1997	1|3	2.00	N/A	3.76	green
Ethical Pacific Rim Fund	1 4 4	43%	1|2	-57.86	06/98	-38.1%	1997	1|2	2.00	N/A	3.15	red
Fidelity Far East Fund	1 2 4 1 1 2 3	56%	4|6	-38.75	06/98	-22.6%	1997	2|6	1.00	1.00	2.82	red
Fidelity Japanese Growth Fund	1 4 3 1 1	47%	1|4	-24.41	06/95	-12.1%	1996	3|4	1.00	3.00	3.00	green
First Canadian Far East Growth Fund	1 1 3 3	49%	2|3	-43.76	06/98	-26.8%	1997	1|3	2.00	N/A	2.39	green
First Canadian Japanese Growth Fund	3 4 2 2	38%	0|3	-34.24	06/98	-25.5%	1997	3|3	3.00	N/A	2.15	green
Global Manager Hong Kong Bear Fund	4 4 1 1 1	39%	1|3	-34.50	01/96	-25.8%	1996	2|3	1.00	N/A	1.82	green
Global Manager Hong Kong Geared Fund	1 1 4 4	43%	2|3	-75.70	06/98	-42.6%	1997	1|3	1.00	N/A	1.82	green
Global Manager Hong Kong Index Fund	1 1 2 3	48%	2|3	-42.13	06/98	-19.1%	1997	1|3	1.00	N/A	0.00	—
Global Manager Japan Bear Fund	4 4 1 2	35%	1|3	-52.34	06/96	-15.2%	1996	2|3	4.00	N/A	1.82	green
Global Manager Japan Geared Fund	3 4 4 2	41%	0|3	-58.89	06/98	-51.6%	1997	3|3	2.00	N/A	1.82	green
Global Manager Japan Index Fund	2 4 3 1	41%	0|3	-37.13	06/98	-30.9%	1997	3|3	3.00	N/A	1.82	green
Global Strategy Asia Fund	3 2 1 4 4	41%	1|4	-53.81	06/98	-39.5%	1997	2|4	3.00	N/A	2.79	orange
Global Strategy Diversified Asia Fund	2 2 4 3	38%	0|3	-49.83	06/98	-39.6%	1997	2|3	4.00	N/A	2.69	orange
Global Strategy Diversified Japan Plus Fund	3 4 3 1	33%	0|3	-30.75	06/98	-26.9%	1997	3|3	3.00	N/A	2.48	green
Global Strategy Japan Fund	4 4 3 1	30%	0|3	-34.00	06/98	-28.4%	1997	3|3	3.00	N/A	2.79	green
S Great-West Life Asian Growth Fund (A) DSC	3	N/A	0|0	0.00	N/A	N/A	N/A	0|0	N/A	N/A	2.61	orange
S Great-West Life Asian Growth Fund (A) NL	3	N/A	0|0	0.00	N/A	N/A	N/A	0|0	N/A	N/A	2.85	red

S = Seg Funds

Performance Trend by Quartiles year columns: 84 85 86 87 88 89 90 91 92 93 94 95 96 97 98 | June 98

16 ASIA-PACIFIC RIM EQUITY

Fund Name	Performance Trend by Quartiles (94 95 96 97 98 June)	Fund Beats GICs %	Fund Beats GICs (Yr)	Worst 12 mo. End	Worst 12 mo. Chng (%)	Worst Calendar Year	Years Fund Lost $	Sharpe 3-Yr	Sharpe 5-Yr	MER
Green Line Asian Growth Fund	2 2 2 2 3 4	39%	1|4	06/98	-49.91	1997 -28.0%	2|4	3.00	N/A	2.60
Green Line Japanese Growth Fund	3 3 1 1	41%	0|3	06/98	-25.35	1997 -15.6%	3|3	2.00	N/A	2.59
Green Line Japanese Index Fund	1	N/A	0|0	N/A	0.00	N/A	0|0	N/A	N/A	0.90
S Growsafe Japanese 225 Index Fund	1	28%	0|0	06/98	-35.86	N/A	0|0	3.00	N/A	2.13
Guardian Asia Pacific Fund	2 2 3 2	38%	0|3	06/98	-40.76	1997 -30.0%	1|3	3.00	N/A	1.72
Hansberger Asian Fund	4 3 2 4 4 4	41%	1|4	06/98	-59.80	1997 -46.9%	3|4	4.00	N/A	2.78
Hongkong Bank Asian Growth Fund	2 1 2 4 3	41%	2|4	06/98	-46.97	1997 -37.3%	2|4	3.00	N/A	2.30
InvestNat Far East Equity Fund	1 1 3 3	45%	2|3	06/98	-42.16	1997 -31.2%	1|3	2.00	N/A	2.51
InvestNat Japanese Equity Fund	3 4 3 1	40%	0|3	06/98	-30.48	1997 -28.9%	3|3	3.00	N/A	2.51
Investors Japanese Growth Fund Ltd.	4 3 1 3 4 2 1	51%	10|21	09/90	-34.94	1990 -27.1%	7|21	3.00	3.00	2.47
Investors Pacific International Fund	2 1 2 2 2 4 4	51%	4|7	06/98	-51.40	1997 -36.5%	2|7	4.00	2.00	2.50
S Maritime Life Pacific Basin Fund (A&C)	2 2 2 4	43%	1|3	06/98	-43.44	1997 -24.8%	2|3	3.00	N/A	2.75
S Maritime Life Pacific Basin Fund Series B	2 4	40%	0|1	06/98	-43.44	1997 -24.9%	1|1	N/A	N/A	2.75
McDonald Asia Plus Fund	2 3	41%	0|1	06/98	-35.22	1997 -20.4%	1|1	N/A	N/A	2.20
McDonald New Japan Fund	2 1	41%	0|1	06/98	-26.92	1997 -22.2%	1|1	N/A	N/A	2.20
S MetLife MVP Asian-Pacific non-RSP Equity Fund	1	N/A	0|0	N/A	0.00	N/A	0|0	N/A	N/A	2.68
S MetLife MVP Asian-Pacific RSP Equity Fund	2	39%	0|0	06/98	-25.50	N/A	0|0	N/A	N/A	2.68
Mutual Alpine Asian Fund	3	8%	0|0	06/98	-47.96	N/A	0|0	N/A	N/A	0.00
S Navigator Asia-Pacific Fund	1 1 2	49%	2|2	06/98	-26.92	1997 15.0%	0|2	1.00	N/A	3.01
NN Can-Asian Fund	3 1 2 2	49%	2|4	06/98	-34.91	1997 -23.9%	2|4	1.00	N/A	2.65
Royal Asian Growth Fund	4 2 2 4 4	42%	1|4	06/98	-50.50	1997 -38.1%	2|4	4.00	N/A	2.97
Royal Japanese Stock Fund	4 3 1 4 4 1 1	50%	4|12	09/90	-34.15	1990 -28.4%	6|12	2.00	3.00	2.82

S = Seg Funds

16 ASIA-PACIFIC RIM EQUITY

Fund Name	Performance Trend by Quartiles (94 95 96 97 98 / June)	Fund Beats GICs %	Fund Beats GICs (Yr)	Worst 12 mo. End Chng (%)	Worst Calendar Year	Years Fund Lost $	Sharpe Ratio Quartile Rankings 3-Yr	Sharpe Ratio Quartile Rankings 5-Yr	MER
Sceptre Asian Growth Fund	3 3 2 4 / 3	48%	1|4	06/98 -54.39	1997 -37.7%	3|4	3.00	2.00	2.45
Scotia Excelsior Pacific Rim Fund	1 2 1 / 2	47%	1|3	06/98 -32.51	1997 -16.0%	1|3	1.00	N/A	2.43
Scudder Pacific Fund	3 1 / 2	45%	0|2	06/98 -33.67	1997 -14.0%	1|2	N/A	N/A	1.91
Spectrum United Asian Dynasty Fund	2 2 2 3 / 3	43%	0|4	06/98 -49.15	1997 -36.3%	2|4	4.00	N/A	2.58
Strategic Value Asia Pacific Fund	2 3 3 / 3	37%	0|3	06/98 -39.93	1997 -26.7%	2|3	4.00	N/A	2.70
Talvest/Hyperion Asian Fund	1 1 4 2 1 2 / 2	51%	4|7	06/98 -34.41	1997 -23.5%	3|7	2.00	1.00	3.26
Talvest/Hyperion China Plus Fund		N/A	0|0	N/A 0.00	N/A 0|0		N/A	N/A	2.75
Trimark Indo-Pacific Fund	1 1 2 / 3	35%	2|3	06/98 -47.67	1997 -26.7%	1|3	2.00	N/A	2.95
Universal Far East Fund	3 2 2 3 / 4	41%	1|4	06/98 -50.71	1997 -34.6%	3|4	3.00	N/A	2.58
Universal Japan Fund	3 3 1 / 1	42%	0|3	06/95 -24.29	1996 -12.7%	3|3	1.00	N/A	2.54

S = Seg Funds

17 CANADIAN LONG/MID-TERM BONDS

Fund Name	84	85	86	87	88	89	90	91	92	93	94	95	96	97	98	June	Fund Beats GICs %	Fund Beats GICs(Yr)	Worst 12 mo. End	Chng (%)	Worst Calendar Year	Years Fund Lost $	Sharpe 3-Yr	Sharpe 5-Yr	MER
Acuity Pooled Fixed Income Fund											1	4	1	1	1	1	55%	3|4	11/94	-0.26	1994 1.5%	0|4	1.00	1.00	0.00
AGF Canadian Bond Fund (S)	1	1	1	1	4	1	1	2	1	1	4	1	1	1	2	3	52%	12|21	01/95	-11.35	1994 -8.5%	1|21	2.00	3.00	1.93
Altamira Bond Fund					2	4	2	2	1	1	1	4	1	3	1	1	59%	6|10	01/95	-10.25	1994 -8.8%	1|10	1.00	1.00	1.30
Altamira Income Fund		3	4	4	1	1	3	1	1	1	4	1	4	3	3	3	56%	11|15	01/95	-9.06	1994 -6.6%	1|15	3.00	2.00	1.00
Apex Fixed Income Fund	4	4	4	1	4	3	1	1	3	1	2	3	3	4	4	4	53%	13|21	01/95	-7.03	1994 -5.2%	1|21	3.00	3.00	2.30
Atlas Canadian Bond Fund				4	3	2	4	4	3	2	4	2	2	3	3	3	54%	6|12	01/95	-7.00	1994 -5.1%	1|12	3.00	2.00	1.97
Atlas Canadian High Yield Bond Fund												4	1	1	3	3	62%	3|3	06/98	7.84	1997 10.5%	0|3	1.00	N/A	1.87
Barreau du Quebec Bond Fund						1	4	2	3	3	2	2	2	1		1	55%	6|8	01/95	-8.15	1994 -6.5%	1|8	2.00	2.00	1.03
Batirente Bond Fund						1	4	1	1	1	2	1	1	1		1	62%	7|9	01/95	-6.20	1994 -4.6%	1|9	1.00	1.00	1.50
Bell Group RRSP Bond (S)											2	3	3	2		2	61%	3|3	11/97	5.93	1997 7.9%	0|3	3.00	N/A	1.15
Beutel Goodman Income Fund							1	1	4	1	1	2	1			1	60%	5|6	01/95	-10.03	1994 -7.2%	1|6	2.00	2.00	0.66
Bissett Bond Fund				2	3	2	3	2	3	1	1	1	1	1	1	2	55%	6|11	01/95	-6.23	1994 -3.8%	1|11	1.00	1.00	0.75
BNP (Canada) Bond Fund								3	2	4	1	2	2	4		4	56%	5|6	01/95	-9.31	1994 -6.9%	1|6	3.00	3.00	1.65
BPI Canadian Bond Fund							1	3	4	3	4	4	1	3		3	53%	4|8	01/95	-9.46	1994 -6.9%	1|8	4.00	4.00	1.50
BPI Corporate Bond Fund														1			N/A	0|0	N/A	0.00	N/A	0|0	N/A	N/A	1.50
C.I. Canadian Bond Fund (S)							1	2	1	1	2			1	1	2	61%	3|4	01/95	-4.89	1994 -4.3%	1|4	1.00	1.00	1.65
C.U. Canadian Bond Index Fund																2	N/A	0|0	N/A	0.00	N/A	0|0	N/A	N/A	2.43
Caisse de Securite du Spectacle fonds obligatoire																2	N/A	0|0	N/A	0.00	N/A	0|0	N/A	N/A	0.94
Caldwell Canadian Income Fund															4		54%	0|0	06/98	8.96	N/A	0|0	N/A	N/A	0.50
Canada Life Fixed Income Fund S-19 (S)		2	3	3	4	2	3	3	3	3	2	4	3	3	3	2	50%	11|21	01/95	-9.26	1994 -7.0%	1|21	2.00	3.00	2.00
Canada Trust Bond Fund		1	4	2	3	1	4	3	4	2	3	3	2	3	3	2	55%	7|11	01/95	-8.69	1994 -6.8%	1|11	3.00	3.00	1.35
Canada Trust Canadian Bond Index Fund																2	N/A	0|0	N/A	0.00	N/A	0|0	N/A	N/A	0.83

S = Seg Funds

17 CANADIAN LONG/MID-TERM BONDS

Risk / Reward-to-Risk / Efficiency

Fund Name	Fund Beats GICs %	Fund Beats GICs (Yr)	Worst 12 mo. End	Worst 12 mo. Chng (%)	Worst Calendar (%)	Worst Calendar Year	Years Fund Lost $	Sharpe Ratio Quartile 3-Yr	Sharpe Ratio Quartile 5-Yr	MER	Efficiency
Canada Trust Monthly Income Fund	N/A	0|0	N/A	0.00		N/A	0|0	N/A	N/A	0.00	—
Canada Trust Short Term Bond Fund	45%	0|1	11/97	2.68	3.5%	1997	0|1	N/A	N/A	1.38	● green
Canso Value Bond Fund	N/A	0|0	N/A	0.00		N/A	0|0	N/A	N/A	1.75	● orange
CCPE Fixed Income Fund (S)	55%	7|11	01/95	-5.61	-4.0%	1994	1|11	2.00	2.00	1.35	● green
CentrePost Bond Fund	54%	4|5	01/95	-7.67	-6.0%	1994	1|5	2.00	3.00	1.00	● green
CIBC Canadian Bond Fund	57%	7|9	01/95	-11.57	-9.2%	1994	1|9	2.00	4.00	1.55	● orange
CIBC Canadian Bond Index Fund	N/A	0|0	N/A	0.00		N/A	0|0	N/A	N/A	0.90	● green
Clean Environment Income Fund	47%	2|4	04/96	1.88	5.0%	1995	0|4	4.00	N/A	1.98	● red
Co-operators Life Fixed Income Fund (S)	56%	4|5	01/95	-8.21	-6.1%	1994	1|5	2.00	1.00	2.06	● red
Cornerstone Bond Fund	53%	7|11	01/95	-6.98	-5.2%	1994	2|11	3.00	2.00	1.41	● green
CUMIS Life Memberfunds Canadian Bond Fund (S)	58%	1|1	12/97	6.83	6.8%	1997	0|1	N/A	N/A	3.00	● red
Desjardins Bond Fund	51%	11|21	07/81	-16.30	-6.5%	1994	3|21	2.00	3.00	1.63	● orange
Desjardins Life Bond Fund (S)	60%	11|14	01/95	-6.78	-4.9%	1994	1|14	1.00	1.00	1.63	● orange
Dynamic Dollar-Cost Averaging Fund	N/A	0|0	N/A	0.00		N/A	0|0	N/A	N/A	0.00	—
Dynamic Income Fund	54%	10|18	09/81	-7.34	-1.1%	1997	1|18	4.00	4.00	1.55	● orange
Elliott & Page Bond Fund	51%	6|9	01/95	-9.44	-8.3%	1994	1|9	4.00	4.00	1.94	● orange
Empire Elite Bond Fund (S)	51%	6|11	01/95	-6.84	-5.7%	1994	2|11	3.00	3.00	2.05	● red
Empire Elite Foreign Currency Canadian Bond Fund (S)	44%	1|3	06/96	-3.70	-1.2%	1996	1|3	4.00	N/A	2.11	● red
Equitable Life Accumulative Income Fund (S)	55%	12|17	01/95	-6.59	-4.7%	1994	1|17	1.00	1.00	0.36	● green
Equitable Life Canadian Bond Fund (S)	55%	4|5	01/95	-7.87	-5.8%	1994	1|5	3.00	3.00	2.00	● red
Ethical Income Fund	57%	9|15	01/95	-9.12	-6.2%	1994	1|15	2.00	2.00	1.63	● green
Ficadre Mortgage Fund	41%	1|2	11/97	2.45	3.4%	1997	0|2	4.00	N/A	1.64	● orange

Consistency — Performance Trend by Quartiles

Fund Name	84	85	86	87	88	89	90	91	92	93	94	95	96	97	98	June
Canada Trust Monthly Income Fund																
Canada Trust Short Term Bond Fund														4	4	4
Canso Value Bond Fund																2
CCPE Fixed Income Fund					4	4	2	2	2	1	1	3	3	3		2
CentrePost Bond Fund						3	3	3	2	2	4	2	2	2	1	
CIBC Canadian Bond Fund						3	3	1	2	2	4	2	2	2	1	2
CIBC Canadian Bond Index Fund																2
Clean Environment Income Fund										1	4	2	2	4		4
Co-operators Life Fixed Income Fund									1	3	1	2	1	1		1
Cornerstone Bond Fund				4	2	1	1	3	3	3	2	2	4	2	1	
CUMIS Life Memberfunds Canadian Bond Fund														4	2	2
Desjardins Bond Fund	4	3	3	3	3	2	3	4	2	3	2	3	2	3	3	3
Desjardins Life Bond Fund	1	1	1	2	1	1	2	1	2	2	1	1	2	2	1	1
Dynamic Dollar-Cost Averaging Fund																
Dynamic Income Fund	1	4	2	1	3	4	1	4	1	4	4	4	4	4	4	3
Elliott & Page Bond Fund						4	1	4	3	4	4	4	4	3	3	3
Empire Elite Bond Fund					4	3	2	2	4	3	2	3	4	3	3	3
Empire Elite Foreign Currency Canadian Bond Fund											4	4	4	4		4
Equitable Life Accumulative Income Fund									4	3	3	3	2	1	1	1
Equitable Life Canadian Bond Fund	2	2	3	1	2	2	1	1	3	2	2	1	1	1	1	2
Ethical Income Fund	3	3	4	2	4	4	4	3	3	3	2	1	2	1	2	2
Ficadre Mortgage Fund														4	4	4

S = Seg Funds

17 CANADIAN LONG/MID-TERM BONDS

Fund Name	Perf. Trend by Quartiles (recent yrs → June)	Fund Beats GICs %	Fund Beats GICs(Yr)	Worst 12 mo. End / Chng (%)	Worst Calendar Year	Years Fund Lost $	3-Yr	5-Yr	MER
Fidelity Canadian Bond Fund	3 4 4 3 1 4 3 2 2 4 / 4	53%	7|9	01/95 -11.66	1994 -9.4%	1|9	3.00	4.00	1.35
First Canadian Bond Fund	4 3 1 2 2 3 1 3 3 3 / 3	54%	7|9	01/95 -8.75	1994 -6.1%	1|9	2.00	2.00	1.50
S Fonds Astra - Obligations	3 /	N/A	0|0	N/A 0.00	N/A	0|0	N/A	N/A	2.20
S Forester Growth Funds - Bond	4 2 4 1 2 3 2 4 1 / 1	56%	5|8	01/95 -6.76	1994 -5.2%	1|8	4.00	3.00	2.00
S GBC Canadian Bond Fund	4 2 2 1 1 2 2 2 1 2 1 1 2 2 / 1	53%	9|13	01/95 -7.59	1994 -5.6%	1|13	2.00	2.00	1.09
General Trust of Canada - Bond Fund	2 1 1 3 3 1 4 1 2 2 4 2 2 3 2 / 2	50%	13|21	01/95 -8.98	1994 -7.1%	1|21	2.00	2.00	1.59
S Great-West Life Bond Fund (B) DSC	3 3 / 3	57%	1|1	11/97 5.36	1997 7.3%	0|1	N/A	N/A	2.08
S Great-West Life Bond Fund (B) NL	3 3 / 3	57%	1|1	11/97 5.09	1997 7.0%	0|1	N/A	N/A	2.32
S Great-West Life Bond Fund (S) DSC	2 1 / 1	63%	1|1	11/97 6.24	1997 8.8%	0|1	N/A	N/A	2.12
S Great-West Life Bond Fund (S) NL	2 1 / 1	63%	1|1	11/97 5.97	1997 8.5%	0|1	N/A	N/A	2.36
S Great-West Life Canadian Bond Investment (G) DSC	3 3 3 / 3	55%	3|3	11/97 5.72	1997 7.9%	0|3	3.00	N/A	1.82
S Great-West Life Canadian Bond Investment (G) NL	3 3 3 4 3 3 3 3 / 3	50%	11|18	01/95 -8.79	1994 -6.7%	1|18	3.00	4.00	2.07
S Great-West Life Government Bond Investment (G) DSC	4 4 4 / 4	55%	2|3	11/97 2.73	1997 4.0%	0|3	4.00	N/A	1.84
S Great-West Life Government Bond Investment (G) NL	4 4 4 / 4	55%	2|3	11/97 2.47	1997 3.7%	0|3	4.00	N/A	2.09
S Great-West Life Income Fund (M) DSC	3 4 / 4	60%	1|1	11/97 5.31	1997 7.5%	0|1	N/A	N/A	2.22
S Great-West Life Income Fund (M) NL	3 4 / 4	60%	1|1	11/97 5.04	1997 7.2%	0|1	N/A	N/A	2.46
S Great-West Life Income Investment Fund (G) DSC	4 1 1 1 / 1	66%	3|3	11/97 8.39	1997 11.2%	0|3	1.00	N/A	1.93
S Great-West Life Income Investment Fund (G) NL	4 1 1 2 / 2	66%	3|3	11/97 8.11	1997 11.0%	0|3	1.00	N/A	2.17
Green Line Canadian Bond Fund	4 4 2 2 2 2 1 1 1 1 / 1	57%	6|9	01/95 -7.95	1994 -5.6%	1|9	1.00	1.00	0.94
Green Line Canadian Government Bond Index Fund	2 1 4 3 3 2 2 2 2 2 / 2	52%	7|10	01/95 -7.24	1994 -5.2%	1|10	2.00	2.00	0.96
Green Line Monthly Income Fund		N/A	0|0	N/A 0.00	N/A	0|0	N/A	N/A	1.25
Green Line Real Return Bond Fund	4 2 4 1 / 1	52%	2|3	04/96 -0.29	1997 4.7%	0|3	4.00	N/A	1.53

S = Seg Funds

17 CANADIAN LONG/MID-TERM BONDS

Fund Name	Performance Trend by Quartiles (84–98 | June)	Fund Beats GICs %	Fund Beats GICs (Yr)	Worst 12 mo. End	Chng (%)	Worst Calendar Year	Worst Calendar %	Years Fund Lost $	Sharpe 3-Yr	Sharpe 5-Yr	Efficiency	MER
S Growsafe Family of Funds Canadian Bond Fund	95=4 96=4 97=3 | Jun=3	51%	3|3	05/96	4.47	1996	5.9%	0|3	4.00	N/A	●	2.25
S Hartford Canadian Income Fund	Jun=1	N/A	0|0	N/A	0.00	N/A	N/A	0|0	N/A	N/A	●	2.40
Hirsch Fixed Income Fund	—	N/A	0|0	N/A	0.00	N/A	N/A	0|0	N/A	N/A	●	1.75
Hongkong Bank Canadian Bond Fund	96=2 97=2 | Jun=2	67%	2|2	11/97	6.55	1997	8.6%	0|2	2.00	N/A	●	1.12
I.G. Sceptre Canadian Bond Fund	97=1 | Jun=1	67%	1|1	11/97	7.48	1997	9.7%	0|1	N/A	N/A	●	2.05
S ICM Bond Fund	3 1 1 1 3 3 4 | Jun=1	62%	6|7	01/95	-5.33	1994	-3.5%	1|7	1.00	1.00	●	0.22
S Industrial Alliance Bond Fund "BNL"	—	N/A	0|0	N/A	0.00	N/A	N/A	0|0	N/A	N/A	●	1.50
S Industrial Alliance Bond Fund Series 2	Jun=4	44%	0|0	02/98	0.73	N/A		0|0	N/A	N/A	●	1.65
S Industrial Alliance Canadian Bond Fund	3 2 1 4 1 1 2 2 3 2 3 3 3 3 | Jun=3	56%	10|14	01/95	-7.32	1994	-5.7%	1|14	2.00	3.00	●	1.50
S Industrial Alliance Ecoflex Bond Fund "BNL"	—	N/A	0|0	N/A	0.00	N/A	N/A	0|0	N/A	N/A	●	2.00
S Industrial Alliance Ecoflex Investment Fund B	3 3 3 4 4 | Jun=4	55%	3|4	01/95	-7.82	1994	-6.2%	1|4	3.00	4.00	●	1.86
S Industrial Alliance Ecoflex Investment Fund R	—	N/A	0|0	N/A	0.00	N/A	N/A	0|0	N/A	N/A	●	1.86
S Industrial Alliance Income Fund R	—	N/A	0|0	N/A	0.00	N/A	N/A	0|0	N/A	N/A	●	1.50
Industrial Bond Fund	4 1 2 1 4 1 1 2 | Jun=2	54%	6|8	01/95	-11.63	1994	-8.7%	1|8	3.00	3.00	●	1.87
InvesNat Protected Canadian Bond Fund	—	N/A	0|0	N/A	0.00	N/A	N/A	0|0	N/A	N/A	●	2.13
Investors Corporate Bond Fund	3 2 2 3 | Jun=3	56%	3|3	11/97	6.64	1997	8.6%	0|3	2.00	N/A	●	1.89
Investors Government Bond Fund	3 2 3 2 3 2 2 3 2 2 2 2 2 | Jun=2	54%	11|18	06/81	-7.72	1994	-5.2%	1|18	2.00	2.00	●	1.90
Investors Income Portfolio	1 4 4 1 4 3 4 3 | Jun=3	61%	5|8	01/95	-5.41	1994	-3.6%	1|8	2.00	3.00	●	2.06
Investors World Growth Portfolio	1 4 2 4 1 | Jun=1	59%	2|4	01/95	-3.96	1997	-0.4%	1|4	4.00	4.00	●	2.62
Jones Heward Bond Fund	4 2 3 3 4 3 3 4 | Jun=4	55%	6|10	01/95	-9.58	1994	-7.6%	1|10	3.00	4.00	●	1.75
Leith Wheeler Fixed Income Fund	3 2 3 2 | Jun=2	62%	3|3	11/97	5.58	1997	7.0%	0|3	1.00	N/A	●	0.80
S London Life Bond Fund	1 1 1 4 2 1 4 2 3 4 2 3 3 | Jun=4	52%	12|21	01/95	-9.25	1994	-6.9%	2|21	3.00	3.00	●	2.00

S = Seg Funds

17 CANADIAN LONG/MID-TERM BONDS

Fund Name		Fund Beats GICs %	Fund Beats GICs(Yr)	Worst 12 mo. End	Chng (%)	Worst Calendar Year	Years Fund Lost $	Sharpe Ratio 3-Yr	Sharpe Ratio 5-Yr	MER
Lotus Bond Fund		58%	3|3	02/95	0.60	1997 8.6%	0|3	1.00	N/A	0.83
Manulife AGF Canadian Bond GIF	S	56%	0|0	06/98	9.14	N/A	0|0	N/A	N/A	2.35
Manulife Cabot Diversified Bond Fund		49%	2|3	02/95	-2.34	1996 5.4%	0|3	4.00	N/A	2.00
Manulife Fidelity Canadian Bond GIF	S	63%	0|0	06/98	8.35	N/A	0|0	N/A	N/A	2.15
Manulife Talvest Income GIF	S	N/A	0|0	N/A	0.00	N/A	0|0	N/A	N/A	2.25
Manulife VistaFund Bond 1	S	52%	10|16	01/95	-11.41	1994 -9.4%	1|16	4.00	4.00	1.63
Maritime Life Bond Fund (A)	S	52%	5|8	01/95	-8.43	1994 -6.1%	1|8	3.00	3.00	1.80
Maritime Life Bond Fund (C)	S	52%	5|8	01/95	-8.43	1994 -6.1%	1|8	3.00	3.00	2.15
Maritime Life Bond Fund Series B	S	50%	1|1	11/97	4.77	1997 6.1%	0|1	N/A	N/A	1.80
Mawer Canadian Bond Fund		59%	5|6	01/95	-7.77	1994 -5.5%	1|6	1.00	2.00	1.00
Mawer Canadian Income Fund		57%	4|5	01/95	-6.51	1994 -4.4%	1|5	1.00	1.00	0.99
Mawer High Yield Bond Fund		56%	1|1	02/98	6.01	1997 7.5%	0|1	N/A	N/A	1.54
Maxxum Income Fund		52%	12|21	01/95	-9.51	1994 -6.7%	1|21	2.00	1.00	1.73
McDonald Enhanced Bond Fund		66%	1|1	11/97	4.94	1997 6.9%	0|1	N/A	N/A	1.00
Mclean Budden Fixed Income - Pooled		56%	12|16	01/95	-6.98	1994 -5.1%	1|16	1.00	1.00	1.00
Mclean Budden Fixed Income Fund		58%	7|9	01/95	-8.30	1994 -6.2%	1|9	1.00	1.00	1.00
MD Bond Fund		58%	7|9	01/95	-7.80	1994 -5.4%	1|9	1.00	1.00	1.02
MetLife MVP Bond Fund	S	54%	5|10	01/95	-8.34	1994 -7.0%	1|10	4.00	4.00	2.19
Millennia III Income Fund Series 1	S	59%	2|2	11/97	4.32	1997 5.8%	0|2	N/A	N/A	2.23
Montrusco Select Bond Index + Fund		65%	1|1	11/97	7.82	1997 9.5%	0|1	N/A	N/A	0.00 –
Montrusco Select High Yield Bonds Fund		50%	0|0	N/A	0.00	N/A	0|0	N/A	N/A	0.00 –
Montrusco Select Income Fund		58%	7|10	01/95	-6.02	1994 -4.4%	1|10	1.00	1.00	0.00 –

S = Seg Funds

17 CANADIAN LONG/MID-TERM BONDS

Fund Name	CONSISTENCY — Performance Trend by Quartiles															RISK — Fund Beats GICs %	Fund Beats GICs(Yr)	Worst 12 mo. End	Worst 12 mo. Chng (%)	Worst Calendar Year	Worst Calendar	Years Fund Lost $	Sharpe 3-Yr	Sharpe 5-Yr	MER
	84	85	86	87	88	89	90	91	92	93	94	95	96	97	98 (June)										
Mutual Bond Fund						3	3	3	3	3	4	4	4	4	3	54%	6|7	01/95	-8.68	1994	-6.2%	1|7	3.00	4.00	1.94
Mutual Premier Bond Fund								4	3	3	3	3	3	3	2	54%	4|5	01/95	-8.69	1994	-6.0%	1|5	3.00	3.00	1.97
S NAL-Investor Canadian Bond Fund					1	3	4	3	2	3	2	4	2	2	4	54%	7|10	01/95	-6.38	1994	-4.6%	1|10	4.00	2.00	1.75
S National Life Fixed Income Fund	2	2	4	2	4	2	2	2	2	3	2	3	2	3	3	50%	12|21	07/81	-9.75	1994	-6.1%	1|21	3.00	2.00	2.00
National Trust Canadian Bond Fund	3	2	4	1	3	3	4	1	2	4	3	1	1	2	1	51%	11|21	07/81	-11.34	1994	-5.9%	2|21	1.00	2.00	1.21
Navigator Canadian Income Fund										4	1	1	1	3		67%	3|3	06/98	8.05	1997	9.9%	0|3	1.00	N/A	2.45
S NN Bond Fund		4	3	2	3	3	4	2	2	1	2	1	1	1		56%	6|11	01/95	-8.91	1994	-4.8%	2|11	2.00	1.00	2.30
S North West Life Ecoflex Bond Fund "BNL"																N/A	0|0	N/A	0.00	N/A		0|0	N/A	N/A	2.00
S North West Life Ecoflex Investment Fund B															4	56%	0|0	02/98	7.63	N/A		0|0	N/A	N/A	1.86
S North West Life Ecoflex Investment Fund R																N/A	0|0	N/A	0.00	N/A		0|0	N/A	N/A	1.86
Northwest Income Fund										4	3	3	4	2	3	57%	4|5	01/95	-8.05	1994	-5.7%	1|5	3.00	3.00	1.75
O.I.Q. FERIQUE Bond Fund	2	3	2	2	3	3	2	2	1	2	2	2	2	2	2	51%	11|21	09/81	-13.54	1994	-4.0%	3|21	1.00	1.00	0.48
O'Donnell High Income Fund												1	1	1	4	55%	2|2	06/98	7.93	1996	11.0%	0|2	N/A	N/A	2.00
Optimum Fonds d'obligations			2	3	1	4	1	1	2	1	1	2	2	4		54%	7|11	01/95	-7.03	1994	-5.5%	1|11	2.00	1.00	1.39
Phillips, Hager & North Bond Fund	2	1	1	1	1	2	1	2	1	1	1	1	1	2	1	53%	12|21	09/81	-11.94	1994	-4.1%	2|21	1.00	1.00	0.57
Pursuit Canadian Bond Fund	4	4	4	4	4	4	4	4	3	1	4	4	1	4	4	45%	4|11	01/95	-6.02	1987	-4.2%	2|11	4.00	4.00	1.00
Quebec Professionals' Bond Fund	4	3	3	1	3	3	2	3	1	4	1	3	1	3	3	55%	11|19	01/95	-4.03	1994	-3.1%	1|19	1.00	1.00	0.95
S Royal & SunAlliance Income Fund							4	1	1	3	4	2	2	2	2	56%	6|7	01/95	-8.74	1994	-7.1%	1|7	2.00	3.00	1.80
Royal Bond Fund	2	2	2	3	2	2	3	1	2	3	2	2	1	3		51%	12|21	01/95	-8.84	1994	-6.5%	1|21	2.00	2.00	1.39
Sceptre Bond Fund		1	3	1	3	1	2	2	4	1	3	2	1	1		60%	9|12	01/95	-6.24	1994	-4.4%	1|12	1.00	1.00	0.95
Scotia CanAm Income Fund									1	4	1	4	1	1		57%	4|6	09/94	-4.05	1996	1.0%	0|6	4.00	3.00	1.60
S Scotia Excelsior Defensive Income Fund					4	4	1	4	4	4	1	4	4	4	4	47%	4|10	01/95	-3.60	1994	-2.6%	1|10	4.00	4.00	1.37

S = Seg Funds

269

17 CANADIAN LONG/MID-TERM BONDS

Risk / Reward-to-Risk / Efficiency

Fund Name	Fund Beats GICs %	Fund Beats GICs (Yr)	Worst 12 mo. End	Worst 12 mo. Chng (%)	Worst Calendar Year	Worst Calendar %	Years Fund Lost $	Sharpe Ratio 3-Yr	Sharpe Ratio 5-Yr	MER	Efficiency
Scotia Excelsior Income Fund	51%	7|10	01/95	-6.76	1994	-5.0%	1|10	4.00	3.00	1.38	● green
Scudder Canadian Bond Fund	58%	0|0	N/A	0.00	N/A	N/A	0|0	N/A	N/A	0.25	● green
Scudder Canadian Short Term Bond Fund	64%	1|2	11/97	2.95	1997	3.5%	0|2	N/A	N/A	0.61	● green
Spectrum United Long-Term Bond Fund	58%	6|8	01/95	-12.67	1994	-9.1%	1|8	3.00	2.00	1.66	● orange
Spectrum United Mid-Term Bond Fund	55%	6|10	01/95	-10.59	1994	-7.6%	1|10	3.00	4.00	1.59	● orange
Standard Life Bond Mutual Fund	55%	4|5	01/95	-7.22	1994	-5.8%	1|5	3.00	2.00	1.50	● orange
S Standard Life Ideal Bond Fund	55%	7|11	01/95	-8.25	1994	-6.4%	1|11	4.00	3.00	2.00	● red
Strategic Value Government Bond Fund	51%	4|9	01/95	-2.30	1994	-1.8%	1|9	4.00	4.00	2.20	● red
Strategic Value Income Fund	53%	10|21	03/80	-10.81	1994	-5.1%	2|21	2.00	2.00	2.20	● red
Synergy Canadian Fund Inc. - Cdn ST Income Class	N/A	0|0	N/A	0.00	N/A		0|0	N/A	N/A	0.00	—
Talvest Bond Fund	54%	11|21	01/95	-7.98	1994	-6.1%	1|21	2.00	2.00	1.99	● red
Talvest Income Fund	50%	10|21	01/95	-3.85	1994	-2.9%	1|21	4.00	4.00	1.50	● orange
Talvest/Hyperion High Yield Bond Fund	62%	1|1	11/97	10.75	1997	12.4%	0|1	N/A	N/A	2.10	● red
Tradex Bond Fund	54%	7|8	01/95	-10.00	1994	-8.0%	1|8	3.00	4.00	1.00	● green
Trans-Canada Bond Fund	46%	4|10	01/95	-3.59	1994	-2.4%	1|10	4.00	4.00	2.92	● red
Trimark Advantage Bond Fund	67%	3|3	11/97	8.38	1997	10.5%	0|3	1.00	N/A	1.24	● green
Trimark Canadian Bond Fund	63%	3|3	11/97	5.97	1997	8.5%	0|3	2.00	N/A	1.24	● green
Trimark Government Income Fund	46%	2|4	01/95	-0.67	1994	0.0%	0|4	4.00	N/A	1.24	● green
Trust Pret et Revenu Bond Fund	56%	6|9	01/95	-7.83	1994	-5.6%	1|9	3.00	2.00	1.58	● orange
Valorem Canadian Bond-Value Fund	59%	0|0	06/98	9.50	N/A		0|0	N/A	N/A	2.16	● red
S Westbury Canadian Life - Bond Fund	47%	5|6	01/95	-8.29	1994	-6.0%	1|6	4.00	4.00	2.06	● red
YMG Income Fund	50%	5|11	01/95	-7.51	1994	-6.0%	1|11	4.00	4.00	1.67	● orange

Consistency — Performance Trend by Quartiles

Fund Name	84	85	86	87	88	89	90	91	92	93	94	95	96	97	98	June
Scotia Excelsior Income Fund					3	3	2	4	3	3	2	1	4	4	4	4
Scudder Canadian Bond Fund																2
Scudder Canadian Short Term Bond Fund													3	4	4	4
Spectrum United Long-Term Bond Fund								4	1	2	1	4	1	1	1	1
Spectrum United Mid-Term Bond Fund										3	4	2	2	3	3	3
Standard Life Bond Mutual Fund										3	3	1	3	3	2	2
S Standard Life Ideal Bond Fund				3	1	3	4	1	2	2	3	2	3	4	3	3
Strategic Value Government Bond Fund						4	1	4	3	4	1	4	4	4	4	4
Strategic Value Income Fund		1	1	3	3	2	3	3	4	3	2	4	3	4	1	1
Synergy Canadian Fund Inc. - Cdn ST Income Class																4
Talvest Bond Fund		1	1	2	2	1	2	3	2	4	1	3	2	3	2	2
Talvest Income Fund		4	4	4	2	1	3	1	4	4	4	1	4	3	4	4
Talvest/Hyperion High Yield Bond Fund														1	4	4
Tradex Bond Fund								1	4	3	4	3	2	3	3	3
Trans-Canada Bond Fund					4	4	1	3	4	4	1	4	4	4	4	4
Trimark Advantage Bond Fund												1	1	1	2	2
Trimark Canadian Bond Fund												1	2	2	3	3
Trimark Government Income Fund												1	4	4	4	4
Trust Pret et Revenu Bond Fund							4	3	2	2	2	2	3	2	2	2
Valorem Canadian Bond-Value Fund																2
S Westbury Canadian Life - Bond Fund									1	4	3	3	4	3	3	3
YMG Income Fund				4	2	2	4	3	4	3	3	2	2	4	4	4

S = Seg Funds

18 CANADIAN SHORT-TERM BONDS

Fund Name	Performance Trend by Quartiles 96 97 98	June	Fund Beats GICs %	Fund Beats GICs(Yr)	Worst 12 mo. End Chng (%)	Worst Calendar Year	Years Fund Lost $	Sharpe Ratio Quartile Rankings 3-Yr	5-Yr	MER	Efficiency
Acadia Bond Fund	1 1 1	1	58%	3|3	05/96 5.74	1997 6.0%	0|3	N/A	N/A	2.16	●
Acuity Pooled Short Term Fund	4 4 4	4	34%	2|4	02/98 0.34	1997 2.5%	0|4	N/A	N/A	0.00	–
AIM GT Short-Term Income Class A	4 4 4	4	16%	0|2	11/97 0.80	1997 0.9%	0|2	N/A	N/A	1.64	●
Altamira Short Term Government Bond Fund	3 2 2	2	59%	2|3	11/97 3.80	1997 4.1%	0|3	N/A	N/A	1.30	●
CIBC Canadian Short Term Bond Fund	2 3 4	4	50%	2|4	01/95 -4.34	1994 -3.4%	1|4	N/A	N/A	0.90	●
Dynamic Government Income Fund	1 2 3	3	47%	2|4	12/94 -3.81	1994 -3.8%	1|4	N/A	N/A	0.85	●
Ficadre Bond Fund	2 1 1	1	57%	7|10	01/95 -7.96	1994 -5.7%	1|10	N/A	N/A	1.62	●
Fidelity Canadian Income Fund	1 1 1	1	62%	1|2	11/97 3.69	1997 4.5%	0|2	N/A	N/A	1.25	●
Global Strategy Bond Fund	3 4 4	4	47%	2|3	02/95 2.05	1997 3.2%	0|3	N/A	N/A	1.50	●
Green Line Short Term Income Fund	4 4 3	3	55%	5|8	01/95 -1.29	1994 -0.7%	1|8	N/A	N/A	1.10	●
Guardian Canadian Income Fund	4 2 3	3	54%	2|3	11/97 2.93	1997 3.6%	0|3	N/A	N/A	1.13	●
InvestNat Short-Term Government Bond Fund	2 3 2	2	51%	5|9	01/95 -2.64	1994 -2.3%	1|9	N/A	N/A	1.33	●
MD Bond and Mortgage Fund	3 3 2	2	56%	1|2	11/97 2.79	1997 3.5%	0|2	N/A	N/A	1.10	●

S = Seg Funds

19 CANADIAN MORTGAGE

Fund Name	CONSISTENCY — Performance Trend by Quartiles (84 85 86 87 88 89 90 91 92 93 94 95 96 97 98 June)	RISK — Fund Beats GICs %	Fund Beats GICs (Yr)	Worst 12 mo. End / Chng (%)	Worst Calendar Year	Years Fund Lost $	Sharpe Ratio 3-Yr	Sharpe Ratio 5-Yr	EFFICIENCY MER
Acadia Mortgage Fund	4 4 2 2 2	30%	0|3	04/97 2.35	1996 3.1%	0|3	4.00	N/A	2.00
S Apex Mortgage Fund	4 4 4 4 4	40%	1|3	11/97 2.06	1997 2.2%	0|3	4.00	N/A	2.00
Canada Trust Mortgage Fund	2 3 4 1 2 2 2 4 2 2 1 3 4 2 2	50%	11|21	01/95 0.01	1994 1.2%	0|21	2.00	2.00	1.59
S CDA Bond & Mortgage Fund (Canagex)	1 1 1 4 1 1 1 4 1 1 1 1	52%	12|21	01/95 -5.60	1994 -3.5%	1|21	1.00	1.00	0.92
CIBC Mortgage Fund	4 4 4 2 4 1 3 1 1 3 2 2 1 3 2	50%	9|18	01/95 -1.40	1994 0.0%	0|18	2.00	2.00	1.69
S Colonia Mortgage Fund	4 2 1 4 4 4	49%	3|5	12/94 -0.11	1994 -0.1%	1|5	3.00	3.00	1.88
S Desjardins Life Mortgage Fund	3 1 1 2 2 1 1 3 4 3 1 2 3 3 1	59%	8|14	01/95 2.09	1994 2.7%	0|14	1.00	1.00	1.61
Desjardins Mortgage Fund	4 2 3 1 2 3 3 4 3 2 3 4 2 1	52%	11|21	01/95 -0.77	1994 0.5%	0|21	2.00	2.00	1.61
First Canadian Mortgage Fund	2 3 2 2 3 2 1 1 2 2 3 2 1 2	49%	13|21	01/95 -2.10	1994 -0.5%	1|21	3.00	2.00	1.40
General Trust of Canada - Mortgage Fund	1 1 2 3 4 2 4 2 3 1 4 4 3	52%	13|21	03/80 -2.01	1994 3.0%	0|21	4.00	3.00	1.57
S Great-West Life Mortgage Investment Fund (G) DSC	1 2 1 1	57%	3|3	11/97 6.30	1997 7.2%	0|3	1.00	N/A	2.16
Great-West Life Mortgage Investment Fund (G) NL	2 2 3 4 2 3 4 2 1 3 1 4 1 2 1 1	47%	11|18	03/80 -5.79	1994 -2.8%	1|18	1.00	1.00	2.40
Green Line Canadian Mortgage Fund	4 4 3 2 1 4 1 2 2 3 3 2 4 2 2	45%	12|21	01/95 -2.04	1994 -0.7%	1|21	3.00	3.00	1.59
Green Line Mortgage-Backed Fund	1 3 3 4 3 3 3 3 4	45%	6|8	01/95 -1.76	1994 -1.1%	1|8	3.00	3.00	1.55
S Hongkong Bank Mortgage Fund	1 1 1 1 4 1 1	58%	2|4	01/95 1.06	1997 2.6%	0|4	2.00	1.00	1.45
S Industrial Alliance Ecoflex Investment Fund H	3 4 4 2 4 4	49%	2|4	01/95 -1.25	1994 -0.4%	1|4	4.00	4.00	1.86
S Industrial Alliance Mortgages Fund	2 2 1 1 3 3 2 3 3 4 2 3 4 1 3 3	60%	10|14	01/95 -0.72	1994 0.1%	0|14	2.00	3.00	1.50
Industrial Mortgage Securities Fund	1 1 3 1 1 4 2 4 1 4 1 1 4 4 3	47%	11|21	01/95 -9.89	1994 -6.2%	2|21	4.00	4.00	1.86
InvesNat Mortgage Fund	1 3 1 4 2 2 3 3	63%	4|6	01/95 0.50	1994 1.7%	0|6	2.00	1.00	1.55
Investors Mortgage Fund	3 3 3 2 3 4 4 3 3 3 2 4 3 3	49%	10|21	01/95 -3.06	1994 -1.7%	1|21	3.00	3.00	1.90
Ivy Mortgage Fund	2 2 2 3 3	46%	2|3	01/95 -2.25	1997 3.3%	0|3	1.00	N/A	1.89
S London Life Mortgage Fund	1 2 1 4 1 2 4 2 1 4 2 2 3 1 1	53%	14|21	04/80 -11.15	1980 0.1%	0|21	1.00	1.00	2.00

S = Seg Funds

19 CANADIAN MORTGAGE

	CONSISTENCY — Performance Trend by Quartiles																RISK					REWARD-TO-RISK — Sharpe Ratio Quartile Rankings		EFFICIENCY
Fund Name	84	85	86	87	88	89	90	91	92	93	94	95	96	97	98	June	Fund Beats GICs %	Fund Beats GICs(Yr)	Worst 12 mo. End Chng (%)	Worst Calendar Year	Years Fund Lost $	3-Yr	5-Yr	MER
Mutual Premier Mortgage Fund											2	3	3	3	3	3	49%	2|4	01/95 -1.13	1994 0.5%	0|4	3.00	3.00	1.65
National Trust Mortgage Fund										4	3	2	1	3	2	2	55%	3|5	01/95 -1.46	1994 -0.6%	1|5	2.00	2.00	1.59
North West Life Ecoflex Investment Fund H															4	4	44%	0|0	02/98 3.95	N/A	0|0	N/A	N/A	1.86
Northwest Mortgage Fund									1	1	3	4	3	2	4	4	46%	4|6	01/95 -3.45	1994 -1.3%	1|6	4.00	4.00	1.75
OTG Investment Fund - Mortgage Income Section										2	1	1	2	1	1	1	68%	4|5	01/95 1.67	1994 2.2%	0|5	1.00	1.00	0.75
Phillips, Hager & North Short Term Bond & Mortgage												1	1	1	2	2	50%	2|3	01/95 -2.02	1997 4.5%	0|3	1.00	N/A	0.64
Royal Mortgage Fund										1	1	4	2	3	3	3	56%	3|5	01/95 -0.73	1994 1.0%	0|5	3.00	2.00	1.56
Scotia Excelsior Mortgage Fund										2	2	2	1	3	2	2	65%	3|5	01/95 -2.33	1994 -0.3%	1|5	2.00	2.00	1.56
Spectrum United Short-Term Bond Fund					3	4	4	3	4	4	4	2	3	3	4	4	39%	8|21	01/95 -4.28	1994 -2.6%	1|21	4.00	4.00	1.45
Templeton Canadian Bond Fund							4	2	3	1	4	4	3	2	3	3	50%	5|8	01/95 -5.56	1994 -3.6%	1|8	3.00	4.00	1.65
Trust Pret et Revenu Mortgage Fund						3	3	2	3	2	2	4	3	3	4	4	48%	12|21	01/95 -3.54	1994 -2.0%	1|21	4.00	4.00	1.68

S = Seg Funds

273

20 INTERNATIONAL BONDS

Fund Name	Perf. Trend by Quartiles (recent, → June)	Fund Beats GICs %	Fund Beats GICs (Yr)	Worst 12 mo. End	Worst 12 mo. Chng (%)	Worst Calendar Year	Worst Cal. %	Years Fund Lost $	Sharpe 3-Yr	Sharpe 5-Yr	MER	Efficiency
ABAX Bradys Bonds Fund	4 4	30%	0|1	06/98	2.21	1997	2.6%	0|1	N/A	N/A	6.50	●
AGF Global Government Bond Fund	3 1 2 2 2 1 1	55%	8|11	03/89	-6.93	1988	-6.4%	1|11	2.00	1.00	1.86	●
AGF RSP Global Bond Fund	4 2 3 2 1 1	48%	2|4	09/94	-7.09	1994	-5.7%	1|4	2.00	N/A	1.97	●
AGF U.S. Income Fund	4 3 4 4 1 1 1	49%	3|5	09/94	-8.37	1994	-2.1%	1|5	3.00	4.00	2.46	●
AGF U.S. Short-Term High Yield Fund	4 1 1 1 1	59%	2|3	12/95	-1.10	1995	-1.1%	1|3	2.00	N/A	2.48	●
AIM Global RSP Income Fund	3 1 4 1 1 1 4	50%	4|5	03/95	1.28	1994	3.1%	0|5	1.00	1.00	2.39	●
AIM GT Global Bond Fund	4 1 3 3 3	49%	2|3	12/97	3.45	1997	3.4%	0|3	2.00	N/A	2.45	●
Altamira Global Bond Fund	3 2 3 2 2 2	51%	2|4	09/94	-5.65	1994	-1.1%	1|4	3.00	N/A	1.81	●
Altamira High Yield Bond Fund	1 1 3	59%	2|2	02/98	11.27	1996	13.0%	0|2	N/A	N/A	1.95	●
Atlas World Bond Fund	3 1 2 3 3 3	51%	2|4	12/94	-4.25	1994	-4.3%	1|4	1.00	N/A	2.06	●
BPI Global RSP Bond Fund	1 1 3	67%	2|2	11/97	6.12	1997	9.9%	0|2	1.00	N/A	1.50	●
C.I. Global Bond RSP Fund	3 1 1 2 3	51%	3|4	09/94	-3.57	1994	-2.9%	1|4	1.00	N/A	2.05	●
C.I. Global High Yield Fund	3 1 1 4	59%	3|3	08/95	-0.18	1997	8.5%	0|3	1.00	N/A	2.16	●
C.I. World Bond Fund	1 3 1 1 3 3	64%	3|5	01/95	-5.73	1994	-4.9%	1|5	1.00	1.00	2.06	●
Canada Life International Bond Fund S-36	3 3 2 1	61%	2|3	01/97	0.66	1996	5.2%	0|3	2.00	N/A	2.00	●
Canada Trust High Yield Income Fund		N/A	0|0	N/A	N/A	N/A		0|0	N/A	N/A	0.00	–
Canada Trust International Bond Fund	3 4 4 3	44%	1|3	01/97	-2.14	1997	0.6%	0|3	4.00	N/A	2.07	●
CIBC Global Bond Fund	3 3 3 3 2	58%	1|3	06/96	2.20	1997	4.6%	0|3	3.00	N/A	1.95	●
CIBC Global Bond Index Fund		N/A	0|0	N/A	N/A	N/A		0|0	N/A	N/A	0.90	●
Dynamic Global Bond Fund	2 1 1 3 4 4 4	49%	4|9	04/98	-5.19	1997	-4.3%	1|9	4.00	3.00	1.78	●
Dynamic Global Income & Growth Fund	4	35%	0|0	06/98	2.11	N/A		0|0	N/A	N/A	2.70	●
Elliott & Page Global Bond Fund	3 4 3 3	48%	1|3	05/96	-0.73	1996	2.9%	0|3	4.00	N/A	1.97	●

Performance Trend by Quartiles columns: 84 85 86 87 88 89 90 91 92 93 94 95 96 97 98 June

S = Seg Funds

20 INTERNATIONAL BONDS

Fund Name	Performance Trend by Quartiles (84–98)	Fund Beats GICs %	Fund Beats GICs(Yr)	Worst 12 mo. End	Chng (%)	Worst Calendar Year (%)	Worst Calendar Year	Years Fund Lost $	Sharpe Ratio 3-Yr	Sharpe Ratio 5-Yr	MER
Ethical Global Bond Fund	2 2 3	64%	2|2	05/96	4.20	6.6%	1997	0|2	2.00	N/A	2.56
FCMI Foreign Bond Fund	3 4	64%	0|1	06/98	0.53	4.2%	1997	0|1	N/A	N/A	0.93
Fidelity Emerging Markets Bond Fund	3 1 1 4	65%	3|3	03/95	-9.84	12.8%	1995	0|3	1.00	N/A	2.23
Fidelity North American Income Fund	4 4 2 3 4	56%	1|4	01/95	-14.98	-12.2%	1994	1|4	2.00	4.00	1.75
First Canadian International Bond Fund	1 1 3 4 1	54%	1|4	08/97	-2.38	-0.8%	1997	1|4	4.00	N/A	2.00
FMOQ Bond Fund	2 2 2 2 2 3	54%	5|6	09/94	-5.06	-1.0%	1994	1|6	2.00	2.00	0.89
Global Manager U.S. Bond Index	1 4 1 2	57%	2|3	01/97	-4.68	-2.9%	1996	1|3	3.00	N/A	1.82
Global Strategy Diversified Bond Fund	3 4 4 2 2 2	56%	6|7	12/94	-7.85	-7.9%	1994	1|7	1.00	4.00	2.20
Global Strategy Diversified Foreign Bond Fund	4 2 3 2	59%	3|3	01/97	2.61	4.8%	1997	0|3	2.00	N/A	2.40
Global Strategy World Bond Fund	3 4 3 2 3 2	54%	5|9	12/94	-8.78	-8.8%	1994	1|9	1.00	4.00	2.10
Great-West Life Global Income Fund (A) DSC	2 2	47%	1|1	01/97	-1.86	5.3%	1997	0|1	N/A	N/A	2.53
Great-West Life Global Income Fund (A) NL	2 2	47%	1|1	01/97	-2.11	5.0%	1997	0|1	N/A	N/A	2.78
Great-West Life International Bond Invest (P) DSC	3 4 2 4	52%	2|3	04/98	-1.51	1.1%	1996	0|3	4.00	N/A	2.80
Great-West Life International Bond Invest (P) NL	4 4 3 4	52%	1|3	04/98	-1.76	0.8%	1996	0|3	4.00	N/A	3.06
Green Line Global Government Bond Fund	1 2 2 3 3 1	49%	2|5	09/94	-1.00	-0.1%	1994	1|5	3.00	2.00	2.07
Green Line Global RSP Bond Fund	1 3 1 2 2	55%	3|4	11/94	0.65	2.2%	1994	0|4	2.00	N/A	2.00
Guardian Foreign Income Fund	2 2 1 1	64%	3|3	01/97	3.81	7.4%	1996	0|3	1.00	N/A	1.68
Guardian International Income Fund	1 4 1 2 2 3	45%	5|11	12/94	-6.31	-6.3%	1994	2|11	1.00	1.00	2.06
Hongkong Bank Global Bond Fund	4 3 3 1	55%	1|3	01/97	-0.21	4.0%	1997	0|3	3.00	N/A	2.10
Industrial Alliance Ecoflex Investment Fund G	4	22%	0|0	04/98	-4.01		N/A	0|0	N/A	N/A	1.86
Industrial Alliance Global Bond Fund	4	22%	0|0	04/98	-3.87		N/A	0|0	N/A	N/A	1.65
InvestNat International RSP Bond Fund	2 3 2	48%	1|2	03/96	0.58	3.9%	1997	0|2	2.00	N/A	2.00

S = Seg Funds

275

20 INTERNATIONAL BONDS

Fund Name	CONSISTENCY — Performance Trend by Quartiles (84–98, June)	RISK Fund Beats GICs %	Fund Beats GICs(Yr)	Worst 12 mo. End	Worst 12 mo. Chng (%)	Worst Calendar Year	Worst Calendar %	Years Fund Lost $	Sharpe Ratio 3-Yr	Sharpe Ratio 5-Yr	EFFICIENCY MER
Investors Global Bond Fund	93:2 94:2 95:4 96:4 97:4 June:2	47%	2|5	09/94	-2.91	1994	1.0%	0|5	4.00	3.00	2.18
Investors North American High Yield Bond Fund	97:1 June:4	63%	1|1	06/98	7.41	1997	10.2%	0|1	N/A	N/A	2.21
Manulife AGF Global Government Bond GIF	June:1	N/A	0|0	N/A	0.00	N/A		0|0	N/A	N/A	2.35
Manulife Dynamic Global Bond GIF		N/A	0|0	N/A	0.00	N/A		0|0	N/A	N/A	2.45
Manulife VistaFund Global Bond 1	95:2 96:4 97:1 June:1	52%	1|2	12/97	-4.77	1997	-4.8%	1|2	4.00	N/A	1.63
MB International Fixed Income - Pooled	97:1 June:1	70%	1|1	11/97	10.56	1997	12.8%	0|1	N/A	N/A	0.00
MD Global Bond Fund	94:2 95:3 96:2 97:2 June:2	45%	2|3	02/97	-1.36	1996	3.0%	0|3	3.00	N/A	1.18
Merrill Lynch World Bond Fund	97:4 June:1	57%	0|1	11/97	1.20	1997	2.3%	0|1	N/A	N/A	2.25
National Trust International RSP Bond Fund	94:1 95:1 96:4 97:1 June:1	65%	2|3	12/97	1.97	1997	2.0%	0|3	2.00	N/A	1.76
NN Can-Global Bond Fund	97:1 June:3	65%	1|1	11/97	5.18	1997	8.1%	0|1	N/A	N/A	2.55
North West Life Ecoflex Investment Fund G	June:4	22%	0|0	04/98	-4.01	N/A		0|0	N/A	N/A	1.86
O'Donnell U.S. High Income Fund		N/A	0|0	N/A	0.00	N/A		0|0	N/A	N/A	2.00
Pursuit Global Bond Fund	95:3 96:4 97:4 June:4	49%	0|2	11/97	-0.23	1997	2.1%	0|2	N/A	N/A	2.00
Rothschild International Bond Fund	96:4 97:4 June:3	50%	0|1	12/97	0.83	1997	0.8%	0|1	N/A	N/A	2.70
Royal Global Bond Fund	92:1 93:2 94:2 95:3 96:3 97:3 June:3	54%	3|6	09/94	-4.07	1994	1.1%	0|6	3.00	2.00	1.87
Scotia Excelsior Global Bond Fund	93:3 94:4 95:3 96:2 June:2	58%	1|3	06/96	-4.48	1996	2.6%	0|3	4.00	N/A	1.99
Spectrum United Global Bond Fund	93:3 94:1 95:3 96:4 97:4 June:3	50%	1|4	11/94	-3.36	1994	-1.0%	1|4	4.00	N/A	2.03
Spectrum United RRSP International Bond Fund	93:1 94:2 95:4 96:4 97:4 June:2	51%	1|4	09/94	-3.05	1997	-1.2%	1|4	4.00	3.00	1.98
Standard Life International Bond Mutual Fund	94:1 95:4 96:1 97:1 June:1	64%	2|3	01/97	-4.42	1996	-0.2%	1|3	3.00	N/A	2.00
Talvest Foreign Pay Canadian Bond Fund	92:2 93:2 94:2 95:2 96:1 97:2 June:2	54%	3|5	09/94	-4.73	1994	-0.1%	1|5	3.00	2.00	2.15
Templeton Global Bond Fund	91:4 92:2 93:3 94:1 95:1 96:4 97:4 June:4	45%	6|9	01/95	-3.56	1997	-0.9%	2|9	3.00	3.00	2.25
Trust Pret et Revenu World Bond Fund	93:3 94:4 95:3 June:3	52%	0|2	01/97	-1.55	1997	0.1%	0|2	4.00	N/A	1.88

S = Seg Funds

20 INTERNATIONAL BONDS

	CONSISTENCY		RISK						REWARD-TO-RISK		EFFICIENCY
Fund Name	Performance Trend by Quartiles 84 85 86 87 88 89 90 91 92 93 94 95 96 97 98	June	Fund Beats GICs %	Fund Beats GICs(Yr)	Worst 12 mo. End / Chng (%)	Worst Calendar Year	Years Fund Last $	Sharpe Ratio Quartile Rankings 3-Yr	5-Yr	MER	
Universal World High Yield Fund		4	N/A	0|0	N/A 0.00	N/A	0|0	N/A	N/A	0.00	—
Universal World Income RRSP Fund	2 1 1 2	2	63%	3|3	01/97 5.08	1996 8.8%	0|3	1.00	N/A	2.15	🟠
Universal World Tactical Bond Fund	1 4 2 1	1	48%	2|3	01/97 -2.97	1996 -0.4%	1|3	3.00	N/A	2.32	🔴

S = Seg Funds

21 U.S./INTERNATIONAL MONEY MARKET

Fund Name	Performance Trend by Quartiles (... 96 97 98 | June)	RISK: Fund Beats GICs %	Fund Beats GICs (Yr)	Worst 12 mo. End	Worst 12 mo. Chng (%)	Worst Calendar Year (%)	Worst Calendar Year	Years Fund Lost $	Sharpe Ratio 3-Yr	Sharpe Ratio 5-Yr	MER	Efficiency
AGF International Short-Term Income Class	1 4 4 4	42%	0|3	07/97	-1.47	1.3%	1997	0|3	2.00	N/A	2.69	●
AGF U.S. Dollar Money Market Account	2 2 1 1	11%	0|6	03/94	2.58	2.7%	1993	0|6	2.00	N/A	0.84	●
Altamira Short Term Global Income Fund	4 1 4 1	51%	4|6	07/97	-1.84	-1.4%	1995	2|6	2.00	N/A	1.22	●
Atlas American Money Market Fund	2 2 2 2	5%	0|10	12/93	2.10	2.1%	1993	0|10	2.00	N/A	1.14	●
BPI U.S. Money Market Fund	2 2	41%	0|1	04/97	4.22	4.6%	1997	0|1	N/A	N/A	0.65	●
C.I. Sector Short-Term Shares	4 4 4 1	9%	0|10	01/97	2.11	2.4%	1996	0|10	4.00	N/A	0.05	●
C.I. US Money Market Fund	1 1 1 1	39%	1|2	01/97	4.70	4.7%	1996	0|2	1.00	N/A	0.51	●
CIBC U.S. Dollar Money Market Fund	3 2 2 3	10%	0|6	01/94	2.11	2.1%	1993	0|6	3.00	N/A	1.08	●
Fidelity U.S. Money Market Fund	3 1 3 3	9%	1|3	09/97	4.32	4.4%	1997	0|3	1.00	N/A	1.25	●
Green Line U.S. Money Market Fund	2 3 3 2	7%	0|9	01/94	2.16	2.2%	1993	0|9	3.00	N/A	1.24	●
Guardian U.S. Money Market Fund	1 2 1 2	16%	1|10	08/93	2.06	2.5%	1993	0|10	1.00	N/A	0.89	●
Hongkong Bank U.S. Dollar Money Market Fund		N/A	0|0	N/A	0.00		N/A	0|0	N/A	N/A	1.06	●
InvesNat U.S. Money Market Fund	3 3 3 3	7%	0|6	12/93	1.90	1.9%	1993	0|6	4.00	N/A	1.11	●
Investors U.S. Money Market Fund	3	36%	0|0	05/98	4.43		N/A	0|0	N/A	N/A	1.06	●
Phillips, Hager & North \$U.S. Money Market Fund	1 1 1 1	20%	1|7	01/94	2.63	2.7%	1993	0|7	1.00	N/A	0.52	●
Royal \$U.S. Money Market Fund	2 3 3 3	7%	0|7	11/93	2.01	2.0%	1993	0|7	3.00	N/A	1.12	●
Scotia CanAm Money Market Fund	2 2	38%	0|1	11/97	4.51	4.6%	1997	0|1	N/A	N/A	1.00	●
Spectrum United U.S. Dollar Money Market Fund	1 3 4 4	2%	0|9	10/92	2.07	2.2%	1992	0|9	3.00	N/A	1.20	●
Universal U.S. Money Market Fund	3 4 4 4	0%	0|3	06/98	3.68	3.7%	1996	0|3	4.00	N/A	1.25	●

S = Seg Funds

278

22 CANADIAN MONEY MARKET

Performance Trend by Quartiles (Consistency)

Fund Name	84	85	86	87	88	89	90	91	92	93	94	95	96	97	98	June
Acadia Money Market Fund												3	4	4	4	4
AGF Money Market Account	2	1	2	2	2	3	3	3	3	3	3	3	4	4	4	4
AIC Money Market Fund												4	4	3	2	2
AIM Cash Performance Fund										4	4	4	3	2	4	4
AIM GT Canada Money Market Fund														4	3	3
Allstar Money Market Fund															3	3
Altamira Short Term Canadian Income Fund															1	1
Altamira T-Bill Fund															1	1
Apex Money Market Fund (S)												2	3	4	4	4
Argentum Short Term Asset Portfolio																
Atlas Canadian Money Market Fund							1	2	2	3	2	3	3	2	2	2
Atlas Canadian T-Bill Fund								2	3	3	4	4	4	4	4	1
Batirente Money Market Fund						4	4	1	1	2	4	1	4	3	1	1
Beutel Goodman Money Market Fund								1	1	1	1	1	1	1	1	1
Bissett Money Market Fund								1	1	1	1	1	1	1	1	1
BNP (Canada) Money Market Fund									4	3	3	3	3	3	4	4
BPI T-Bill Fund				1	1	1	1	2	2	2	2	1	1	1	1	1
BPI T-Bill Segregated Fund (S)															2	
C.I. Money Market Fund								2	1	2	1	1	2	1	2	2
C.I. Money Market Segregated Fund (S)															4	
C.U. Canadian Money Market Fund (S)																
Canada Life Money Market S-29 (S)				3	4	4	4	2	4	3	3	3	2	4	3	3

Risk / Reward-to-Risk / Efficiency

Fund Name	Fund Beats GICs %	Fund Beats GICs (Yr)	Worst 12 mo. End	Worst 12 mo. Chng (%)	Worst Calendar Year Chng	Worst Calendar Year	Years Fund Lost $	Sharpe 3-Yr	Sharpe 5-Yr	MER	Efficiency
Acadia Money Market Fund	2%	0|3	10/97	1.72	1.8%	1997	0|3	4.00	N/A	1.56	● (red)
AGF Money Market Account	24%	6|21	11/97	1.71	1.7%	1997	0|21	4.00	4.00	1.42	● (red)
AIC Money Market Fund	6%	0|3	11/97	2.25	2.3%	1997	0|3	3.00	N/A	1.00	● (orange)
AIM Cash Performance Fund	3%	0|5	11/97	2.49	2.5%	1997	0|5	4.00	4.00	1.03	● (orange)
AIM GT Canada Money Market Fund	0%	0|1	10/97	1.12	1.5%	1997	0|1	N/A	N/A	0.75	● (orange)
Allstar Money Market Fund	0%	0|0	01/98	1.86		N/A	0|0	N/A	N/A	1.15	● (red)
Altamira Short Term Canadian Income Fund	36%	0|0	05/98	4.30		N/A	0|0	N/A	N/A	0.35	● (green)
Altamira T-Bill Fund	0%	0|0	05/98	3.38		N/A	0|0	N/A	N/A	0.24	● (green)
Apex Money Market Fund (S)	4%	0|3	11/97	1.63	1.7%	1997	0|3	4.00	N/A	1.56	● (red)
Argentum Short Term Asset Portfolio	N/A	0|0	N/A	0.00		N/A	0|0	N/A	N/A	0.00	—
Atlas Canadian Money Market Fund	17%	2|12	11/97	2.33	2.4%	1997	0|12	3.00	3.00	1.09	● (orange)
Atlas Canadian T-Bill Fund	16%	2|10	11/97	1.86	1.9%	1997	0|10	4.00	4.00	1.29	● (red)
Batirente Money Market Fund	26%	3|9	10/97	2.30	2.4%	1997	0|9	3.00	2.00	0.75	● (green)
Beutel Goodman Money Market Fund	19%	1|6	10/97	2.91	2.9%	1997	0|6	1.00	1.00	0.58	● (green)
Bissett Money Market Fund	12%	0|6	12/97	3.19	3.2%	1997	0|6	1.00	1.00	0.50	● (green)
BNP (Canada) Money Market Fund	2%	0|6	11/97	2.02	2.2%	1997	0|6	3.00	3.00	1.32	● (red)
BPI T-Bill Fund	21%	4|15	11/97	2.88	2.9%	1997	0|15	1.00	2.00	0.65	● (green)
BPI T-Bill Segregated Fund (S)	N/A	0|0	N/A	0.00		N/A	0|0	N/A	N/A	0.00	—
C.I. Money Market Fund	14%	1|7	11/97	2.79	2.8%	1997	0|7	2.00	2.00	0.75	● (green)
C.I. Money Market Segregated Fund (S)	N/A	0|0	N/A	0.00		N/A	0|0	N/A	N/A	1.50	● (red)
C.U. Canadian Money Market Fund (S)	N/A	0|0	N/A	0.00		N/A	0|0	N/A	N/A	1.15	● (red)
Canada Life Money Market S-29 (S)	21%	7|21	11/97	1.98	2.1%	1997	0|21	3.00	3.00	1.25	● (red)

S = Seg Funds

22 CANADIAN MONEY MARKET

Fund Name	Performance Trend by Quartiles (84–98, June)	Fund Beats GICs %	Fund Beats GICs (Yr)	Worst 12 mo. End	Worst 12 mo. Chng (%)	Worst Calendar Year	Worst Calendar %	Years Fund Lost $	Sharpe 3-Yr	Sharpe 5-Yr	MER	Efficiency
Canada Trust Money Market Fund	1 1 2 1 3 4 3 4 3 3 3 | 3	25%	3|11	11/97	2.27	1997	2.3%	0|11	4.00	4.00	0.98	yellow
Canada Trust Premium Money Market Fund	2 2 | 2	0%	0|1	11/97	2.68	1997	2.7%	0|1	N/A	N/A	0.57	green
Capstone Cash Management Fund	4 2 1 1 1 1 1 2 1 2 1 | 1	35%	4|10	12/97	2.39	1997	2.4%	0|10	1.00	1.00	0.60	green
CCPE Money Market Fund	2 3 1 | 1	7%	0|2	12/97	2.23	1997	2.2%	0|2	1.00	N/A	0.75	green
CDA Money Market Fund (Canagex)	1 1 1 3 3 2 1 2 2 1 1 1 1 1 1 | 1	25%	7|21	12/97	2.69	1997	2.7%	0|21	1.00	1.00	0.66	green
CentrePost Short Term Fund	1 2 3 2 1	3%	0|5	09/97	2.48	1997	2.6%	0|5	2.00	3.00	0.75	green
CIBC Canadian T-Bill Fund	4 4 3 3 3 2 3 | 1	4%	0|7	11/97	2.35	1997	2.4%	0|7	4.00	4.00	0.99	yellow
CIBC Money Market Fund	2 2 3 4 3 3 3 2 3	23%	2|9	11/97	2.42	1997	2.4%	0|9	3.00	4.00	0.99	green
CIBC Premium Canadian T-Bill Fund	2 3 1 2 1 | 1	7%	0|6	11/97	2.72	1997	2.8%	0|6	2.00	2.00	0.55	green
Clarington Money Market Fund	3 | 2	0%	0|1	11/97	2.21	1997	2.2%	0|1	N/A	N/A	0.75	yellow
Colonia Money Market Fund	3 4 1 2 3 3	10%	0|5	12/97	2.35	1997	2.3%	0|5	2.00	2.00	1.00	yellow
Co-operators Life Money Market Fund	4	N/A	0|0	N/A	0.00	N/A		0|0	N/A	N/A	1.88	red
Cornerstone Government Money Market Fund	2 3 3 3 2 4 3 | 3	16%	1|7	10/97	2.09	1997	2.2%	0|7	3.00	3.00	1.14	red
CUMIS Life Memberfunds Canadian Money Market	2 2	0%	0|1	12/97	2.62	1997	2.6%	0|1	N/A	N/A	0.75	green
Desjardins Money Market Fund	4 4 3 4 4 3 4 3 3	12%	1|8	10/97	2.06	1997	2.2%	0|8	4.00	4.00	1.11	red
Dynamic Money Market Fund	4 1 1 2 2 3 3 3 2	15%	2|13	11/97	2.18	1997	2.2%	0|13	3.00	3.00	0.80	yellow
Elliott & Page Money Fund	2 1 1 1 1 1 1 2 2 2	33%	5|13	11/97	2.42	1997	2.6%	0|13	2.00	2.00	0.27	green
Elliott & Page T-Bill Fund	4 4 4 4	0%	0|3	11/97	1.22	1997	1.4%	0|3	4.00	N/A	1.75	red
Empire Elite Money Market Fund	4 2 4 3 4 4 4 4 4 3	19%	2|8	11/97	1.79	1997	1.9%	0|8	4.00	4.00	1.43	red
Equitable Life Money Market Fund	4 4 2 4	2%	0|3	05/97	2.24	1997	2.6%	0|3	3.00	N/A	1.75	red
Ethical Money Market Fund	2 2 2 2 1 1 1 3 3 3 3 3 2 3 4	19%	2|15	01/98	2.33	1997	2.3%	0|15	3.00	4.00	1.25	red
Ficadre Money Market Fund	3 2 2 3 3 3 2 1 3	11%	1|7	11/97	2.69	1997	3.2%	0|7	2.00	2.00	1.11	red

S = Seg Funds

22 CANADIAN MONEY MARKET

Fund Name	CONSISTENCY — Performance Trend by Quartiles (84 85 86 87 88 89 90 91 92 93 94 95 96 97 98 | June)	RISK — Fund Beats GICs %	Fund Beats GICs(Yr)	Worst 12 mo. End	Chng (%)	Worst Calendar Year	Years Fund Lost $	Sharpe 3-Yr	Sharpe 5-Yr	MER	Efficiency
Fidelity Canadian Short-Term Asset Fund	3 4 4 4 1 4 | 3	3%	0|6	10/97	2.01	2.1% / 1997	0|6	1.00	1.00	1.25	● red
First Canadian Money Market Fund	4 3 3 2 3 3 3 2 3 | 3	16%	2|9	11/97	2.29	2.3% / 1997	0|9	3.00	4.00	1.09	● orange
First Canadian Premium Money Market Fund	1	N/A	0|0	N/A	0.00	N/A	0|0	N/A	N/A	0.40	● green
First Canadian T-Bill Fund	3 3 3 3 3 3 | 1	0%	0|4	12/97	2.19	2.2% / 1997	0|4	3.00	N/A	1.13	● red
FMOQ Money Market Fund	4 1 1 1 1 1 1 1 1 | 1	32%	2|8	11/97	3.01	3.0% / 1997	0|8	1.00	1.00	0.68	● green
S Fonds Astra - Marche monetaire	4	N/A	0|0	N/A	0.00	N/A	0|0	N/A	N/A	1.30	● red
GBC Money Market Fund	3 2 2 2 2 2 1 3 3 1 | 1	23%	3|9	11/97	2.20	2.3% / 1997	0|9	2.00	2.00	0.75	● orange
General Trust of Canada - Money Market Fund	1 4 4 3 1 2 1 3 2 2 3 4 | 4	24%	4|11	11/97	2.44	2.4% / 1997	0|11	2.00	3.00	1.15	● red
Global Strategy Money Market Fund	4 4 4 2 2 2 4 2 3 | 3	14%	2|9	10/97	2.43	2.5% / 1997	0|9	4.00	3.00	0.84	● green
S Great-West Life Money Market Investment (G) DSC	4 4 4 3 | 3	0%	0|3	10/97	1.78	1.9% / 1997	0|3	4.00	N/A	1.38	● red
S Great-West Life Money Market Investment (G) NL	1 1 2 1 4 4 4 4 4 3 | 3	22%	4|17	10/97	1.52	1.7% / 1997	0|17	4.00	4.00	1.64	● red
Green Line Canadian Money Market Fund	1 1 2 1 2 2 2 1 2 | 2	24%	3|9	11/97	2.92	2.9% / 1997	0|9	2.00	2.00	0.84	● orange
Green Line Canadian T-Bill Fund	4 2 3 2 2 2 2 2 3 | 3	3%	0|5	11/97	2.69	2.7% / 1997	0|5	2.00	3.00	0.86	● orange
Green Line Premium Money Market Fund	1	N/A	0|0	N/A	0.00	N/A	0|0	N/A	N/A	0.30	● green
S Growsafe Family of Funds Canadian Money Market	4 2 2 2 2 | 2	0%	0|3	01/98	2.54	2.5% / 1997	0|3	4.00	N/A	0.96	● orange
Guardian Canadian Money Market Fund	2 3 2 1 1 2 2 2 3 2 2 | 2	29%	5|21	10/97	2.34	2.4% / 1997	0|21	3.00	1.00	0.86	● orange
Harford Money Market Fund	4	N/A	0|0	N/A	0.00	N/A	0|0	N/A	N/A	1.75	● red
Hongkong Bank Money Market Fund	4 4 4 3 4 2 2 2 2 | 2	13%	1|8	11/97	2.57	2.6% / 1997	0|8	2.00	3.00	0.90	● red
ICM Short Term Investment Fund	1 1 1 1 1 1 1 1 | 1	38%	4|9	12/97	3.33	3.3% / 1997	0|9	1.00	1.00	0.12	● green
S Imperial Growth Money Market Fund	4 4 4 4 4 4 4 4 4 | 4	10%	1|9	11/97	1.54	1.7% / 1997	0|9	4.00	4.00	1.50	● red
S Industrial Alliance Ecoflex Investment Fund M	4 4 4 | 3	2%	0|3	11/97	1.82	2.0% / 1997	0|3	4.00	N/A	1.36	● red
S Industrial Alliance Money Market Fund	4 2 4 4 4 4 4 | 4	5%	0|6	11/97	1.60	1.7% / 1997	0|6	4.00	4.00	1.50	● red

S = Seg Funds

22 CANADIAN MONEY MARKET

Fund Name	Performance Trend by Quartiles (84 85 86 87 88 89 90 91 92 93 94 95 96 97 98 June)	Fund Beats GICs %	Fund Beats GICs(Yr)	Worst 12 mo. End	Worst 12 mo. Chng (%)	Worst Calendar Year (%)	Worst Calendar Year	Years Fund Lost $	Sharpe Ratio 3-Yr	Sharpe Ratio 5-Yr	MER	Efficiency
Industrial Cash Management Fund	2 2 2 2 2 2 1 1 1 1 1 2 2 2 2	22%	3|13	11/97	2.59	2.6%	1997	0|13	2.00	2.00	0.50	●
Industrial Short-Term Fund	4 4 4 4 4 4 4 4	1%	0|6	11/97	1.73	1.8%	1997	0|6	4.00	4.00	1.25	●
Infinity T-Bill Fund	1 1 1 1	6%	0|0	01/98	2.36		N/A	0|0	N/A	N/A	1.00	●
InvesNat Corporate Cash Management Fund	4 2 3 3 3 3 2 2 3	12%	0|2	11/97	3.08	3.1%	1997	0|2	1.00	N/A	0.52	●
InvesNat Money Market Fund	3	4%	0|7	11/97	2.51	2.5%	1997	0|7	3.00	3.00	1.05	●
InvesNat Presumed Sound Investments Fund	3	N/A	0|0	N/A	0.00		N/A	0|0	N/A	N/A	1.11	●
InvesNat Treasury Bill Plus Fund	3 2 2 2 2 2 1 2	8%	0|7	11/97	2.77	2.8%	1997	0|7	2.00	2.00	0.77	●
InvesNat Treasury Management Fund	1	N/A	0|0	N/A	0.00		N/A	0|0	N/A	N/A	0.27	●
Investors Money Market Fund	4 3 2 3 3 4 3 2 3 3 3 2	17%	2|12	10/97	2.17	2.2%	1997	0|12	3.00	3.00	1.07	●
Jones Heward Money Market Fund	2 3 2	7%	0|3	12/97	2.23	2.2%	1997	0|3	2.00	N/A	0.50	●
Leith Wheeler Money Market Fund	3 2 2 2	0%	0|3	10/97	2.30	2.4%	1997	0|3	2.00	N/A	0.64	●
S London Life Money Fund	2 1 1 3 1 3 3 4	26%	3|8	12/97	2.24	2.2%	1997	0|8	2.00	2.00	1.30	●
Lotus Income Fund	1 1 1 2 2 3 1 1 3	25%	3|9	01/98	2.84	2.9%	1997	0|9	2.00	3.00	0.81	●
Manulife Cabot Money Market Fund	2 4 4 4	4%	0|3	11/97	2.09	2.1%	1997	0|3	4.00	N/A	1.25	●
S Manulife Elliott & Page Money Market GIF	4	6%	0|0	03/98	2.09		N/A	0|0	N/A	N/A	1.25	●
S Manulife Elliott & Page Money Market NL GIF	3	6%	0|0	04/98	2.08		N/A	0|0	N/A	N/A	1.35	●
S Manulife VistaFund ShortTerm Securities 1	3 3 3 3 2 4 1 2 4 4	26%	4|13	01/98	1.75	1.8%	1997	0|13	2.00	2.00	1.63	●
Marathon Performance Canadian Cash Manager		N/A	0|0	N/A	0.00		N/A	0|0	N/A	N/A	0.75	●
S Maritime Life Money Market Fund (A)	4 4 3 4 4 4 2 4 4 4 4 4 3	15%	2|15	12/97	1.96	2.0%	1997	0|15	4.00	4.00	1.00	●
S Maritime Life Money Market Fund (C)	4 4 3 4 4 4 2 4 4 4 4 4 4	15%	2|15	12/97	1.69	1.7%	1997	0|15	4.00	4.00	2.00	●
S Maritime Life Money Market Fund Series B	4	0%	0|1	11/97	1.82	1.9%	1997	0|1	N/A	N/A	1.00	●
Mawer Canadian Money Market Fund	3 2 4 3 2 2 2 2 2 1	20%	2|9	11/97	2.57	2.6%	1997	0|9	2.00	2.00	0.67	●

S = Seg Funds

22 CANADIAN MONEY MARKET

Fund Name	Performance Trend by Quartiles (84 85 86 87 88 89 90 91 92 93 94 95 96 97 98 June)	Fund Beats GICs %	Fund Beats GICs(Yr)	Worst 12 mo. End	Worst 12 mo. Chng (%)	Worst Calendar %	Worst Calendar Year	Years Fund Lost $	Sharpe 3-Yr	Sharpe 5-Yr	MER
Maxxum Money Market Fund	1 1 3 2 1 1 1 2 1 2	23%	3|11	12/97	2.96	3.0%	1997	0|11	1.00	2.00	0.84
McLean Budden Money Market Fund	1 3 3 4 2 1 1 1 3	24%	2|9	01/98	2.69	2.9%	1997	0|9	1.00	2.00	0.75
MD Money Fund	3 3 4 3 4 3 2 3 1 1 1 2 1 1	22%	7|21	11/97	2.82	2.9%	1997	0|21	2.00	1.00	0.52
S MetLife MVP Money Market Fund	4 4 4 4 4 4 4	0%	0|6	02/98	1.49	1.6%	1997	0|6	4.00	4.00	1.68
Middlefield Money Market Fund	3 4	0%	0|1	06/98	0.93	2.3%	1997	0|1	N/A	N/A	0.55
S Millennia III Money Market Fund Series 1	4 4 4	6%	0|2	10/97	1.74	1.9%	1997	0|2	N/A	N/A	1.45
Montrusco Select T-Max Fund	1 1 1	29%	0|2	10/97	3.32	3.9%	1997	0|2	1.00	N/A	0.00
Mutual Money Market Fund	4 4 4 3 4 4 3 2 2 3 3 2	13%	2|12	10/97	2.22	2.3%	1997	0|12	3.00	3.00	1.07
S NAL-Investor Canadian Money Market Fund	2 3 3 4 4 3 4 1	20%	1|8	11/97	1.78	1.8%	1997	0|8	1.00	1.00	1.25
S National Life Money Market Fund	4 4 4 4 4 4	1%	0|5	10/97	1.65	1.7%	1997	0|5	4.00	4.00	1.60
National Trust Money Market Fund	4 3 3 4 4 2 2 3	8%	0|7	12/97	2.48	2.5%	1997	0|7	3.00	4.00	1.14
S NN Money Market Fund	2 1 2 1 1 1 1	19%	1|7	11/97	2.89	3.0%	1997	0|7	1.00	1.00	1.00
S NN T-Bill Fund	4 4 4 2 2 4 4 4 3 4 3	9%	1|10	12/97	2.13	2.1%	1997	0|10	4.00	4.00	1.30
S North West Life Ecoflex Investment Fund M	4	0%	0|0	01/98	1.98		N/A	0|0	N/A	N/A	1.36
Northwest Money Market Fund	2 2 3 3 2 2	5%	0|5	12/97	2.50	2.5%	1997	0|5	3.00	3.00	1.00
O.I.Q. FERIQUE Short Term Income Fund	1 1 2 2 3 3 1 1 1 1 1 2	30%	6|21	01/98	3.27	3.3%	1997	0|21	1.00	1.00	0.35
O'Donnell Money Market Fund	3 4 3	3%	0|2	12/97	2.10	2.1%	1997	0|2	N/A	N/A	1.10
O'Donnell Short Term Fund	4 4 4	0%	0|2	12/97	1.93	1.9%	1997	0|2	N/A	N/A	1.35
Optimum Fonds d'epargne	1 2 4 1 3 1 4 2 2	25%	1|11	10/97	2.50	2.7%	1997	0|11	3.00	2.00	0.71
OTG Investment Fund - Fixed Value Section	1 1 2 1 1 1	20%	0|5	11/97	3.00	3.0%	1997	0|5	1.00	1.00	0.50
Phillips, Hager & North Canadian Money Market Fund	3 3 1 1 1 1 2 1 1	24%	3|11	10/97	2.81	2.9%	1997	0|11	2.00	2.00	0.48
Pursuit Money Market Fund	3 3 1 1 1 2 1 1 1 2	29%	3|9	12/97	3.42	3.4%	1997	0|9	1.00	1.00	0.50

S = Seg Funds

22 CANADIAN MONEY MARKET

Fund Name	Fund Beats GICs %	Fund Beats GICs(Yr)	Worst 12 mo. End	Worst 12 mo. Chng (%)	Worst Calendar Year %	Worst Calendar Year	Years Fund Lost $	Sharpe Ratio Quartile 3-Yr	Sharpe Ratio Quartile 5-Yr	MER
Quebec Professionals' Short Term Fund (S)	44%	4|10	12/97	2.99	3.0%	1997	0|10	1.00	1.00	0.30
Royal & SunAlliance Money Market Fund	11%	0|4	12/97	2.88	2.9%	1997	0|4	1.00	1.00	1.00
Royal Canadian Money Market Fund	18%	2|11	10/97	2.42	2.5%	1997	0|11	4.00	4.00	0.95
Royal Canadian T-Bill Fund	3%	0|6	11/97	2.40	2.4%	1997	0|6	3.00	3.00	0.92
Royal Premium Money Market Fund	25%	0|0	03/98	3.47	N/A	N/A	0|0	N/A	N/A	0.30
Sceptre Money Market Fund	21%	2|9	01/98	2.91	2.9%	1997	0|9	2.00	2.00	0.75
Scotia Excelsior Money Market Fund	12%	0|7	11/97	2.24	2.3%	1997	0|7	3.00	3.00	1.00
Scotia Excelsior Premium T-Bill Fund	4%	0|5	11/97	2.71	2.7%	1997	0|5	2.00	2.00	0.52
Scotia Excelsior T-Bill Fund	2%	0|6	11/97	2.19	2.2%	1997	0|6	3.00	3.00	1.00
Scudder Canadian Money Market Fund	33%	0|0	N/A	0.00	N/A	N/A	0|0	N/A	N/A	0.25
Spectrum United Canadian Money Market Fund	22%	3|10	11/97	2.35	2.4%	1997	0|10	1.00	1.00	0.92
Spectrum United Savings Fund	23%	3|10	12/97	2.18	2.2%	1997	0|10	3.00	3.00	1.00
Standard Life Ideal Money Market Fund (S)	27%	1|4	12/97	3.03	3.0%	1997	0|4	1.00	N/A	1.00
Standard Life Money Market Mutual Fund	13%	0|5	12/97	2.49	2.5%	1997	0|5	1.00	1.00	0.90
Stone & Co Flagship Money Market Fund Canada	0%	0|1	12/97	2.23	2.2%	1997	0|1	N/A	N/A	1.00
Strategic Value Money Market Fund	19%	3|12	11/97	2.04	2.0%	1997	0|12	4.00	4.00	0.99
Talvest Money Fund	28%	3|10	10/97	2.79	2.8%	1997	0|10	1.00	1.00	0.75
Talvest/Hyperion Cash Management Fund	N/A	0|0	N/A	0.00	N/A	N/A	0|0	N/A	N/A	1.00
Templeton Treasury Bill Fund	23%	3|9	11/97	2.17	2.2%	1997	0|9	3.00	3.00	0.75
Trans-Canada Money Market Fund	14%	1|14	03/98	3.07	3.2%	1997	0|14	1.00	1.00	0.65
Trimark Interest Fund	21%	2|11	10/97	2.60	2.7%	1997	0|11	2.00	2.00	0.75
Trust Pret et Revenu Money Market Fund	16%	2|8	12/97	2.39	2.4%	1997	0|8	3.00	3.00	1.14

S = Seg Funds

284

22 CANADIAN MONEY MARKET

Fund Name	CONSISTENCY — Performance Trend by Quartiles (84 85 86 87 88 89 90 91 92 93 94 95 96 97 98 June)	RISK Fund Beats GICs %	Fund Beats GICs(Yr)	Worst 12 mo. End	Chng (%)	Worst Calendar Year		Years Fund Lost $	REWARD-TO-RISK Sharpe Ratio Quartile Rankings 3-Yr	5-Yr	EFFICIENCY MER
University Avenue Money Fund	2 3	0%	0|1	10/97	2.40	1997	2.5%	0|1	N/A	N/A	● 0.75
Valorem Government Short Term Fund	4	0%	0|0	01/98	1.41	N/A		0|0	N/A	N/A	● 1.65
YMG Money Fund	1 2 3 2 2 2 2 2 1 1 2 2	23%	3|10	11/97	2.66	1997	2.7%	0|10	2.00	1.00	● 0.62

S = Seg Funds

23 CANADIAN TACTICAL BALANCED

Fund Name	CONSISTENCY / RISK Fund Beats GICs %	Fund Beats GICs(Yr)	Worst 12 mo. End Chng (%)	Worst Calendar Year	Years Fund Lost $	Sharpe Ratio 3-Yr	Sharpe Ratio 5-Yr	MER
AGF Canadian Tactical Asset Allocation Fund	56%	5|8	01/95 -9.68	1994 -4.1%	1|8	2.00	2.00	2.42
AGF Growth and Income Fund Limited	55%	14|21	06/82 -21.94	1990 -12.5%	3|21	4.00	3.00	2.50
AIM Canadian Balanced Fund	56%	3|5	01/95 -4.26	1994 0.3%	0|5	3.00	4.00	2.71
Altamira Balanced Fund	53%	6|12	08/88 -20.15	1990 -10.6%	3|12	4.00	4.00	2.00
Altamira Growth & Income Fund	57%	5|11	11/97 -11.48	1997 -6.2%	1|11	4.00	4.00	1.40
S Apex Balanced Fund (AGF)	53%	11|21	03/82 -26.50	1990 -15.5%	4|21	4.00	4.00	3.00
Caldwell Associate Fund	61%	6|7	01/93 -5.87	1992 -3.4%	1|7	4.00	2.00	2.36
CIBC Balanced Fund	54%	6|9	01/95 -9.74	1994 -5.6%	1|9	1.00	3.00	2.24
Clean Environment Balanced Fund	64%	4|5	01/95 -11.54	1994 -8.0%	1|5	1.00	1.00	2.60
S Co-operators Life Balanced Fund	59%	4|5	01/95 -6.99	1994 -2.4%	1|5	1.00	1.00	2.06
Dynamic Partners Fund	58%	7|9	01/95 -5.18	1990 -2.5%	2|9	3.00	3.00	2.30
Dynamic Team Fund	52%	6|11	01/95 -9.43	1990 -6.5%	2|11	4.00	4.00	0.52
Elliott & Page Balanced Fund	54%	6|9	01/95 -8.35	1994 -3.0%	2|9	3.00	3.00	1.80
S Empire Elite Asset Allocation Fund	54%	3|3	05/95 5.34	1997 8.2%	0|3	2.00	N/A	2.46
S Equitable Life Asset Allocation Fund	51%	3|3	11/97 5.32	1997 8.8%	0|3	3.00	N/A	2.25
S First Canadian Asset Allocation Fund	51%	6|9	01/95 -10.76	1994 -6.1%	2|9	2.00	4.00	1.94
Hongkong Bank Balanced Fund	48%	6|8	01/95 -10.14	1994 -5.4%	1|8	1.00	1.00	1.81
S Industrial Alliance Diversified Fund Series 2	50%	0|0	01/98 0.36	N/A	0|0	N/A	N/A	2.82
S Industrial Alliance Diversified Fund	54%	6|10	01/95 -4.86	1994 -0.7%	1|10	3.00	2.00	1.57
S Industrial Alliance Ecoflex Investment Fund D	65%	3|4	01/95 -5.37	1994 -1.3%	1|4	3.00	3.00	2.48
Investors Asset Allocation Fund	56%	3|3	01/95 -7.64	1997 8.8%	0|3	2.00	N/A	2.73
S Manulife Dynamic Partners GIF	N/A	0|0	N/A	N/A	0|0	N/A	N/A	3.37

S = Seg Funds

THE MONSTER FUND TABLES ●

THE MONSTER FUND TABLES ●

THE MONSTER FUND TABLES ●

THE MONSTER FUND TABLES ●

THE MONSTER FUND TABLES ●

23 CANADIAN TACTICAL BALANCED

Fund Name	Performance Trend by Quartiles (84–98, June)	Fund Beats GICs %	Fund Beats GICs(Yr)	Worst 12 mo. End	Worst 12 mo. Chng (%)	Worst Calendar Year	Worst Calendar %	Years Fund Lost $	Sharpe 3-Yr	Sharpe 5-Yr	MER	Efficiency
Mawer Canadian Diversified Investment Fund	4 1 2 2 4 3 2 3 1	2	55%	6|9	01/95	-6.25	1994	-3.2%	1|9	1.00	1.00	1.08	●
Mutual Diversifund 40	3 3 2 3 4 2 1 2 2	2	55%	7|12	10/90	-10.94	1990	-6.0%	2|12	1.00	1.00	1.85	●
Mutual Premier Diversified Fund	1 1 2	2	63%	3|3	08/95	7.67	1997	10.0%	0|3	2.00	N/A	2.38	●
S North West Life Ecoflex Investment Fund D	3		61%	0|0	01/98	7.10	N/A		0|0	N/A	N/A	2.48	●
Northwest Balanced Fund	2 4	1	59%	2|2	01/98	3.24	1997	5.9%	0|2	3.00	N/A	2.00	●
Royal Balanced Fund	2 2 3 2 2 3 2 2 4 2	3	57%	7|10	01/95	-7.73	1990	-2.5%	2|10	2.00	2.00	2.20	●
Scotia Excelsior Total Return Fund	1 1 1 2 4 3 2 2	2	55%	6|8	01/95	-11.25	1994	-4.8%	1|8	2.00	1.00	2.27	●
Spectrum United Asset Allocation Fund	3 3 3 4 1	2	61%	4|5	01/95	-8.63	1994	-3.6%	1|5	1.00	2.00	2.22	●
Templeton Canadian Asset Allocation Fund	3 3 3 2	4	53%	3|3	06/98	6.60	1997	10.2%	0|3	1.00	N/A	2.15	●
Trans-Canada Pension Fund	3 3 4 1 3 4 1 1 1	4	41%	8|14	01/93	-20.58	1992	-15.4%	5|14	4.00	4.00	3.48	●
Trust Pret et Revenu Retirement Fund	4 1 1 2 4 3 1 1 3	4	52%	12|21	03/82	-10.03	1981	-4.8%	2|21	3.00	2.00	1.95	●
S Westbury Canadian Life - Balanced Fund	3 4 2 1 2 2	1	48%	4|6	01/95	-6.23	1994	-1.3%	1|6	2.00	3.00	2.41	●

S = Seg Funds

287

24 CANADIAN STRATEGIC BALANCED

Fund Name	Performance Trend by Quartiles (84–98 June)	Fund Beats GICs %	Fund Beats GICs (Yr)	Worst 12 mo. End	Worst 12 mo. Chng (%)	Worst Calendar Year %	Worst Calendar Year	Years Fund Lost $	Sharpe 3-Yr	Sharpe 5-Yr	MER
A.P.M. Balanced Fund	2 3 4 3 ‖ 1	55%	3|4	01/95	-4.94	-1.7%	1994	1|4	2.00	1.00	1.13
A.P.P.Q. (Fonds equilibre)	4 1 3 3 3	53%	3|4	01/95	-7.10	-5.1%	1994	1|4	3.00	3.00	0.24
ABC Fully-Managed Fund	1 3 4 1 1 1 1 3 4	55%	6|9	01/95	-6.47	-1.5%	1992	1|9	2.00	1.00	2.00
Acadia Atlantic Fund		N/A	0|0	N/A	0.00	N/A	N/A	0|0	N/A	N/A	0.00
Acadia Balanced Fund	4 2 4 ‖ 4	49%	2|3	06/98	-7.45	4.3%	1997	0|3	4.00	N/A	2.42
Acadia Diversified Fund		N/A	0|0	N/A	0.00	N/A	N/A	0|0	N/A	N/A	0.00
Acuity Pooled Canadian Balanced Investment Fund	2 2 1 1 1 1	66%	3|4	01/95	-4.49	-2.3%	1994	1|4	1.00	1.00	0.00
Acuity Pooled Conservative Asset Allocation Fund	4 4 1 1 1 ‖ 1	56%	2|4	01/95	-14.54	-11.6%	1994	1|4	1.00	4.00	0.00
AIC Income Equity Fund	1 ‖ 4	N/A	0|0	N/A	0.00	N/A	N/A	0|0	N/A	N/A	2.46
AIM GT Canada Income Class	1 4	69%	1|1	06/98	11.88	17.3%	1997	0|1	N/A	N/A	2.10
S Apex Growth & Income Fund	4 4	53%	1|1	01/98	7.18	7.9%	1997	0|1	N/A	N/A	2.54
Atlas Canadian Balanced Fund	3 3 4 4 2 1 3 1 1 1	51%	5|8	10/90	-6.56	-2.4%	1990	2|8	1.00	1.00	2.21
Azura Balanced RRSP Pooled Fund	3 4	60%	1|1	01/98	5.25	8.7%	1997	0|1	N/A	N/A	2.22
Azura Conservative Fund	4 4 3	53%	2|2	07/96	5.60	7.5%	1996	0|2	4.00	N/A	2.08
Barreau du Quebec Balanced Fund	2 1 1 1 1 3 4 2 4 2 2	54%	7|10	01/95	-6.52	-4.4%	1994	1|10	1.00	2.00	0.78
S Bell Group RRSP Balanced	3 4 4 4	59%	2|3	11/97	2.54	4.4%	1997	0|3	4.00	N/A	1.15
Beutel Goodman Balanced Fund	4 1 1 4 3 2 3	56%	4|6	01/95	-6.37	-0.3%	1994	1|6	2.00	2.00	2.11
Bissett Retirement Fund	2 2 2 1 1 1 ‖ 2	62%	4|6	01/95	-5.29	-1.8%	1994	1|6	1.00	1.00	0.44
BPI Canadian Balanced Fund	2 4 3 1 2 4 4 4 4	52%	7|9	01/95	-12.28	-6.9%	1994	2|9	4.00	4.00	2.22
BPI Global Balanced RSP Fund	4 1 4 2 1 1 4 4 1 4	48%	4|9	04/90	-2.25	0.9%	1990	0|9	4.00	3.00	2.25
S BPI Global Balanced RSP Segregated Fund		N/A	0|0	N/A	0.00	N/A	N/A	0|0	N/A	N/A	0.00
BPI Income & Growth Fund	2	85%	0|0	06/98	40.32		N/A	0|0	N/A	N/A	2.49

S = Seg Funds

24 CANADIAN STRATEGIC BALANCED

S = Seg Funds

Fund Name	Performance Trend by Quartiles (84–98 | June)	Fund Beats GICs %	Fund Beats GICs (Yr)	Worst 12 mo. End	Chng (%)	Worst Calendar Year		Years Fund Lost $	Sharpe Ratio 3-Yr	Sharpe Ratio 5-Yr	MER	Efficiency
S BPI Income & Growth Segregated Fund	1 2 4 4 | 1	N/A	0|0	N/A	0.00	N/A	N/A	0|0	N/A	N/A	0.00	—
C.I. Canadian Balanced Fund	1 2 4 4 | 1	55%	3|4	01/95	-4.72	1994	1.1%	0|4	4.00	3.00	2.30	●
C.I. Canadian Income Fund	1 3 3 | 4	62%	3|3	06/98	7.48	1997	10.1%	0|3	2.00	N/A	1.82	●
S C.I. Harbour Growth & Income Segregated	| 4	N/A	0|0	N/A	0.00	N/A	N/A	0|0	N/A	N/A	2.97	●
C.S.F.P.Q. Balanced Fund	1 2 3 3 | 2	56%	3|4	01/95	-2.69	1994	0.1%	0|4	2.00	2.00	0.99	●
Caisse de Securite du Spectacle Equilibre	3 2 3 2 2 1 2 2 3 3 1 |	52%	10|17	01/95	-6.03	1994	-1.5%	1|17	3.00	2.00	0.76	●
Cambridge Balanced Fund	2 1 1 2 4 1 2 1 1 4 4 4 4 4 |	48%	9|21	11/97	-33.54	1997	-27.5%	2|21	4.00	4.00	3.48	●
S Canada Life Managed Fund S-35	2 2 2 1 2 4 2 2 3 2 2 2 2 3 2 |	55%	9|13	09/90	-8.80	1990	-5.3%	2|13	2.00	3.00	2.25	●
Canada Trust Balanced Fund	1 3 2 2 4 2 3 4 2 3 1 |	54%	7|10	01/95	-10.58	1994	-6.8%	1|10	2.00	3.00	2.13	●
Canada Trust Balanced Index Fund	| 2	N/A	0|0	N/A	0.00	N/A		0|0	N/A	N/A	2.13	●
Canada Trust Retirement Balanced Fund		57%	0|0	06/98	12.34	N/A		0|0	N/A	N/A	1.69	●
Capstone International Investment Trust Fund	4 1 2 1 1 2 2 4 2 4 1 |	53%	7|10	09/90	-10.41	1988	-4.3%	2|10	4.00	3.00	2.00	●
S CCPE Diversified Fund	3 2 2 3 2 4 4 1 3 2 2 | 3	52%	7|11	01/95	-4.87	1990	-0.7%	2|11	2.00	2.00	1.35	●
S CDA Balanced Fund (KBSH)	2 2 1 2 2 1 2 3 3 2 3 2 3 2 |	55%	9|19	06/82	-22.71	1981	-6.8%	3|19	2.00	2.00	0.96	●
CentrePost Balanced Fund	4 2 2 1 4 | 4	59%	3|5	06/94	-5.40	1994	-2.2%	1|5	3.00	4.00	1.00	●
Clarington Canadian Balanced Fund	3 | 3	59%	1|1	06/98	9.04	1997	11.0%	0|1	N/A	N/A	2.75	●
Clarington Canadian Income Fund	3 | 3	58%	1|1	06/98	10.59	1997	11.0%	0|1	N/A	N/A	2.09	●
S Colonia Strategic Balanced Fund	1 | 3	50%	2|2	01/98	11.36	1997	14.8%	0|2	N/A	N/A	2.04	●
S Common Sense Asset Builder Fund I	2 2 1 | 3	64%	3|3	02/95	4.47	1995	15.4%	0|3	1.00	N/A	2.25	●
S Common Sense Asset Builder Fund II	3 1 1 | 1	64%	3|3	02/95	5.08	1995	14.8%	0|3	1.00	N/A	2.26	●
S Common Sense Asset Builder Fund III	3 1 1 | 1	64%	3|3	02/95	4.46	1995	13.1%	0|3	1.00	N/A	2.25	●
S Common Sense Asset Builder Fund IV	4 1 1 | 1	60%	3|3	02/95	4.57	1995	11.9%	0|3	1.00	N/A	2.25	●

24 CANADIAN STRATEGIC BALANCED

Fund Name		Fund Beats GICs %	Fund Beats GICs(Yr)	Worst 12 mo. End	Chng (%)	Worst Calendar Year	Worst Calendar %	Years Fund Lost $	Sharpe Ratio 3-Yr	Sharpe Ratio 5-Yr	MER
Common Sense Asset Builder Fund V	S	60%	3|3	02/95	3.07	1995	12.8%	0|3	1.00	N/A	2.26
Cormel Balanced Fund		54%	7|10	01/95	-5.96	1994	-3.0%	1|10	2.00	2.00	0.92
Cornerstone Balanced Fund		55%	11|21	06/82	-31.61	1987	-8.8%	5|21	4.00	4.00	2.38
CUMIS Life Memberfunds Balanced Fund	S	58%	0|1	06/98	1.15	1997	2.1%	0|1	N/A	N/A	3.00
Desjardins Balanced Fund		51%	6|11	01/95	-7.97	1994	-2.4%	3|11	3.00	3.00	1.93
Desjardins Diversified Ambitious Fund		56%	0|0	01/98	8.73	N/A	N/A	0|0	N/A	N/A	1.98
Desjardins Diversified Audacious Fund		64%	2|2	11/97	7.07	1997	8.4%	0|2	3.00	N/A	1.91
Desjardins Diversified Moderate Fund		62%	2|2	11/97	5.32	1997	6.2%	0|2	3.00	N/A	1.79
Desjardins Diversified Secure Fund		55%	1|2	11/97	3.84	1997	4.3%	0|2	4.00	N/A	1.70
Desjardins Life Diversified Fund	S	55%	5|8	01/95	-7.04	1994	-2.5%	1|8	2.00	2.00	0.00
Desjardins Quebec Fund		62%	0|0	06/98	22.99	N/A	N/A	0|0	N/A	N/A	2.20
Empire Elite Balanced Fund	S	54%	5|8	01/95	-7.38	1994	-3.3%	1|8	3.00	3.00	2.44
Ethical Balanced Fund		54%	4|8	01/95	-9.13	1994	-4.1%	1|8	2.00	1.00	2.08
Ficadre Balanced Fund		52%	13|21	08/88	-14.55	1994	-4.0%	3|21	3.00	3.00	2.18
Fidelity Canadian Asset Allocation Fund		60%	3|3	07/96	10.81	1996	22.6%	0|3	1.00	N/A	2.48
FMOQ Omnibus Fund		52%	12|18	01/95	-3.97	1994	0.0%	0|18	1.00	1.00	0.62
Fonds Astra - 110(s)	S	N/A	0|0	N/A	0.00	N/A		0|0	N/A	N/A	2.50
Fonds Astra - Equilibre	S	N/A	0|0	N/A	0.00	N/A		0|0	N/A	N/A	2.40
Fonds Remec Equilibre		55%	7|9	01/95	-4.04	1994	-0.8%	1|9	2.00	2.00	1.67
Forester Growth Funds - Balanced	S	54%	5|8	10/90	-5.87	1990	-3.9%	2|8	3.00	2.00	2.00
General Trust of Cda - Balanced Fund		49%	6|11	09/90	-10.06	1990	-5.4%	3|11	4.00	4.00	2.12
Global Strategy Income Plus Fund		65%	4|5	01/95	-4.91	1994	-3.0%	1|5	1.00	1.00	2.40

S = Seg Funds

24 CANADIAN STRATEGIC BALANCED

		CONSISTENCY — Performance Trend by Quartiles																RISK							REWARD-TO-RISK — Sharpe Ratio Quartile Rankings		EFFICIENCY
	Fund Name	84	85	86	87	88	89	90	91	92	93	94	95	96	97	98	June	Fund Beats GICs %	Fund Beats GICs(Yr)	Worst 12 mo. End	Worst 12 mo. Chng (%)	Worst Calendar Year	Worst Cal. %	Years Fund Lost $	3-Yr	5-Yr	MER
S	Great-West Life Balanced Fund (B) DSC														2	4		63%	1|1	11/97	10.12	1997	13.6%	0|1	N/A	N/A	2.56
S	Great-West Life Balanced Fund (B) NL														2	4		60%	1|1	11/97	9.84	1997	13.3%	0|1	N/A	N/A	2.80
S	Great-West Life Balanced Fund (M) DSC														4	4		57%	1|1	06/98	2.15	1997	7.8%	0|1	N/A	N/A	2.70
S	Great-West Life Balanced Fund (M) NL														4	4		57%	1|1	06/98	1.88	1997	7.5%	0|1	N/A	N/A	2.94
S	Great-West Life Balanced Fund (S) DSC														2	2		60%	1|1	06/98	9.51	1997	12.5%	0|1	N/A	N/A	2.64
S	Great-West Life Balanced Fund (S) NL														2	2		60%	1|1	06/98	9.23	1997	12.2%	0|1	N/A	N/A	2.89
S	Great-West Life Diversified Investment (G) DSC											4	3	2	2	2		57%	3|3	08/95	5.64	1995	13.1%	0|3	3.00	N/A	2.40
S	Great-West Life Diversified Investment (G) NL					3	2	3	3	3	3	4	4	4	2	3		49%	6|12	01/95	-8.81	1994	-4.3%	2|12	3.00	4.00	2.64
S	Great-West Life Equity/Bond Investment (G) DSC												3	2	2	3		60%	3|3	08/95	4.94	1997	11.9%	0|3	4.00	N/A	2.40
S	Great-West Life Equity/Bond Investment Fund (G) NL						2	2	3	2	4	3	2	3	3		56%	6|9	01/95	-11.34	1994	-5.8%	1|9	4.00	4.00	2.64
S	Great-West Life Growth & Income Fund (M) DSC													1	3			70%	1|1	01/98	12.10	1997	14.8%	0|1	N/A	N/A	2.52
S	Great-West Life Growth & Income Fund (M) NL													2	3			70%	1|1	01/98	11.81	1997	14.5%	0|1	N/A	N/A	2.77
	Green Line Balanced Growth Fund					3	1	4	4	3	4	3	1	1	2	2		55%	6|10	01/95	-8.92	1990	-4.2%	2|10	1.00	2.00	1.95
	Green Line Balanced Income Fund						2	4	3	4	4	3	2	2	2	2		53%	6|9	09/90	-9.91	1994	-5.4%	2|9	2.00	3.00	1.95
	Greystone Managed Wealth Fund												4	3	1	1		58%	3|3	07/96	0.57	1995	11.5%	0|3	2.00	N/A	2.46
S	Growsafe Canadian Balanced Fund												4	3	4	3		55%	3|3	04/95	3.46	1997	6.7%	0|3	3.00	N/A	2.46
	Guardian Canadian Balanced Fund	1	4	4	1	1	4	1	3	1	4	1	4	1	4	4	4	49%	8|21	06/82	-17.85	1981	-12.1%	1|21	4.00	4.00	1.66
	Guardian Growth & Income Fund																	44%	0|0	06/98	7.13	N/A		0|0	N/A	N/A	2.00
	Harbour Growth & Income Fund														3			38%	0|0	06/98	4.40	N/A		0|0	N/A	N/A	2.33
	Hartford Asset Allocation Fund														4			N/A	0|0	N/A	0.00	N/A		0|0	N/A	N/A	2.50
	Hirsch Balanced Fund																	N/A	0|0	N/A	0.00	N/A		0|0	N/A	N/A	2.50
	I.G. Beutel Goodman Canadian Balanced Fund														2	4		63%	1|1	11/97	9.50	1997	12.7%	0|1	N/A	N/A	2.71

S = Seg Funds

24 CANADIAN STRATEGIC BALANCED

CONSISTENCY — Performance Trend by Quartiles

Fund Name	84	85	86	87	88	89	90	91	92	93	94	95	96	97	98	June
I.G. Sceptre Canadian Balanced Fund															3	2
ICM Balanced Fund					2	3	4	1	1	1	1	1	2	4	2	
S Imperial Growth Diversified Fund						4	2	3	3	4	2	3	3	2	3	
S Industrial Alliance Diversified Fund "DNL"																
S Industrial Alliance Ecoflex Diversified Fund "DNL"																
Industrial Balanced Fund									3	1	3	3	3	3	3	4
Industrial Income Fund Class A Units	1	1	3	1	1	2	3	2	1	3	4	1	4	4	4	
Industrial Income Fund Class B Units																
Industrial Pension Fund	3	1	4	1	1	4	4	4	4	1	4	1	1	1	1	2
InvesNat Protected Growth Balanced Fund																
InvesNat Protected Retirement Balanced Fund																
InvesNat Retirement Balanced Fund						4	3	3	2	4	2	2	3	4	1	
Investors Income Plus Portfolio							1	2	3	4	2	4	4	3	3	
Investors Mutual of Canada	4	3	4	2	1	1	4	3	4	1	1	4	2	2	1	
Investors Retirement Plus Portfolio							3	3	4	3	1	4	3	4	3	
Ivy Growth & Income Fund										4	1	1	1	1	1	2
Jones Heward Canadian Balanced Fund	1	4	1	3	3	4	2	2	1	2	4	3	4	3	4	
LaSalle Balanced Fund									2	4	3	4	2	4		
Leith Wheeler Balanced Fund						1	4	1	1	1	2	4	2	1	2	
S London Life Diversified Fund						1	4	2	1	3	3	3	2	2	2	
Lotus Balanced Fund		4	2	4	4	2	4	3	1	1	4	3	2	3	1	
S Manulife AGF Growth & Income GIF																4

RISK / REWARD-TO-RISK / EFFICIENCY

Fund Name	Fund Beats GICs %	Fund Beats GICs (Yr)	Worst 12 mo. End	Worst 12 mo. Chng (%)	Worst Calendar %	Worst Calendar Year	Years Fund Lost $	Sharpe Ratio 3-Yr	Sharpe Ratio 5-Yr	MER	Efficiency
I.G. Sceptre Canadian Balanced Fund	67%	1|1	06/98	9.19	11.5%	1997	0|1	N/A	N/A	2.73	red
ICM Balanced Fund	55%	7|10	08/88	-7.82	-3.0%	1990	2|10	2.00	1.00	0.26	green
S Imperial Growth Diversified Fund	52%	6|9	01/95	-4.75	-1.7%	1994	1|9	3.00	3.00	2.00	orange
S Industrial Alliance Diversified Fund "DNL"	N/A	0|0	N/A	0.00		N/A	0|0	N/A	N/A	1.50	green
S Industrial Alliance Ecoflex Diversified Fund "DNL"	N/A	0|0	N/A	0.00	N/A	N/A	0|0	N/A	N/A	2.40	red
Industrial Balanced Fund	53%	4|6	01/95	-8.49	-3.5%	1994	1|6	4.00	4.00	2.37	orange
Industrial Income Fund Class A Units	53%	14|21	03/80	-15.11	-5.5%	1994	4|21	3.00	4.00	1.86	green
Industrial Income Fund Class B Units	N/A	0|0	N/A	0.00	N/A	N/A	0|0	N/A	N/A	0.00	–
Industrial Pension Fund	53%	11|21	10/90	-23.46	-20.4%	1990	5|21	1.00	1.00	2.40	orange
InvesNat Protected Growth Balanced Fund	N/A	0|0	N/A	0.00	N/A	N/A	0|0	N/A	N/A	2.99	red
InvesNat Protected Retirement Balanced Fund	N/A	0|0	N/A	0.00	N/A	N/A	0|0	N/A	N/A	3.05	red
InvesNat Retirement Balanced Fund	49%	5|9	09/90	-6.02	-2.3%	1994	2|9	3.00	4.00	2.10	orange
Investors Income Plus Portfolio	61%	5|8	01/95	-5.52	-2.5%	1994	1|8	1.00	2.00	2.29	orange
Investors Mutual of Canada	53%	13|21	06/82	-19.67	-6.3%	1990	4|21	3.00	3.00	2.37	orange
Investors Retirement Plus Portfolio	51%	5|8	09/90	-5.56	-2.0%	1990	1|8	3.00	3.00	2.41	red
Ivy Growth & Income Fund	65%	4|5	01/95	-1.64	-0.7%	1994	1|5	1.00	1.00	2.12	orange
Jones Heward Canadian Balanced Fund	50%	9|14	01/95	-11.17	-6.4%	1994	2|14	4.00	4.00	2.40	orange
LaSalle Balanced Fund	55%	4|5	01/95	-8.45	-4.7%	1994	1|5	4.00	4.00	2.29	orange
Leith Wheeler Balanced Fund	54%	7|10	09/90	-6.31	-3.1%	1990	2|10	1.00	1.00	1.18	green
S London Life Diversified Fund	55%	7|9	10/90	-9.08	-5.8%	1990	2|9	2.00	3.00	2.00	orange
Lotus Balanced Fund	55%	9|13	01/95	-12.54	-8.1%	1994	3|13	2.00	4.00	2.16	orange
S Manulife AGF Growth & Income GIF	56%	0|0	06/98	1.96		N/A	0|0	N/A	N/A	2.95	red

S = Seg Funds

24 CANADIAN STRATEGIC BALANCED

Fund Name	Performance Trend by Quartiles (84–98)	June	Fund Beats GICs %	Fund Beats GICs (Yr)	Worst 12 mo. End	Worst 12 mo. Chng (%)	Worst Calendar Year	Worst Calendar %	Years Fund Lost $	Sharpe 3-Yr	Sharpe 5-Yr	MER
S Manulife Elliott & Page Balanced GIF		3	N/A	0|0	N/A	0.00	N/A		0|0	N/A	N/A	2.75
S Manulife Fidelity Canadian Asset Allocation GIF		1	63%	0|0	06/98	19.29	N/A		0|0	N/A	N/A	2.95
S Manulife Harbour Growth & Income GIF			N/A	0|0	N/A	0.00	N/A		0|0	N/A	N/A	2.95
S Manulife Talvest Canadian Asset Allocation GIF		4	N/A	0|0	N/A	0.00	N/A		0|0	N/A	N/A	2.95
S Manulife Trimark Select Balanced GIF			56%	0|0	06/98	3.67	N/A		0|0	N/A	N/A	2.85
S Manulife VistaFund Diversified 1	3 4 4 1 2 1 4 4 2 3 3 2 4 4 3		51%	9|17	01/95	-8.24	1990	-4.3%	2|17	4.00	4.00	1.63
Marathon Performance Canadian Balanced Fund			N/A	0|0	N/A	0.00	N/A		0|0	N/A	N/A	2.15
S Maritime Life Balanced Fund (A&C)	2 3 3 2 4 4 4 2 2 3 3 1		55%	6|11	01/95	-5.52	1994	-1.5%	1|11	2.00	2.00	2.45
S Maritime Life Balanced Fund Series B	3 1		60%	1|1	11/97	7.45	1997	9.6%	0|1	N/A	N/A	2.45
Mawer Canadian Balanced Retirement Savings Fund	3 1 3 3 2 2 2 2 1 1 1		56%	6|9	01/95	-6.13	1994	-2.3%	1|9	2.00	1.00	0.99
Maxxum Canadian Balanced Fund	3 3 1 2 1 4 1 1 4 1		56%	6|9	01/95	-14.22	1994	-8.4%	2|9	3.00	4.00	2.13
McDonald Canada Plus Fund	4 4 4 4 3 2		53%	3|4	02/95	-9.19	1994	-7.4%	1|4	4.00	N/A	2.88
McLean Budden Balanced - Pooled	2 2 1 3 1 1 2 1 1 2 3 1 1 1 1 3		54%	10|14	01/95	-7.46	1994	-2.7%	1|14	1.00	1.00	1.00
McLean Budden Balanced Fund	3 2 1 3 3 3 1 1 1 3		51%	6|9	01/95	-8.81	1994	-4.2%	2|9	1.00	2.00	1.75
MD Balanced Fund	2 2 2 2 2 1		64%	4|5	01/95	-6.38	1994	-2.4%	1|5	3.00	2.00	1.29
Members Mutual Fund		4	50%	0|0	06/98	-5.21	N/A		0|0	N/A	N/A	3.41
S MetLife MVP Balanced Fund	4 3 4 3 4 4 4 2 3		53%	6|10	01/95	-10.12	1994	-5.0%	2|10	3.00	4.00	2.20
S Millennia III Canadian Balanced Fund Series 1	4 3 3	3	59%	2|2	01/98	8.38	1997	11.0%	0|2	N/A	N/A	2.74
Millennium Diversified Fund	4 1 3 1 3		55%	3|4	01/95	-9.25	1994	-6.4%	1|4	2.00	N/A	2.50
Montrusco Select Balanced + Fund	2 1 1 1		65%	3|4	01/95	-6.28	1994	-1.7%	1|4	1.00	1.00	0.00
Montrusco Select Balanced Fund	4 1 2 2 1 1 1 4 1 3 3		57%	7|10	09/90	-4.71	1994	-0.3%	1|10	4.00	3.00	0.00
Mutual Summit Growth & Income Fund		2	62%	0|0	06/98	13.96	N/A		0|0	N/A	N/A	0.00

S = Seg Funds

293

24 CANADIAN STRATEGIC BALANCED

Fund Name	Performance Trend by Quartiles (84–June)	Fund Beats GICs %	Fund Beats GICs (Yr)	Worst 12 mo. End	Worst 12 mo. Chng (%)	Worst Calendar %	Worst Calendar Year	Years Fund Lost $	Sharpe 3-Yr	Sharpe 5-Yr	MER	Efficiency
S NAL-Investor Balanced Growth Fund	1 1 2 3 / 2 3	61%	3|3	06/98	10.56	14.4%	1997	0|3	1.00	N/A	2.00	● orange
S NAL-Investor Canadian Diversified Fund	3 2 3 4 3 3 1 2 4 2 2	54%	5|10	01/95	-7.73	-3.0%	1990	2|10	4.00	4.00	1.75	● green
S National Life Balanced Fund	1 3 2 1 2 2	57%	4|5	01/95	-9.02	-3.7%	1994	1|5	1.00	2.00	2.25	● orange
National Trust Balanced Fund	1 3 3 4 2 2 1 1	56%	5|7	01/95	-9.33	-4.5%	1994	1|7	1.00	2.00	1.74	● green
Navigator Canadian Growth & Income Fund	4	N/A	0|0	N/A	0.00		N/A	0|0	N/A	N/A	2.75	● red
S NN Asset Allocation Fund	4 4 3 4 2 2 3 2 1 2 1	50%	7|10	01/95	-7.78	-3.4%	1994	2|10	1.00	2.00	2.65	● red
S North West Life Ecoflex Diversified Fund "DNL"		N/A	0|0	N/A	0.00		N/A	0|0	N/A	N/A	2.40	● red
O.I.Q. FERIQUE Balanced Fund	3 1 2 1 2 3 1 1 4 2 1 1	53%	9|17	06/82	-14.86	-0.3%	1994	1|17	2.00	1.00	0.34	● green
O.I.Q. FERIQUE Equity Fund	4 1 3 1 1 4 1 4 1 1 3 1 2 1	55%	13|21	06/82	-37.64	-13.1%	1981	4|21	4.00	3.00	0.54	● green
O'Donnell Balanced Fund	4 4	47%	0|1	06/98	3.57	4.7%	1997	0|1	N/A	N/A	2.40	● orange
Optimum Croissance et revenus	4	N/A	0|0	N/A	0.00		N/A	0|0	N/A	N/A	0.00	—
Optimum Fonds Equilibre	3 2 3 2 3 3 1 4 3 3	52%	6|11	01/95	-6.82	-4.1%	1994	2|11	2.00	2.00	1.46	● green
OTG Investment Fund - Balanced Section	3 2 2 1 3 4 2 3 3 2 2 1 2	54%	7|12	01/95	-6.85	-2.9%	1994	2|12	1.00	1.00	1.00	● green
Phillips, Hager & North Balanced Fund	2 1 2 2 1 2 2 2	**58%**	**4|5**	**01/95**	**-4.37**	**0.4%**	**1994**	**0|5**	**2.00**	**1.00**	**0.91**	● green
Phillips, Hager & North Balanced Pension Trust	1 3 2 1 1 2 1 1 1 1 2 2	58%	7|9	10/90	-5.99	-0.6%	1990	1|9	1.00	1.00	1.52	● green
Quebec Professionals' Balanced Fund	1 3 2 3 3 3 1 1 2 4 2 3 4 3 2	52%	11|19	01/95	-3.61	-1.6%	1994	1|19	1.00	1.00	0.95	● green
Quebec Professionals' Growth and Income Fund	3 4 4 2	57%	3|3	07/96	7.40	8.3%	1997	0|3	3.00	N/A	0.95	● green
Rothschild Canadian Balanced Fund	1 4	71%	1|1	06/98	14.83	20.4%	1997	0|1	N/A	N/A	2.68	● red
S Royal & SunAlliance Balanced Fund	1 1 3 4 2 2 3 2 3	58%	6|7	01/95	-9.20	-4.6%	1994	1|7	2.00	3.00	2.34	● green
Royal Trust Advantage Balanced Fund	3 3 1 2 3 2 3 2 3 3 3 2	55%	6|11	01/95	-7.11	-2.4%	1994	1|11	3.00	3.00	1.75	● green
Royal Trust Advantage Growth Fund	3 4 1 3 4 2 2 3 3 3 3 3	55%	6|11	08/88	-10.66	-2.5%	1990	2|11	3.00	4.00	1.90	● green
Royal Trust Advantage Income Fund	3 3 2 1 2 2 4 3 3 4 3 3	55%	6|11	01/95	-5.97	-2.7%	1994	1|11	2.00	2.00	1.63	● green

S = Seg Funds

24 CANADIAN STRATEGIC BALANCED

Fund Name	84	85	86	87	88	89	90	91	92	93	94	95	96	97	98 (June)	Fund Bears GICs %	Fund Beats GICs (Yr)	Worst 12 mo. End Chng (%)	Worst Calendar Year	Years Fund Lost $	Sharpe 3-Yr	Sharpe 5-Yr	MER	Efficiency
Saxon Balanced Fund				2	4	4	4	4	1	1	3	1	1	3	2	52%	7|12	03/88 -19.27	1987 -15.8%	3|12	3.00	2.00	1.75	●
Sceptre Balanced Growth Fund		1	2	1	3	2	2	3	1	1	3	1	1	2	4	53%	8|12	01/95 -8.75	1994 -4.2%	2|12	2.00	1.00	1.44	●
Scotia Excelsior Balanced Fund							1	3	4	2	2	2	3	4	2	49%	5|8	01/95 -8.04	1994 -2.2%	1|8	3.00	3.00	1.90	●
Spectrum United Canadian Balanced Portfolio							4	3	2	2	1	3	3	3	3	57%	5|9	01/95 -8.03	1994 -4.0%	2|9	3.00	3.00	2.16	●
Spectrum United Canadian Conservative Portfolio															2	N/A	0|0	N/A 0.00		0|0	N/A	N/A	2.00	●
Spectrum United Canadian Growth Portfolio															3	N/A	0|0	N/A 0.00	N/A	0|0	N/A	N/A	2.22	●
Spectrum United Canadian Income Portfolio														3		N/A	0|0	N/A 0.00	N/A	0|0	N/A	N/A	1.85	●
Spectrum United Diversified Fund					3	3	3	3	4	3	4	3	3	2	2	52%	6|10	01/95 -10.46	1994 -4.8%	2|10	2.00	3.00	2.08	●
S Standard Life Balanced Mutual Fund									3	3	1	1	1	1	2	61%	4|5	01/95 -7.18	1994 -3.6%	1|5	1.00	1.00	2.00	●
Standard Life Ideal Balanced Fund				4	3	3	1	1	2	4	2	1	3	2	1	56%	6|11	03/88 -4.99	1987 -1.3%	2|11	2.00	1.00	2.00	●
Stone & Co Flagship Growth & Income Fund Canada														3	4	47%	1|1	01/98 7.11	1997 8.6%	0|1	N/A	N/A	2.85	●
Strategic Value Canadian Balanced Fund							3	2	4	4	4	3	3	3	3	52%	6|9	01/95 -6.31	1994 -2.7%	2|9	3.00	4.00	2.70	●
Talvest Canadian Asset Allocation Fund					2	1	2	3	4	3	1	4	3	2	1	52%	7|11	01/95 -4.26	1994 -0.5%	1|11	3.00	3.00	2.42	●
The Hemisphere Value Fund											4	3	4	4	4	61%	3|3	01/98 4.94	1997 7.2%	0|3	4.00	N/A	1.80	●
S Transamerica Balanced Investment Growth Fund	1	4	4	1	3	4	1	4	1	4	1	3	4	4	3	45%	9|18	06/82 -4.18	1994 1.6%	0|18	4.00	2.00	1.80	●
Trimark Income Growth Fund					1	1	4	1	3	1	1	1	2	2	4	61%	6|10	09/90 -11.53	1990 -7.1%	1|10	4.00	3.00	1.56	●
Trimark Select Balanced Fund							2	2	2	1	1	2	2	4	3	59%	5|8	01/95 -4.99	1990 -0.1%	1|8	3.00	2.00	2.23	●
Universal Canadian Balanced Fund													1	1	1	60%	1|1	06/98 19.35	1997 23.9%	0|1	N/A	N/A	2.41	●
Universal World Asset Allocation Fund											1	4	4	3	1	52%	3|4	01/97 -13.33	1996 -7.5%	1|4	4.00	N/A	2.47	●
University Avenue Balanced Fund																N/A	0|0	N/A 0.00		0|0	N/A	N/A	2.25	●
Valorem Diversified Fund															1	47%	0|0	01/98 11.40	N/A	0|0	N/A	N/A	2.51	●
YMG Balanced Fund			2	3	4	1	2	3	4	4	2	4	3	4	4	53%	12|21	01/95 -10.56	1994 -5.1%	3|21	4.00	4.00	1.78	●

S = Seg Funds

25 GLOBAL BALANCED

Fund Name	Performance Trend by Quartiles (84–98, June)	Fund Beats GICs %	Fund Beats GICs(Yr)	Worst 12 mo. End	Worst 12 mo. Chng (%)	Worst Calendar Year	Worst Calendar %	Years Fund Lost $	Sharpe 3-Yr	Sharpe 5-Yr	MER	Efficiency
Acuity Pooled Global Balanced Fund	4 2 4 1 1	52%	2|4	02/95	-8.10	1994	-6.2%	1|4	2.00	3.00	0.00	—
AGF American Tactical Asset Allocation Fund	2 1 3 1 1	54%	6|9	09/94	-5.10	1994	0.6%	0|9	1.00	1.00	2.56	orange
AGF European Asset Allocation Fund	2 4 1 1 1	60%	2|4	01/95	-5.49	1994	1.7%	0|4	1.00	N/A	2.56	orange
AGF World Balanced Fund	3 4 2 2 1	49%	6|10	09/90	-19.62	1990	-15.2%	2|10	2.00	4.00	2.46	orange
AIM GT Global Growth & Income Fund	2 2 2 1	64%	3|3	10/95	6.14	1996	11.9%	0|3	1.00	N/A	2.87	red
Altamira Global Diversified Fund	1 4 2 4 1	51%	5|12	08/88	-28.17	1990	-21.7%	2|12	3.00	3.00	2.00	green
Azura Balanced Fund	3 2 4	61%	2|2	07/96	4.35	1996	9.2%	0|2	4.00	N/A	2.30	green
C.I. International Balanced Fund	1 2 2 2	69%	3|3	10/96	9.65	1996	13.0%	0|3	1.00	N/A	2.41	green
C.I. International Balanced RSP Fund	1 3 2 2	67%	3|3	10/96	8.02	1996	10.5%	0|3	2.00	N/A	2.40	green
Caldwell International Fund	2 3 3 4	56%	3|7	01/93	-8.01	1994	0.3%	0|7	4.00	4.00	2.64	orange
Canada Trust Global Asset Allocation Fund		N/A	0|0	N/A	0.00	N/A		0|0	N/A	N/A	1.93	green
Co-operators Life U.S. Diversified Fund(s)	2	N/A	0|0	N/A	0.00	N/A		0|0	N/A	N/A	2.37	green
CUMIS Life Memberfunds Global Balanced Fund	4 3	63%	0|1	12/97	4.36	1997	4.4%	0|1	N/A	N/A	3.00	red
Desjardins World Wide Balanced Fund	3 3	47%	1|1	01/97	1.88	1997	9.8%	0|1	N/A	N/A	2.19	green
Dynamic Global Partners Fund	3 2 4 3	56%	3|3	08/95	1.22	1997	6.8%	0|3	4.00	N/A	2.47	green
Elliott & Page Global Balanced Fund	3 4 3 2	58%	3|3	07/96	1.76	1997	6.9%	0|3	4.00	N/A	2.74	red
Fidelity Global Asset Allocation Fund	3 4 1 1 2	67%	3|4	01/95	-7.27	1994	-4.1%	1|4	1.00	2.00	2.70	orange
FMOQ Investment Fund	2 1 1 1	56%	8|14	08/88	-7.55	1994	0.6%	0|14	1.00	1.00	0.64	green
Global Manager Tactical Growth Fund	1	67%	0|0	N/A	0.00	N/A		0|0	N/A	N/A	0.00	—
Global Strategy World Balanced Fund	3 4 4 1	67%	3|3	01/97	3.07	1997	6.3%	0|3	3.00	N/A	2.32	green
Growsafe International Balanced	4 3 2 3	55%	3|3	04/95	1.00	1995	8.1%	0|3	3.00	N/A	2.79	red
Guardian International Balanced Fund	4 3 3 3 4	53%	3|4	01/95	-10.49	1994	-6.8%	1|4	3.00	N/A	2.12	green

S = Seg Funds

25 GLOBAL BALANCED

CONSISTENCY — Performance Trend by Quartiles

Fund Name	84	85	86	87	88	89	90	91	92	93	94	95	96	97	98	June
Investors Growth Plus Portfolio											1	1	2	2	3	3
Merrill Lynch Capital Asset Fund														1	3	3
Merrill Lynch World Allocation Fund														4	3	3
NN Elite Fund **S**												4	2	3	4	4
Spectrum United Global Diversified Fund										3	1	4	3	2		2
Strategic Value Global Balanced Fund										1	2	4	3	2		2
Strategic Value Global Balanced RRSP Fund														4	3	3
Talvest Global Asset Allocation Fund										1	4	4	4	2		2
Templeton Balanced Fund									3	2	1	1	1	4		4
Templeton Global Balanced Fund											2	1	2	4		4
Templeton International Balanced Fund											3	1	3	4		4
Universal World Balanced RRSP Fund											2	1	3	3		3
Zweig Global Managed Assets												3	1	2		2

RISK / REWARD-TO-RISK / EFFICIENCY

Fund Name	Fund Beats GICs %	Fund Beats GICs (Yr)	Worst 12 mo. End / Chng (%)	Worst Calendar Year	Years Fund Lost $	Sharpe Ratio Quartile Rankings 3-Yr	5-Yr	MER
Investors Growth Plus Portfolio	53%	5|8	09/90 -8.44	1990 -3.2%	1|8	1.00	1.00	2.45
Merrill Lynch Capital Asset Fund	60%	1|1	01/97 6.90	1997 21.7%	0|1	N/A	N/A	2.80
Merrill Lynch World Allocation Fund	63%	1|1	11/97 5.02	1997 6.2%	0|1	N/A	N/A	2.75
NN Elite Fund	49%	2|3	10/95 0.90	1995 4.3%	0|3	4.00	N/A	2.30
Spectrum United Global Diversified Fund	60%	7|9	09/90 -8.60	1994 -4.5%	1|9	2.00	2.00	2.30
Strategic Value Global Balanced Fund	51%	5|8	12/90 -2.83	1990 -2.8%	1|8	3.00	3.00	2.70
Strategic Value Global Balanced RRSP Fund	55%	1|1	01/98 3.50	1997 5.2%	0|1	N/A	N/A	2.79
Talvest Global Asset Allocation Fund	50%	5|10	07/91 -8.71	1990 -3.6%	1|10	4.00	4.00	2.75
Templeton Balanced Fund	53%	5|7	01/95 -9.98	1994 -3.0%	2|7	2.00	2.00	2.44
Templeton Global Balanced Fund	64%	3|3	10/95 6.60	1997 10.9%	0|3	2.00	N/A	2.55
Templeton International Balanced Fund	58%	3|3	10/95 3.20	1997 8.3%	0|3	3.00	N/A	2.55
Universal World Balanced RRSP Fund	58%	3|3	02/95 -5.76	1997 8.3%	0|3	3.00	N/A	2.41
Zweig Global Managed Assets	64%	2|2	01/97 4.73	1996 8.9%	0|2	2.00	N/A	2.75

S = Seg Funds

297

26 ASSET ALLOCATION SERVICES

Fund Name	Performance Trend by Quartiles (84–98, June)	Fund Beats GICs %	Fund Beats GICs (Yr)	Worst 12 mo. End / Chng (%)	Worst Calendar Year	Years Fund Lost $	Sharpe Ratio Quartile Rankings 3-Yr	5-Yr	MER	Efficiency
Ambassador Aggressive Global RRSP Portfolio	1	N/A	0|0	N/A / 0.00	N/A	0|0	N/A	N/A	0.97	● green
Ambassador Aggressive Portfolio	1	N/A	0|0	N/A / 0.00	N/A	0|0	N/A	N/A	0.95	● green
Ambassador Balanced Global RRSP Portfolio	1	N/A	0|0	N/A / 0.00	N/A	0|0	N/A	N/A	0.98	● green
Ambassador Balanced Portfolio	1	N/A	0|0	N/A / 0.00	N/A	0|0	N/A	N/A	0.96	● green
Ambassador Conservative Global RRSP Portfolio	1	N/A	0|0	N/A / 0.00	N/A	0|0	N/A	N/A	0.98	● green
Ambassador Conservative Portfolio	2	N/A	0|0	N/A / 0.00	N/A	0|0	N/A	N/A	0.97	● green
S C.U. Asset Allocation Fund	2	N/A	0|0	N/A / 0.00	N/A	0|0	N/A	N/A	2.73	● red
S Goldtrust	1 4 4	47%	9|21	11/81 / -42.50	1981 / -37.5%	8|21	N/A	N/A	0.79	● green
S Great-West Life Advanced Portfolio Fund (G) DSC	1 3	59%	1|1	01/98 / 11.04	1997 / 14.0%	0|1	N/A	N/A	2.64	● orange
S Great-West Life Advanced Portfolio Fund (G) NL	1 3	59%	1|1	01/98 / 10.76	1997 / 13.7%	0|1	N/A	N/A	2.88	● red
S Great-West Life Aggressive Portfolio Fund (G) DSC	1 2	59%	1|1	01/98 / 12.31	1997 / 15.8%	0|1	N/A	N/A	2.70	● orange
S Great-West Life Aggressive Portfolio Fund (G) NL	1 2	59%	1|1	01/98 / 12.02	1997 / 15.5%	0|1	N/A	N/A	2.94	● orange
S Great-West Life Balanced Portfolio Fund (G) DSC	1 2	59%	1|1	11/97 / 10.47	1997 / 12.7%	0|1	N/A	N/A	2.58	● orange
S Great-West Life Balanced Portfolio Fund (G) NL	1 2	59%	1|1	11/97 / 10.19	1997 / 12.4%	0|1	N/A	N/A	2.82	● red
S Great-West Life Conservative Portfolio (G) DSC	3 4	59%	1|1	11/97 / 6.82	1997 / 8.5%	0|1	N/A	N/A	2.47	● orange
S Great-West Life Conservative Portfolio Fund (G) NL	3 4	59%	1|1	11/97 / 6.55	1997 / 8.2%	0|1	N/A	N/A	2.71	● orange
S Great-West Life Growth & Income Fund (A) DSC	4 4	53%	0|1	01/98 / -1.69	1997 / 3.8%	0|1	N/A	N/A	2.62	● orange
S Great-West Life Growth & Income Fund (A) NL	4 4	53%	0|1	01/98 / -1.94	1997 / 3.5%	0|1	N/A	N/A	2.86	● red
S Great-West Life Moderate Portfolio Fund (G) DSC	2 3	68%	1|1	11/97 / 8.22	1997 / 10.2%	0|1	N/A	N/A	2.52	● orange
S Great-West Life Moderate Portfolio Fund (G) NL	2 3	64%	1|1	11/97 / 7.94	1997 / 9.9%	0|1	N/A	N/A	2.76	● red
Keystone Registered Balanced Income & Growth		N/A	0|0	N/A / 0.00	N/A	0|0	N/A	N/A	0.00	—
Keystone Registered Conservative Income & Growth		N/A	0|0	N/A / 0.00	N/A	0|0	N/A	N/A	0.00	—

S = Seg Funds

26 ASSET ALLOCATION SERVICES

	CONSISTENCY		RISK							REWARD-TO-RISK		EFFICIENCY
Fund Name	Performance Trend by Quartiles 84 85 86 87 88 89 90 91 92 93 94 95 96 97 98	June	Fund Beats GICs %	Fund Beats GICs(Yr)	Worst 12 mo. End	Worst 12 mo Chng (%)	Worst Calendar Year		Years Fund Lost $	Sharpe Ratio Quartile Rankings 3-Yr	5-Yr	MER
Keystone Registered Long-Term Growth			N/A	0|0	N/A	0.00	N/A		0|0	N/A	N/A	0.00 —
Keystone Registered Maximum Equity Growth			N/A	0|0	N/A	0.00	N/A		0|0	N/A	N/A	0.00 —
Keystone Registered Maximum Long-Term Growth			N/A	0|0	N/A	0.00	N/A		0|0	N/A	N/A	0.00 —
MatchMaker Strategic Balanced Port 1		3 3	57%	1|1	11/97	8.25	1997	9.6%	0|1	N/A	N/A	0.00 —
MatchMaker Strategic Balanced Port 2		2 2	60%	1|1	11/97	10.13	1997	12.1%	0|1	N/A	N/A	0.00 —
MatchMaker Strategic Growth Port 1		2 4	57%	1|1	06/98	6.32	1997	12.0%	0|1	N/A	N/A	0.00 —
MatchMaker Strategic Growth Port 2		1 4	57%	1|1	06/98	4.19	1997	12.6%	0|1	N/A	N/A	0.00 —
MatchMaker Strategic Security Port 1		4 3	60%	1|1	11/97	4.17	1997	5.3%	0|1	N/A	N/A	0.00 —
MatchMaker Strategic Security Port 2		3 3	70%	1|1	11/97	7.11	1997	9.1%	0|1	N/A	N/A	0.00 —
Primerica Canadian Aggressive Growth Portfolio		4	N/A	0|0	N/A	0.00	N/A		0|0	N/A	N/A	0.00 —
Primerica Canadian Balanced Portfolio Fund		2	N/A	0|0	N/A	0.00	N/A		0|0	N/A	N/A	0.00 —
Primerica Canadian Conservative Portfolio Fund		4	N/A	0|0	N/A	0.00	N/A		0|0	N/A	N/A	0.00 —
Primerica Canadian Growth Portfolio Fund		3	N/A	0|0	N/A	0.00	N/A		0|0	N/A	N/A	0.00 —
Primerica Canadian High Growth Portfolio Fund		4	N/A	0|0	N/A	0.00	N/A		0|0	N/A	N/A	0.00 —
Primerica Canadian Income Portfolio Fund		4	N/A	0|0	N/A	0.00	N/A		0|0	N/A	N/A	0.00 —
Primerica International Aggressive Growth Portfol		1	N/A	0|0	N/A	0.00	N/A		0|0	N/A	N/A	0.00 —
Primerica International Growth Portfolio Fund		1	N/A	0|0	N/A	0.00	N/A		0|0	N/A	N/A	0.00 —
Primerica International High Growth Portfolio Fund		1	N/A	0|0	N/A	0.00	N/A		0|0	N/A	N/A	0.00 —
Registered MatchMaker Strategic Balanced Port 1		3 3	60%	1|1	11/97	7.85	1997	9.7%	0|1	N/A	N/A	0.00 —
Registered MatchMaker Strategic Balanced Port 2		2 3	60%	1|1	11/97	8.73	1997	11.0%	0|1	N/A	N/A	0.00 —
Registered MatchMaker Strategic Growth Port 1		2 4	57%	1|1	06/98	4.63	1997	11.8%	0|1	N/A	N/A	0.00 —
Registered MatchMaker Strategic Growth Port 2		1 4	57%	1|1	06/98	6.24	1997	12.8%	0|1	N/A	N/A	0.00 —

S = Seg Funds

299

26 ASSET ALLOCATION SERVICES

Fund Name	Performance Trend by Quartiles (recent)	Fund Beats GICs %	Fund Beats GICs(Yr)	Worst 12 mo. End	Worst 12 mo. Chng (%)	Worst Calendar Year	Worst Calendar %	Years Fund Lost $	Sharpe Ratio 3-Yr	Sharpe Ratio 5-Yr	MER	Efficiency
Registered MatchMaker Strategic Security Port 1	4 4	53%	0|1	11/97	3.16	1997	3.6%	0|1	N/A	N/A	0.00	—
Registered MatchMaker Strategic Security Port 2	4 3	60%	1|1	11/97	4.36	1997	5.5%	0|1	N/A	N/A	0.00	—
* STAR Canadian Balanced Growth & Income	2 2	60%	1|1	06/98	10.19	1997	11.9%	0|1	N/A	N/A	0.00	—
* STAR Canadian Conservative Income & Growth	3 4	55%	1|1	11/97	6.42	1997	8.4%	0|1	N/A	N/A	0.00	—
* STAR Canadian Long-Term Growth	1 2	60%	1|1	06/98	10.51	1997	13.7%	0|1	N/A	N/A	0.00	—
* STAR Canadian Maximum Equity Growth	1 2	63%	1|1	06/98	10.32	1997	15.4%	0|1	N/A	N/A	0.00	—
* STAR Canadian Maximum Long-Term Growth	1 2	60%	1|1	06/98	10.53	1997	14.1%	0|1	N/A	N/A	0.00	—
* STAR Foreign Balanced Growth & Income	4 3 1	67%	2|2	01/97	1.57	1996	8.4%	0|2	N/A	N/A	0.00	—
* STAR Foreign Maximum Equity Growth	3 3 1	65%	2|2	04/97	4.96	1997	9.2%	0|2	N/A	N/A	0.00	—
* STAR Foreign Maximum Long-Term Growth	4 4 1	62%	1|2	06/98	1.38	1997	3.1%	0|2	N/A	N/A	0.00	—
* STAR Investment Balanced Growth & Income	4 2 2	62%	2|2	07/96	6.91	1996	10.8%	0|2	N/A	N/A	0.00	—
* STAR Investment Conservative Income & Growth	1 3 2	64%	2|2	11/97	6.95	1997	8.0%	0|2	N/A	N/A	0.00	—
* STAR Investment Long-Term Growth	3 2 1	64%	2|2	07/96	7.99	1997	11.6%	0|2	N/A	N/A	0.00	—
* STAR Investment Maximum Long-Term Growth	4 4 1	67%	1|2	11/97	2.53	1997	2.7%	0|2	N/A	N/A	0.00	—
* STAR Registered Balanced Growth & Income	2 2 3	69%	2|2	06/98	7.38	1997	10.5%	0|2	N/A	N/A	0.00	—
* STAR Registered Conservative Income & Growth	3 4 3	62%	2|2	11/97	6.35	1997	7.8%	0|2	N/A	N/A	0.00	—
* STAR Registered Long-Term Growth	2 3 3	67%	2|2	06/98	6.11	1997	9.3%	0|2	N/A	N/A	0.00	—
* STAR Registered Maximum Equity Growth	1 2 2	65%	2|2	06/98	7.71	1997	11.9%	0|2	N/A	N/A	0.00	—
* STAR Registered Maximum Long-Term Growth	2 3 1	67%	2|2	04/97	7.39	1997	7.9%	0|2	N/A	N/A	0.00	—

S = Seg Funds   * = Mackenzie Star Funds

27 OTHER

Fund Name	Perf. Trend (Quartiles 96/97/98·June)	Fund Beats GICs %	Fund Beats GICs(Yr)	Worst 12 mo End	Chng (%)	Worst Calendar Year	Worst Cal. Value	Years Fund Lost $	Sharpe 3-Yr	Sharpe 5-Yr	MER
20/20 Managed Futures Value Fund	3 1 4	45%	1|2	06/98	-34.25	1996	4.0%	0|2	3.00	N/A	3.94
B.E.S.T. Discoveries Fund	3	20%	0|0	06/98	-3.14	N/A		0|0	N/A	N/A	4.33
C.I. Covington Fund Inc. (LSVCC)	1 2 3	22%	2|2	03/98	0.34	1997	7.5%	0|2	2.00	N/A	4.84
Canadian Medical Discoveries Fund Inc. (LSVCC)	3 3 2	33%	0|2	01/98	-1.95	1997	1.2%	0|2	3.00	N/A	4.91
Canadian Science & Technology Growth Fund Inc.	3	17%	0|0	01/98	-1.70	N/A		0|0	N/A	N/A	5.50
Canadian Venture Opportunities Fund (LSVCC)	4 2 4	23%	1|3	11/95	-22.32	1995	-18.8%	2|3	4.00	N/A	6.37
Capital Alliance Ventures Inc. (LSVCC)	2 3 3	20%	2|2	06/97	-7.34	1997	4.9%	0|2	3.00	N/A	4.04
Centerfire Growth Fund Inc.	4	36%	0|0	05/98	2.18	N/A		0|0	N/A	N/A	1.60
Crocus Investment Fund	3 1 2	28%	1|2	06/97	1.44	1996	5.7%	0|2	1.00	N/A	3.78
DGC Entertainment Ventures Corp. (LSVCC)	1 4 1	29%	1|3	01/98	-4.49	1997	-0.9%	1|3	2.00	N/A	5.00
ENSIS Growth Fund Inc. (LSVCC)		N/A	0|0	N/A	0.00	N/A		0|0	N/A	N/A	0.00
FCMI Diversified Fund	1 4	36%	1|1	06/98	-8.16	1997	24.8%	0|1	N/A	N/A	5.09
FCMI Futures Fund		N/A	0|0	N/A	0.00	N/A		0|0	N/A	N/A	2.39
FCMI Toronto Trust Equity-Hedge Fund		N/A	0|0	N/A	0.00	N/A		0|0	N/A	N/A	2.00
FCMI Toronto Trust Intl Sec Fund		N/A	0|0	N/A	0.00	N/A		0|0	N/A	N/A	2.00
FESA Enterprise Venture Cap of Cda. Ltd. (LSVCC)	2 4 4	24%	1|2	06/98	-10.86	1997	-4.3%	1|2	4.00	N/A	0.00
First Ontario Fund (LSVCC)	4 3 1	27%	0|2	09/96	1.63	1996	2.9%	0|2	3.00	N/A	4.75
S Horizons Multi-Asset Fund	3 2 2	44%	2|4	07/95	-1.95	1994	4.6%	0|4	2.00	N/A	3.60
S Horizons RRSP Hedge Fund	1	N/A	0|0	N/A	0.00	N/A		0|0	N/A	N/A	2.00
Innovacap Capital Corporation	3	14%	0|0	05/98	-14.86	N/A		0|0	N/A	N/A	12.00
Retrocom Growth Fund Inc. (LSVCC)	4 2 2	24%	1|2	05/96	-0.87	1996	1.4%	0|2	4.00	N/A	4.24
Sportfund Inc. (LSVCC)	1 1 4	18%	2|3	05/98	-6.94	1995	2.2%	0|3	2.00	N/A	4.85

S = Seg Funds

27 OTHER

Fund Name	CONSISTENCY — Performance Trend by Quartiles (84 85 86 87 88 89 90 91 92 93 94 95 96 97 98 June)	RISK — Fund Beats GICs %	Fund Beats GICs(Yr)	Worst 12 mo. End Chng (%)	Worst Calendar Year	Years Fund Lost $	REWARD-TO-RISK — Sharpe Ratio Quartile Rankings 3-Yr	5-Yr	EFFICIENCY — MER
The Friedberg Currency Fund	1 4 1	55%	1|2	11/97 -20.65	1997 -1.5%	1|2	1.00	N/A	● 4.21
Triax Growth Fund Inc. (LSVCC)	3 2	57%	0|1	05/97 -1.61	1997 2.9%	0|1	N/A	N/A	● 3.60
Trillium Growth Capital Inc. (LSVCC)	4 4 3	20%	0|2	04/98 -11.22	1997 -9.3%	2|2	4.00	N/A	● 5.60
VenGrowth Investment Fund Inc. (LSVCC)	2 1 2	33%	2|2	08/96 2.50	1996 7.1%	0|2	1.00	N/A	● 3.90
Working Opportunity Fund (EVCC) Ltd.	2 2 1	37%	2|3	03/95 1.94	1995 5.0%	0|3	1.00	N/A	● 3.30
Working Ventures Canadian Fund Inc. (LSVCC)	4 3 1	26%	1|7	05/97 -3.64	1994 0.3%	0|7	4.00	N/A	● 2.41

$ = Seg Funds

GLOSSARY

Asset allocation. The relative proportions of equities, bonds, cash, real estate, and other asset types held in a portfolio at a given time. In a mutual fund, the portfolio manager often varies these proportions in order to maximize return when economic conditions change.

Automatic reinvestment. An option available to investors in a mutual fund or other investment whereby income (dividends, interest, or capital gains) distributions are used to purchase additional units of the fund.

Balanced portfolio. A balanced portfolio is the distribution of investments into several asset categories to help increase returns and reduce risk. The basic components of a balanced portfolio are cash, bonds, Canadian and international equities, real estate, oil, gas, and gold. The weighting of the different components varies depending on one's age and aggressiveness as an investor.

Bear market. A stock market whose index of representative stocks, such as the Toronto Stock Exchange 300 Composite Index, is declining in value. A "bearish" investor believes share prices will fall.

Blue-chip stocks. Stocks with good investment qualities. They are usually common shares of well-established companies with good earning records and regular dividend payments that are known nationally for the quality and wide acceptance of their products and services.

Bond. A debt instrument issued by governments and corporations. A bond is a promise by the issuer to pay the full amount of the debt on maturity, plus interest payments at regular intervals.

Bottom-up. A style of investing which places a priority on examining companies that may be appropriate for investment. Less emphasis is placed on macroeconomic considerations. See also *Top-down.*

Bull market. A stock market whose index has been rising in value. A "bullish" investor believes share prices will rise.

Canada Deposit Insurance Corporation (CDIC). An agency of the Government of Canada which insures the deposits of Canadians in banks and trust companies up to $60,000.

Capital Cost Allowance (CCA). A tax deduction available to reflect the depreciation of various types of assets. Applied to buildings (either commercial or residential), CCA can be used to shelter rental income from real estate investment trusts (REITs).

Capital gain (loss). A profit (or loss) made on the sale of an asset when the market price rises above or falls below the purchase price — usually in real estate, stocks, bonds, or other capital assets.

Closed-end fund. A mutual fund in which the total number of units is limited. If units are not purchased when the fund is initially offered, they can only be purchased from another owner. They often trade on stock exchanges.

Common share. A class of stock that represents ownership, or equity, in a company. Common shares entitle the holder to a share in the company's profits, usually as a dividend. They may also carry a voting privilege.

Consumer Price Index (CPI). A statistical measure of the cost of living for consumers. Often used to demonstrate general increases in the level of inflation over a period of time.

Current yield. As applied to money market funds, it refers to the actual rate of return over the past seven days, annualized.

Cyclical stock. A stock within a specific industry sector that is particularly sensitive to changes in economic conditions. The natural resources sector tends to be cyclical, as do particular stocks in the sector.

Deferred sales charge (DSC). An increasingly popular alternative to mutual funds that charge front-end acquisition fees. Here, a fee is paid when the investor sells units in the fund. This usually begins at 4.5% of the unit's value in the first year and declines by 0.5% to 1% per year, eventually reaching 0% several years into the future. Sometimes called an Exit Fee.

Distribution fees. Fees levied by some mutual fund companies on the value of units purchased with a back-end load or deferred sales charge. While most funds have stopped charging these fees, a few hold-outs remain.

Distributions. The payments made by a mutual fund to its unitholders of the interest, dividends, and/or capital gains earned during the year. Shareholders may either take distributions in cash or reinvest them in additional shares of the fund.

Diversification. Spreading investment risk by investing in a variety of asset categories (stocks, bonds, gold) in different industries and/or countries.

Dividend tax credit. A special tax credit applied to reduce the effective rate of tax paid on Canadian dividend income.

Dividend. A portion of a company's profit paid out to common and preferred shareholders, the amount having been decided on by the company's board of directors. A dividend may be in the form of cash or additional stock. A preferred dividend is usually a fixed amount, while a common dividend may fluctuate with the earnings of the company.

Dollar cost averaging. An investment program in which contributions are made at regular intervals with specific and equal dollar amounts. This often results in a lower average cost per unit because more units are purchased when the prices are depressed than when they are high.

Equity funds. Mutual funds that invest in common and preferred shares.

Ex-dividend. The date on which distributions that have been declared by a mutual fund are deducted from total net assets. The price of the fund's shares or units will be reduced by the amount of the distribution.

Fixed asset mix. For balanced funds, an approach which fixes the asset mix to be maintained in the fund: often 50–60% equity and 40–50% fixed income. Compare to an asset allocation fund, where there is no pre-set fixed asset mix.

Fixed income funds. Mutual funds that invest in mortgages, bonds, or a combination of both. Mortgages and bonds are issued at a fixed rate of interest and are known as fixed-income securities.

Front-end commission charge. An acquisition fee based on the total value of mutual fund units purchased. The fees can range from 2% to 9%, but average 4% to 5% on most purchases.

GIC (Guaranteed Investment Certificate). A deposit certificate usually issued by a bank or trust company. An interest-bearing investment that matures after a specified term, usually anywhere from 30 days to 5 years. The interest remains fixed during this period.

Growth investing. An approach to investing which places greater emphasis on a stock's future growth potential than on its current price. A growth manager may therefore be prepared to pay a higher price for a stock than a value manager would, if he or she believes it has attractive future growth potential. It is seen as a more aggressive style of management than value investing.

Growth stock. Shares of a company whose earnings are expected to grow faster than average.

Hedging. The strategy of taking positions in more than one commodity, security, or asset category in an attempt to reduce investment risk. An investment in gold or oil/natural gas, for example, is often seen as a hedge or protection against inflation.

Income splitting. The process of diverting taxable income from an individual in a high tax bracket to one in a lower tax bracket.

Index fund. A mutual fund designed to match the performance of a recognized group of publicly traded stocks, such as those represented by the TSE 300 Index or the Standard & Poor 500 Index in the U.S.

Index. For stocks, an indicator of broad market performance. The Dow Jones industrial average includes the shares of 30 large companies; the Toronto Stock Exchange's composite index includes 300 companies; the Standard & Poor index contains 500 companies. Developed from statistics that measure the state of the economy, based on the performance of stocks or other key indicators such as the Consumer Price Index.

Investment fund. See *Mutual fund.*

Leverage. Using borrowed funds to maximize the rate of return on investment. A potentially dangerous strategy if the investment declines in value.

Limited partnership. See *Tax shelter.*

Liquidity. The ease with which an asset can be sold and converted into cash at its full value.

Management expense ratio (MER). The total of all management and other fees charged to the fund, shown as a percentage of the fund's total assets, or as a dollar amount per $100 of assets.

Management fee. The amount paid annually by a mutual fund to its managers. The average annual fee in Canada is between 1% and 2% of the value of the fund's assets.

Marginal tax rate. The rate at which tax is calculated on the next dollar of income earned. This rate increases at progressively higher income brackets.

Market timing. The process of shifting from one type of investment to another with the intention of maximizing the return as market conditions change.

MBS (Mortgage-backed securities). These provide higher yields than many other savings options by investing in first mortgages on residential properties.

Money market fund. Fixed-income mutual funds that invest in short-term securities (maturing within one year).

Mortgage. A legal instrument given by a borrower to the lender entitling the lender to take over pledged property if conditions of the loan are not met.

Multi-Period Composite (MPC). The mathematical model used in this book to compare the returns of similar types of funds over one-year calendar time frames. This model eliminates end date bias associated with the more traditional use of average annual compound rates of return.

Mutual fund. A professionally managed pool of assets, representing the contributions of many investors, which is used to purchase a portfolio of securities that meets specific investment objectives. See *Open-end fund and Closed-end fund.*

Net asset value (NAV). The value of a fund's assets, less its liabilities. The NAV is used to calculate the buying or selling price of shares or units in a fund, usually expressed as the net asset value per share (NAVPS).

Net asset value per share (NAVPS). The total market value of all securities owned by a mutual fund, less its liabilities, divided by the number of units outstanding.

No-load fund. A mutual fund that does not charge a fee for buying or selling its units.

Open-end fund. A mutual fund whose units are offered for sale on a continuous basis; the fund will also buy back units at their current price (net asset value per share). Sometimes called an investment fund. The most common type of mutual fund.

Portfolio. A group of securities held or owned for investment purposes by an individual or institution. An investor's portfolio may contain common and preferred shares, bonds, options, and other types of securities.

Prospectus. A legal document describing a new issue of securities or a mutual fund that is to be sold to the public. The prospectus must be prepared in accordance with provincial securities commission regulations. It must contain information on any material facts that can have an impact on the value of the investment, such as the fund's investment objectives and policies, services offered, or fees charged. It must also identify any investment restrictions, as well as the officers of the company.

Real estate investment trust (REIT). A form of real estate mutual fund with the difference that the REIT trades on a stock exchange. As a result, it provides greater liquidity than is usually available through a traditional real estate mutual fund. The units generally trade at a discount from net asset value.

Real rate of return. The stated rate of return, less inflation and taxes.

Registered investment. A security held in a tax-sheltered plan — most often an RRSP or RRIF — which has been approved by Revenue Canada.

Risk tolerance. The ability of a person to tolerate risk. Risk tolerance is a function of the individual's personality and other factors, and is an important element in determining investment strategy.

Risk-free return. The return available from securities that have no risk of loss. Short-term securities issued by the government (such as Treasury Bills) normally provide a risk-free return.

Risk. The possibility that some or all of the money put into an investment will be lost.

RRIF (Registered Retirement Income Fund). A non-annuity investment vehicle for maturing RRSPs. One of the options available to RRSP holders upon cashing in their retirement funds at age 69 or sooner. RRIFs generally provide for a series of payments that increase each year.

RRSP (Registered Retirement Savings Plan). A savings program approved by Revenue Canada that permits tax-deferred saving for retirement purposes. Contributions to an RRSP are tax-deductible. Earnings on contributions are sheltered from tax while they remain in the plan.

Sector rotation. A style of investing that identifies prospective investments (or the weighting of an investment portfolio) according to which sectors of the economy are poised to do well. Often associated with the "top-down" approach to investing.

Segregated funds. Funds sold and administered by life insurance companies.

Self-directed RRSP. An RRSP whose investments are controlled by the plan holder. A self-directed RRSP may include stocks, bonds, residential mortgages, or other types of investments approved by Revenue Canada.

Sharpe Ratio. Invented by Nobel prize winner Dr. William Sharpe, this ratio is a means of measuring risk-adjusted returns. It is calculated by taking the annual compounded returns of a fund **minus** the annual compounded return of T-Bills (a "risk free" investment) **divided by** the annualized standard deviation. The higher the Sharpe Ratio the better.

Systematic withdrawal plan (SWP). A plan for withdrawing money from a mutual fund on a regular basis — monthly, quarterly, semi-annually, or annually. Used mostly by investors who require a steady stream of income from their investments.

Tax shelter. An investment that, by government regulation, can be made with untaxed or partly taxed dollars. The creation of tax losses in order to offset an individual's taxable income from other sources thereby reduces tax liability.

Taxable income. The amount of annual income that is used to calculate how much income tax must be paid: total earnings for the year, minus deductions.

Term deposit. Similar to a guaranteed investment certificate. An interest-bearing investment to which an investor commits funds for a specified term and rate of interest.

Top-down. A style of investing that considers the economic "big picture" to identify sectors of the economy that are expected to outperform. Less importance is attached to identifying individual companies which may do well. See also *Bottom-up.*

Total return. The amount of income earned from an investment, together with its capital appreciation, expressed as a percentage of the original amount invested. It indicates an investment's performance over a stated period.

Treasury Bills. Short-term debt securities sold by governments, usually with maturities of three months to one year. They carry no stated interest rate, but trade at a discount to their face value. The discount represents the market's valuation of the future return at maturity.

Unit. In mutual funds, a unit represents a portion, or share, of the total value of the fund. Units are purchased by investors, and rise or fall proportionately with the net asset value of the fund.

Value investing. An approach to investing that attempts, through the use of various analytical models, to identify companies which are fundamentally strong but which may be out of favour in the marketplace and trading at prices which represent a good 'buy.' This conservative approach is often associated with Sir John Templeton and is one which many investment managers claim to use.

Volatility. A measure of a mutual fund's tendency to fluctuate in value. More volatile funds are traditionally considered to have a greater degree of risk, although the fluctuation in value may, in fact, be either up or down.

INDEX

Q

Quartile — 42-43, 50-51, 64

R

Real Estate Funds — 5, 11, 12, 174, 176, 181-185

Real Estate Investment Trust (REIT) — 15, 308

Rebalancing, portfolio — 196-198, 201-202

Redemption Charges — 23-24

Reward-to-Risk, fund criterion — 50-51

Risk, fund criterion — 48-51, 206-207

Risk Tolerance — 175-176

RRIF (Registered Retirement Income Fund) — 309

RRSP (Registered Retirement Savings Plan) — 309

S

Sales charges — 21-28

SROs (Self-Regulatory Organizations) — 187

Sector Equity — 231

    Canadian Sector Equity Funds — 231

Sector Rotation — 58

Segregated Funds — 18-19, 189-190

Sharpe Ratio — 51, 207

Similar fund — 55, 64, 68-167

Small/ Mid-Cap Funds — 13-14

    Canadian Small/Mid-Cap Equity Funds — 13, 82-86, 223-226

    U.S. Small Cap Equity Funds — 14, 103, 241

Spread trading — 60-61

Standard Deviation — 48-50

STAR, Mackenzie — 18, 167, 180, 182, 300

Stock market, world — 14

Style, fund criterion — 54-62

TOP FUNDS 1999

The following is a list of the 100 Top Funds of 1999, arranged by **category** and in **alphabetical order** within each category. An (✓) beside a fund indicates that it is a new Top Fund in 1999.

CANADIAN LARGE CAP/DIVERSIFIED BLEND

✓Atlas Canadian Large Cap Growth Fund	68
Bissett Canadian Equity Fund	69
Ethical Growth Fund	70
✓First Canadian Growth Fund	71
✓Green Line Canadian Equity Fund	72
✓Investors Summa Fund	73
McLean Budden Equity Growth Fund	74
✓Phillips, Hager & North Canadian Equity Fund	75
✓Standard Life Equity Mutual Fund	76

CANADIAN LARGE CAP/DIVERSIFIED VALUE

Ivy Canadian Fund	77
✓Spectrum United Canadian Investment Fund	78

CANADIAN LARGE CAP/DIVERSIFIED GROWTH

✓AIC Diversified Canada Fund	79
✓Clean Environment Equity Fund	80
Phillips, Hager & North Vintage Fund	81

CANADIAN SMALL/MID-CAP EQUITY

Bissett Small Cap Fund	82
✓Chou RRSP Fund	83
Colonia Special Growth Fund	84
✓Fidelity Canadian Growth Company Fund	85
✓Millennium Next Generation Fund	86

CANADIAN DIVIDEND

AGF Dividend Fund	87
Bissett Dividend Income Fund	88
Industrial Dividend Growth Fund	89
Maxxum Dividend Fund of Canada	90
Phillips, Hager & North Dividend Income Fund	91
Royal Dividend Fund	92

CANADIAN SECTOR EQUITY

AIC Advantage Fund	93

CANADIAN RESOURCES & PRECIOUS METALS

20/20 Canadian Resources Fund	94
Maxxum Natural Resource Fund	95
Royal Precious Metals Fund	96
✓Universal Canadian Resource Fund	97

U.S. LARGE CAP/DIVERSIFIED EQUITY

AGF American Growth Class Fund	98
AIC Value Fund	99
Fidelity Growth America Fund	100
✓Green Line U.S. Index Fund	101
✓Spectrum United American Growth Fund C$	102

U.S. SMALL CAP EQUITY

BPI American Small Companies Fund	103

INTERNATIONAL EQUITY

✓AIC World Equity Fund	104
✓Great West Life International Equity Inv (P) DSC	105
Templeton International Stock Fund	106

GLOBAL EQUITY

AGF International Value Fund	107
✓BPI Global Equity Value Fund	108
Canada Life U.S. & Int'l Equity Fund S-34	109
Fidelity International Portfolio Fund	110
✓Investors Growth Portfolio Fund	111
Templeton Global Smaller Companies Fund	112
Templeton Growth Fund Ltd.	113
Trimark Fund	114

GLOBAL SECTOR

AIM Global Health Sciences Fund	115
Dynamic Real Estate Equity Fund	116

NORTH AMERICAN EQUITY

✓Chou Associates Fund	117

EUROPEAN EQUITY

✓AGF International Group Germany Class Fund	118
Dynamic Europe Fund	119
Fidelity European Growth Fund	120
✓Universal European Opportunities Fund	121

LATIN AMERICAN & EMERGING MARKETS

20/20 Latin America Fund	122
✓AIM GT Latin America Growth Class Fund	123
✓C.I. Emerging Markets Fund	124
Spectrum United Emerging Markets Fund	125
Templeton Emerging Markets Fund	126

319